North Carolina's Revolutionary Founders

North Carolina's Revolutionary Founders

Edited by

Jeff Broadwater
& Troy L. Kickler

The University of North Carolina Press
Chapel Hill

© 2019 The University of North Carolina Press

All rights reserved

Designed by Jamison Cockerham
Set in Arno, Dear Sarah, IM Fell English, and Scala Sans
by codeMantra, Inc.

Manufactured in the United States of America

The University of North Carolina Press has been a member
of the Green Press Initiative since 2003.

Cover illustration: *Grunge North Carolina State Flag*; © Allexxandar, iStockphoto.com.

LIBRARY OF CONGRESS CATALOGING-IN-PUBLICATION DATA
Names: Broadwater, Jeff, editor. | Kickler, Troy, editor.
Title: North Carolina's revolutionary founders /
    edited by Jeff Broadwater and Troy L. Kickler.
Description: Chapel Hill : The University of North Carolina Press, [2019] |
    Includes bibliographical references and index.
Identifiers: LCCN 2018046424 | ISBN 9781469651194 (cloth : alk. paper) |
    ISBN 9781469651200 (pbk : alk. paper) | ISBN 9781469651217 (ebook)
Subjects: LCSH: North Carolina—History—Revolution, 1775–1783. | North Carolina—
    History—Revolution, 1775–1783—Biography. | Politicians—North Carolina—
    History—17th century. | Politicians—North Carolina—Biography.
Classification: LCC E263.N8 N83 2019 | DDC 975.6/03—dc23
LC record available at https://lccn.loc.gov/2018046424

Contents

Introduction: North Carolina in an Age of Revolution   1
Jeff Broadwater & Troy L. Kickler

I THE REVOLUTIONARIES

1 Treasonous Tea: The Edenton Tea Party of 1774   25
Maggie Hartley Mitchell

2 Declaring Independence: William Hooper, Joseph Hewes, and John Penn   43
Jeff Broadwater

II THE WEST

3 Caught between Two Fires: The Catawba and the Cherokee Choose Sides in the American Revolution   67
James MacDonald

4 Our Common Country: John Sevier and the American Revolution   88
Michael Toomey

III THE FEDERALISTS

  5 Hugh Williamson: North Carolina Federalist   113
     Jennifer Davis-Doyle

  6 An Ordinary Founder: Richard Dobbs Spaight Sr.   132
     Karl Rodabaugh

  7 The Political Views of Richard Caswell and
     the Founding of the New Nation   159
     Lloyd Johnson

  8 James Iredell: Revolutionist, Constitutionalist, Jurist   178
     Willis P. Whichard

IV THE ANTI-FEDERALISTS

  9 Samuel Spencer, Anti-Federalist   199
     Jason Stroud

 10 Willie Jones   217
     Kyle Scott

V THE LEGATEES OF THE REVOLUTION

 11 William R. Davie: North Carolina's Patriot Partisan   237
     Scott King-Owen

 12 John Chavis: Quiet Leader of an Early Revolution   257
     Benjamin R. Justesen

 13 Two North Carolinians, Same Goal, Different Approaches:
     An Examination of the Political Lives and Philosophies
     of Nathaniel Macon and Archibald D. Murphey   279
     Troy L. Kickler

     Afterword   301
     Jeff Broadwater & Troy L. Kickler

     Contributors   305

     Index   307

Figure

Satirical illustration of the Edenton Tea Party
attributed to the English artist Philip Dawe   36

Introduction

North Carolina in an Age of Revolution

Jeff Broadwater & Troy L. Kickler

Why a collection of essays devoted, for the most part, to a representative group of North Carolina political leaders during the era of the American Revolution? For one reason, America's decentralized political system meant that the success of the Revolution in North Carolina, and elsewhere, depended in great part on the efforts of an influential cadre of provincial leaders, or "ordinary founders," as Karl Rodabaugh has described North Carolina's Richard Dobbs Spaight. From its very beginning, the United States had something like a federal system. From 1776, when thirteen North American colonies declared their independence from Great Britain, until the United States Constitution took effect in 1789, political power in the new American republic lay largely with the states. If we define federalism to mean a system in which power is divided between a central administration and political entities on the national or imperial periphery, which seems reasonable, federalism in America has a long history.[1]

That history can be traced through three stages. The first would be an imperial stage in which colonial assemblies struggled for autonomy from the British Parliament. The second would be a revolutionary stage in which a weak central government attempted to manage a war for independence but generally deferred to state governments operating under their respective state constitutions. The ratification of the U.S. Constitution marked the beginning of a third stage, in which a lengthy list of enumerated powers was bestowed upon a national government that would exercise a dual sovereignty with the individual states.

The Constitution reinvigorated the national government and gave Congress, among other powers, the authority to tax and to regulate commerce. Yet, with its elaborate system of checks and balances and its Bill of Rights, the Constitution created a government devoted to "negative liberty," or in other words, a government designed to respect the rights of its white citizens. By contrast, the states retained broad, and often coercive, powers in areas not subject to exclusive federal jurisdiction. Very different legal regimes were allowed to coexist. Article VI of the U.S. Constitution, for example, provided that "no religious Test shall ever be required as a Qualification to any Office or public Trust under the United States." Meanwhile, Article 32 of the North Carolina Constitution of 1776 prohibited Catholics, Jews, or atheists from holding state office.[2]

In addition to the critical role played by the states in the American founding, a second consideration motived this volume. The figures profiled in the succeeding pages have been relatively neglected by historians and virtually forgotten by the general public. North Carolina's ordinary founders have almost, if not quite, disappeared from our collective memory. Only a few of our founders have been the subject of even one full-length, published biography. Others have received little more scholarly attention than an encyclopedia entry. More typical of their fates in the secondary literature would be a solid but dated article in a regional journal. William Hooper and William R. Davie have inspired excellent dissertations, but dissertations do not circulate widely.

North Carolina's unique history and distinctive political culture offer a final reason to look closely at its founders. By adopting the Halifax Resolves in April 1776, North Carolina became the first American colony to call for independence from Great Britain. Yet Tar Heels refused to ratify the United States Constitution until November 1789, months after the new federal government had begun to function. Only Rhode Island, the last state to vote for ratification, showed more resistance to the new regime. Isolation; a lack of economic development; sectional, ethnic, and religious tensions; and political corruption and dysfunction had bred in many North Carolinians an intense localism and a distrust of government in general.

Events specific to North Carolina, including the "foreign attachment" controversy over the jurisdiction of colonial courts, fanned the flames of independence as anti-British sentiment grew throughout the colonies in 1775 and 1776. In 1789, North Carolinians bowed to the inevitable and accepted the Constitution, giving the state's Federalists a brief ascendancy, but a small-government ideology deeply rooted in North Carolina's history and culture would soon reassert itself.

Since its founding in the mid-1600s, the colony had been racked by coups, countercoups, piracy, and Indian wars. The establishment of a royal government and the appointment of a royal governor in 1729 brought a degree of order, but a series of governors faced stubborn opposition from a local assembly determined to protect what it understood to be its prerogatives under North Carolina's colonial charter. By 1750 or so, politics in most of the colonies had stabilized under the leadership of a fairly responsible provincial elite. Yet North Carolina lagged behind. In North Carolina, the acerbic Anglican cleric Charles Woodmason complained, "The Civil Police is hardly yet established."[3]

The lack of a deep-water harbor, a scarcity of navigable rivers, and a generally poor transportation system retarded economic development. Shortages of capital and skilled labor presented additional obstacles. A classic colonial economy, North Carolina exported the products of its fields and forests: corn, salt pork and beef, animal skins and wooden shingles. Cash crops included tobacco and rice, but North Carolina did not produce either on the scale seen in Virginia or South Carolina. Raising livestock, which usually roamed free, was the most lucrative activity in the backcountry. North Carolina did produce the bulk of the colonies' naval stores—the tar, pitch, and turpentine used to caulk and seal the timbers and ropes of the era's wooden sailing ships. Wealth typically took the form of land and slaves, but probably less than a third of the colony's white families owned slaves before the Revolution.[4]

A certain lack of social development went hand in hand with the primitive economy. Only about a third of the population could read or write. The colony had no newspaper until 1751 and no regular post roads before 1770. The "average North Carolinian," Alice Mathews has written, "had little money, was indebted, lived in a small frame house or log cabin, was often deemed slovenly and lazy by contemporary visitors, and had little contact with the outside world." Backcountry white farmers could complain bitterly about high taxes and political corruption, with, as we shall see, good reason. They did not, however, normally challenge the established order. By their standards, they lived well enough, most owned their own land, and they rarely demanded radical reform.[5]

The primitive economy did not produce an impressive, indigenous elite. Officeholders often lacked the social status to command respect or the personal integrity to inspire confidence; many were newcomers to the colony. Although adult white men who owned land and paid taxes could vote after living in North Carolina for a year, the political process was hardly democratic. Voters selected assembly members by county, which favored the smaller, more numerous counties of the east. Local officials were not elected; the governor, for example, appointed justices of the peace upon the recommendation of other local officeholders. Two-thirds of the members of the assembly also served as justices, thus concentrating power in notorious "courthouse rings." The colonial government, meanwhile, collected from its subjects quitrents, tonnage duties, import duties on liquor, and an especially unpopular poll tax that placed a proportionally greater burden on small farmers than on large planters. The poll tax was, according to historian Lindley Butler, "the most inefficient and corrupt aspect of the provincial administration."[6]

North Carolina's size—it was 150 miles from New Bern west to Hillsborough—and its diversity aggravated sectional tensions and contributed to the colony's political instability. The population swelled from 36,000 settlers in the 1730s to 250,000 by 1770, in large part as a result of emigration from Britain's other North American colonies. Charles Woodmason believed, with obvious exaggeration, that North Carolina's "People are composed of the Out Casts of all the other Colonies." Most newcomers were English, Scottish, Scotch Irish, or German. The Scots included Highlanders and the less numerous Lowlanders, who were nevertheless highly visible because many of them became merchants. White Virginians had introduced slavery to the Albemarle region in the 1600s; white South Carolinians, meanwhile, brought the institution to the Cape Fear area. North Carolina's slave population grew rapidly after about 1750. Enslaved blacks, evenly divided between the native born and those imported from Africa, may have constituted a quarter of the population by 1775. A few free blacks lived in the region; Benjamin R. Justesen's essay on the African American minister and educator John Chavis illustrates the challenges they faced. White society divided itself into the gentry, a "middling class," and a "meaner" or "lower sort."[7]

Large planters of English descent dominated the east; Scotch Irish and German farmers settled in the west. If the east-west divide has long dominated the historiography, one of the most thorough recent studies of Revolutionary North Carolina has identified six distinct regions within the colony: Edenton and the Albemarle Sound, the oldest area of white settlement; the coastal port towns, principally New Bern and Wilmington; the Upper Cape Fear, a rapidly growing area that would be a center of Loyalist disaffection; Halifax and the old Granville District, which had been the colony's original backcountry; a newer backcountry, centered in Hillsborough but stretching from the Haw River to the eastern slope of the Appalachians; and finally a frontier beyond the mountains, where conflicts with Native Americans overshadowed other issues.[8]

In an age in which denominational differences mattered greatly, religion further divided the colony. The Anglican Church, North Carolina's established faith, had always been, in the words of Robert Calhoon, "underfinanced and understaffed." Anglicans had long competed with a substantial Quaker population for influence in the colony, and Presbyterian and Baptist ranks grew dramatically during the First Great Awakening, a religious revival that swept the colonies in the 1740s. In the 1750s and 1760s, Moravians established settlements around Bethabara and Salem. Methodists would enjoy explosive growth in the 1780s. Especially in the backcountry, Andrew Denson has written, "religion was a basic element of the political culture . . . and thus thoroughly intertwined with political life." The dissenting faiths tended to emphasize each individual's right to make moral judgments and encouraged resistance to oppressive governments. Backcountry rebels like Herman Husband combined religious nonconformity with radical Whig ideas to produce a powerful ideology of resistance that historians may only now be coming to appreciate fully.[9]

On the very eve of the American Revolution, North Carolina experienced one more spasm of unrest. What became known as the Regulator movement began in 1766 when backcountry farmers organized the Sandy Creek Association to challenge their exploitation by corrupt local officials. Pressed by rising taxes and the failure of peaceful protest, the movement eventually turned violent; the tumult included an attack on the Hillsborough courthouse. One of the most spectacular episodes of civil disobedience in American history ended in May 1771 with a pitched battle at Alamance between eastern militia units, led by Governor William Tryon, and armed Regulators. The fighting left eighteen men dead, not including six Regulators who were hanged afterward. The Regulator movement illustrated the instability of a political system in which backcountry farmers were underrepresented and unfairly taxed by a government too feeble to maintain law and order through normal channels.[10]

The end of the French and Indian War in 1763 left Great Britain with a war debt to pay and an expensive new empire in Canada to administer. British authorities responded with a "new colonial policy" that tightened the reins on Britain's American colonies and ultimately provoked a revolution. To avoid another Indian war, the Proclamation of 1763 banned white settlement west of the Appalachian Mountains; North Carolinians generally ignored it. The Sugar Act of 1764 attempted to improve the collection of duties on imported sugar and molasses by, among other things, trying alleged smugglers in a vice admiralty court in Halifax, Nova Scotia, thus denying them the right to a jury trial. The law had limited impact in North Carolina. Parliament's 1764 Currency Act proved more irritating. It prohibited most of the colonies, including North Carolina, from printing their own bills of credit, essentially paper money of dubious value. In an underdeveloped agrarian economy with an unfavorable balance of trade and a chronic shortage of specie, the Currency Act helped make debt and taxes especially explosive issues.[11]

The explosion came after Parliament, on 22 March 1765, passed the Stamp Act, the first direct tax to be imposed by Great Britain on America. The act taxed most printed documents. Rates varied, but some were high; a law license cost ten pounds, and the tax had to be paid in sterling.[12] Maurice Moore, an associate justice on the colonial superior court and occasional legislator, provided the intellectual rationale for the Stamp Act's opponents. Skillfully blending legal and practical arguments, and a touch of sarcasm, his pamphlet *The Justice and Policy of Taxing the American Colonies* has been called "the most complete expression of North Carolina political thought of the Stamp Act period." English law prohibiting taxation without representation went back to the days of the Saxons, and Moore argued that the colonists did not forfeit their rights by coming to America.[13]

He ridiculed the concept of "virtual representation," the idea that Parliament represented all parts of the empire whether or not particular subjects elected any of its members. It was a recent innovation inconsistent with the rights of freeholders. Inhabitants of Great Britain who lacked the vote might have the same interests as their members of Parliament and could easily petition them, but Americans did not and could not. Extrapolating from the composition of Parliament, Moore suggested the British ought to divide the colonies into 558 districts and give each district a representative. More realistically he asked why, if Parliament represented the colonies, their charters gave them their own assemblies, each with the power to tax. More realistically still, Moore predicted arbitrary taxes and regulations would ruin Anglo-American trade and foment "a spirit of rebellion."[14]

On 19 October 1765, 500 people gathered in Wilmington to protest the act. The tax was supposed to take effect on 1 November, but when the stamped paper did not arrive from Britain, Governor Tryon closed the Wilmington port and the courts. The closings drove home the severity of the crisis and provoked more protest. In mid-November a mob—"beating drums and flying colors," according to one observer—forced the local stamp agent to resign. Later in the month, when the *Diligence* arrived in Brunswick with stamped paper, it could not unload its controversial cargo.[15] With opposition throughout the colonies making tax collections virtually impossible, Parliament, in March 1766, repealed the Stamp Act.[16]

"North Carolinians," according to one student of the crisis, "carried Stamp Act protest further than most other American colonists because they had more at stake." The controversy, Donna Spindel has written, disrupted "the maritime trade upon which the livelihood of the Lower Cape Fear depended." To make matters worse, the Cape Fear ports remained closed until 12 February 1766, later than any others in the colonies. Few regions in the colonies displayed more hostility to the new colonial policy than did the Lower Cape Fear, and Whig radicalism eventually spread to other parts of North Carolina. Ironically, however, North Carolina had little influence on its neighboring colonies. It went unrepresented, for example, at the Stamp Act Congress, which met in New York in October 1765 to coordinate opposition to the stamp tax. North Carolina could not elect delegates because Tryon, amid the crisis, refused to convene the assembly.[17]

Repeal of the Stamp Act defused the immediate controversy, but Britain's war debt and the costs of empire persisted. Accordingly, in 1767, Parliament passed the Townshend Acts, imposing import duties on wine, tea, paper, glass, and lead. Unlike the stamp tax, the Townshend Duties would not fall directly on consumers, but they were no more acceptable to Americans. In November 1768, the North Carolina assembly, led by House Speaker John Harvey, passed a resolution condemning the measure. When official protests failed to produce relief, the assembly, at its fall 1769 session, approved a Virginia resolution calling for "non-importation," or a boycott of British goods.[18]

Governor Tryon responded by dissolving the assembly, at which point Harvey and virtually every other lawmaker reassembled in an extralegal convention and approved a "non-importation association" intended to enforce the boycott. William Powell, for years the dean of North Carolina historians, called the 1769 convention "the first such legislative body in any of the colonies."[19] In March 1770, Parliament repealed the Townshend Duties, except for the tax on tea, and took much of the momentum out of the nonimportation movement. The Regulator uprising briefly overshadowed the conflict with Britain, but an issue unique to North Carolina would further radicalize the colony and contribute to a collapse of royal authority months before fighting broke out between Massachusetts militia and British redcoats at Lexington and Concord.

Since 1746, North Carolina courts had enjoyed the power of foreign attachment, the jurisdiction to seize the North Carolina property of British debtors of North Carolina creditors. But North Carolinians were more likely to be debtors, so the power was rarely used. According to a study of the Edenton district superior court, among the largest and presumably busiest courts in the colony, from 1760 to 1773, only 2.8 percent of debt actions began as foreign attachments, and they collected little money. The Board of Trade had urged Governor Tryon to end the practice. Tryon apparently moved cautiously, but his replacement, the less sagacious Josiah Martin, received more specific instructions, and he was determined to implement them.[20]

When the assembly refused to approve a judicial appropriations bill without a provision for foreign attachments and Martin refused to accept a bill with it, many of the colony's courts were forced to close. Martin's attempt to create courts on his own initiative made matters worse. Foreign attachments assumed an enormous symbolic importance in North Carolina, comparable to the issue of taxation. Beyond question, lawmakers saw Martin's instructions as another assault on their prerogatives, and the controversy aggravated popular discontent with imperial rule.[21]

In the middle of the court crisis, Parliament, hoping to rescue the financially troubled East India Company, passed the Tea Act, which gave the company tax breaks and other privileges that would allow it to undersell its American competitors. American merchants resented the law. Patriots saw it as a subterfuge to entice them to buy tea bearing the hated tax. Unrest in Boston led to the famous Boston Tea Party in 1773. In response Parliament passed the punitive Coercive Acts, one of which closed the port of Boston effective 1 June 1774.[22]

In North Carolina, a newly created Committee of Correspondence, composed of nine established eastern politicians, endorsed a widespread demand for a general meeting of the colonies and for a boycott of British goods until Boston's harbor was reopened. A mass meeting in Wilmington on 21 July called for a provincial congress to debate North Carolina's response to the worsening crisis. Governor Martin tried to dissuade delegates from attending, but in August 1774, representatives from most of the colony's towns and counties met in New Bern in what became known as the First Provincial Congress. William Powell considered it "the first such congress held in any of the colonies." They condemned parliamentary taxation; endorsed a boycott of Great Britain; agreed not to buy slaves imported after 1 November; and elected delegates to the First Continental Congress.[23]

The First Provincial Congress also proposed that committees of safety be established in each county to enforce the boycott, and the volume of Anglo-American trade soon plummeted. The implementation of economic sanctions required the mobilization of those who might not normally have been engaged in public life. As described in Maggie Hartley Mitchell's essay, in October 1774 a group of Edenton women, led by Elizabeth King and Penelope Barker, published a statement endorsing the Continental Congress's call to suspend trade with Great Britain. In Wilmington, women burned tea to express their opposition to British policy.[24]

As trade collapsed, so did Martin's authority. In an effort to forestall another provincial congress, the colonial governor called a meeting of the assembly for April 1775 in New Bern. Whig leaders outmaneuvered him by combining the meetings: John Harvey served as both moderator of the Second Provincial Congress and as Speaker of the lower house of the assembly. Martin attempted to dissolve the assembly, but he had already lost control. In May, the Mecklenburg Committee of Safety adopted the Mecklenburg Resolves denying the validity of royal commissions and calling for the organization of militia units independent of royal authority. The committee had no authority to bind the colony, but its resolves were further evidence of the radicalization of North Carolina politics. Fearing for his safety, Martin fled to Fort Johnston, at the mouth of the Cape Fear River, and later to a British warship off the coast.[25]

Fighting had erupted at Lexington and Concord on 18 and 19 April, so by the time Martin left New Bern, North Carolina was effectively at war. The Third Provincial Congress, meeting in August 1775, declared that because Martin had "deserted" his post, it would assume the functions of government. It probably did not, however, represent a majority of the colony's population. Many remained loyal to the king. Loyalist ranks included Anglican clergy, wealthy merchants, colonial officials, some large planters and professionals, most Scottish Highlanders, and an unknown number of ex-Regulators. Carole Troxler has found that Loyalists "tended to be members of minority groups within their immediate environment." In a "Fiery Proclamation" issued on 8 August 1775, Governor Martin called on Loyalists to take up arms to suppress the rebellion in the southern colonies. They did, and they suffered a crushing defeat at Moore's Creek Bridge near Wilmington in February 1776. The Battle of Moore's Creek Bridge doomed British hopes for a quick victory in the South and dampened Loyalist sentiment in North Carolina. It also made a military hero, as Lloyd Johnson explains in his essay, out of patriot leader Richard Caswell, one of Revolutionary North Carolina's most popular politicians.[26]

Except for the Catawba, as James MacDonald explains in his essay, Native Americans who took sides generally supported the British; the royal Proclamation of 1763 had at least tried to slow white expansion westward.[27] More common than outright hostility to the Revolution may have been ambivalence or apathy. The provincial congress worried especially about the pacifism of the Quakers and Moravians. Enslaved African Americans had little reason to support either side. The Crown had blocked efforts to end the foreign slave trade, and Governor Martin had vetoed a bill to treat the murder of a slave as the murder of a free person would be treated. Yet the patriots' record hardly inspired support. North Carolina, for example, did not permit private manumissions until 1790, making it the last southern state to allow owners to free their slaves without the approval of colonial officials. Josiah Martin and other

British officials actively recruited blacks for the British cause. They offered slaves their freedom if they enlisted, but "relatively few" North Carolina slaves, Jeffrey J. Crow has concluded, "apparently earned their freedom by fighting for the patriot cause." Free blacks, by contrast, may have been more apt to join the Continental army or state militia units.[28]

War and especially their victory at Moore's Creek, however, radicalized white patriots. Most of them initially seemed to have hoped armed resistance would merely force the British to repeal the unpopular reforms adopted since 1763, but the change in public opinion can be tracked through the petitions and resolves issued by local groups throughout the colonies from 1774 to 1776. Over time they became more militant. At least ninety state and local declarations of independence were adopted between April and July 1776. In the two years before the war, patriots could complain about Parliament and still express loyalty to the king, but George III eventually became a target. Whigs criticized his refusal to negotiate, his willingness to enlist Indians and slaves, his hiring of German mercenaries, and his acceptance of a blockade against American trade.[29]

When the Fourth Provincial Congress met at Halifax on 4 April 1776, independence was the main issue confronting the delegates. Joseph Hewes, one of the colony's representatives to the Continental Congress, had asked for instructions; Hewes anticipated he might soon have to vote on a declaration of independence.[30] After a brief debate on 12 April, all eighty-three of the Halifax delegates approved a committee report empowering North Carolina's congressional delegation to support independence.[31] Jeff Broadwater's essay profiling Hewes and the other North Carolina signers of the Declaration of Independence, William Hooper and John Penn, questions their commitment to its soaring rhetoric.

The Continental Congress, anticipating the approval of a declaration of independence, had recommended to the states that they draft new constitutions to replace their soon-to-be obsolete colonial charters. Here the unanimity among the Halifax delegates collapsed, and the Fourth Provincial Congress could not reach agreement. Historians have traditionally divided North Carolina Whigs into two camps, radicals and conservatives. Radicals, whose leaders included Willie Jones, the subject of Kyle Scott's chapter, feared overbearing governors and judges; favored legislative power, especially when it was concentrated in the lower house of the assembly; and advocated frequent elections, the separation of church and state, a free press, and modest property requirements for voting and office-holding. Conservatives, led by men like James Iredell, profiled in this volume by Willis P. Whichard, worried about mob rule and wanted a strong executive; independent, appointed judges; protection for property rights; and substantial property requirements to vote or hold office.[32]

The inability of the Halifax delegates to agree on a constitution shifted the responsibility to the Fifth Provincial Congress, which would be elected in October for a November session. Some historians have seen the October elections as a violent struggle for power between conservatives and radicals. Others disagree. Robert Ganyard has argued that the radicals lacked the organization to mount a coherent challenge to the conservatives and that the evidence does not support a clear radical versus conservative split among ordinary voters, or even, in some cases, among the candidates. Conservatives and radicals, as we shall see, often found common ground, and radicals sometimes disagreed among themselves. Mecklenburg County radicals demanded a unicameral legislature, while reformers in Orange County supported a bicameral assembly, a more conservative institution that would place an additional check on the popular will.[33]

Voters, in any event, failed to remake the provincial congress. Chowan County did not return conservative stalwart Samuel Johnston, but overall turnover among the delegates, about a third of the assembly, was typical for the four previous congresses. Events, more than the election returns, may have strengthened the conservative position. By the time the Fifth Provincial Congress met, Virginia and South Carolina had adopted fairly conservative constitutions along the lines advocated by John Adams in his *Thoughts on Government*, and William Hooper, an erudite and highly respected member of North Carolina's congressional delegation, had written a series of letters back home condemning unchecked democracy.[34]

When the Fifth Provincial Congress met on 12 November, the large radical faction could not be ignored, and the delegates, apparently committed to achieving a rough consensus, produced a constitution that historians have struggled to characterize. The constitution created a two-house legislature; only Pennsylvania would adopt the more radical unicameral assembly. All free adult men, including African Americans, who headed their own households and paid a poll tax could vote for members of the lower house, but only men who owned fifty acres of land could vote for state senators. Officeholders had to own larger estates. The constitution reduced but did not eliminate the advantage the eastern counties had enjoyed in the colonial assembly; westerners would not begin to press for proportional representation until the 1790s. The constitution banned dual officeholding but exempted justices of the peace, thus allowing the courthouse rings to survive. The assembly appointed most public officials, including the governor, a practice radicals generally disliked, but the governor was weak, serving a single one-year term and exercising no veto power. Radicals appreciated the limits on executive discretion.

The constitution ended imprisonment for debt, included a bill of rights, and authorized the legislature to provide for a state university system and public schools, reforms radicals wanted and conservatives, with varying degrees of enthusiasm, could accept. It also disestablished the Anglican Church. Radicals pushed for one of the constitution's most illiberal provisions: Article 32 banned atheists, Catholics, and Jews from "any Office or Place of Trust or Profit in the Civil Department, within this state." Conservatives like Johnston and Hooper, as well as some reformers, opposed religious tests, but most Whig leaders believed only Protestant churches, in the words of Robert Calhoon, "could promote the virtue and self-discipline needed to sustain republican government."[35]

Milton Ready has seen the 1776 constitution as a victory for the radicals while admitting it cannot be judged by modern standards. William Link has called it a "mixed document" that "did little to change the political structure of power in place since the colonial era." Despite "an intense obsession with liberty," North Carolina's revolutionaries left slavery intact and preserved an "oligarchic political structure."[36] Robert Ganyard has concluded the constitution was "only vaguely democratic," although it laid the foundation for future reform. Other historians have said North Carolina's first state constitution was democratic in theory or appearance but not in practice. It has perhaps been most commonly assessed as a compromise in which conservatives maintained a tenuous advantage.[37]

A new government had been created, but the war remained to be won. Whigs and Tories fought a vicious civil war. Both sides resorted to robbery, rape, murder, and arson. In May 1780, 1,400 North Carolina soldiers and militia became prisoners of war when Charleston, South Carolina, fell to British troops under Lord Charles Cornwallis. An American victory over a small Tory army at Ramsour's Mill the following month was soon overshadowed by Horatio Gates's devastating defeat at Camden, South Carolina, in August 1780. A surprising American victory at King's Mountain in October temporarily relieved the threat to North Carolina. John Sevier's participation in the battle, as described in Michael Toomey's essay, helped advance Sevier's remarkable and checkered political career. After playing cat-and-mouse for months, a gifted new American general, Nathanael Greene, fought Cornwallis to a bloody stalemate at Guilford Courthouse in March 1781. Cornwallis's heavy losses led him to abandon North Carolina for Virginia, but the war in North Carolina continued. In September 1781, the Tory David Fanning took 200 prisoners, including

Governor Thomas Burke, during a raid on Hillsborough. The British occupied Wilmington until 18 November 1781. Relative stability did not prevail until the following May, when Fanning left the state, long after the Battle of Yorktown had made a final American victory virtually inevitable.[38]

Amid the carnage of war, state government barely functioned. In the words of Milton Ready, "North Carolina had become a Jeffersonian state long before Thomas Jefferson's political and social philosophy [of limited government] took shape." For many North Carolinians, the weak government had its advantages. If it could not always maintain law and order, for example, neither could it regularly collect taxes.[39]

Under the 1776 constitution, ordinary citizens did become more involved in politics. Although veteran politicians continued to hold most major offices, the number of small farmers in the assembly grew. According to one study, of the men who served in the state senate between 1776 and 1788, 30 percent were "remarkable only for their anonymity."[40] Factionalism also increased, especially as the war came to an end, and new issues arose to divide radicals and conservatives. Radicals, mainly backcountry farmers, demanded generous emissions of paper money, the confiscation and redistribution of Tory property, the cancellation or abatement of prewar debts to British merchants, and easy access to western land. Hoping eventually to restore normal trade with Great Britain, conservatives favored sound money and more conciliatory policies toward the British and their allies.[41]

Next to the war itself, finances presented the new state government with its most vexing problem. North Carolina struggled to pay its bills and meet congressional requisitions. The provincial congress began printing paper money in 1775, and emissions continued well into the 1780s. The state had no good options, and at least in the short term, paper money made it easier for farmers to pay their debts and taxes, but rampant inflation resulted. Despite a few periods of monetary stability, by 1782, 800 North Carolina paper dollars equaled 1 dollar in specie. An inability to support its troops dramatized the state's financial plight. Hugh Rankin has described the demobilization of North Carolina's Continental Line at the end of the war as "a gradual melting away of vagabond soldiers, making their way to their homes, satisfying the gnawing in their bellies by begging, stealing, or using force."[42]

The Treaty of Paris of 1783 ended the war and recognized American independence. It also called for the return of confiscated Loyalist property and the payment of prewar debts to British merchants, even though Congress could not enforce those provisions on the states. North Carolina lawmakers generally opposed them. The feeble central government created by the wartime

Articles of Confederation had no chief executive and no national courts, and it lacked the power to tax or to regulate commerce. When the Articles were being drafted, North Carolina's delegates to the Continental Congress, especially Thomas Burke, had fought successfully, as Section 2 of the Articles provided, for the "sovereignty, freedom, and independence" of each state.[43]

North Carolina, however, was not well situated to enjoy its independence. Exports, especially of tobacco, increased after the Revolution, but the state's almost entirely agricultural economy depended heavily on imported manufactured goods. An unfavorable balance of trade made consumers reliant on credit and drained specie from the state. Monetary policy and debt, both public and private, continued to be hotly contested political issues and on balance seemed to reinforce North Carolina's commitment to a very limited central government. Radicals feared a Congress strong enough to regulate or suppress state emissions of paper money. Nationally minded conservatives hoped Congress would assume much of the states' Revolutionary War debt, but assumption, when it came, did not benefit North Carolina. The state had by then paid its own debt and much of Congress's obligation for the back wages of the state's Continental army veterans. Giving Congress the power to tax would have profited congressional creditors by making repayment more likely, thus raising the market value of their holdings, but few North Carolinians owned securities from the central government.[44]

In the immediate aftermath of the Revolution, radicals probably won more legislative battles than they lost, but they did not win them all, and they did not invariably oppose the expansion of congressional authority. Karl Rodabaugh's chapter on Richard Dobbs Spaight sheds light on the state's political divisions. In April 1784, radicals passed a Cession Act that would have transferred control of North Carolina's western territory, essentially the modern state of Tennessee, to Congress. Westerners tended to favor the cession; they hoped Congress would sell the land cheaply to small farmers and provide more protection against Indians. Conservatives, hoping to use proceeds from land sales to pay off the state debt, repealed the act at the October 1784 assembly session. Frustrated westerners attempted to establish their own state of Franklin, which neither North Carolina nor Congress recognized. The status of western lands, as well as the issues of paper money, Loyalist property, and British debts, would fester throughout the decade.[45]

When the Virginia legislature called for a September 1786 convention in Annapolis, Maryland, to discuss amending the Articles of Confederation and empowering Congress to regulate trade, North Carolina governor Richard Caswell appointed delegates, but only one, Hugh Williamson, attempted to attend, and he arrived the day the convention adjourned.[46] Poor attendance prevented the Annapolis convention from accomplishing anything of substance, although it did issue a call for a meeting in Philadelphia to discuss more thoroughgoing reform, a proposal Congress later endorsed. Jennifer Davis-Doyle's essay analyzes the career of the versatile Williamson, a doctor, scientist, and political operative sometimes called "North Carolina's Benjamin Franklin."

On 6 January 1787, the North Carolina assembly elected Richard Caswell, Alexander Martin, William R. Davie, Richard Dobbs Spaight, and Willie Jones to represent the state at the Philadelphia convention. Jones and Caswell declined to serve; Caswell, who was then governor, appointed Williamson and William Blount as replacements. All five North Carolina delegates went to Philadelphia, but only Blount, Williamson, and Spaight stayed until the end and signed the Constitution. Federalists, as supporters of constitutional reform came to be known, tended to be conservatives with ties to the commercial economy, or in other words, eastern planters, merchants, and professionals. Martin, Davie, Spaight, Williamson, and Blount have been described as "lukewarm conservatives." Only Martin, who grew up among the Scotch Irish, had much in common with the small farmers who made up the bulk of the state's population.[47]

Except for Williamson—who, according to one count, spoke seventy-three times and made twenty-three motions—the North Carolinians played at best a modest role at the convention.[48] The North Carolina delegates had their greatest influence as a force for compromise. On the critical issue of congressional representation, the states divided according to size, with larger states favoring representation based on population and the smaller states demanding equal representation, as they had enjoyed under the Articles of Confederation. Early in the convention the North Carolina delegates voted with the large states in favor of proportional representation. Yet they had reasons not to be dogmatic. The 1790 federal census would show North Carolina to be the fourth most populous state, but in 1787 it was not quite clear how big the state was, and finding out carried risks. North Carolina's representatives in the Confederation Congress worried a larger population would obligate the state to carry a larger share of the national debt.[49]

Accordingly, North Carolina supported the Great Compromise, resolving the thorny issue of representation by providing for a two-house legislature in which each state would have two votes in the Senate while seats in the House of Representatives would be allocated based on population. The North Carolinians also supported the Three-Fifths Compromise, counting a slave as three-fifths of a free person for purposes of representation and taxation, and the slave trade compromise, allowing the foreign slave trade to continue for another twenty years.[50]

The Philadelphia convention finished its work on 17 September, and the *North Carolina State Gazette* published the Constitution in full on 4 October. A vigorous debate began immediately. In order for the document to take effect, it had to be ratified by nine state conventions. Anti-Federalists, largely ex-radicals, complained that the Constitution would create a remote and aristocratic central government that would undermine the states and threaten individual liberties; they decried especially the omission of a bill of rights. In December, over some dogged opposition, the legislature scheduled an election for March 1788 for delegates to a convention that would consider ratification.[51]

After a spirited campaign, the newly elected delegates met in Hillsborough and voted 184 to 83 not to ratify the Constitution, even though, by the time the convention adjourned, eleven other states had approved it. Instead, led by Anti-Federalists Samuel Spencer and Willie Jones, the subjects of essays by Jason Stroud and Kyle Scott, respectively, the convention recommended the adoption of a bill of rights and twenty-six other amendments. The Hillsborough vote showed "how much the conservatives were out of touch with the majority of the state's voters," but it left North Carolina in an untenable position—outside the union with only Rhode Island for company.[52]

Anti-Federalist leaders apparently wanted to hold out as long as they could to extract whatever amendments they could get from Congress. As Kyle Scott notes, Jones saw no rush to act; he understood North Carolina could join the union whenever it wished. In November 1788, the General Assembly called for a new election in August 1789 for a second convention to meet in Fayetteville the following November. Events were running in the Federalists' favor. In September 1789, Congress sent the states that had ratified the Constitution a proposed bill of rights for their approval. Historians disagree on its significance in swaying public opinion, and other forces were at work. Prominent Federalists like James Iredell conducted an effective propaganda campaign on behalf of the new government. The economy seemed to be improving, but some voters feared the imposition of federal import and tonnage duties if North Carolina remained outside the union. George Washington's election as president went a long way to relieve fears about the abuse of executive power. Some westerners believed the new government could protect them from Indian attacks better than the state could. To the surprise of no one, the Fayetteville convention ratified the Constitution by a vote of 195 to 77.[53]

Most Tar Heels, despite joining the union, retained their suspicion of government in general and of centralized government in particular. Many may have soon come to regret the decision in Fayetteville. Secretary of the Treasury Alexander Hamilton's fiscal policies, which included refinancing the federal debt and assuming the state's war debts, raised taxes without providing visible benefits to backcountry farmers. North Carolina leaders hoped that when wartime accounts were settled, Congress would owe the state about $2 million; Congress eventually adopted an accounting formula that instead found that North Carolina owed *it* money. Almost immediately after ratifying the Constitution, Alan Watson has written, North Carolina "retreated to its time-honored insularity."[54] Many of the state's Federalist leaders fared badly after the Revolution. Nationalists struggled to maintain a local political base. William Hooper's influence declined rapidly before his untimely death. Richard Dobbs Spaight became a Democratic-Republican, only to find himself ensnared in a partisan feud that led to a fatal duel. Some of our "ordinary founders" continued founding. Iredell served on the United States Supreme Court in the 1790s. As Scott King-Owen explains, William R. Davie helped establish the University of North Carolina and negotiate an end to the Quasi-War with France but then left North Carolina in disgust after losing a race for Congress. Hugh Williamson had already retired to New York.

North Carolina's Revolutionary Founders is not a comprehensive history of North Carolina in the American Revolution. Our focus is on individuals who either actively supported the Revolution or who participated publicly in the debates over the adoption of the U.S. Constitution. James MacDonald's essay on the Catawba is the one exception; scant records in their case do not permit a biographical approach. Our definition of founders excludes Loyalists as well as enslaved African Americans whose involuntary labor helped support North Carolina's economy. Fortunately, they have received careful attention elsewhere.[55]

We gave the contributors considerable flexibility in shaping their essays. In an effort to understand why colonial elites would risk "their lives, their fortunes, and their sacred honor," as Thomas Jefferson put it, to throw off British rule and establish a new state government and in less than a decade replace a new national government under the Articles of Confederation with another one under the Constitution, we did encourage contributors to consider just what kind of political order the North Carolina founders hoped to create.

As a whole, the essays suggest considerable diversity of opinion among our founders, with immediate and practical needs, if not self-interest, as salient as republican principles. Michael Toomey argues that for a westerner like John Sevier, freedom meant access to western land. Sevier supported ratification of the Constitution but considered a scheme to transfer territory in the

West to Spain before he became the first governor of Tennessee. By contrast, Jennifer Davis-Doyle describes Hugh Williamson as an "aggressive nationalist." A second theme also occurs repeatedly: the extent to which the battles of the era—literal, intellectual, and political—were fought out at the state level by ordinary founders of demonstrable skill, resourcefulness, and resilience. Even our often-maligned Anti-Federalists fare well. As Kyle Scott points out, Willie Jones's faith in the small republic as the surest defender of individual rights had a respectable intellectual pedigree stretching back to Aristotle. Jason Stroud finds Samuel Spencer to be an articulate and insightful critic of the Constitution who deserves to be taken seriously.

Finally, ratification of the Constitution represented only a temporary victory for North Carolina's Federalists. As Troy L. Kickler concludes in the volume's final chapter, the debate among Federalists and Anti-Federalists and later between a new Federalist Party and the Democratic-Republicans over the role of government in a republican society was carried on by the legatees of the Revolutionary generation. After the War of 1812, Orange County judge and legislator Archibald Murphey made the case for a more energetic state government as an engine of social reform and economic progress. Longtime congressman and senator Nathaniel Macon best represented the Anti-Federalist tradition in his fear of the abuse of political power and, in particular, unwarranted assumptions of authority by the general government. In Jacksonian North Carolina, Macon's views generally prevailed, but the debates over personal freedom versus the common good, regulation versus laissez-faire, and states' rights versus more centralized authority went on and may never be resolved.

NOTES

1. Views of federalism as a post-1787 phenomenon include Jack R. Rakove, *Original Meanings: Politics and Ideas in the Making of the Constitution* (New York: Alfred A. Knopf, 1997), 161–202; Forrest McDonald, *Novus Ordo Seclorum: The Intellectual Origins of the Constitution* (Lawrence: University Press of Kansas, 1985), 276–84; and Gordon S. Wood, *The Creation of the American Republic, 1776–1787* (New York: W. W. Norton, 1969), 545. For a longer view of federalism as an idea rooted in America's colonial past, see Andrew Shankman, "Toward a Social History of Federalism: The State and Capitalism to and from the American Revolution," *Journal of the Early Republic* 37, no. 4 (2017): 615–53; Jack P. Greene, *The Constitutional Origins of the American Revolution* (New York: Cambridge University Press, 2011); and Alison L. LaCroix, *The Ideological Origins of American Federalism* (Cambridge, Mass.: Harvard University Press, 2010).

2. Gary Gerstle, *Liberty and Coercion: The Paradox of Republican Government from the Founding to the Present* (Princeton, N.J.: Princeton University Press, 2015). For an argument that federalism and state sovereignty were virtually synonymous in the early republic and that they were the foundation of the new constitutional order, see Aaron

N. Coleman, *The American Revolution, State Sovereignty, and the American Constitutional Settlement, 1765–1800* (Lanham, Md.: Lexington Books, 2016).

3. Milton Ready, *The Tar Heel State: A History of North Carolina* (Columbia: University of South Carolina Press, 2005), 89–92; A. Roger Ekirch, *"Poor Carolina": Politics and Society in Colonial North Carolina, 1729–1776* (Chapel Hill: University of North Carolina Press, 1981), 215–20; Richard Hooker, ed., *The Carolina Backcountry on the Eve of Revolution: The Journal and Other Writings of Charles Woodmason, Anglican Itinerant* (Chapel Hill: University of North Carolina Press, 1953), 81.

4. Alan D. Watson, *Society in Colonial North Carolina* (Raleigh: North Carolina Department of Cultural Resources, 1996), 8–12; William S. Powell, *North Carolina through Four Centuries* (Chapel Hill: University of North Carolina Press, 1989), 131–38; Guion Griffis Johnson, *Ante-bellum North Carolina: A Social History* (Chapel Hill: University of North Carolina Press, 1937), 14–15.

5. Walter F. Pratt, "Oral and Written Cultures: North Carolina and the Constitution, 1787–1791," in *The South's Role in the Creation of the Bill of Rights*, ed. Robert J. Hawes (Jackson: University Press of Mississippi, 1991), 77–99; Alice E. Mathews, *Society in Revolutionary North Carolina* (Raleigh: North Carolina Department of Cultural Resources, 1976), 3–23 (quote on 19).

6. Ekirch, *"Poor Carolina,"* 25, 45; William S. Price Jr., "'There Ought to Be a Bill of Rights': North Carolina Enters a New Nation," in *The Bill of Rights and the States: The Colonial and Revolutionary Origins of American Liberties*, ed. Patrick T. Conley and John P. Kaminksi (Madison, Wis.: Madison House, 1991), 424–42; Hugh T. Lefler and William S. Powell, *Colonial North Carolina: A History* (New York: Charles Scribner's Sons, 1973), 217–20; Lindley S. Butler, *North Carolina and the Coming of the American Revolution, 1763–1776* (Raleigh: North Carolina Department of Cultural Resources, 1976), 12–13.

7. Wayne E. Lee, *Crowds and Soldiers in Revolutionary North Carolina: The Culture of Violence in Riot and War* (Gainesville: University Press of Florida, 2001), 69–70; Hooker, *Carolina Backcountry on the Eve of Revolution*, 80; Watson, *Society in Colonial North Carolina*, 4–8.

8. Dan Higginbotham, "Decision for Independence," in *The North Carolina Experience: An Interpretive and Documentary History*, ed. Lindley S. Butler and Alan D. Watson (Chapel Hill: University of North Carolina Press, 1984), 125–46; John R. Maass, "'A Complicated Scene of Difficulties': North Carolina and the Revolutionary Settlement, 1776–1789" (Ph.D. diss., Ohio State University, 2007), 16–24. On Edenton, which competed with the Lower Cape Fear region for political and intellectual leadership within the colony, see Troy Kickler, *The King's Trouble Makers: Edenton's Role in Creating a Nation and a State* (Edenton, N.C.: Edenton Historical Commission, 2013).

9. Marjoleine Kars, *Breaking Loose Together: The Regulator Rebellion in Pre-Revolutionary North Carolina* (Chapel Hill: University of North Carolina Press, 2002), 5–6, 77, 98, 113–14; Andrew C. Denson, "Diversity, Religion, and the North Carolina Regulators," *North Carolina Historical Review* 72, no. 1 (1995): 30–53 (quote on 31); Robert W. Calhoon, *Religion and the American Revolution* (Raleigh: North Carolina Department of Cultural Resources, 1976), vii–x, 1, 7–16.

10. Ready, *Tar Heel State*, 95–100; W. Lee, *Crowds and Soldiers*, 46–96; Alan D. Watson, "Revolutionary North Carolina, 1765–1789," in *Writing North Carolina History*, ed. Jeffrey J. Crow and Larry E. Tise (Chapel Hill: University of North Carolina Press, 1979), 47–50; James P. Whittenburg, "Planters, Merchants, and Lawyers: Social Change and the Origins

of the North Carolina Regulation," *William and Mary Quarterly*, 3rd ser., 34, no. 2 (1977): 20–36. See generally Kars, *Breaking Loose Together*; and Abby Chandler, "'Unawed by the Laws of Their Country': Local and Imperial Legitimacy in North Carolina's Regulator Rebellion," *North Carolina Historical Review* 93, no. 2 (2016): 119–96.

11. Jeffrey J. Crow, *A Chronicle of North Carolina during the American Revolution, 1763–1789* (Raleigh: North Carolina Division of Cultural Resources, 1975), 5; William A. Link, *North Carolina: Change and Tradition in a Southern State* (Wheeling, Ill.: Harlan Davidson, 2009), 96–100; Alan D. Watson, *Money and Monetary Problems in Early North Carolina* (Raleigh: North Carolina Department of Cultural Resources, 1980), 51–53; Enoch Lawrence Lee Jr., "Days of Defiance: Resistance to the Stamp Act in the Lower Cape Fear," *North Carolina Historical Review* 43, no. 2 (1966): 186–202; Johnson, *Ante-bellum North Carolina*, 15–16. For a contrary view that the Sugar Act provoked more opposition in North Carolina than anywhere else, except for New York, see Ready, *Tar Heel State*, 92–95. The New England colonies had been prohibited from issuing paper money since 1751. See John R. Alden, *A History of the American Revolution* (New York: De Capo, 1969), 62–63.

12. Link, *North Carolina*, 97; Ready, *Tar Heel State*, 94–95; E. Lee, "Days of Defiance," 188–89.

13. William S. Price, ed., *Not a Conquered People* (Raleigh: North Carolina Department of Cultural Resources, 1975), 1–7, 35–48; C. Robert Haywood, "The Mind of the North Carolina Opponents of the Stamp Act," *North Carolina Historical Review* 29, no. 3 (1952): 317–43 (quote on 329).

14. Price, *Not a Conquered People*, 35–48, 46.

15. W. Lee, *Crowds and Soldiers*, 37; Powell, *North Carolina*, 163–65; Donna J. Spindel, "Law and Disorder: The North Carolina Stamp Act Crisis," *North Carolina Historical Review* 57, no. 1 (1980): 1–16.

16. E. Lee, "Days of Defiance," 189–202; Crow, *Chronicle of North Carolina*, 7.

17. Spindel, "Law and Disorder," 15; Edmund S. Morgan and Helen M. Morgan, *The Stamp Act Crisis: Prologue to Revolution* (Chapel Hill: University of North Carolina Press, 1953), 165; Hugh T. Lefler and Albert Ray Newsome, *North Carolina: The History of a Southern State*, rev. ed. (Chapel Hill: University of North Carolina Press, 1963), 182.

18. Crow, *Chronicle of North Carolina*, 9–10.

19. Powell, *North Carolina*, 165–67; Charles G. Sellers Jr., "Making a Revolution: The North Carolina Whigs, 1765–1775," in *Studies in Southern History: James Sprunt Studies in History and Political Science*, vol. 39, ed. J. Carlyle Sitterson (Chapel Hill: University of North Carolina Press, 1957), 23–46; Crow, *Chronicle of North Carolina*, 10.

20. H. Broughn Taylor, "The Foreign Attachment Law and the Coming of the Revolution in North Carolina," *North Carolina Historical Review* 52, no. 1 (1975): 20–36; Link, *North Carolina*, 101. On Martin, see Vernon O. Stumpf, *Josiah Martin: The Last Royal Governor of North Carolina* (Durham, N.C.: Carolina Academic Press, 1986).

21. Taylor, "Foreign Attachment Law," 36; Sellers, "Making a Revolution," 27; Butler, *North Carolina and the Coming of the American Revolution*, 48–52; Ready, *Tar Heel State*, 105–6.

22. Crow, *Chronicle of North Carolina*, 14.

23. Ibid., 15–17; Ready, *Tar Heel State*, 107; Powell, *North Carolina*, 171.

24. Crow, *Chronicle of North Carolina*, 17–18. On the committees of safety, see Alan D. Watson, "The Committees of Safety and the Coming of the American Revolution in North Carolina, 1774–1776," *North Carolina Historical Review* 73, no. 2 (1996): 131–55. For more on the "Edenton Tea Party," see Cynthia A. Kierner, "The Edenton Ladies: Women, Tea,

and Politics in Revolutionary North Carolina," in *North Carolina Women: Their Lives and Times*, ed. Michele Gillespie and Sally G. McMillen, 2 vols. (Athens: University of Georgia Press, 2014), 1:12–33.

25. Crow, *Chronicle of North Carolina*, 19–21.

26. Watson, "Revolutionary North Carolina," 58–59; Ready, *Tar Heel State*, 97–114; Link, *North Carolina*, 105–12; Carole Troxler, *The Loyalist Experience in North Carolina* (Raleigh: North Carolina Department of Cultural Resources, 1976), viii–ix.

27. Powell, *North Carolina*, 184.

28. Link, *North Carolina*, 106; Higginbotham, "Decision for Independence," 130–36; Jeffrey J. Crow, *The Black Experience in Revolutionary North Carolina* (Raleigh: North Carolina Department of Cultural Resources, 1983), 25, 55–62, 64, 69, 82.

29. Powell, *North Carolina*, 182–84; Lefler and Newsome, *North Carolina*, 203; David A. Norris, "Resolves, Prerevolutionary," in *Encyclopedia of North Carolina*, ed. William S. Powell (Chapel Hill: University of North Carolina Press, 2006), 965–66; Pauline Maier, *American Scripture: Making the Declaration of Independence* (New York: Alfred A. Knopf, 1997), 48, 76–80.

30. North Carolina Delegates to the North Carolina Committee of Safety, 10 February 1776, in Paul H. Smith et al., eds., *Letters to Delegates to Congress, 1774–1789*, 25 vols. (Washington: Library of Congress, 1976–2000), 3:28–29; Joseph Hewes to Samuel Johnston, 20 March 1776, ibid., 3:416–17.

31. William L. Saunders, ed., *Colonial and State Records of North Carolina*, 26 vols. (Raleigh: P. M. Hale, 1886–1907), 10:504–5, 510–13; Lefler and Newsome, *North Carolina*, 204–5.

32. Ready, *Tar Heel State*, 116–17; Elisha P. Douglass, *Rebels and Democrats: The Struggle for Equal Political Rights and Majority Rule during the American Revolution* (Chapel Hill: University of North Carolina Press, 1955), 118–21.

33. Robert L. Ganyard, "Radicals and Conservatives in Revolutionary North Carolina: A Point at Issue, the October Election, 1776," *William and Mary Quarterly*, 3rd ser., 24, no. 4 (1967): 568–87; Douglass, *Rebels and Democrats*, 115–18, 125–29; Saunders, *Colonial Records*, 9:699–700, 10:239.

34. Douglass, *Rebels and Democrats*, 121–25; Robert L. Ganyard, *The Emergence of North Carolina's Revolutionary State Government* (Raleigh: North Carolina Department of Cultural Resources, 1978), 68–70.

35. Saunders, *Colonial Records*, 23:980–84; Calhoon, *Religion and the American Revolution*, 69–70. See generally Douglass, *Rebels and Democrats*, 129–35; and Ganyard, *North Carolina's Revolutionary State Government*, 80–89.

36. Ready, *Tar Heel State*, 118; Link, *North Carolina*, 109–11, 121–22.

37. Ganyard, *North Carolina's Revolutionary State Government*, 89; Edwin Hendricks, "Joining the Federal Union," in *North Carolina Experience*, 149–50; Lefler and Newsome, *North Carolina*, 210; Watson, "Revolutionary North Carolina," 52–53.

38. Powell, *North Carolina*, 207–8; Crow, *Chronicle of North Carolina*, 39–48. On the Revolutionary War in North Carolina, see also Lawrence E. Babits and Joshua Howard, *Long, Bloody, and Obstinate: The Battle of Guilford Courthouse* (Chapel Hill: University of North Carolina Press, 2009); John Buchanan, *The Road to Guilford Courthouse: The American Revolution in the Carolinas* (New York: Wiley, 1997); and John S. Pancake, *This Destructive War: The British Campaign in the Carolinas, 1780–1782* (Tuscaloosa: University of Alabama Press, 1985).

39. Ready, *Tar Heel State*, 143; Watson, "Revolutionary North Carolina," 70–71.

40. Mathews, *Society in Revolutionary North Carolina*, 44–45, 75. See also Powell, *North Carolina*, 188–89.

41. Lefler and Newsome, *North Carolina*, 215, 240; Powell, *North Carolina*, 209–11; Ready, *Tar Heel State*, 145–47; Link, *North Carolina*, 122–28; Maass, "'Complicated Scene,'" 6–10.

42. Hendricks, "Joining the Federal Union," 151–52; Watson, *Money and Monetary Problems*, 37–43, 51–53; Hugh Rankin, *North Carolina Continentals* (Chapel Hill: University of North Carolina Press, 1971), 390–91.

43. Hendricks, "Joining the Federal Union," 147–50; Maass, "'Complicated Scene,'" 589–90.

44. James R. Morrill, *The Practice of Fiat Finance: North Carolina in the Confederation, 1783–1789* (Chapel Hill: University of North Carolina Press, 1969), 3–14, 127–31, 167–68; Watson, *Money and Monetary Problems*, 43–50.

45. Link, *North Carolina*, 128–30.

46. Burton Craige, *The Federal Convention of 1787: North Carolina in the Great Crisis* (Richmond, Va.: Expert Graphics, 1987), 11–12.

47. Craige, *Federal Convention*, 15–18; Ready, *Tar Heel State*, 147–48; Link, *North Carolina*, 130–33; Charles D. Rodenbough, *Governor Alexander Martin: Biography of a North Carolina Revolutionary War Statesman* (Jefferson, N.C.: McFarland, 2004), 11–16.

48. Ready, *Tar Heel State*, 148; Powell, *North Carolina*, 223–29.

49. Craige, *Federal Convention*, 20.

50. Link, *North Carolina*, 130–33; Craige, *Federal Convention*, 23–45.

51. Lefler and Newsome, *North Carolina*, 266–67. The most thorough treatment of the ratification debate in North Carolina remains Louise Irby Trenholme, *The Ratification of the Federal Constitution in North Carolina* (New York: Columbia University Press, 1932). See also John C. Cavanagh, *Decision at Fayetteville: The North Carolina Ratification Convention and General Assembly of 1789* (Raleigh: North Carolina Department of Cultural Resources, 1989); and Price, "'There Ought to Be a Bill of Rights.'"

52. Ready, *Tar Heel State*, 148–50. Of the six major regions of the state, as identified by John Maass, only the Albemarle supported ratification. See Maass, "'Complicated Scene,'" 551.

53. Link, *North Carolina*, 134; Albert Ray Newsome, "North Carolina's Ratification of the Federal Constitution," *North Carolina Historical Review* 17, no. 4 (1940): 287–301; Watson, "Revolutionary North Carolina," 72–75.

54. Ready, *Tar Heel State*, 150; Morrill, *Fiat Finance*, 167–68, 215–19; Watson, "Revolutionary North Carolina," 36.

55. On Loyalists, see Maya Jasanoff, *Liberty's Exiles: American Loyalists in the Revolutionary World* (New York: Vintage: 2011); and Troxler, *Loyalist Experience in North Carolina*. On the concept of "forced founders," see Woody Holton, *Forced Founders: Indians, Debtors, Slaves, and the Making of the American Revolution in Virginia* (Chapel Hill: University of North Carolina Press, 1999). See also Crow, *Black Experience in Revolutionary North Carolina*; and more generally Douglas R. Egerton, *Death or Liberty: African Americans and Revolutionary America* (New York: Oxford University Press, 2009).

I

The Revolutionaries

1

Treasonous Tea

The Edenton Tea Party of 1774

Maggie Hartley Mitchell

The Edenton Tea Party, an intentional gathering of women who were economically and geographically situated to make a bold statement on colonial politics, occurred on 25 October 1774 and produced a petition signed by fifty-one North Carolina women.[1] Infuriated by taxes imposed by Parliament, the women of Edenton, Chowan County, and the surrounding area joined forces to sign a petition against purchasing British goods, including tea. Despite facing adversity and potential charges of treason, these women flexed their political muscles, joined the patriot cause, and garnered colonial and European attention. While the Edenton petition did not change British policy, it helped to mobilize the opposition in North Carolina. Perhaps more importantly, the protests of the Edenton women provided an almost unprecedented example of female activism. If they could not vote or hold office in 1774, their petition foreshadowed a new political order in the future in which women would have a voice in public affairs.

From the mid-1600s to the early 1700s, colonists flocked from Virginia to what is now northeastern North Carolina for a chance to own land and acquire wealth.[2] The growth of the region and its natural harbor drew the attention of North Carolina's government. The unincorporated town called Queen Anne's Creek was renamed Edenton, after Governor Charles Eden's death in 1722.[3] Due to Edenton's position on the Albemarle Sound and the fertile land in the region, most of the occupations of men in the town revolved around shipping and agriculture.

Abundant land in northeastern North Carolina and the tobacco crop in the Chesapeake area prompted many men to become planters. This richness of land fueled rapid expansion in Edenton and created a local elite.[4] Several Edenton men held significant positions in the colonial government.[5]

Edenton enhanced the shipping and commerce of North Carolina by serving as a complementary port to Wilmington during the eighteenth century. The town exported items such as tar, pitch, turpentine, corn, pork, beans, black-eyed peas, hog's lard, deerskins, timber, and tobacco.[6] Not only did these exports improve North Carolina's economy, but trade raised the standard of living for many families in Edenton and allowed them and other North Carolinians to import items such as cheese, brandy, coffee, chocolate, Chinese black tea, iron, molasses, and sugar.[7]

Many Edenton traders and merchants benefited financially from the town's role in the Atlantic trading world. John Horniblow owned an inn, the King's Arms, which hosted visiting merchants and politicians.[8] Some of the merchants held public office. Joseph Hewes, one such merchant, engaged in politics and was later one of North Carolina's signatories to the Declaration of Independence.[9] Whether a planter or a merchant or a lawyer, the typical Albemarle area politician was affluent; public service imposed explicit traveling costs and implicit opportunity costs.

Edenton's economic importance eventually led to it becoming one of the colonial capitals of North Carolina until 1743. It would not be until 1770, when the governor's residence moved to New Bern, that North Carolina had a permanent capital. Edenton was also the home to several prominent political families with ties to colonial governors, including the Eden family and the Johnston clan. It was even said that Edenton rivaled Williamsburg in political activity and style prior to the Revolution.[10]

As a prosperous port city and county seat of Chowan County, Edenton became a hub of Revolutionary sentiment. Edentonians, men and women, enjoyed the luxury of being in the forefront of political developments. As the cries for independence stirred in the air following the French and Indian War, Edenton's men did not stand idly by. In a town where many men possessed enough wealth and leisure to actively engage in politics, news of unrest elsewhere, including perhaps a tea boycott organized by Boston women in 1770, would have been commonplace.

The more prominent women in Edenton and the surrounding area had an affluence and access to political news that helped to set the stage for their political engagement. Not only did many of the women of the Edenton Tea Party have a privileged socioeconomic status, but many of their husbands were active in North Carolina political circles as well. These women's economic and political condition provided public opportunities to address their grievances with the British. Their roles as managers of their household economies made their cooperation critical to the effectiveness of any boycott of British goods.[11]

Although Edenton was a thriving port during the eighteenth century, Chowan County's population was fairly sparse by modern standards, and historian Richard Dillard claimed that it was "very probable that fifty-one names compromised most of the ladies living in and around Edenton then."[12] Only twelve women left sufficient records for a detailed, individual analysis. Yet enough information survives to offer insight into the beliefs of all the Edenton Tea Party participants, who were among the elite and middling sorts, not the lower classes. In contrast to the predominantly urban nature of colonial resistance to British taxation in the North, many of the signers of the Edenton petition were from rural areas. A number were the wives of planters; as a consequence many of the signers' husbands were slaveholders.[13]

Mary Blount, one of the signers of the Edenton Tea Party petition, was the first wife of Charles Pettigrew, a prominent Edentonian. Starting out as the local schoolmaster in Edenton, Pettigrew converted to Anglicanism and became the rector of St. Paul's Episcopal Church. Not only was he a well-educated and religious man, he also was a planter with land in North Carolina and Tennessee and thirty-four slaves.[14] Due to the Blounts' wealth and Charles's role in the community, Mary Blount was probably also well known within Edenton and Chowan County.

Also well known throughout Edenton was another signer, Anne Horniblow, wife of innkeeper John Horniblow.[15] Together, Anne and John had five sons and three daughters and owned seven slaves.[16] The number of slaves owned by the Horniblows suggests that they either owned a small farm in addition to the inn or employed slaves as hotel staff.

Elizabeth Beasley, the sister of signer Mary Blount, also stepped into the public sphere as a petition signatory. She was married to John Beasley.[17] According to the 1790 census, the Beasleys had two slaves.[18] At the time of John's death in 1806, he left the family in debt, but his belongings indicated they lived a modest farmer's life with seventy-one hogs, twenty-seven head of cattle, three plows, and domestic goods including six teaspoons and one tablecloth.[19] Unlike many of the women who married attorneys, Elizabeth was from the middling sorts.

Signatories Sarah Littlejohn, Elizabeth Ormond, and Ruth Benbury left a few records that shed light on their lives prior to the Edenton Tea Party. Sarah Littlejohn was married to attorney William Littlejohn. She was well known for caring for the sick and poor, so much so that the *Edenton Gazette* wrote of her virtue following her death in 1807.[20] Elizabeth Ormond was the wife of attorney Wyriot Ormond, who worked closely with Thomas Barker in the North Carolina General Assembly in New Bern during 1749.[21] Finally, Ruth Benbury, according to the census of 1790, had ten slaves in her household.[22] Although she had the same last name, she was not related to Thomas Benbury, a planter and the sheriff of Chowan County.[23]

Two of the signers, Margaret Cathcart and Penelope Dawson, had familial connections to the Johnston family; Royal Governor Gabriel Johnston resided in Edenton with his daughter Penelope Dawson and his nephew Samuel Johnston.[24] Margaret Cathcart was Samuel Johnston's cousin and often wrote to him. One letter in particular—written a year after the Edenton Tea Party—thanked him for his gift after her "misfortune to be deprived of my Dear Father."[25] Penelope Dawson not only was the royal governor's daughter but also was the mother of William Johnston Dawson, who later served in the U.S. Congress.[26] After taking a public political stance by signing the petition, she remained interested in public affairs. In November 1775, Dawson wrote to a friend about the naval "skirmish at Hampton," emphasizing the "spirit of our country men" while praying that "God in his goodness put a stop to these terrible doings, & restore to us Peace once more for indeed it is beyond description shocking to see or hear of friends and fellow subjects destroying one another."[27]

Finally, two of the signers, Sarah (Winfried) Hoskins and Penelope Barker, were the presumed leaders of the Edenton Tea Party. Sarah served as the secretary of the meeting and Penelope led it.[28] Sarah Hoskins was the wife of Richard Hoskins, and they lived just outside Edenton on a farm named Paradise. She was known for her spinning, sewing, and weaving.[29] Sarah and John had eight sons, eight daughters, and twenty slaves.[30] Not only did Sarah's participation in the Edenton Tea Party associate the Hoskins family with the patriot cause, but she managed the farm during the Revolution while Richard joined "the American army at the first sound to arms [and] served with signal bravery and courage until its close."[31]

Penelope Barker's role in the Edenton Tea Party raises a question: What in her past empowered her to play a leading part in an act of rebellion? Penelope was born in Edenton in 1728 to Dr. Samuel Pagett and his wife of gentry background.[32] She grew up alongside the Blount family in Chowan County.[33] To care for her nieces and nephews after her sister's death, a sixteen-year-old Penelope married her brother-in-law John Hodgson. In 1747, during her first marriage, she petitioned for the division of her father's estate.[34] In 1752 John passed away, leaving Penelope with three stepchildren, Isabella, John, and Robert, and her children, Samuel and Thomas.³⁵ At the time of John Hodgson's death, he owned twenty-five slaves: five men, seven boys, eight women, and five girls.³⁶

In typical eighteenth-century fashion, Penelope quickly remarried. This time, she wed James Craven, a merchant, planter, and well-known politician.³⁷ During her second marriage, she supplemented her household income by selling spices, such as nutmeg, cinnamon, and sugar, as well as hiring out her slaves.³⁸ When James passed away in 1756, Penelope became the wealthiest woman in North Carolina.³⁹

Penelope's final marriage was to Thomas Barker, who established himself as a prominent lawyer in eastern North Carolina. Barker had prepared Penelope's first husband's estate and also tutored Samuel Johnston, who was elected but refused to serve as the first president of Congress under the Articles of Confederation. Johnston was also the sixth governor of North Carolina.⁴⁰ Thomas functioned in the colonial assembly and was the colonial treasurer for many years.⁴¹ At this point in her life, Penelope continued managing her household and purchased such luxury items as chocolate, sugar, rum, salt, and molasses.⁴² Thomas passed away in 1789, leaving Penelope with slaves and a plantation as well as identifiably upper-class items, including thirty-three chairs, four large tables, four tea tables, a mahogany plate tray, twelve pewter dishes, twelve pairs of pillowcases, two tea kettles, two tea boxes, twenty-six damask tablecloths, five kitchen tables, and three large china punch bowls.⁴³

Throughout her life, Barker faced some difficult obstacles despite her affluence. Reflecting on her portrait, historian Richard Dillard described her as "one of those lofty, intrepid, high-born women peculiarly fitted by nature to lead; fear formed no part of her composition. Her face bears the expression of sternness without harshness, which a cheap novelist would describe as hauteur. She was a brilliant conversationalist, and a society leader of her day."⁴⁴ Her socioeconomic status, persistent drive, and life experiences positioned her to challenge the status quo, regarding not only female political participation but also Britain's taxation of the colonies.

The timing of the Edenton Tea Party indicates that many of these women had followed the proceedings of the North Carolina Provincial Congress and the Continental Congress, especially concerning trade.⁴⁵ Delegates from Edenton participated in the First Provincial Congress in New Bern on 25 August 1774. There, delegates approved a resolution threatening a trade boycott against the British.⁴⁶ The Edenton Tea Party was a purposeful and not spontaneous response occurring exactly two months after the provincial congress's decision. It was no coincidence that the Edenton Tea Petition used similar phrasing to express similar political concepts.

The Tea Act of 1773 had begun the series of events that led to the Edenton Tea Petition. The Tea Act authorized the British East India Company to sell tea directly to American consumers, thus bypassing colonial merchants. The act also gave the company certain tax breaks that allowed it to sell tea, which was still subject to the Townshend Duties, more cheaply than could its competitors. American merchants resented the competition. Patriots saw the act as an attempt to entice Americans into paying a tax that had not been approved by their elected representatives. After the Boston Tea Party protested the Tea Act in December 1773, the British responded in 1774 with the Coercive Acts, which tightened the reins on the colonists in Boston. In port cities along the East Coast, including Philadelphia, tea parties and boycotts of British goods ensued to protest British taxation and other policies. However, unlike the Boston Tea Party, the women of Edenton did not actually dump tea into a harbor or resort to violence.

According to local tradition, the Edenton Tea Party occurred on 25 October 1774 at the home of Elizabeth King. Penelope Barker, who had called on 23 October for a meeting, presided, with Winifred Hoskins serving as the secretary.[47] As we shall see, the traditional account is questionable in some parts. All fifty-one women supposedly attended the meeting in King's home and thereafter signed the petition to boycott British goods. Barker reportedly said directly after the meeting that "maybe it has only been men who have protested the king up to now. That only means we women have taken too long to let our voices be heard. We are signing our names to a document, not hiding ourselves behind costumes like the men in Boston did at their tea party. The British will know who we are."[48] Barker's passion in this statement, as the presumed leader of the tea party, showed the conviction of the Edenton women and their desire to express their political beliefs through the signing of a petition.

Placing their names on a political document went against traditional gender roles for that period, but the women explained their action: "As we cannot be indifferent on any occasion that appears nearly to affect the peace and happiness of our country, and as it has been thought necessary, for the public good, to enter into several particular resolves by a meeting of Members deputed from the whole Province, it is a duty which we owe, not only to our near and dear connections who have concurred in them, but to ourselves who are essentially interested in their welfare, to do every thing as far as lies in our power to testify our sincere adherence to the same; and we do therefore accordingly subscribe this paper, as a witness of our fixed intention and solemn determination to do so."[49]

The introduction of the petition alludes to the North Carolina Provincial Congress's resolutions that had been adopted two months earlier and acknowledged that the women were following in the footsteps of those Edenton men who were a part of the First Provincial Congress (prominent lawyers and politicians including Samuel Johnston, Thomas Oldham, Thomas Benbury, Thomas Jones, Luke Sumner, and Jacob Hunter) in taking a stand against British policy. They also insisted that this petition was a duty not only to themselves but also to their family, friends, and North Carolina. By signing this document, the women of Edenton and Chowan County ensured that their views were made public and would be long-lasting. Their petition was more than an expression of political opinion; it showcased their claim to certain rights as English citizens, even though society deemed them unfit to engage in politics.[50]

The women also carefully used the first-person point of view throughout the petition. By doing so, they strengthened their argument by claiming the same rights as Englishmen without asking for them as women or appealing to other women. In a sense, they built upon the momentum of the First Provincial Congress, reinforcing the ideals and boycotts embraced by the men. However, the Edenton Tea Party, unlike the resolutions, expressed the views of the consumers of British goods and of those who held the purse strings within the family.

Prior tea parties involved either the boycott or destruction of tea. As a popular beverage and the only import still subject to the Townshend Duties, tea had assumed enormous political significance, but the Edenton petition did not mention it specifically. While a tea boycott was implied by the document, the First Provincial Congress's resolutions targeted not only tea but almost every British good. The delegates wanted to inflict as much economic pain on Great Britain as they could. The petition was signed after the passage of the Intolerable Acts, which tightened Britain's grip on the colonies, not in direct response to the Tea Act, making the traditional description of the event as a tea party misleading. Perhaps it is more appropriate to refer to the Edenton Resolves, but Richard Dillard's decision to call it the Edenton Tea Party provided more notoriety and allure than a set of resolves would probably command.

Most importantly, the petition was republished in other colonies and across the Atlantic Ocean. This small place had created an international affair. One of the signers, Penelope Dawson, supposedly sent the petition to the *Virginia Gazette*, a popular colonial newspaper, perhaps in an effort to exploit her ties in Williamsburg. She had resided with Virginia's lieutenant governor, Robert Dinwiddie, after being orphaned by her father, Governor Johnston.[51] As with any petition, a broad audience, including that of the government it targeted, was needed.

Penelope Barker sent the petition to a British newspaper, the *Morning Chronicle and London Advertiser*, and boldly attached a letter from herself to the king: "The Provincial Deputies of North Carolina having resolved not to drink any more tea, nor wear any more British cloth, etc. many ladies of this Province have determined to give a memorable proof of their patriotism, and have accordingly entered into the following honourable and spirited association. I send it to you, to shew your fair countrywomen, how zealously and faithfully American ladies follow the laudable example of their husbands, and what opposition your Ministers may expect to receive from a people thus firmly united against them."[52]

The beginning of the letter provided the context for the petition: not only did they give up tea and British goods, including clothing, in accordance with the First Provincial Congress's resolutions, but they wanted to make their views known. Effective protest required publicity, both to win support and to attract the attention of British policy makers. Barker emphasized the Edenton women's opposition to the acts implemented by Parliament since the French and Indian War, and she criticized the British government. Her letter included the only mention of tea associated with the Edenton Tea Party.

She continued: "American ladies follow the laudable example of their husbands." Because the women of the Edenton Tea Party respected the model of their politically active husbands, Barker assumed, presumably due to her own limited sphere, that other women would do so. Unlike the petition, Barker's letter was specific regarding gender, almost like a call for other women to rise up against British policy. Women elsewhere had written to protest British rule, usually anonymously. Few had written so forthrightly. Barker may have hoped that by departing from a conventional female role she might impress upon her British readers the gravity of the crisis.

She closed with a challenge to the British government that could have been perceived as a threat of treason, warning the British of "what opposition your Ministers may expect to receive from a people thus firmly united against them." If it was unacceptable for a male to make such statements, it was shocking to hear them from a woman, even though some might perceive them as less threatening coming from a woman. The bluntness of the letter, along with the petition, garnered tremendous criticism from the British. For the era, it was a radical statement. While the petition eventually provoked a patronizing response, her message was clear.

When analyzing the Edenton Tea Party, it is important to evaluate the effectiveness of both the petition and the letter. Because of the petition's gender neutrality—except for the names of its signatories—it is highly likely that the women of Edenton intended for it to supplement the actions of North Carolina's First Provincial Congress. On the other hand, Barker's letter was more provocative because it explicitly mentioned gender. Could it be that Barker intended to sabotage the petition with her letter? That seems improbable. Because she signed the petition, it would not be logical for her to sabotage something she had a stake in. More than likely, she wanted to draw attention to the petition but did not anticipate the adverse effect it would have.

The petition and the letter Barker attached to it are the only definitive sources supporting the existence of the Edenton Tea Party, which can create reasonable doubt about the details of the traditional narrative. Not only were there no other records of the event, but the sources subsequently uncovered over the decades contradict one another. The three most notable details that need examination involve the tea party's leader, its location, and the use of the petition.

The first challenge is determining who actually led the Edenton Tea Party. As Fred Olds observed in 1922 in "The Celebrated Edenton, N.C. Tea Party," and as it is traditionally assumed, Penelope Barker was the presumed ringleader.[53] However, it seems that the only evidence for that claim was a painting of the tea party, which is now lost.[54] Further, the petition itself suggests that Barker may not have led the event after all. Typically, the first signature on a petition indicates leadership. For example, the Declaration of Independence was first signed by John Hancock, the president of the Continental Congress. The first signer of the Edenton Tea Party's petition was Abigail Charlton.[55] Barker, however, was well known throughout Edenton and therefore was one of the most notable of the signers. The dearth of information regarding Charlton and the abundance of evidence concerning Barker's elite status may explain the assumption of her leadership in the traditional narrative.

This assumption of Barker's leadership has important implications. When examining the petition alone, without regard to the issue of gender, the Edenton Tea Party was simply a statement of opinion. There were no direct mentions of boycotts, merely a general condemnation of British policy. However, Barker's letter changes everything if she was the leader of the tea party. By signing their names to the petition under her leadership, the women of Edenton indirectly agreed with Barker's stance in her subsequent letter. If Barker was not the leader of the tea party, then she was acting alone and her actions and words did not necessarily reflect those of the other women.

Over the years, some scholars have challenged the exact location of the Edenton Tea Party. Tradition says that it was held in the home of Elizabeth King. However, this is unlikely. Her home served as a boardinghouse and was not listed on the tax rolls in 1774.[56] Another possible location could be the home of Penelope Barker.[57] But even though she was a member of the elite, fifty-one women could not fit easily into any Edenton home.[58] The Barkers' larger house was not built until 1782. Because of these factors, it is highly unlikely that a single residence was the site of the signing on 25 October 1774.

More than likely, some of the women passed the petition around town or placed it in a prominent place, such as the courthouse, for the rest of the women to sign. Although it is missing, the painting of the Edenton Tea Party shows only fifteen women, with Penelope Barker presiding.[59] This corroborates Cynthia Kierner's hypothesis that leans toward the Edenton Tea Party being a literal petition instead of a single signing. In addition, the women of Edenton supposedly associated themselves as Edenton's Ladies Patriotic Guild.[60] An organized association of political women would have made it easier for the women of the town to disseminate information and gather signatures for a circulating petition.

No matter how the petition was signed, it still denoted an important political event that set a precedent for all other women. According to Kierner, it was "the first recorded case in which a group of women asserted their political principles in writing and in their own names ... [representing a] pivotal moment in the history of women's relationship to public life."[61] This petition marked the beginning of women organizing to participate in politics.[62] (While the petition did influence women to organize in its immediate aftermath, most female petitions during the American Revolution were actually individual requests for financial aid or help in familial matters.)[63]

The Edenton Tea Party paved the way for petitions to become a familiar political tool for women, especially for female antislavery societies, during the early nineteenth century.[64] One such nineteenth-century society was the Philadelphia Female Anti-Slavery Society. Formed in 1833 because women could not join the American Anti-Slavery Society, the Philadelphia Female Anti-Slavery Society was racially integrated from its beginning. The society supported the Underground Railroad financially and logistically and circulated petitions for the abolition of slavery and boycotts of southern and slave-made goods.[65]

Modern-day petitions have lost much of their radical, political significance. They can seem a waste of time. Petitions, for instance, can be for almost any issue, including a plea to resurrect a personal favorite television show that was canceled. But for the women of Edenton, signing a petition was a major event. They performed a bold and potentially treasonous action when stepping outside of their traditional roles.[66] They willingly affixed their names to a document that challenged the authority of Great Britain when women were not generally allowed to participate in politics.

In mezzotint and in transatlantic correspondence, these women endured insults and criticism, but they encouraged more women to stand up for themselves and their country, creating one of America's first organized female political movements. The women of Edenton, however, did not foresee how their tea party would influence others or the criticism they would receive within the colonies and throughout Britain. Nor did they anticipate that Barker's letter would become more influential than the petition they signed.

Instead of effectively aiding reconciliation in London, the petition and accompanying letter, according to Carol Berkin, seemed "to conservative men to signal the same social anarchy as the Boston Tea Party's destruction of private property."[67] This event was interpreted as a violation of the established gender roles; matters of state were only for men.[68] Because of this, the women of Edenton subjected themselves to hostility and ridicule, as seen through a cartoon distributed throughout Britain and the colonies.[69]

Arguably, the most recognizable aspect of the Edenton Tea Party is the famous cartoon of the women that pokes fun at them as they engage in the male-dominated sphere of politics. The cartoon is a wood etch produced by an English artist, Philip Dawe, in response to the Edenton Tea Party and Barker's letter, which was later reproduced in newspapers. In a condescending style, the artist intentionally distorted the women's features to make them resemble men.

The cartoon portrays them as unfit mothers, as shown by the child playing unattended underneath the table. One of the petition signers is entertaining a male suitor who is presumably not her husband, thus further depicting the women as promiscuous. The women in the background are drinking from a bowl and ignoring proper societal norms. The slave in the picture is not shown serving but fraternizing with the ladies. Finally, in the bottom right corner of the cartoon, a dog is urinating on one of the ladies in a blatant sign of British disrespect for the women of Edenton.

The cartoon also summarized Barker's letter, not the petition, as a resolution that stated, "We the ladies of Edenton do hereby solemnly engage not to conform to ye pernicious Custom of Drinking Tea or that we, the aforesaid Ladies, will not promote ye wear of any manufacture from England, until such time that all Acts which tend to enslave this our Native Country shall be repealed."[70] This resolution within the cartoon demonstrates that Barker's letter was more offensive than the petition itself. Creating the women to look imprudent had just as much to do with the fact that the British were unsympathetic to the colonial cause as it did with the fact that the signers of the petition were women.

The only contemporary image of the Edenton Tea Party is a satirical print attributed to the English artist Philip Dawe. (Library of Congress)

However, it was not just the British who made sport of the Edenton Tea Party; so did fellow Edentonians who were in Britain at the time. At the beginning of 1775, sixteen-year-old Arthur Iredell wrote a critical letter from London to his brother James Iredell, an Edenton resident who later became the first North Carolinian to serve on the United States Supreme Court. In his letter, Arthur mocked the women's action:

> I see, by the News Papers, the Edenton Ladies have signalized themselves, by their protest against Tea Drinking. The name Johnston among others; are any of my sister's relations patriotic heroines? Is there a Female Congress at Edenton too? I hope not, for we Englishmen are afraid of the male Congress, but if the ladies, who have ever, since the Amazonian era, been esteemed the most formidable enemies, if they, I say, should attack us, the most fatal consequences to be dreaded. So dexterous in the handling of dart, each wound they give is mortal; whilst we, so unhappily formed by nature, the more we strive to conquer them, the more are conquered! The Edenton ladies, conscious, I suppose, of this superiority on their side, by former experience, are willing I imagine, to crush us into atoms, by their omnipotency; the only security, on our side, to prevent the impending ruin, that I can perceive, is the probability that there are but few places in America which possess so much female artillery as Edenton. Pray let me know all the particulars when you favor me with a letter.[71]

At the time of the Edenton Tea Party and the publication of the petition and Barker's letter, Arthur Iredell, in England, witnessed the hostile reactions. His mention of tea drinking indicates that Barker's letter was influential in developing his opinion, and presumably the general public's opinion, toward the Edenton Tea Party. Iredell responded in the same sarcastic way most of the British responded.

His letter's undertones reveal symptoms of the tension between patriot and Loyalist opinion within families that became more evident as the hostilities broke out.[72] Iredell's letter demonstrates that, as historian Mary Beth Norton explains, "he dismissed the first stirrings of political awareness among American women as a joke, refusing to recognize the ways in which their concept of their role was changing."[73] While this displays his assertion of gender roles, class interests may have played a role in his response. The Edenton Tea Party involved not only elite women but middling sorts as well.[74] It was not proper for elite women to openly defy gender roles, and Iredell revealed his disdain by comparing the Edenton Tea Party to the Amazon myth. But while colonists such as Arthur Iredell disapproved of the Edenton Tea Party, the women inspired others to stand for liberty in Edenton.

Less than a year after the Edenton Tea Party, another group of North Carolina women followed the example of the women in Edenton and took a political stand in Wilmington. The best glimpse into the Wilmington Tea Party comes from the journal of a traveler from Europe, Janet Schaw, who recorded the events of her journey to visit relatives in North Carolina. When she first arrived in what was then "Wilmingtown" in the latter part of 1775, she attended a ball, which she described as miserable: "[I was] dressed out in all my British airs with a high head and a hoop and trudging thro' the unpaved streets in embroidered shoes by the light of a lanthorn carried by a black wench half naked. No chair, no carriage—good leather shoes need none. The ridicule was the silk shoes in such a place."[75] Although she did not like the barbaric feel of the ball, particularly her walk to it, she did meet a few respectable women. Little did she know at the time that those same women were not as proper, in the British sense, as she had assumed.

Schaw believed she had witnessed the opposite of cordiality and propriety when she observed the Wilmington Tea Party. In her journal, she wrote that "the Ladies have burnt their tea in a solemn procession, but they had delayed however till the sacrifice was not very considerable, as I do not think any one offered above a quarter of a pound."[76] Even though the women of Wilmington did not write a petition to King George, they wanted to protest what they considered unconstitutional acts passed by Parliament, including the Tea and Intolerable Acts. By choosing to burn tea in a public square at an unknown date sometime between late March and early April 1775, around five months after the Edenton Tea Party, the women of Wilmington took a political stance against the king and his Parliament's legislation.[77] The Wilmington Tea Party was similar in deed to the Boston Tea Party but similar in spirit to the Edenton petition.

While the women of Wilmington chose a more provocative route for their tea party, its ideological roots were in Edenton. Both towns are coastal port cities in North Carolina that witnessed female tea parties just five months apart. More than likely, the women of Edenton inspired their female counterparts in Wilmington. Popular colonial newspapers, such as the *Virginia Gazette*, published the Edenton Tea Party petition. The exploits in Wilmington also suggest Barker's letter might have been circulated throughout the colonies; her letter was more of a call to women for action than was the petition.[78]

Other than for students of North Carolina history and women's history, the Edenton Tea Party eventually faded into obscurity, typically receiving only a brief mention in books regarding the role of women in the Revolution. However, these women deserve to be remembered not only for their impact on the Revolution but also for their influence on later feminism. In October 1774, fifty-one women agreed publicly to boycott tea and other British products as a result of their common opposition to Britain's taxation policies and their support for North Carolina's First Provincial Congress. The Edenton Tea Party was not an isolated event, nor did it happen spontaneously, as is commonly assumed. This event was an intentional action that rippled throughout the British Empire.

These women of Edenton were indeed patriots. They embodied the values of the American Revolution and those of the future feminist movement. Demonstrating courage, they signed a petition that defied both societal norms in regard to politics and also the British government. Undoubtedly, they knew that their actions could be considered treasonous. The women of the Edenton Tea Party demonstrated loyalty not only to their colony and families but also to each other as they stood together by signing their names to the petition. Ultimately, sacrifice is found in the actions of the Edenton Tea Party participants by their recognition that stepping across the political boundaries set in place by society could isolate them from their families, friends, and community. It was through the courage, loyalty, and sacrifice of these fifty-one women that the groundwork was laid for feminism and gender equality.[79] It is because of these character traits that the women of the Edenton Tea Party should be remembered throughout the generations as revolutionaries. They can also be listed among the founders of the new American republic.

NOTES

1. Although the petition contains fifty-one signatures, there is some debate regarding the actual number of women who may have signed the petition.

2. Jonathan Martin, "Chowan County (1681)," North Carolina History Project, accessed 10 September 2015, http://www.northcarolinahistory.org/encyclopedia/627/entry/.

3. John H. Wheeler, *Historical Sketches of North Carolina from 1584 to 1851* (Philadelphia: Lippincott, Grambo, 1851), 88.

4. One example is John Hodgson, the first husband of tea party leader Penelope Barker. See "A Division of the Negros Belonging to the Estate of John Hodgson (19 April 1752)," in Edenton (N.C.) Papers, Southern Historical Collection, the Wilson Library, University of North Carolina at Chapel Hill.

5. "Deposition of James Durham Concerning Sectional Dispute over the Location of the North Carolina General Assembly Sessions (1746)," in Colonial and State Records of North Carolina, Documenting the American South, accessed October 2015, https://docsouth.UNC.edu/csr/index.php/document/csr04-0380.

6. "Produce of North Carolina (1770)," in Johnston Family Papers, Hayes Collection, Southern Historical Collection.

7. "A Scheme of Goods Suitable for North Carolina (1770)," in ibid.

8. Oil portrait of John Horniblow of Edenton (1770), in North Carolina Division of Archives and History Photograph Collection, Raleigh.

9. Wheeler, *Historical Sketches*, 94.

10. Richard Dillard, *The Historic Tea-Party of Edenton, October 25th, 1774: Incident in North Carolina Connected with Taxation* (New York: A. S. Barnes, 1892), 8.

11. For more on the history of women and household consumption, see Ellen Hartigan-O'Connor, *The Ties That Buy: Women and Commerce in Revolutionary America* (Philadelphia: University of Pennsylvania Press, 2011); and Laurel Ulrich, *A Mid-wife's Tale, Based on Her Diary: 1785–1812* (New York: Vintage, 1991).

12. Dillard, *Historic Tea Party of Edenton*, 5.

13. Cynthia Kierner, "The Edenton Ladies: Women, Tea, and Politics in Revolutionary North Carolina," in *North Carolina Women: Their Lives and Times*, ed. Michelle Gillespie and Sally McMillen, 2 vols. (Athens: University of Georgia Press, 2014), 1:19–22.

14. Meredith Malburne-Wade, "Charles Pettigrew, 1744–1807, Last Advice of the Rev. Charles Pettigrew to His Sons, 1797 Summary," in Documenting the American South, accessed 10 April 2015, http://docsouth.unc.edu/nc/pettigrew/summary.html.

15. Oil portrait of John Horniblow of Edenton (1770).

16. "Chowan County Census of 1790," in Documenting the American South, accessed 3 April 2015, http://docsouth.unc.edu/csr/index.html/document/csr26-0011.

17. Sarah McCulloh Lemmon, "Beasley, Frederic," NCPedia, accessed 20 October 2015, http://ncpedia.org/biography/beasley-frederic.

18. "Chowan County Census of 1790."

19. "The Estate of John Beasley," in Edenton District Court: Estate Records, State Archives of North Carolina.

20. Guion Griffis Johnson, *Ante-bellum North Carolina: A Social History* (Chapel Hill: University of North Carolina Press, 1937), 699.

21. "Deposition of Wyriot Ormond and Thomas Barker Concerning Copies of Acts of the North Carolina General Assembly," in Documenting the American South, accessed 3 October 2015, http://docsouth.unc.edu/csr/index.html/document/csr04-0397.

22. Walter Clark, William Laurence Saunders, and Stephen Beauregard Weeks, eds., *Census 1790*, in *The State Records of North Carolina* (Goldsboro, N.C.: Nash Brothers Book and Job Printers, 1905), 26:3–4.

23. Elmer D. Johnson, "Benbury, Thomas," NCPedia, accessed 20 October 2015, http://ncpedia.org/biography/benbury-thomas.

24. Kierner, "Edenton Ladies," 13.

25. Margaret Cathcart to Samuel Johnston, Edenton, 29 September 1775, in Cathcart Family Papers, State Archives of North Carolina.

26. James Elliot Moore, "Dawson, William Johnston," NCPedia, accessed 20 October 2015, http://ncpedia.org/biography/dawson-william-johnston.

27. Penelope Dawson to Mrs. Lee, 2 November 1775, in British Records, State Archives of North Carolina.

28. Fred A. Olds, "The Celebrated Edenton, N.C. Tea Party," *Daughters of the American Revolution* 56, no. 6 (June 1922): 328.

29. Dillard, *Historic Tea Party of Edenton*, 14.

30. "Chowan County Census of 1790."

31. Dillard, *Historic Tea Party of Edenton*, 13.

32. Joseph Cummins, *Ten Tea Parties: Patriotic Protests That History Forgot* (Philadelphia: Quirk Books, 2012), 165.

33. "Map of Land," in Edenton (N.C.) Papers.

34. "Petition of Division of Samuel Paget's Estate," in ibid.

35. "August 1752 Apportionment of the Estate of John Hodgson," in ibid.

36. "Division of the Negros Belonging to the Estate of John Hodgson (19 April 1752)."

37. William S. Price Jr., "Craven James," NCPedia, accessed 10 September 2015, http://ncpedia.org/biography/craven-james.

38. "Mrs. Penelope Craven to William Sorother & Company," in Edenton (N.C.) Papers.

39. Cummins, *Ten Tea Parties*, 165.

40. Dillard, *Historic Tea Party of Edenton*, 12.

41. "Dr. Thomas Barker Esq. Public Treasurer in Account with the Public of North Carolina as Settled by the Committee of Accounts April 1762," in Edenton (N.C.) Papers.

42. "Account of Thomas Barker Esq. in 1764," in ibid.

43. "Inventory of Sundries Taken This 1st Day of January 1788 Belonging to the Estate of Thomas Barker Esq. Deceased," in ibid.

44. Dillard, *Historic Tea Party of Edenton*, 12.

45. Kierner, "Edenton Ladies," 16.

46. Wheeler, *Historical Sketches*, 90.

47. Olds, "Celebrated Edenton, N.C. Tea Party," 328.

48. Debra Michals, ed., "Penelope Barker (1728–1796)," National Women's History Museum, accessed 15 April 2013, http://www.nwhm.org/education-resources/biography/biographies/penelope-barker/.

49. "Extract of a letter from North Carolina, Oct. 27," *Morning Chronicle and London Advertiser*, 31 January 1775, reprinted by the Edenton Woman's Club in *Historic Edenton and Countryside* (*The Chowan Herald*, 1959), 3–4, in Eastern North Carolina Digital Library at East Carolina University, Greenville, N.C.

50. Ibid.

51. Kierner, "Edenton Ladies," 13.

52. Penelope Barker, "Extract of a Letter from North Carolina, Oct. 27," in *The North Carolina Experience: An Interpretive and Documentary History*, ed. Lindley S. Butler and Alan D. Watson (Chapel Hill: University of North Carolina Press, 1984), 136–37.

53. Olds, "Celebrated Edenton, N.C. Tea Party," 328.

54. Mary Dawes Staples, "The Edenton Tea Party," *American Monthly Magazine*, August 1907, 360.

55. "Extract of a letter from North Carolina, Oct. 27," *Morning Chronicle and London Advertiser*, 3–4.

56. Kierner, "Edenton Ladies," 20.

57. Staples, "Edenton Tea Party," 358.

58. Kierner, "Edenton Ladies," 19.

59. Olds, "Celebrated Edenton, N.C. Tea Party," 332.

60. Cummins, *Ten Tea Parties*, 168.

61. Kierner, "Edenton Ladies," 12.

62. Mary Beth Norton, *Liberty's Daughters: The Revolutionary Experience of American Women* (Boston: Little, Brown, 1980), 161.

63. Robert J. Dinkin, *Before Equal Suffrage: Women in Partisan Politics from Colonial Times to 1920* (Westport, Conn.: Greenwood Press, 1995), 12.

64. Linda K. Kerber, *Women of the Republic: Intellect and Ideology in Revolutionary America* (Chapel Hill: University of North Carolina Press, 1980), 41.

65. "Philadelphia Female Anti-Slavery Society," Historical Society of Philadelphia, accessed 20 November 2015, https://hsp.org/sites/default/files/philadelphiafemaleantislaverysociety.pdf.

66. Troy Kickler, *The King's Trouble Makers: Edenton's Role in Creating a Nation and State* (Edenton, N.C.: Edenton Historical Commission, 2013), 18.

67. Carol Berkin, *Revolutionary Mothers: Women in the Struggle for America's Independence* (New York: First Vintage Books, 2004), 22.

68. Dinkin, *Before Equal Suffrage*, 10.

69. Kerber, *Women of the Republic*, 279.

70. "Extract of a letter from North Carolina, Oct. 27," *Morning Chronicle and London Advertiser*, 3–4.

71. *The Papers of James Iredell*, ed. Don Higginbotham (Raleigh: North Carolina Historical Commission, 1976), 1:282.

72. Sally Smith Booth, *Women of '76* (New York: Hastings House, 1973), 12.

73. Norton, *Liberty's Daughters*, 163.

74. Margaret Supplee Smith and Emily Herring Wilson, *North Carolina Women: Making History* (Chapel Hill: University of North Carolina Press, 1999), 50–51.

75. Janet Schaw, *Journal of a Lady of Quality: Being the Narrative of a Journey from Scotland to the West Indies, North Carolina, and Portugal, in the Years 1774 to 1776*, ed. Evangeline Walker Andrews (New Haven, Conn.: Yale University Press, 1921), 153–54.

76. Ibid., 155.

77. Cummins, *Ten Tea Parties*, 176.

78. There is an opportunity for future research to find definitive connections between the Edenton and Wilmington Tea Parties.

79. Smith and Wilson, *North Carolina Women*, x.

2

Declaring Independence

William Hooper, Joseph Hewes, and John Penn

Jeff Broadwater

Whatever their other accomplishments, William Hooper, Joseph Hewes, and John Penn can be called founders for one reason: they signed the Declaration of Independence on North Carolina's behalf. We should be careful not to read too much into that act. They did not take literally the Declaration's assertion of human equality; the American Revolution would not be a social revolution. Their support for American independence did not reflect a consensus behind a new political order. Thomas Jefferson's recollections, which give Penn too much credit, capture the tensions surrounding them. "You remember as well as I do," he wrote fellow ex-president John Adams in 1819, "that we had not a greater tory in Congress than Hooper, that Hughes [sic] was very wavering, sometimes firm, sometimes feeble, according as the day was clear or cloudy." Jefferson considered Richard Caswell, a member of North Carolina's original delegation to the Continental Congress, to be a sound Whig who kept Hooper and Hewes in check, but after he left, "their line of conduct became then uncertain until Penn came, who fixed Hughes and the vote of the State."[1] Independence would not resolve their differences.

Born in Boston in June 1742, William Hooper enjoyed every advantage the American colonies could offer. His father, William Hooper Sr., a Scottish Congregationalist turned Anglican, was rector of Boston's Trinity Church. As a boy, William attended the exclusive Boston Latin School and later went to Harvard, where he earned a master's degree. From the fall of 1760 until the fall of 1764, Hooper clerked in the law office of James Otis, who was then emerging as an early critic of British imperial policy. Hooper and Otis had much in common: Harvard degrees, an interest in the classics, keen intellects, and excitable temperaments. Otis's influence on his clerk seems undeniable.[2]

It was not, however, wholly welcome. The Reverend Hooper apparently disapproved of Otis's Whig politics, and he may have hatched a plot to send William to Wilmington, North Carolina. The elder Hooper was a friend of James Murray, a Boston merchant who had an agent, Thomas Clark, in Wilmington. William Hooper Sr. wanted to get his son away from Otis, and North Carolina made an attractive refuge. Murray's connections would help William establish himself in Wilmington; young lawyers there faced less competition than they did in Boston, and Clark had a single daughter, Anne, whom William had begun courting while she was staying in Boston. William arrived in Wilmington in October 1764 and was elected borough recorder two years later. He and Anne married in August 1767.[3]

North Carolina presented Hooper opportunities for personal gain in a toxic political climate. Rapid growth after about 1715 and the lack of a well-entrenched landed gentry, similar to those that dominated Virginia and South Carolina, allowed favored newcomers like Hooper to move up quickly. Most of North Carolina's population growth since 1745 had been in its Piedmont and backcountry counties. By 1775, they contained two-thirds of the colony's population, but malapportionment allowed the eastern counties to control the colonial assembly.[4]

Corruption in local politics probably generated more resentment than malapportionment did. Royal governors appointed new sheriffs and justices of the peace based on the recommendations of incumbent justices. Sheriffs supervised elections to the colonial legislature, while most lawmakers also served on the county courts, thus creating an incestuous alliance between the eastern-dominated assembly and local courthouse rings.[5]

Dishonest and unrepresentative government bred endemic financial irregularities. Sheriffs and other officials charged citizens exorbitant fees for routine services while embezzling money from colonial coffers. According to one estimate, sheriffs pocketed over half the colony's annual tax revenues.[6] Discontent in the west produced the Regulator movement, which began with peaceful protests, escalated into violent demonstrations, and culminated in the Battle of Alamance in May 1771, an armed confrontation between western farmers and eastern militia under the command of William Tryon, the royal governor. Hooper supported Tryon, and Regulators associated the Wilmington lawyer with the eastern establishment. In May 1768, a mob disrupted proceedings at the Anson County courthouse and reportedly drove Hooper from the courtroom.[7]

Not vindictive by nature, Hooper made some effort to address the Regulators' concerns. After Tryon appointed him a temporary deputy attorney general for the Salisbury District, he prosecuted an attorney, John Frohick, for overcharging a local widow, but a jury ruled against him. At Hillsborough in March 1769, Regulators wanted Hooper to bring charges against an inferior court clerk, but Hooper was lodging with their bête noire, Judge Edmund Fanning; this situation, the Regulator Herman Husband complained, discouraged "men of common Modesty" from asking him for help. A few of the more intrepid did approach Hooper; he asked them to prepare a complaint and then, according to Husband, made trivial objections to multiple drafts. A year later a mob attacked the Hillsborough courthouse, dragging Fanning from the bench. After threatening and assaulting other lawyers and officials, according to a Boston newspaper, "they then seized Mr. Hooper, a gentleman of the law, dragged & paraded him through the streets and treated him with every mark of contempt and insult."[8]

No respectable figure condoned the violence, but Tryon's successor, Josiah Martin, concluded after a tour of the backcountry that westerners "have been provoked by insolence and cruel advantages taken of the peoples ignorance by mercenary tricking Attornies, clerks and other little officers who have practiced upon them every sort of rapine and extortion." Bitterness toward the eastern elite would persist long after the Regulator movement had collapsed.[9]

William Hooper first appeared in the North Carolina assembly in January 1773 as a representative of the tiny borough of Campellton and almost immediately established himself as one of the legislature's most influential members. He won passage of bills eliminating the death penalty for horse stealing, at least for first offenders; prohibiting the "willful and malicious" killing of slaves; and limiting the sentences of people imprisoned for debt. He also supported the creation of a judiciary independent of royal control. His position on court reform brought Hooper, and the rest of the assembly, into conflict with Governor Martin. The assembly refused to fund a court system without a provision for "foreign attachments," a procedure that would have allowed colonial courts to seize the North Carolina property of debtors who did not live in the colony. Martin vetoed the measure and then attempted to establish new courts on his own initiative, an unpopular step that marked the beginning of the end of royal authority in North Carolina. Meanwhile, Martin vetoed Hooper's bills on horse stealing and the murder of slaves, and the Board of Trade disallowed his bill protecting insolvent debtors.[10]

At its December 1773 session, the assembly refused to recognize the legitimacy of the governor's courts and appointed a Committee of Correspondence to coordinate opposition to British policies with the other colonies. Hooper was named to the committee and so was Joseph Hewes. Hewes had grown up a Quaker on his family's plantation near Kingston in what was then West Jersey. In 1749, at age nineteen, he decided against attending the College of New Jersey, now Princeton, electing instead to apprentice himself to Joseph Ogden, a Philadelphia merchant who had married Hewes's cousin Jemina. Hewes spent five years with Ogden, learning his trade and traveling throughout the colonies.[11]

Hewes attempted to establish a mercantile business of his own in Philadelphia but soon began to look for opportunities elsewhere. His work for Ogden had taken him to Edenton, a prosperous coastal town that seemed ideal, in the words of the contemporary writer John Brickell, for men of "small beginnings." Moving to Edenton about 1755, Hewes impressed the locals with his relentlessly practical mind and a fierce Puritan work ethic, although his friend James Iredell said later he was "a professed Deist." In a few months Hewes formed a mercantile partnership with George Blair and Charles Worth Blount; an even closer personal and political relationship with Samuel Johnston came later. He eventually became engaged to Johnston's sister Isabella. She died before their wedding day. Hewes never married, and Johnston considered him a member of the family for the rest of his life. The Quaker turned Deist became an alderman at St. Paul's Anglican Church, and in 1760 Johnston engineered his election to the colonial assembly. If assessments vary as to Hewes's effectiveness as a legislator, no one ever questioned his business acumen. By the eve of the Revolution his wealth, according to one biographer, put him "among the top three percent of the population in colonial America."[12]

Governor Martin prorogued the assembly until March 1774, leaving the court controversy unresolved and the colony, the Anglican minister James Reed wrote from New Bern, "in great confusion." As relations with Martin and Parliament deteriorated, William Hooper emerged as one of the Whigs' most reliable draftsmen. He wrote a series of newspaper essays, which have not survived, under the pseudonym "Hampden," to assert American rights, and when the assembly reconvened in March he was appointed to one committee to draft a rebuttal to Martin on the foreign attachment issue and to another to prepare a petition to King George III pleading for the colony's right to issue paper currency.[13]

Martin and the assembly reached a partial compromise, allowing a few courts to reopen, but what little rapprochement they achieved was immediately undone by Parliament's passage, in the wake of the Boston Tea Party, of the Coercive Acts, which among other punitive measures closed the port of Boston to most traffic. The imperial crisis put Whig leaders like Hooper and Hewes in an awkward position. They did not want a revolution—they had too much to lose—but they would not compromise American rights, or more precisely the prerogatives of the assembly they controlled.[14]

In April 1774, Hooper produced one of the two or three most revealing of his extant papers. In a long letter to the Edenton lawyer James Iredell, Hooper demonstrated a prescient understanding of where the resistance movement was headed, a commitment to classical republicanism, and an inability to envision an alternative to the British constitution. At a time when virtually all Americans were denying any interest in severing ties with Britain, Hooper told Iredell the colonies "are striding fast to independence, and ere long will build an empire upon the ruins of Great Britain; will adopt its constitution purged of its impurities, and from an experience of its defects will guard against those evils which have wasted its vigor and brought it to an untimely end." Commerce had produced "wealth, and luxury, and corruption" in Great Britain. "Good fortune," Hooper believed, "is a powerful enemy to virtue." Acquisition of an empire that was "too unwieldy" had led to Britain's decline, just as it had done in Rome. Essentially an Anglophile, Hooper linked the defense of freedom in America with the survival of English liberties anywhere. As British subjects lost their rights, he hoped they might find America "the asylum of liberty too."[15]

That the Coercive Acts targeted Hooper's hometown undoubtedly contributed to his radicalization. "I am absorbed," he wrote Iredell in June, "by the distress of my native country." On 21 July, he chaired a mass meeting in Wilmington, the first of its kind in North Carolina, that passed a series of resolutions calling for a meeting of delegates from throughout the colony to discuss "the present alarming State of British America" and for a "General Congress" of "the several Colonies" in Philadelphia. The Wilmington Resolves, which Hooper likely drafted, also pledged to support Boston's embattled patriots; "we consider the cause of the Town of Boston as the common cause of British America."[16]

Over the course of the next month, other counties held similar meetings, and in late August, thirty of the colony's thirty-five counties sent delegates to New Bern for what would become known as the First Provincial Congress; a series of provincial congresses would govern the colony in the interim between the collapse of royal authority and the creation of a new state government.

Hooper represented New Hanover County. Edenton sent Hewes. The New Bern congress adopted its own resolves, usually attributed to Hooper, which pledged loyalty to the king and to the British constitution but complained that "our most essential rights" have been invaded by Parliament. Because Americans could not be represented in Parliament, any taxes it imposed were "illegal and unconstitutional." The resolves mentioned the Tea Act specifically, condemned the preferential treatment Parliament had given tea exported by the East India Company, and assailed the Coercive Acts, in particular a provision allowing royal officials accused of capital offenses in America to be tried in England. They also called for an aggressive economic boycott of British trade, cutting off British imports as of 1 January 1775 and, if no relief was forthcoming, embargoing the export of tobacco and naval stores the following October.[17]

Much in the resolves was predictable, but two points stand out. First, echoing the Wilmington resolves, was the commitment to British liberty. "We claim no more than the rights of Englishmen," and "liberty is the spirit of the British constitution, and it is the duty, and will be the Endeavour of us British Americans to transmit this happy constitution to our posterity in a state if possible better than we found it." Second, North Carolina's delegates to the upcoming Continental Congress in Philadelphia were given broad authority to make "a firm and resolute defence of our persons and properties against all unconstitutional encroachments whatever."[18]

The New Bern delegates also elected three representatives to the First Continental Congress. Hooper's education and the role he had played in the resistance movement made him a virtually inevitable choice, although there was apparently opposition from western delegates who preferred one of their own. Hewes's personal popularity probably aided his election; James Iredell called him "one of the best and most agreeable men in the world." Richard Caswell completed the delegation. Governor Josiah Martin believed Caswell accepted the appointment "purely for the sake of maintaining his popularity" so he could retain his post as colonial treasurer. The governor dismissed Hooper and Hewes as "professed champions of all popular measures." He might have been more sympathetic. As historians David Morgan and William Schmidt have written, the North Carolina delegates went "to Philadelphia to prevent a revolution, not to start one."[19]

They arrived in September. The Connecticut delegate Silas Deane shared his first impressions of Hooper in a letter to his wife, Elizabeth. He "is a Bostonian bred & Educated at Cambridge college . . . a Lawyer by profession, ingenious, polite, spirited, & tolerably eloquent." Deane described Hewes as "about forty"—in reality he was thirty-four—"sedate, & settled . . . well affected to the general cause." Hooper proved to be one of the most active delegates in Congress; John Adams classified him as an "orator," along with the Virginians Richard Henry Lee and Patrick Henry. Hewes, less equipped by education or experience to argue fine points of constitutional theory, rarely participated in congressional debates, but he did useful work in committee.[20]

In the First Continental Congress, the North Carolina delegates joined with Maryland and Virginia to defeat a proposal from the New Englanders to address objections to imperial policy going back to 1607. They knew challenging the Navigation Acts regulating American trade would make reconciliation more difficult. At the same time, they supported the Continental Association, Congress's plan to impose economic sanctions on Great Britain. Congress adjourned in October, but over the next year, Hooper and Hewes would serve together in a colonial assembly and a Second Provincial Congress in New Bern in April 1775, in the Second Continental Congress in May, and in a Third Provincial Congress in Hillsborough in August.[21]

Through it all, even after fighting erupted at Lexington and Concord in April 1775, the North Carolina delegates talked publicly and privately of reconciliation, denying any interest in independence, but they left themselves no room for compromise. "I am not," Hooper wrote his mother, "a licentious demagogue, but think coolly & dispassionately upon the conduct of Government." Yet he could never accept Parliament's decision to close the port of Boston.[22] Hooper may well have envisioned the reformation of the British Empire into something akin to its late twentieth-century form, with Parliament exercising no real power over its foreign dominions and the monarch serving as a figurehead.[23]

In Philadelphia after the war erupted, Hewes wrote almost frantic letters home, encouraging colonial leaders to prepare for armed resistance. As he wrote Samuel Johnston, "I had rather perish ten thousand times than they [the people] should give up the matter now in the time of trial."[24] Worried about the loyalty of ex-Regulators in the backcountry, many of whom were Presbyterians, Hewes worked to recruit ministers from their denomination to mobilize support for the war effort. He had his own bill of particulars against the British: they had attempted to incite Canadians, Indians, and slaves against American Whigs; they had sought to destroy colonial trade and to prevent Americans from acquiring arms from Europe; and they had "sent a formidable Fleet and Army to seize our Vessels and cut our throats." Then they "charge us with Rebellion because we will not believe that they have a right to make Laws to bind us in all cases whatsoever."[25]

He and Hooper had reputations as moderates, but by July 1775, Hewes was advising Samuel Johnston, who was then serving as moderator of the provincial congress, to expel Governor Martin and Chief Justice Martin Howard if they attempted "to do anything" and was predicting a new, popular government must soon be established. "I consider myself now over head & Ears in what the ministry call Rebellion," he told Johnston.[26]

Hooper and Hewes continued, however, to profess their loyalty to the British system. Hooper, writing in the third person, claimed he had "never taken a step which has not been dictated by the honesty of his heart & a sincere love for the Constitution of G. Britain." Their identification with Great Britain made the rebellion more than a struggle for American rights. If America succumbed to tyranny, Hooper and Hewes agreed, "Britain must go hand in hand with her to destruction." Hewes wrote an undoubtedly public letter to London merchants, pleading, "We do not want to be independent, we want no revolution . . . ," yet "we are convinced, nothing can restore peace to this unhappy country, and render the liberty of your's secure, but a total change of the present Ministry."[27]

Britain's preeminence as a world power sometimes seemed to endow American resistance with global significance, as when Hooper wrote his mother in November 1774, "The liberties of mankind are at stake." More typical was language in an address to the assembly of Jamaica, which was produced for the Second Continental Congress by a committee that Hooper chaired. The restrictions placed on the British colonies in North America were merely part of "a deliberate plan to destroy, in every part of the empire, the free constitution, for which Britain has been so long and so justly famed." To Hooper's committee, "ministerial barbarity . . . has plunged us in all the horrors and calamities of civil war."[28] Note the term "civil war." Hooper, Hewes, and countless other moderate and conservative Whigs were not fighting for a revolution; they saw themselves engaged in a contest over the nature of the British constitution.

On 8 September 1775, the Third Provincial Congress elected John Penn to replace Richard Caswell, who had resigned to accept a position as one of North Carolina's two new colonial treasurers. Penn's selection suggests the delegates had come to see a need for greater unity in the midst of a worsening crisis. A westerner, Penn owed his nomination to another Granville County delegate, the ex-Regulator Thomas Person. Penn's selection was seen as an attempt to placate former Regulators who had opposed William Hooper's election a year earlier.[29]

Penn had been born near Port Royal, Virginia, in May 1740. His father, Moses Penn, put little stock in formal education, so Penn went to school for only two or three years, but after his father died, the jurist Edmund Pendleton, a distant relative, allowed John to use his library, and Penn apparently read law under the eminent judge. Family connections brought him to North Carolina. Moses's widow, Catherine Taylor Penn, remarried and moved to Granville County, home of Penn's future wife, Susannah Lyme. They married in 1763. By June 1774, Penn had moved to North Carolina and, in Pendleton's words, "by the law, trade and planting acquired a handsome fortune." Penn immediately involved himself in Whig politics and was elected to the Third Provincial Congress. Penn's qualifications for his post, apart from geography, a certain likability, and a willingness to serve, are not immediately apparent. An early twentieth-century historian charitably summarized his congressional career: Penn "made no conspicuous public display," but his "services were highly efficient and useful, and entirely acceptable to the people he represented."[30]

Penn is usually described as the first of the North Carolina delegates to embrace independence, but by the fall of 1775, Hewes had given up almost all hope of reconciliation with Great Britain.[31] Among other ominous signs, George III had by then rejected Congress's Olive Branch Petition proposing a ceasefire. Hewes busied himself serving on three committees dealing with naval affairs and on 30 October was appointed to the Naval Board. The board drafted regulations for the new American navy, bought ships, and commissioned officers; Hewes helped John Paul Jones, the Revolution's greatest naval hero, secure a commission. The ever-practical Hewes kept the board's books and managed its correspondence. When the Naval Board was superseded by a new Marine Committee, Hewes became its most active member.[32]

Hewes did not, however, speak up in favor of independence, and Hooper, although he had earlier recognized the almost unstoppable momentum toward a complete break with Britain, still hoped to avoid it. He successfully opposed efforts to create a formal union of the thirteen colonies, which was seen as a step toward independence, and he worked with conservatives like John Dickinson of Pennsylvania on a wholly futile effort to develop a new peace plan.[33] Frustrated with his inability to find a political compromise to the imperial crisis, Hooper expected the worst. "From newspapers & private letters," he wrote Samuel Johnston in December 1775, "we are assured that next Summer will be a bloody one." The strain left North Carolina's most influential delegate, at the age of thirty-three, contemplating political retirement. In a long letter to Iredell he complained he was "weary of politicks, it is a study that corrupts the human heart, degrades the Idea of human nature, and drives men to expedients that morality must condemn." Politics made vice a virtue. "Deep stratagems, dark disguise, Fiction, falsehood, are but the fair side of a perfect, politician. . . . Hide the picture! 'tis a horrid one."[34]

February 1776 represents something of a turning point for Hooper, Hewes, and Penn. In December, two months earlier, an American attack on Quebec, led by Benedict Arnold and Richard Montgomery, had failed. On New Year's Day, Lord Dunmore, Virginia's royal governor, had ordered British warships to shell Norfolk. Less than two weeks later, Thomas Paine's revolutionary pamphlet *Common Sense* appeared in Philadelphia. Penn's reputation as the first of the North Carolina delegates to endorse independence rests largely on a February letter to Thomas Person in which he argued that the colonies needed trade to finance the war effort, that trade would require foreign alliances, and that alliances might lead "to a total separation with Britain," a result he seemed prepared to accept.[35]

As rumors of a new British peace initiative proved unfounded, Hooper and Hewes sounded hardly more conciliatory than Penn. "I think everything is now at stake," Hooper wrote, "must not every man a friend to the Cause, and capable of duty turn out with his musquet." Hewes agreed, reporting to Samuel Johnston, "I have furnished my self with a good Musket & Bayonet and when I can no longer be useful in Council I hope I shall be willing to take to the field."[36]

Yet their reactions to *Common Sense* indicated divisions existed within the delegation. Paine not only called for independence but also attacked the British constitution that Hooper revered as "the base remains of two ancient tyrannies . . . monarchial tyranny in the person of the king" and "aristocratical tyranny in the persons of the peers." To further unnerve traditionalists, Paine called for a continental union and for more equitable representation in what would be the new state legislatures. Loading a wagon headed for North Carolina, Hewes hesitated to include copies of *Common Sense*—he called it "a Curiosity"—and then changed his mind, explaining rather sheepishly to Samuel Johnston that Penn liked the pamphlet and that local officials "can Judge the propriety" of distributing it.[37]

How Hooper, Hewes, and Penn came to sign the Declaration of Independence turned out to be less dramatic than might be assumed. On 20 March 1776, Hewes, anticipating a vote in Congress on independence and reporting that he saw no hope for a negotiated settlement, wrote Johnston asking for instructions from the Fourth Provincial Congress. It convened in Halifax on 4 April, and Hooper and Penn attended the meeting. The destruction of a Loyalist force at Moore's Creek Bridge in February had emboldened North Carolina's Whigs, and on his journey home Hooper reported finding strong support for independence. He advised Hewes, "One had better swim on the democratic flood than vainly attempt to check it." For his part, Penn "heard nothing praised in the course of his Journey, but *Common Sense* and Independence." Governor Martin's efforts to recruit slaves to the Loyalist cause, he thought, had helped turn public opinion against the British.[38]

On 12 April 1776, the Halifax convention passed the Halifax Resolves, making North Carolina the first colony to authorize its congressional delegates to support independence, but Hooper and Penn did not arrive in Halifax until three days later. Hewes received a copy of the resolves in late April, but he did not present them to Congress until 27 May, when the Virginia delegates presented similar resolutions. Hooper and Penn had not yet returned to Philadelphia, and it was not Hewes's nature to take the lead on so bold a measure.[39]

Besides a characteristic reserve, Hewes had other reasons to hesitate. As always, he spent much of his time on more prosaic matters, "raising men, making cannon, Muskets & Money, finding out ways & means of supplying our Troops with cloaths, provisions & ammunition." He had hoped Congress could have secured a foreign alliance and approved a plan for a confederation of the states before declaring independence. Finally, under the stress of representing North Carolina by himself for almost three months, his health began to fail.[40]

But Penn returned to Congress about 20 June, and by the end of the month, Hewes had concluded a resolution declaring "Independency" would pass "by a great Majority." On the critical vote of 2 July on Richard Henry Lee's motion that "these united colonies are and of right ought to be free and independent states," Hewes voted with Penn in the affirmative. Penn's vote was never in doubt, but as John Adams, who was prone to exaggeration, remembered years later, "The unanimity of the States finally depended on the Vote of Joseph Hewes, and was finally determined by him." Hooper, who did not return to Congress until 23 July, missed the vote. An official signing ceremony was held, rather anticlimactically, in August.[41]

Independence required North Carolina to replace its colonial charter with a new form of government. Fear of what that government might look like had given Hooper and Hewes another reason to hope for reconciliation with Great Britain. North Carolinians would almost certainly demand a more egalitarian, republican system, a prospect conservatives did not relish. "I hate republicks and would almost prefer the Government of Turkey to live under," Hewes wrote in March 1776 as prospects for a quick peace faded. At the same time, he believed he could accept any regime the people supported. For the more philosophical Hooper, the transition from monarchy to republic would not come so easily.[42]

On 13 April 1776, the Fourth Provincial Congress had appointed a committee to draft North Carolina's new constitution. Hooper and Penn joined the committee after they reached Halifax later in the month. The delegates found themselves bitterly divided. Reformers or radicals, on the one hand, wanted a more liberal franchise, a powerful and more representative assembly, and a government generally responsive to public opinion. On the other hand, moderates or conservatives, in the words of a sympathetic nineteenth-century historian, saw "the dangers of an irresponsible legislature, representing not the property, but the mere will of the people," and opposed giving the vote "to every '*biped*' of the forest."[43]

Hooper sided with the conservatives, while Penn played a small role in the production of one of the first important documents to emerge from the era of Revolutionary constitution-making, John Adams's *Thoughts on Government*. Penn had written Adams for advice. Always ready to instruct others—the subject of constitution-making, he thought, "seems not to have been sufficiently considered in the southern colonies"—Adams responded with a letter that, to satisfy popular demand, according to Adams, he later expanded into his famous essay. Adams intended his remarks as a response to *Common Sense*; he believed Paine's thoughts on government were too democratic. Adams recommended the creation of a bicameral legislature, with a governor selected by the assembly. The governor would possess a veto and could appoint judges with the consent of a council, or the upper house of the legislature. To ensure their independence, judges would serve during good behavior. Adams's plan was conservative in the sense that it created checks and balances to limit the power of popular majorities, but it had its progressive features, including provisions for "equitable" representation, public education, and at some future day the possibility the governor might be selected by a vote of the people.[44]

Penn presumably had hoped for a more democratic blueprint; we have little direct evidence of his role at the Halifax convention, but his mentor, Thomas Person, was a key leader of the reformers. The committee charged with drafting a constitution proposed a two-house assembly. Both houses would be popularly elected, but only freeholders could vote for members of the upper house. The governor and county court judges would also be chosen by the people. The committee could not, however, agree on a complete draft, and efforts to proceed on the convention floor failed. The records of the debate are spotty, but Hooper opposed the reformers' proposal that the governor's council be popularly elected and serve one-year terms. He wanted a council more insulated from popular pressure. On 30 April, the convention suspended its efforts to produce a new charter.[45]

A Fifth Provincial Congress returned to Halifax in November 1776 and tried again. Hooper wanted to attend, but Hewes and Penn went instead. Someone had to stay in Philadelphia. At Halifax, Hewes sided with the conservatives and Penn with the reformers. Ironically, however, we know more about Hooper's views on a new constitution than about the views of Penn and Hewes because in the fall of 1776, Hooper wrote a series of letters that are far more informative than the records of the congress.[46]

Hooper continued to admire the British constitution, although he admitted the Crown might now "be too independent of the people." He envisioned a system of checks and balances rooted in classical republican terms. A viable government required virtue, which he associated with the masses; wisdom, which would come from the upper classes; and power, which would be provided by the executive. The lower house of the assembly, he recommended, should represent the people. The upper house would represent the more affluent, and the governor and a council would provide the requisite power. He disliked Rhode Island's more democratic constitution and criticized Pennsylvania's liberal charter, with its unicameral legislature and weak governor, as "the motley mixture of limited monarchy, and an execrable democracy—a Beast without a head." He much preferred the more conservative constitutions adopted in South Carolina and New Jersey, and he singled out Delaware's for praise. It ensured the independence of judges and was "as nearly similar as possible to the old one, abolishing little else but the regal & proprietary powers and deriving all power from the people."[47]

In December, the Halifax delegates agreed on a compromise constitution that might, on balance, have satisfied Hooper. To be sure, it created a weak governor chosen annually by the assembly with little patronage and no power to override the assembly, but Hooper had by then abandoned his earlier preference for an executive veto. Many of the new constitution's progressive features enjoyed some conservative support: it limited multiple officeholding, disestablished the Anglican Church, restricted entails, ended imprisonment for debt, authorized the creation of public schools and a state university, and included a bill of rights. Power remained, however, with the planters, merchants, and lawyers of the east. Voters in elections for the state senate had to own fifty acres. The ban on multiple officeholding did not apply to justices of the peace, who were still appointed by the governor upon the recommendation of the incumbents, thus allowing the courthouse rings to survive. Most important, the east remained overrepresented in the assembly, although western delegates did not press in 1776 for representation based on population.[48]

One historian has described North Carolina's first state constitution, with perhaps unintended irony, as a relatively democratic document, compared with those of other states, that "did little to advance the cause of democracy."[49]

The debate over the constitution created lingering wounds. William Hooper resented the defeat of his friend the conservative icon Samuel Johnston in his race for a seat in the Fifth Provincial Congress. "Past services," he complained to Hewes, "seem to be no security for future preferment." It is "the greatest Example of Ingratitude that ever marked a people."[50]

More would come. Illness, infighting, and an inability to adjust to the new political order created by independence would undo the congressional delegation. In December 1776, the Halifax congress replaced John Penn with Thomas Burke. The strain of representing the state alone began to take its toll on Hooper. He apparently contracted yellow fever early in 1777, and isolated in Baltimore, where the Continental Congress had fled to avoid the British, he chafed at his own uncertain prospects. "If the services I have rendered Carolina in a publick Character will not secure me the unsolicited unanimous reappointment of my country I want it not."[51]

On 28 April 1777, the new General Assembly reelected Hooper, but in a nasty contest Penn defeated Hewes. Even though he had led Hooper to believe he would support his former colleague, Penn challenged Hewes's reappointment, alleging the Edenton merchant, by serving as a delegate to the Continental Congress and as its commercial agent, had violated the state constitution's limits on multiple officeholding, neglected his congressional duties, and enriched himself with commissions on transactions he executed for Congress. The first two charges lacked merit; the third was problematic. In the absence of explicit rules governing conflicts of interest and without a bureaucracy to handle administrative tasks, members of Congress often took on assignments better left to others. John Adams, for one, considered Hewes to be "a man of Honour and Integrity," but Hewes had made huge profits doing the public's business. He had also made enemies among reformers during the debate over the new constitution.[52]

Hooper resigned a few days after Hewes's defeat. His family wanted him to stay home, and he had other reasons to leave Congress. His health and his finances were declining—the British had burned Hooper's Finian estate outside Wilmington—and his letters reveal a man shaken by defeat on the battlefield, frustrated by the rise of Loyalist opposition, and worried about the collapse of the Continental currency.[53]

Returned to Congress after a brief absence, Penn left many of his colleagues unimpressed. He developed a reputation as a social butterfly. Thomas Burke suggested, presumably tongue in cheek, that since Philadelphia "is a scene of gaiety and Dissipation, public assemblies every fortnight and private Balls every night, in all such business as this we propose that Mr. Penn shall represent the whole state."[54] Penn carried on a feud with Henry Laurens from South Carolina that included a duel in which each man fired a shot and missed. Presiding at a session of Congress, Laurens later ridiculed Penn by singing, "Poor little Penny, poor little Penny."[55] Some delegates made Penn's name a synonym for leaking confidential information, as when James Lovell wrote Sam Adams "that I can pennize . . . enough" to provide a few details about an upcoming campaign. After Cornelius Harnett joined the North Carolina delegation, he felt compelled to defend Penn's character to Governor Richard Caswell. Two modern historians, by contrast, have described Penn, when he served with Burke and Harnett, as a "pygmy between two giants."[56]

Whatever his limitations, Penn combined natural political skills with a commitment to democracy in a way that allowed him to stay in public office for about as long as his health would permit. He remained in Congress until 1780; his 1,038 days of service made him the longest-tenured North Carolina delegate of the Revolutionary era. In 1781–82 he served on the state Board of War and spent two more years on the governor's council. Appointed a federal tax collector in 1784, he resigned after a month, citing poor health. He died in 1788, at the age of forty-eight.[57]

Hewes's loss of his congressional seat effectively ended his political career. Edenton elected him to the General Assembly in 1779, and the assembly almost immediately voted to send him back to Philadelphia. Tragically for him, he had never fully recovered from an apparent case of malaria years earlier. Arriving in Philadelphia in mid-July, he wrote Richard Caswell, "I . . . find my health injured rather than repaired by the long Journey in such Violent hot weather." He tried to work, but by late October the forty-nine-year-old Hewes was bedridden. He died in Philadelphia in November.[58]

Hewes's death depressed William Hooper. "It prays upon my feelings," he wrote James Iredell, and left him "effeminately affected."[59] A natural aristocrat, Hooper struggled to adjust to the less deferential politics the Revolution created. Democracy, he railed, was "a vortex that will soon sweep within it the characters, property, and person too of every man whose family, fortune or connections have placed above the rabble." As the Revolutionary War ground on, he waxed and waned about the prospects for an American victory.[60] He returned to the General Assembly, but minus the influence he once exercised. He lost his seat in 1780 and then in 1782 won a close, contested race that the assembly overturned. Hooper moved to Hillsborough—he may have expected it to become the state capital—and in 1783 lost another race for the assembly, this time to a local tavern keeper.[61]

Finally, in 1784 Hooper won an assembly election that he called "the most warmly contested of any which ever happened in this county." Hooper advocated compliance with those provisions in the 1783 Treaty of Paris providing for the collection of prewar British debts and for the return of confiscated Loyalist property. He also favored the cession of North Carolina's western land claims to Congress and the creation of a professional and independent judiciary.[62] But his views did not enjoy broad support, and he left the assembly after one term. Returned for the January 1787 session, Hooper seemed poised to revive his career, but his support for constitutional reform at the federal level alienated his constituents. He lost a race for a seat in the state convention called to consider ratification of the Constitution.[63]

As did Penn's and Hewes's, Hooper's heath failed prematurely. He had been seriously ill in 1777. In July 1781, he complained his right arm had swollen "to a size not much less than my leg." An overdose of laudanum a few weeks later, he said, "threw me into a delirium." His wife, Anne, had to send their son Billy to bring him home from Edenton in the summer of 1788. Some evidence suggests he had begun to drink heavily, and he suffered from reoccurring bouts of malaria. By October 1790, James Iredell reported to his wife, Hannah, that "poor Hooper has been at times, and is now part of every day a raving madman, but fortunately his health declines so fast that he cannot probably last much longer." Hooper, forty-eight, died in Hillsborough on 14 October.[64]

What kind of political order had Hooper, Hewes, and Penn intended to create? Perhaps all that can be said with certainty about John Penn is that he hoped the new republic would provide the small farmers of the west with an honest and responsive government. Hewes deferred to Hooper on matters of political theory, and Hooper's republican philosophy taught that nations went through inevitable cycles of rise and decline, with virtue routinely giving way to corruption. To Hooper, republicanism required eternal vigilance, not fundamental reform. He would have been content to replicate the British constitution in America, or at least a modernized, rationalized version of it.

Always identified with the conservatives among American Whigs, Hooper was no reactionary. At different stages in his career, he defended freedom of the press and the equity of progressive taxation and condemned proposals to restrict public offices to Protestants, a provision reformers inserted into the North Carolina Constitution.[65] In an August 1776 speech in the Continental Congress, Hooper expressed his opposition to slavery. He hoped, he said, "to see the day that slaves are not necessary." Yet Hooper did not believe that "all men are created equal" in their capacity for politics.[66] In short, he longed for the creation in America of an enlightened republic governed by prudent aristocrats, a vision his fellow North Carolinians, for the most part, did not share.

NOTES

1. Thomas Jefferson to John Adams, 9 July 1819, in *The Adams-Jefferson Letters: The Complete Correspondence between Thomas Jefferson and Abigail and John Adams*, ed. Lester J. Cappon, 2 vols. (Chapel Hill: University of North Carolina Press, 1959), 2:543–44.

2. Mary Claire Engstrom, "Hooper, William," in *Dictionary of North Carolina Biography* (hereafter *DNCB*), ed. William S. Powell (Chapel Hill: University of North Carolina Press, 1979–91), 3:199–202; Robert Charles Kneip, "William Hooper, 1742–1790: Misunderstood Patriot" (Ph.D. diss., Tulane University, 1980), 1–19.

3. Kneip, "William Hooper," 20–32; Patrick G. Williams, "Hooper, William," in *American National Biography* (hereafter *ANB*), ed. John A. Garraty and Mark C. Carnes (New York: Oxford University Press, 1999), 11:145–47.

4. Jack P. Greene, *The Quest for Power: The Lower Houses of the Assembly in the Southern Royal Colonies, 1689–1776* (Chapel Hill: University of North Carolina Press, 1962), 41; Elisha P. Douglass, *Rebels and Democrats: The Struggle for Equal Political Rights and Majority Rule during the American Revolution* (Chapel Hill: University of North Carolina Press, 1955), 72–79: Memory F. Mitchell, *North Carolina's Signers: Brief Sketches of the Men Who Signed the Declaration of Independence and the Constitution* (Raleigh: North Carolina Department of Cultural Resources, 1964), 2.

5. Douglass, *Rebels and Democrats*, 72–79; Robert L. Ganyard, *The Emergence of North Carolina's Revolutionary State Government* (Raleigh: North Carolina Department of Cultural Resources, 1978), 6–12.

6. Ganyard, *North Carolina's Revolutionary State Government*, 12–13; Douglass, *Rebels and Democrats*, 72–79.

7. Kneip, "William Hooper," 32–44.

8. Carole Watterson Troxler, *Farming Dissenters: The Regulator Movement in Piedmont North Carolina* (Raleigh: North Carolina Department of Cultural Resources, 2011), 76–78; James Hunter et al. to Herman Husband, 14 September 1769, in Walter Clark, ed., *The Colonial Records of North Carolina* (hereafter *CRNC*), 26 vols. (Raleigh: P. M. Hale, 1886–1907), 8:68–70; "An Account of the Regulators," *Boston Evening Post*, 12 November 1770, in William S. Powell et al., eds., *The Regulators of North Carolina: A Documentary History, 1759–1776* (Raleigh: North Carolina Department of Cultural Resources, 1971), 253–55.

9. Josiah Martin to Secretary Hillsborough, 30 August 1772, *CRNC*, 9:329–33; Josiah Martin to Lord Dartmouth, 28 November 1772, ibid., 9:357–58; Douglass, *Rebels and Democrats*, 99–100. See generally Marjoleine Kars, *Breaking Loose Together: The Regulator Rebellion in Pre-Revolutionary North Carolina* (Chapel Hill: University of North Carolina Press, 2002).

10. Joseph S. Jones, *A Defence of the Revolutionary History of the State of North Carolina from the Aspersions of Mr. Jefferson* (Boston: C. Bowen, 1834), 79–80; Kneip, "William Hooper," 45–64, 94–97; Jeffrey J. Crow, *A Chronicle of North Carolina during the American Revolution, 1763–1789* (Raleigh: North Carolina Department of Cultural Resources, 1975), 13–14.

11. Michael G. Martin, "Hewes, Joseph," *DNCB*, 3:123–25; Michael G. Martin, "Joseph Hewes, Reluctant Revolutionary? A Study of a North Carolina Whig and the War for American Independence, 1730–1779" (M.A. thesis, University of North Carolina–Chapel Hill, 1969), 1–8.

12. Brickell quoted in Martin, "Joseph Hewes," 19. See also Mitchell, *North Carolina's Signers*, 5–7; and Martin, "Joseph Hewes," 14–15, 20–26, 31–32. In the absence of more detailed records, Martin, extrapolating from Hewes's committee assignments, ranks him as one of the assembly's more influential members. See Martin, "Joseph Hewes," 32–33. By contrast, Greene, *Quest for Power*, 463–95, puts him in the second tier.

13. Reverend James Reed to the Secretary, 7 January 1774, *CRNC*, 9:815; Assembly Proceedings, 2 March 1774, ibid., 9:875–88; Kneip, "William Hooper," 66–67, 78–89. The "Hampden" essays were reportedly so inflammatory that Hooper's law license was suspended for a year. See Richard H. Rayburn, "Infallible Power: The 'Musquetoe,' the Wilmington–New Hanover County Safety Committee, and the Coming of the Revolution in the Lower Cape Fear, 1774–1776," *North Carolina Historical Review* 92, no. 3 (2015): 387–425, 394n26.

14. Samuel Johnston to William Hooper, 5 April 1774, *CRNC*, 9:968–69; William Hooper to James Iredell, 21 June 1774, in Griffith J. McRee, ed., *Life and Correspondence of James Iredell*, 2 vols. (New York: Peter Smith, 1857), 1:197–98; Martin, "Joseph Hewes," 41–42.

15. William Hooper to James Iredell, 26 April 1774, *CRNC*, 9:983–86. See also William Hooper to James Iredell, 5 August 1774, in McRee, *Iredell*, 1:199–201, for another classic statement of republican thought, including the idea that the decay of the British constitution was part of an inevitable cycle.

16. William Hooper to James Iredell, 21 June 1774, in McRee, *Iredell*, 1:197–98; Wilmington Resolves, 21 July 1774, *CRNC*, 9:1016–17; Kneip, "William Hooper," 102–8.

17. Ganyard, *North Carolina's Revolutionary State Government*, 29; Proceedings of the First Provincial Congress, *CRNC*, 9:1041–49; Andrew Miller to Thomas Burke, 4 September 1774, *CRNC*, 9:1063–64. On James Otis's influence on the resolves, see Kneip, "William Hooper," 119–24.

18. Proceedings of the First Provincial Congress, *CRNC*, 9:1043–49.

19. Samuel Ashe, "William Hooper," in *Biographical History of North Carolina from Colonial Times to the Present*, ed. Samuel Ashe (Greensboro, N.C.: C. L. Van Noypen, 1905–17), 7:237; Alan D. Watson, Dennis R. Lawson, and Donald R. Lemon, *Harnett, Hooper and Howe: Revolutionary Leaders of the Lower Cape Fear* (Wilmington, N.C.: Lower Cape Fear Historical Society, 1979), 41; Andrew Miller to Thomas Burke, 4 September 1774, *CRNC*, 9:1063–64; Josiah Martin to Earl of Dartmouth, 1 September 1774, *CRNC*, 9:1050–61; David T. Morgan and William J. Schmidt, *North Carolinians in the Continental Congress* (Winston-Salem, N.C.: John F. Blair, 1976), 17. Iredell quoted in Morgan and Schmidt, *North Carolinians*, 7.

20. Silas Deane to Elizabeth Deane, 23 September 1774, in Paul H. Smith et al., eds., *Letters of Delegates to Congress, 1774–1789*, 25 vols. (Washington, D.C.: Library of Congress,

1976–2000), 1:91–92; John Adams's diary, 10 October 1774, in ibid., 1:168; Morgan and Schmidt, *North Carolinians*, 5–7.

21. Martin, "Joseph Hewes," 47–52; Kneip, "William Hooper," 128–37; *The Journals of the Continental Congress, 1776-1789* (hereafter *JCC*), ed. Worthington C. Ford et al., 34 vols. (Washington, D.C.: Government Printing Office, 1904–37), 1:42–43.

22. William Hooper to Mary Hooper, 7 November 1774, in Smith, *Letters*, 1:255–56; Proceedings of the Second Provincial Congress, 5 April 1775, *CRNC*, 9:1181–82. See also "Address to the Inhabitants of the British Empire," 8 September 1775, *CRNC*, 10:202–3. It is generally attributed to Hooper. See Jones, *Defence of the Revolutionary History*, 227–28.

23. See Kneip, "William Hooper," 162–72, 212.

24. Joseph Hewes to James Iredell, 23 May 1775, in McRee, *Iredell*, 1:204–5; Joseph Hewes to Samuel Johnston, 11 May 1775, *CRNC*, 9:1246–47.

25. North Carolina Delegates to the Presbyterian Ministers of Philadelphia, circa 3–8 July 1775, in Smith, *Letters*, 1:575–76; Joseph Hewes to James Iredell, 8 July 1775, in ibid., 1:611–12; North Carolina Delegates to Elihu Spencer, 8 December 1775, in ibid., 2:459–61.

26. Joseph Hewes to Samuel Johnston, 8 July 1775, in ibid., 1:612.

27. William Hooper to Mary Hooper, 20 June 1775, in ibid., 1:523–24; North Carolina Delegates to the North Carolina Committees, 19 June 1775, in ibid., 1:511–15; Joseph Hewes and Robert Smith to a London Mercantile Firm, 31 July 1775, in ibid., 1:684–86.

28. William to Mary Hooper, 7 November 1774, in ibid., 1:255–56; "Address to the Assembly of Jamaica," in *JCC*, 2:204–6; Kneip, "William Hooper," 185–88.

29. Thomas A. Pittman, "John Penn," in Ashe, *Biographical History of North Carolina*, 8:414–18; David T. Morgan, "Penn, John," *ANB*, 17:290–91; George Troxler, "Penn, John," *DNCB*, 5:65–66; Douglass, *Rebels and Democrats*, 107–14. On Person, see Sue Dossett Skinner, "Person, Thomas," *DNCB*, 5:74–75.

30. Edmund Pendleton to Joseph Chew, 20 June 1774, in *The Letters and Papers of Edmund Pendleton, 1734–1803*, ed. David J. Mays, 2 vols. (Charlottesville: University Press of Virginia, 1767), 1:92–95; Mitchell, *North Carolina's Signers*, 9–10; Pittman, "John Penn," 420.

31. G. Troxler, "Penn, John," 65–66; Joseph Hewes to James Iredell, 9 November 1775, in Smith, *Letters*, 2:322–23; Joseph Hewes to James Iredell, 9 November, 1775, in Smith, *Letters*, 2:323–24; Joseph Hewes to Samuel Johnston, 16 November 1775, in Smith, *Letters*, 2:353–54; Joseph Hewes to Samuel Johnston, 1 December 1775, in Smith, *Letters*, 2:420–21.

32. Martin, "Joseph Hewes," 64–66.

33. Richard Smith's diary, 16 January 1776, in Smith, *Letters*, 3:102–3; "John Dickinson's Draft Address to the Inhabitants of America," circa 24 January 1776, in ibid., 3:139–46.

34. William Hooper to Samuel Johnston, 2 December 1775, in ibid., 2:424–25; William Hooper to James Iredell, 6 January 1776, in ibid., 3:44–46.

35. Smith, *Letters*, 144n1; John Penn to Thomas Person, 14 February 1776, in ibid., 3:254–56.

36. William Hooper to Joseph Hewes and John Penn, 6 February 1776, in ibid., 3:208–10; William Hooper to Samuel Johnston, 6 February 1776, in ibid., 210–11; Joseph Hewes to Samuel Johnston, 11 February 1776, in ibid., 3:229–30; Joseph Hewes to Samuel Johnston, 20 March 1776, in ibid., 3:416–17.

37. Thomas Paine, *Common Sense*, ed. Isaac Kramick (New York: Penguin, 1986), 68–69, 86, 96–97; Joseph Hewes to Samuel Johnston, 13 February 1776, in Smith, *Letters*, 3:246–48; Joseph Hewes to Samuel Johnston, 20 February 1776, in Smith, *Letters*,

3:289–90. Hewes may not have fully appreciated the revolutionary significance of *Common Sense*; many of his colleagues ignored it in their letters home. Richard R. Beeman, *Our Lives, Our Fortunes, and Our Sacred Honor: The Forging of American Independence, 1774–1776* (New York: Basic Books, 2013), 320–21.

38. Joseph Hewes to Samuel Johnston, 20 March 1776, in Smith, *Letters*, 3:416–17; Kneip, "William Hooper," 254–55; William Hooper to Joseph Hewes, 17 April 1776, Hayes Collection, North Carolina State Archives, Raleigh; Watson, Lawson, and Lemon, *Harnett, Hooper and Howe*, 47; John Adams to James Warren, 20 April 1776, in Smith, *Letters*, 3:558–60; Smith, *Letters*, 596n1.

39. G. Troxler, "Penn, John," 65–66; Morgan and Schmidt, *North Carolinians*, 19–25.

40. Joseph Hewes to James Iredell, 17 May 1776, in Smith, *Letters*, 4:26–27; Joseph Hewes to Samuel Johnston, 4 June 1776, in ibid., 4:138–49; Joseph Hewes to Samuel Johnston, 8 July 1776, in ibid., 4:409–11; Joseph Hewes to Samuel Johnston, 28 July 1776, in ibid., 4:555–56.

41. Joseph Hewes to James Iredell, 28 June 1776, in ibid., 4:331–33; Morgan and Schmidt, *North Carolinians*, 19–25; John Adams to Thomas Jefferson, 2 June 1819, *Adams-Jefferson Letters*, 2:542; Kneip, "William Hooper," 268.

42. Joseph Hewes to Samuel Johnston, 26 March 1776, in Smith, *Letters*, 3:443–44; Pittman, "John Penn," 419; Morgan and Schmidt, *North Carolinians*, 28.

43. Ganyard, *North Carolina's Revolutionary State Government*, 61–62; Jones, *Defence of the Revolutionary History*, 276, 284.

44. John Adams to John Penn, circa 19–27 March 1776, in Smith, *Letters*, 3:399–406; John Adams to James Warren, 20 April 1776, in ibid., 3:558–60; John Adams to John Penn, 28 April 1776, in ibid., 3:595–96.

45. Ganyard, *North Carolina's Revolutionary State Government*, 61–62; Martin, "Joseph Hewes," 75; Douglass, *Rebels and Democrats*, 120–24.

46. William Hooper to North Carolina Provincial Convention, 26 October 1776, in Smith, *Letters*, 5:396–403; Martin, "Hewes, Joseph," 123–25.

47. William Hooper to Samuel Johnston, 26 September 1776, in Smith, *Letters*, 5:245–49; William Hooper to North Carolina Provincial Convention, 26 October 1776, in ibid., 5:396–403; William Hooper to Joseph Hewes, 27 October 1776, in ibid., 5:407–11. See generally Kneip, "William Hooper," 309–25. Kneip concludes that Hooper "did not fully see the implications of his having severed power from its landed moorings and . . . was totally unprepared for democracy when it came thundering across the piedmont North Carolina" (321).

48. See Ganyard, *North Carolina's Revolutionary State Government*, 80–89; Douglass, *Rebels and Democrats*, 129–35; Marc W. Kruman, *Between Authority and Liberty: State Constitution Making in Revolutionary America* (Chapel Hill: University of North Carolina Press, 1997), 124. According to Kruman, North Carolinians "associated county representation with 'equal representation'" (67).

49. Douglass, *Rebels and Democrats*, 124, 133.

50. William Hooper to Joseph Hewes, circa 16 November 1776, in Smith, *Letters*, 5:497–500.

51. G. Troxler, "Penn, John," 65–66; Engstrom, "Hooper, William," 199–202; William Hewes to Joseph Hewes, 3 December 1776, in Smith, *Letters*, 5:564; William Hewes to Joseph Hewes, 1 January 1777, in Smith, *Letters*, 6:7–10; William Hooper to Robert Morris, 1 February 1777, in Smith, *Letters*, 6:191–93.

52. Martin, "Joseph Hewes," 77–82; Martin, "Hewes, Joseph," 123–25; John Adams to Abigail Adams, 11 July 1777, in Smith, *Letters*, 7:334. According to David T. Morgan, "Hewes, Joseph," *ANB*, 10:711–12, Hewes had rented ships he owned to Congress and arranged to be paid in Spanish gold dollars, not in inflated Continental currency. William Aylett, Congress's deputy commissary of purchases in Virginia, later claimed Hewes had sold spoiled pork to the army, but the issue was apparently never resolved. See Henry Laurens to William Aylett, 22 April 1778, in Smith, *Letters*, 9:468–70. For more on Hewes's self-dealing, see David T. Morgan and William J. Schmidt, "From Economic Sanctions to Political Separation: The North Carolina Delegation to the Continental Congress, 1774–1776," *North Carolina Historical Review* 52, no. 3 (1975): 215–34, 232–33.

53. See Smith, *Letters*: William Hooper to Robert Livingston, 17 August 1776, 5:14–15; William Hooper to Samuel Johnston, 26 September 1776, 5:245–49; William Hooper to Joseph Hewes, 1 November 1776, 5:424–26; William Hooper to Joseph Hewes, 5 November 1776, 5:443–40; William Hooper to Joseph Hewes, 29 November 1776, 5:552–54; Joseph Hewes to Richard Caswell, 30 March 1777, 6:511–12.

54. Thomas Burke to Richard Caswell, 20 December 1778, in ibid., 11:361–62; Morgan and Schmidt, *North Carolinians*, 16, 27–28.

55. See Smith, *Letters*, Henry Laurens' Notes of Debates, 26 March 1779, 12:249–52; Henry Laurens' Notes of Debates, 29 March 1779, 12:260–61; Henry Laurens' Notes on His Remarks in Congress, 9 January 1779, 11:439–41; Charles Thomson to a Committee of Congress, 6 September 1779, 13:458–66.

56. James Lovell to Samuel Adams, 28 January 1780, in ibid., 14:381; Cornelius Harnett to Richard Caswell, 20 March 1778, in ibid., 9:316–17; Morgan and Schmidt, *North Carolinians*, 43.

57. G. Troxler, "Penn, John," 66; Mitchell, *North Carolina's Signers*, 10–11; Pittman, "John Penn," 422–24. Congress, under the Articles of Confederation, could not impose taxes, but Superintendent of Finance Robert Morris appointed agents in each state to receive, he hoped, state taxes collected on behalf of the national government. See Clarence L. Ver Steeg, *Robert Morris, Revolutionary Financier* (New York: Octagon Books, 1976), 98–105.

58. Joseph Hewes to Richard Caswell, 27 July 1779, in Smith, *Letters*, 13:296–97; Joseph Hewes to Richard Caswell, 17 August, 1779, in ibid., 13:377–78; Cornelius Harnett and William Sharpe to Richard Caswell, 4 November 1779, in ibid., 14:150–52; *JCC*, 15:1252.

59. McRee, *Iredell*, 1:436–38.

60. Morgan and Schmidt, *North Carolinians*, 28–32; William Hooper to James Iredell, 17 December 1778, in McRee, *Iredell*, 1:404–6; William Hooper to James Iredell, 15 June 1779, in McRee, *Iredell*, 1:426–27; William Hooper to John Penn, 15 August 1779, Hayes Collection.

61. William Hooper to James Iredell, 8 July 1784, in McRee, *Iredell*, 2: 105–108; Kneip, "William Hooper," 406, 441–42, 448–61; Engstrom, "Hooper, William," *DNCB*, 199–202.

62. See McRee, *Iredell*: William Hooper to James Iredell, 4 January 1744, 2:82–85; William Hooper to James Iredell, 1 May 1784, 2:99–100; William Hooper to James Iredell, 15 March 1784, 2:94–96; William Hooper to James Iredell, 8 July 1784, 2:105–8; William Hooper to James Iredell, 6 July 1785, 2:125–27.

63. Kneip, "William Hooper," 483–96; William Hooper to James Iredell, 31 December 1787, in McRee, *Iredell*, 2:184–85.

64. William Hooper to James Iredell, 13 July 1781, in McRee, *Iredell*, 1:526–27; William Hooper to James Iredell, 25 August 1781, in ibid., 1:532–33; Anne Hooper to James Iredell,

2 June 1788, in ibid., 2:259–60; James Iredell to Hannah Iredell, 8 October 1790, in ibid., 2:298; Engstrom, "Hooper, William," 199–202; Williams, "Hooper, William," 147.

65. William Hooper to James Duane, 22 November 1774, in Smith, *Letters*, 1:262–63; William Hooper to Samuel Johnston, 26 September 1776, in ibid., 5:245–49; William Hooper to James Iredell, 29 March 1781, in McRee, *Iredell*, 1:496–97.

66. *JCC*, 9:1080–81; Watson, Lawson, and Lemon, *Harnett, Hooper and Howe*, 47; David Alan Shain, ed., *The Declaration of Independence in Historical Context: American State Papers, Petitions, Proclamations, and Letters of the Delegates to the First National Congresses* (New Haven, Conn.: Yale University Press, 2014), 8–13.

II

The West

3

Caught between Two Fires

*The Catawba and the Cherokee
Choose Sides in the American Revolution*

James MacDonald

At a conference in Charleston in 1775, representatives from the colony of South Carolina met with Catawba Indians to explain the deteriorating relations between themselves and the British government. Rebel leaders were engaged in a race against agents from the English Crown who also hoped to enlist or keep neutral the Native Americans living in the South. At the Charleston meeting, William Henry Drayton offered a not-so-veiled threat that the Indians would face serious retaliation if they sided against the Whigs. Drayton need not have been concerned—British superintendent of Indian Affairs John Stuart made little headway in his attempt to bring the Catawba to the English side. Joseph Kershaw, assigned by the South Carolina Council of Safety as the delegate to the Catawba, assured the rebel assembly that the Catawba "are hearty in our Interest." After generations of toleration and sometime cooperation between the two peoples, the Catawba knew their continued survival would be better guaranteed by an alliance with their American neighbors.[1]

As Catawba leaders were being hosted by the South Carolina revolutionary government, the Cherokee Indians met with agents from the Transylvania Land Company in North Carolina at an Overhill Cherokee town. When it concluded, accommodationist leaders Attakullakulla and Oconostota signed over 31,000 square miles of land between the Kentucky and Cumberland Rivers to the North Carolinians in exchange for a cabin full of trade goods. The infamous land swindle—known as the Sycamore Shoals Treaty—brought to the breaking point a generational gulf in the Cherokee towns. Attakullakulla's headstrong son Dragging Canoe attempted to prevent the agreement, arguing the colonists' land-grabbing ways had to be stopped once and for all.[2]

Dragging Canoe was not alone. A significant number of younger Cherokee came of age at a time when the pace of land cessions to the colonies increased dramatically, especially in the decade before the Revolution. Desiring to avoid bloodshed and for the sake of peace, elders hoped a policy of accommodation would avert a prolonged conflict, spelling an almost certain doom for the Cherokee.[3] The divide among the Cherokee represented a generational split between older leaders ready to give ground and keep the peace and younger Cherokee opposed to any land concessions. In 1775, Dragging Canoe and his faction prepared to go to war because it seemed the only method to stop future surrenders of territory. Storming out of the treaty council in disgust, he promised that the ceded lands would become "dark and bloody." His actions created the possibility of an insurgent, militant faction among the Cherokee who rejected the peaceful path of their traditional leaders.[4]

Scholars today face serious challenges when researching a detailed history of the Catawba. Evidence is fragmentary and scattered at best, and typical of the colonial period, we rely only on references about the Indians made by white colonial writers. Historians who chronicle the Catawba often use anecdotal information that places "Indians" at locations during the conflict yet does not identify a particular Native American group. Credible accounts of the colonial period agree the Catawba lived on the present-day borders of North and South Carolina. War with their neighbors and disease took a heavy toll on the Catawba, and except for a period of hostility during the Yamassee War of 1715–16, the Catawba traded with and accommodated colonists during the middle decades of the 1700s. Disease decimated the nation during the decades before the Revolution. From a population estimated to be 4,600 in 1682, the Catawba numbers diminished to 1,400 in 1728. Smallpox epidemics in 1738 and 1759 nearly wiped out the nation, as its numbers fell to below 500.[5]

By this time, the Catawba established closer ties to the South Carolina colonial government, deciding that resistance to the Carolina governments would spell doom for the survivors. Shifting their towns farther south along the Catawba River in 1760, they allied with Carolina colonists during the Cherokee War of 1761. During an expedition into the Cherokee towns, Catawba warriors joined a force of 2,600 militia under British general James Grant that burned houses and destroyed corncribs. Tribal leaders such as King Hagler realized the only recourse for the survival of the Catawba lay in allying themselves with the Carolina governments.[6]

At the conclusion of the French and Indian War in 1763, British authorities met with the southeastern Indians at Augusta to negotiate a treaty. Fewer than 100 Catawba attended, leading British superintendent John Stuart to comment that the Catawba had "an absolute dependence upon it [South Carolina] and are inseparably connected with its interests."[7] After the conference, the Catawba were granted a fifteen-square-mile reservation exclusively in South Carolina, including 144,000 acres in the present counties of Lancaster, York, and Chester. Under the treaty, the Catawba were given land recognized in Anglo-American law that prevented settlers from moving the Indians aside. If they wished, the Catawba could rent tracts to planters moving to the Carolina frontier.[8]

Unlike the Catawba, who were surrounded by colonial settlers, the Cherokee occupied mountainous areas in western North and South Carolina, Virginia, and Georgia. At the beginning of the Revolution, some 15,000 lived in forty different towns. Cherokee towns were divided into four groups, designated Lower, Middle, Valley, and Overhill settlements, based on their geographic locations. Lower settlements were in western South Carolina and Middle settlements in the western tip of North Carolina. Valley towns took up the region in eastern Tennessee, and Overhill towns were the farthest west on the lower reaches of the Little Tennessee River.[9] With a sizable population and sensing the tension between England and its colonists, the Cherokee could take one of several paths to enhance their chance of survival should war break out in North America. While the Catawba solidified their position in South Carolina by serving as slave catchers for the colony, the Cherokee remained bitter at the end of the French and Indian War.[10]

Native Americans throughout the continent were neither monolithic in their response nor united in allegiances when it came to choosing sides in the American rebellion. The Revolution made Indian communities confront new challenges after 1775—decisions that could aid in their survival or risk their destruction at the hands of their neighbors. The coming of the conflict forced Indians into alliances with either British or Whig forces. Some Native Americans attempted neutrality, delayed a commitment, or simply became riven with divided loyalties. That the decisions happened in the middle of an American rebellion allowed several instances of an Indian civil war to take place within a revolution. American independence or the continuity of the British Empire mattered little except when it directly affected Native Americans' way of life. In the colonial southeast during 1775 and 1776, several factors influenced whether or not a particular nation sided with the British or Revolutionary

Whig governments. The British commanded a network of trade in the royal system. Furthermore, Native Americans felt that British efforts since 1763 effectively discouraged white settlement into western lands, as opposed to colonial land deals that took land. Finally, most Indians believed the English would win the war. As fighting commenced around Boston, Cherokee and Catawba leaders participated in meetings that would profoundly affect their future in North America.[11]

As a recent historian of the Revolution has noted, Indians "were caught between two social forces: pan-Indianism and inter-tribal and intra-tribal division." Most nations sided with the British, recognizing that their preservation could be ensured by a victory of the Crown's forces. Other groups, like the Catawba, understood that both staying out of the conflict and resistance to Whig shadow governments would guarantee their annihilation. Whether the main factor was the security of their families, of their land, or of their culture, each group carefully considered an alliance with the Whigs or British. Indian peoples in the Revolutionary era, according to Colin Calloway, "were doing pretty much the same thing as the American colonists: fighting for their freedom in tumultuous times." If the threat for Native Americans did not come from distant capitals, it as easily could come from their neighbors. Divisions that already existed before 1775 were exacerbated by the colonial rebellion, which had a direct impact on Indian worlds.[12]

During the course of the American Revolution, the Catawba Nation participated in several critical campaigns in the South. In 1776, Catawba warriors fought with militia and Continentals at the defense of Charleston on Sullivan's Island. Later that summer, South Carolina forces recruited the Catawba as scouts in an expedition to the Cherokee towns across the Appalachian Mountains. These campaigns successfully parried British and Indian threats to the eastern and western borders of the Carolinas. In 1780, after the British captured Charleston, the interior of the state became a battleground of sustained conflict between British and American forces. As English armies attempted to pacify the state, the Catawba homeland came under the sword. When armies maneuvered in the Carolina backcountry, the Catawba were fighting not only with their patriot allies but for the very existence of their nation and their homes.

Southeastern Indian groups like the Catawba and Cherokee constituted two of several nations occupying the contentious borderlands of Virginia, the Carolinas, and Georgia. Numbering 50,000–60,000 Indians, the Catawba, Cherokee, Creek, Choctaw, and Chickasaw could put thousands of warriors in the field in the service of either the British or the Whigs. Both British and patriot belligerents hoped to keep Native Americans out of the conflict. Yet even before independence, southeastern Indians like the Creek and Seminole were dividing over which side to take. In the Cherokee Nation, nothing short of a leadership rift was taking place.[13]

Though modest in numbers and not feared as a direct military threat, the Catawba were courted by rebel leaders of both Carolinas in the months after Lexington and Concord.[14] In his study of the American Revolution in the South, John Alden concedes that the Catawba "were not to be despised" just because the nation could field close to only 300 warriors. The diminished numbers belied their importance to the colonists during previous generations. Occupying a small enclave in South Carolina, the Catawba, Alden continues, "were brave and loyal friends of the Carolinians, had protected their frontiers, [and] had been valuable allies to the colonials in the harassing Anglo-Cherokee war of 1760–1761." Whig militia would ask the Catawba again to serve as allies against the longtime Catawba enemy the Cherokee.[15]

Concerned with the allegiances of the people living on their frontiers, the South Carolina Whig government took action to counter efforts by John Stuart. On 17 June 1775, the First Provincial Congress resolved to authorize the Council of Safety—part of an enforcement arm of the congress—to "invite fifty men of the Catawba Indians, or so many more, as upon any emergency may appear needful, to enter service of this colony." Volunteers from the nation would be organized under "the command of one or more proper white men."[16] Under this open-ended recruitment, the Catawba could be used in several capacities, including as auxiliary troops or scouts or to track and capture runaway slaves. In the postscript to a letter from William Thomson to the Council of Safety dated 22 June, Thomson was made aware that King Prow and fifty Catawba were visiting Camden in the central part of the colony. Thomson told the council that he and Joseph Kershaw "are both at a loss what to do with regard to taking some of them into pay for want of Your Instructions." Colonial leaders appeared amenable to offer cash bounties to any Catawba willing to serve South Carolina.[17]

South Carolina acted quickly to secure the allegiance of its Indian allies within the colony. Formal action may have been prompted by a visit from two Catawba representatives to Charleston in the summer of 1775. William Moultrie acknowledged that military preparations in all regions of the colony created a sense of alarm among the Catawba. According to Moultrie, "they had been told different stories and they came down to know the truth."[18] The Catawba representatives wanted a note that could be carried back to their king and explain the Whigs' point of view concerning the deteriorating situation between colonies and mother country. The Council of Safety for South Carolina took up the measure in July and gave the task to William Henry Drayton.[19]

Drayton took only a day to respond. In the letter with the salutation "Friends and Brothers," Drayton spoke in paternalistic—one might argue patronizing—tones, as the council chronicled the deteriorating relationship between the colonies and Great Britain. Increased tax burdens from the Crown hurt colonists and Indians alike, Drayton made clear. Raising more revenue in North America would have an adverse effect on the price of trade goods. As the letter states, "If the Great King makes the white people give so much more for the same kind of goods than they used to," prices for everything, from blankets, shirts, and rum, would increase. After relaying news about the battles near Boston where the "people in New-England killed a great many of the red coats," Drayton and the council then proposed a military alliance: "Now we hope you have opened your eyes, and that you see plainly that your case and our case is just the same: and therefore we expect that your warriors will join our warriors in this business, which concerns you as much as it does us: and we acquaint you, that we are willing to pay some of your warriors, in order to show that we look upon your nation as brother warriors. We are willing to hold you fast by the hand and we think it is best to tell you, that we have heard a bad talk about you: and we tell you this, because we hope you will let us see that you will hold us fast by the hand also." The council letter closed with a not-so-veiled threat directed at both the Catawba and their Cherokee neighbors. Officials in South Carolina considered a move out of Catawba towns an act of war. Moultrie warned, "Our warriors will set up the war-whoop, and look upon you as enemies." It was the hope of the council that the letter handed to the Catawba representatives would also make its way to the Cherokee Indians during the upcoming weeks.[20]

Within three weeks of the letter to the Catawba, more news arrived in Charleston relating to the potential military use of Indian allies. A month before, the provincial congress approved the idea of organizing the Catawba under a white officer. Henry Laurens asked the Whig representative to the Catawba, Joseph Kershaw, to choose a qualified individual for the task. Kershaw chose Samuel Boykin of Granby, a Camden merchant, to lead the company. At the end of July, Moultrie and the Council of Safety received an answer from the Catawba concerning their allegiance in the upcoming conflict. Council president Henry Laurens addressed a letter to Kershaw, expressing the gratitude of the council concerning his efforts with the old men and warriors of the Indians. According to Kershaw, the Catawba "were hearty in our interest" and seemed more than willing to supply forty to fifty men in the service of the colony.

Skilled as they were in woodland tactics, the Catawba who enlisted would be attached to the ranger regiment of South Carolina. Offered a chance to show their allegiance, and with the promise of pay, the Catawba Indians were put to work immediately.[21]

When his company was assembled, Boykin commanded thirty-four Catawba, who were charged by the council to "scout and attempt to take runaway negroes about the Parishes of St. George, Dorchester, St. Paul, and St. Bartholomew." Council members put Boykin's company at the disposal of the committees of the several parishes to "perform other public service in the line of their duty" until 10 March 1776. Having rendered the necessary service to the colony, Boykin's Catawba were dismissed with the promise that further service to the public would be expected if the Indian warriors were needed again. In the meantime, Boykin was issued £1,503 for his own pay and for the Catawba who marched with him in the apprehension of escaped slaves. As promised, South Carolina paid the Indians in the manner they would compensate white militia. Within three months, the Catawba returned to the Charleston area—this time defending the city from a significant British fleet.[22]

In May 1776, the South Carolina Provincial Congress was notified that a British fleet of some fifty ships could be seen off the coast of Charleston. Desiring to protect the fort on Sullivan's Island, Major General Charles Lee and South Carolina's own Colonel William Moultrie stationed 780 soldiers at the eastern end of the island behind recently completed breastworks with several cannon. From the backcountry, Lieutenant Colonel William "Danger" Thompson arrived with 300 militia from the Third Regiment of rangers. Bolstering the rangers were North Carolina Continentals, 200 South Carolina militia, and a detachment of assorted soldiers, including 30 Catawba Indians.[23] On 28 June, British forces under General Henry Clinton and Commodore Peter Parker sent combined naval and infantry forces from nearby Long Island in an unsuccessful attempt to capture the fort on Sullivan's Island. Separating the two islands was a seventy-five-yard inlet known as the "Breach." Positioned 500 yards from the Breach, safely out of range of British artillery, Thompson's forces waited. Attempting to make their way across the marsh in an amphibious landing, the British soldiers made no headway against the concentrated rifle and cannon fire coming from Sullivan's Island. A Charleston Tory who served on one of the landing craft commented, "It was impossible for any set of men to sustain so destructive a fire as the Americans poured in . . . on this occasion." Clinton spent several days after the failed attack contemplating a next move but in early July sailed for New York. The British southern campaign of 1775–76 proved to be an utter disaster. For a time, the Carolinas appeared safe. The victory on Sullivan's Island meant the Lower South would be free from the king's troops for more than two years.[24]

For the Cherokee living along the border of four southern states, resentments from the demoralizing land swindle at Sycamore Shoals had not ebbed in the ensuing year. In a meeting with Henry Stuart, the brother of British Indian superintendent John Stuart, Dragging Canoe maintained that land speculator Richard Henderson and the Transylvania group had purchased the land from elderly, infirm chiefs who were too old to fight the encroaching white settlement. Attakullakulla and his allies, in other words, did not speak for the Cherokee. During the talk with Stuart, Dragging Canoe complained that his people "were almost surrounded by White People, that they had but a small spot of ground left for them to stand upon and that it seemed to be the Intention of White People to destroy them from being a people." He intimated that his warriors planned to drive off the pioneers living in the Watauga settlements along the North Carolina–Tennessee border in the spring of 1776.[25]

Events during the next several months determined that the militant faction headed by Dragging Canoe would dictate Cherokee policy. Though warned of an impending attack of Indian warriors, colonists in the Carolina backcountry refused to leave their homes. Then, in May, a delegation of northern Indians from the Mohawk, Shawnee, and Delaware Nations arrived in the Overhill town of Chota to call for a unified front against American settlers. Dragging Canoe accepted the war belt of the northern Indian representatives and prepared for battle.[26] The decision for war—a revolution within a revolution—was not a rash one made by bloodthirsty, crazed Indians. Present at the council meeting were both moderate and militant Cherokee. Both sides recognized the high stakes, and during the previous year, each group had proposed its own solution to deal with encroaching settlers. Cherokee factions realized that the consequences for attacking settlements were enormous. Once angered, retaliation from the Revolutionary state governments would be swift and severe. The Cherokee could expect that their homes, crops, and lives might be lost. And critically, Indian attacks might not guarantee that the British would come to the aid of the Cherokee or their Shawnee-led allies from the north.[27] It is not unlikely that elders like Attakullakulla reminded the more militant members of their people of the devastation of the Cherokee War. Yet against what appeared to be insurmountable odds, Dragging Canoe's party chose war. As Colin Calloway has noted, the decision in the Overhill towns in May 1776 was as dramatic as those in Philadelphia in June and July: "Dragging Canoe committed the Cherokees to war and issued a resounding renunciation of Attakullakulla's policies." Neither the colonists nor the British had asked Indians to choose sides, though Stuart did provide gunpowder to the Cherokee. The militant group could claim equipment, men, and initiative to take the offensive against the aggressive colonists. Sporadic and isolated attacks began almost immediately.[28]

In the spring of 1776, Cherokee Indian warriors struck western areas of the southern backcountry. The violence started with irregular assaults on isolated families scattered around the frontier. Although these were at first intermittent, the news nevertheless terrified residents as far east as the Moravian communities in Salem. Reports indicated residents near the Holston River were fleeing the area or gathering together in a defensive stance. Attacks became more widespread and coordinated in July, as warriors also moved toward Crooked Creek, near present day Rutherfordton.[29]

Charged with defending the foothills and mountains, Brigadier General Griffith Rutherford drafted a letter to the North Carolina Council of Safety containing a blunt assessment about conditions in his district. The Indians, Rutherford explained, were "making Grate prograce, in Distroying & Murdering, in the frunteers of this County." He claimed 37 settlers were killed the week before and that a militia officer along with 120 women and children were under siege on the Catawba River. Rutherford fully expected them to perish and implored the council to send him more supplies. Finally, he asked for men from the neighboring Hillsborough District to join the proposed expedition to the Cherokee towns.[30]

The council pledged to Rutherford "every assistance" to "put an end to this cruel unjust & wicked Indian War." Rutherford also learned that more powder was coming, and the letter closed with the civil authorities stating, "All other matters we leave entirely to your discretion."[31] Historian Thomas Hatley has argued the North Carolina delegates actually contemplated a cultural conquest of the Cherokee Nation. The delegates spoke in near-biblical terms, believing the mission into the Cherokee towns allowed the combined armies "to extinguish the very race of them and scarce to leave enough of existence to be a vestige in proof that a Cherokee nation once was." But they concluded that their duty as Christians prevented wanton destruction and hoped the North Carolina force would spare noncombatants.[32]

In an unprecedented showing of colonial unity, the Carolinas and Virginia organized military expeditions to counter the threats from the frontier. Though General Charles Lee, commander of the Continental troops in the South, could spare no soldiers at the time, since he was occupied with the defense of Charleston, he hoped all of the affected states could send men against the Cherokee. Sensing more urgency than their southern neighbors, South Carolina did not waste time coordinating plans. Colonel Andrew Williamson at the end of July recruited a significant force of 1,120 men including militia, Continentals, and 20 Catawba scouts. Commissioned to lead the South Carolina soldiers into the Cherokee Lower Towns, Williamson sent scouts out of his Twenty-Three Mile Creek camp to look for occupied towns, Loyalists, or British official Alexander Cameron.[33]

During the next several weeks, Williamson often split his forces into fast-moving units that could strike individual towns or groups of villages. In the course of the Cherokee campaign, the Catawba scouts constituted part of an advance patrol of rangers and cavalry. At the end of July, Williamson pushed toward the Cherokee town of Seneca along the Keowee River. On 1 August a substantial force of Cherokee attacked his main force, and Williamson's horse was shot from beneath him. Only a desperate counterattack and the onset of darkness prevented a rout of the militia. As Williamson and his main force fought the Cherokee at Seneca, two of his regiments marched cautiously toward the upper Lower Towns. Detached from this force, a group of 125 militia with 25 Catawba scouts pushed ahead. The Cherokee were known to assign groups of warriors to climb trees and others to serve as runners to relay news of oncoming enemies, so the Catawba, according to Maurice Moore, a Carolina soldier, were placed at the head of a column and "would often pause in the march, and examine with the greatest care the bark of the tallest trees, to ascertain if they had been recently ascended." Descending a cove, the Indian scouts hesitated: "The Catawbas made a halt, and pointing to the wild peavine, and rank weeds freshly broken and trampled upon, which gave evidence of some numbers of feet had recently traversed this place, they advised that the advance guard should remain here until the main body of the army came up. But the whites were impatient to go on; and, although the Indians insisted on going no further, they were finally overcome by persuasion, and again took up the line of march." When a closer look at the terrain showed fresh footprints on smooth rocks near a spring, the Catawba again refused to move forward until Williamson's main body came up. The soldiers of the militia ignored the warnings, however, and proceeded several hundred yards when a force of Cherokee attacked. The firefight did not become a sustained battle because of the difficulty the Cherokee had with maneuvering through the thick ground cover. The main force of militia also moved to the sound of musket fire, and probably their numbers prevented the Cherokee from remaining on the attack.[34]

Over the next several weeks, elements of the South Carolina militia marched through the Lower Towns and encountered sporadic fighting with Cherokee warriors. Mostly, however, the towns were abandoned, and rumors of Loyalists, British officials, or large parties of Cherokee were unfounded.

During August, the Catawba were typically assigned to the regiments of Thomas Neel and John Thomas. Both officers recruited from the northwestern part of the state, and their soldiers often separated from Williamson's main force. Through August 1776, Neel's and Thomas's regiments marched through the Lower Towns, sometimes engaging in firefights but most often finding abandoned villages. By the end of the month, Williamson called upon the regiments to again rally near Seneca.

While his soldiers built a fortified supply depot, more militia arrived at Williamson's camp, including 20 Catawba under a Captain Smith. On 30 August 1776, Williamson sent 13 Catawba and 150 cavalry to proceed to Sugartown on the upper Keowee River to capture prisoners and gather intelligence. Catawba scouts spotted a Cherokee camp near the village of Qualhatchee. Before reinforcements could be brought up, the impatient Catawba and militia attacked.[35] The Cherokee warriors fled, returning only a scattered fire. One Cherokee was "so confounded by the surprise," he ran into a Catawba who immediately dispatched the Indian. During the skirmish, one Catawba was killed while attempting to capture a Cherokee horse as a prize. Even though they had been stunned by the Carolina force, the Cherokee inflicted several casualties on the army as it returned back to Williamson's camp near Seneca. One of the wounded was a Catawba.[36]

By mid-September, Williamson knew General Griffith Rutherford was on the move from North Carolina and decided to push into the Valley towns. On 19 September, near the town of Canucca, the army moved into a mountainous valley, perfectly suited for an attack from the surrounding high ground. The area seemed a good place to cross the Nantahala Mountains, but Williamson's Catawba scouts told him the Cherokee were in the area. Lead troops had almost reached the steepest part of the trail when musket fire erupted. The Cherokee at first mistook the Catawba for some of their own warriors before noticing the distinctive deer tails in their hair, which helped white militia distinguish them from the Cherokee. Before long, the Waya Gap valley became the scene of a prolonged battle.[37]

Williamson's soldiers spent the next six hours fighting anywhere from 600 to 1,200 Cherokee in a contest later known as the Battle of Black Hole. South Carolina troops lost 60 killed, including at least one Catawba, with several Catawba being wounded. John Drayton, who wrote about the battle in his memoirs, claimed the Cherokee casualties would have been higher if many of them had not been mistaken for Catawba. In the fog of battle, Carolina militia showed rare restraint in not wanting to cause what today might be labeled a friendly fire accident.[38]

On 26 September, the meeting of Williamson's forces with those of the North Carolina troops under Griffith Rutherford finally took place. Between the two forces, most of the Middle and Valley towns were destroyed, and because they assumed soldiers from Virginia were on the way to the Overhill towns farther west, the officers decided to return to their respective states. The North Carolina forces destroyed eleven towns during the campaign. Williamson's South Carolina army, in the field longer than Rutherford's, destroyed thirty-one Cherokee towns. The Carolinians were home by October.[39]

Richard D. Blackmon, who has written one of the most extensive studies of the Cherokee War of 1776, states that the combined Carolina forces destroyed scores of Cherokee towns and damaged the Indian ability to make war. Unfortunately for the Whig governments, the Cherokee were wise enough to avoid pitched battles with the Carolina armies. Though damaged, the Cherokee were not annihilated as some had hoped. Blackmon credits the Catawba in their role as scouts in advance guards. He correctly criticizes commanders who routinely discounted or ignored Catawba advice about woodland warfare. If the Catawba allies had been heeded, "casualties would not have been so great, and the expeditions might have been more effective."[40]

If the Catawba equivocated in support of the Whig cause during 1776, the nation could consider the fate of the Cherokee. Carolina and Virginia forces organized 6,000 soldiers to march into the foothills and lay waste to villages during the fall. Though Williamson and Rutherford were unable to fight Cherokee warriors in extended engagements, the result was satisfactory. Cherokee war-making ability became seriously compromised because of the devastation to dwellings and food stores. In the aftermath of the Cherokee War, British superintendent for Indian Affairs John Stuart funneled gifts and cash to Native Americans but in the end was unable to use them as allies. Quite simply, the coordinated expeditions into the mountain villages of the Cherokee knocked them out of the war. As one historian of the British strategy concludes, Indian cooperation "turned out to be a dead end for the British cause in the South."[41]

After months of devastation, older leaders of the Cherokee attempted to sue for peace. In October 1776, as another column of militia from Virginia, commanded by William Christian, moved into the Overhill towns, the Raven from the Cherokee approached his camp. Battered from a season of Whig campaigns, the accommodationist group of the Cherokee came to terms with the southern states in two treaties in 1777. For the Carolina settlers, the Treaty of Long Island on Holston effectively ratified the land grab at Sycamore Shoals from two years before.[42]

The generational conflict that had plunged the Cherokee into war in 1776 did not end after the withdrawal of American militias. Refusing to surrender after many of their towns were destroyed by Carolina militia, Dragging Canoe and his allies continued to fight. They wisely did not give battle to the columns commanded by Williamson, Rutherford, and Christian, opting to remove themselves further into lands near the Chickamauga Creek, which flows north and west into the Tennessee River in northern Georgia. Chickamauga towns after 1777 formed a core of resistance that brought in Indians from other towns. In 1778, having pledged allegiance to the British Crown, English superintendents for Indians in the south began outfitting the militants with supplies for the 1,000 Cherokee who called themselves "the real people."[43]

In almost a decade of conflict after the Sycamore Shoals Treaty in 1775, several more campaigns and rearguard actions continued to weaken the Chickamauga resistance. One such campaign was headed by Colonel Evan Shelby of Virginia; the 600 militia he led burned eleven towns and carried off corn supplies. Later, in 1782, even after the surrender of Charles Cornwallis to Washington at Yorktown, North Carolina dispatched troops to the Chickamauga towns in retaliation for "their late Disaffection and the Murders and Ravages they have committed upon our peaceable, inoffensive citizens." Final settlement took place at the Treaty of Hopewell in 1785, one of the first formal treaties between southern Indians and the newly independent United States.[44] For James O'Donnell, who has written extensively on the Cherokee and southern Indians, the Revolution started with "a group of North Carolinians negotiating for tribal land (the Henderson Purchase) and thus it was ending with North Carolinians and Virginians again bargaining for tribal lands." In the meantime, the choice of war in 1776 destroyed villages and diminished the power of the Cherokee Nation.[45]

During the aftermath of the surrender of Charleston in May 1780, the Carolina interior became a battleground. Lacking a significant presence of Continental army forces, leaders in North and South Carolina relied on partisan militia bands to resist British forces pushing into the backcountry. One of the latest studies on the Waxhaw upcountry concludes, "Between 1780 and 1782 the people of the upcountry fought British and American regulars as well as each other in a bloody inland civil war, exchanging atrocities and leaving one another embittered and exhausted." Irregular fighters like Thomas Sumter, Andrew Pickens, and Francis Marion constituted the only fighting force left to stop the British from marching to the Carolina interior.[46]

From the rallying point in Salisbury, North Carolina, Sumter along with William Richardson Davie recruited Carolina militia to harass and attack dispersed soldiers under British general Charles Cornwallis. Beginning in June 1780, Sumter and his lieutenants recruited along the Catawba River and near the Catawba reservation south of Charlotte, North Carolina. Sumter used the Catawba lands as a mobilization area in the summer of 1780. Veterans from earlier campaigns in the South and militia in the South Carolina New Acquisition District made their way to his camp. As many as 100 Catawba may have been a part of the Whig forces along the border of the two states.[47]

Though Sumter did not have the might to attack strong British positions, he hoped that he and Davie could deter Loyalist foraging parties around the Waxhaws. Joining Davie's forces, General New River of the Catawba with thirty-five warriors came to the encampment on the north side of Waxhaw Creek. Because the Whig forces lay within eighteen miles of the British position at Hanging Rock, Davie relates that "skirmishes happened every day for some time." The plan ultimately succeeded, for Davie's forces were able to drive Loyalist parties back to the safety of British lines.[48] The South Carolina government also put a company of Catawba under the command of Thomas Drennan to serve with General Sumter. Records of the comptroller general attest to the service provided by Drennan's company, made up of forty-one Catawba and three white men. The company was led by General New River.[49]

For the service of the Catawba, South Carolina offered pay at ten shillings a day over the twenty-five to ninety-eight days of service during the campaigns of 1780 and 1781. Along with New River, the names of forty other Catawba are listed in the comptroller general's records. They include militia members such as Sugar Jamey, Quash, and Billy Redhead. Attempts made by survivors of the war to collect pensions further attest to their service. Patriot fortunes seemed the bleakest in the Carolinas in the aftermath of the defeat at Camden, South Carolina, in August. With a second Continental army defeated and scattered, the role of the state militia became even more critical.

During the remainder of 1780, the Catawba continued in the service of the state and provided sustenance to the partisan forces. Richard Winn, who campaigned in the Carolinas, indicates the important role the Catawba played: "When we took the field after the fall of Charleston, we often encamped on their lands for days together. Those friendly Indians drove us beef from their own stocks and several times brought out their whole force and encamped near us." Robert Wilson, a resident of Chester on the Broad River, joined Sumter's forces in June 1780. Camping near the Catawba, he attested to a unique defense mechanism to secure the Indian camp: Wilson noticed the Catawba stretched out cowhides between trees in an effort to prevent a cavalry attack. The knowledge that Banastre Tarleton and his Loyalist horse soldiers were in the area and had cut down Continental soldiers trying to surrender probably brought on this unique practice. Fighting with Sumter in his various engagements, the Catawba participated in the battles at Hanging Rock and Rocky Mount.[50]

Continuing to show their faith in the patriot cause, the Catawba paid a price for their loyalty. Lieutenant Colonel Francis Rawdon, serving under General Cornwallis, heard from local Tories about their fears of both Whigs and Catawba forces in the vicinity of Charlotte. Rawdon proceeded to issue a proclamation attempting to affect the return of the Catawba, who took refuge in North Carolina. Under Rawdon's offer, the British would protect the Indians but promised destruction of homes and crops if they did not return to the reservation. Probably during the summer, many members of the nation chose to seek temporary refuge in North Carolina.[51]

By December 1780, the Catawba faced dire circumstances as the patriot forces moved into North Carolina. That month, General New River arrived with a letter of introduction from General Horatio Gates to General Nathanael Greene. Greene was new on the scene, only recently replacing Gates after his loss at Camden. Gates, in a 10 December letter, told Greene that General New River believed his people had been unfairly treated by the inhabitants of South Carolina and hoped to relocate to Charlotte. Gates also spoke of the "faithfulness" of the Catawba, which he believed obliged the country to "mitigate their wants." As Richard Winn observed, "Those Indians were so fraid of the British that they deserted their country, men, women, and children, with a few exceptions, and moved towards Virginia." The Catawba, in effect, were moving with Greene's army as he attempted to stretch the British resources by forcing Cornwallis to pursue him toward the Dan River.[52]

The following spring, after Greene had bloodied Cornwallis at Guilford Courthouse, the Catawba returned to their lands in South Carolina. As Rawdon had warned, their village was destroyed: everything from crops to fowl and cattle. With British forces retreating to the North Carolina coast and eventually to Virginia at the end of 1781, an immediate military threat to the Carolinas and the Catawba appeared to be less likely. The scars of war, however, were deep. In 1782, the Catawba appealed to the state of South Carolina for relief. Records from the state House of Representatives and Senate show that upon the governor's request, 500 bushels of corn were to be purchased for the use of the nation. Both legislative bodies acceded to this bill, a small gesture that would help the nation until summer and fall crops could be harvested.[53] The Catawba benefited from the respect earned by leaders in power after the war. Because army veterans often served in the state government, the Catawba could rely on advocates who remembered their service and sacrifice. In one example, the

House of Representatives in 1784 introduced a bill to deliver nearly £300 for nearly two months to individual Catawba in various campaigns. A further sum of £125 was voted for "Horses, Cattle, Hogs &ca. which has been taken from them for the use of the Army during the War." Governor William Moultrie, Joseph Kershaw, and Thomas Sumter, who fought alongside the Catawba, attempted to make their transition to peacetime neighbors in South Carolina a bit easier.[54]

Scholars have neglected and downplayed the role of Native Americans who allied themselves with Whig forces during the Revolution. In the case of the Catawba, the modest numbers of soldiers contributing to the patriot forces might help explain this oversight. Perhaps the lack of a substantial paper trail concerning Catawba involvement in different theaters presents a second factor. Even Douglas Summers Brown, who wrote extensively about the nation, concludes that "the full extent of the Catawbas' participation in the Revolution will probably never be known." James Merrell, author of *The Indians' New World*, concedes that while the nation's warriors never determined the fate of a battle, numbers do not tell the whole story. Merrell concludes his brief section on the American Revolution by stating, "The significance of the Indians' contribution lay, not in the size of the Catawba company or the number of cattle they herded into Sumter's camp, but in their active and visible participation in the cause." The sacrifices made in lives, fortunes, and homes made an impression on thousands of settlers in the Carolinas. In 1781, their friend and advocate Joseph Kershaw told the Catawba leaders he looked forward to the end of "this Long and Bloody War, in which You have taken so Noble a part and have fought and Bled with your white Brothers of America." Nearly eliminated only a generation before because of disease and the encroachment of whites, the Catawba endured. Their service in the American Revolution guaranteed a level of respect and recognition in the centuries after independence.[55]

Two Indian nations who made their home in the Carolinas, the Catawba and the Cherokee, fought in the American Revolution for different reasons. Surrounded by white settlers and confined to a small reservation at the start of the war, the Catawba believed their best chance to endure as a nation would happen by offering aid to the leaders of the resistance in North and South Carolina. The nation never represented a barrier to expansion by white settlers, but it can be argued that allying with the Carolina governments *was* effectively their only choice. Nevertheless, by heeding the warning of the Whig governments and joining campaigns during the Revolution, the Catawba were able to earn grudging respect in the new republic. During the course of the war, Catawba warriors fought in numerous engagements in the southern theater as part of a militia force or as scouts. In addition to providing soldiers in numerous campaigns, the Catawba lands became a place of refuge and comfort for partisan bands when the British moved in force through the Carolinas in 1780 and 1781. In the years after the war, the Catawba remained on their modest reservation in South Carolina. But in spite of their service to the Revolutionary cause, the Catawba reservation shrunk to 8,000 acres in the 1790s as corrupt trustees swindled away more tracts of land. Settlers who coveted Catawba lands resorted to intimidation in order to get it. Victims of the political weakness of a national government and incoherent Indian policy in the early republic, the Catawba nevertheless endured through quiet resignation.[56]

Greater in number and living in four southern states, the Cherokee chose a different path in 1776. Accommodationist leaders attempted to enact a buffer to keep the peace with their white neighbors. They hoped surrendering land in the decade before the Revolution would allow them to remain on an ever-decreasing part of North America and show their fidelity to southern colonial governments. But when a splinter group of younger Cherokee chose war, they fashioned a different response to help ensure the survival of their nation. The Chickamauga insurgency represented a part of what has been called the "largest most unified Native American effort the continent would ever see."[57] By continuing to attack settlers long after their elder leaders made peace in 1777, the Chickamauga Cherokee militants assumed that the only option to preserve their land and keep their way of life was to fight. In the new republic, moderate leaders such as Oconostota reasserted control and sued for peace. Lacking British resources after 1781, elements of the Chickamauga secessionists wanted hostilities to end.[58] And yet, the very fact that the Cherokee went to war without a strong British alliance is proof that the young warriors in 1776 carried the day in the beginning, risking all to protect their homes. At the beginning of the American Revolution, the Cherokee could choose one of two paths. The so-called leading men hoped compromise and a legitimate buffer state would prevent violence with the land-hungry southern colonists. The Chickamauga dissenters claimed to walk the "truer path." They hoped to assert independence by fighting the American encroachment on their land and thereby rebuild their nation in an effort to ensure its survival.[59] While accommodationist leaders signed the Treaty of Hopewell in 1785 in an attempt to permanently fix a Cherokee border with the United States, Dragging Canoe continued to resist sporadically well into the 1790s. When federal treaties failed to protect their land from the encroachment of whites, frustrated Cherokee opted to join the Chickamauga faction.[60]

NOTES

1. Jim Piecuch, *Three Peoples, One King: Loyalists, Indians, and Slaves in the Revolutionary South, 1775–1782* (Columbia: University of South Carolina Press, 2008), 63.

2. Colin G. Calloway, *Pen and Ink Witchcraft: Treaties and Treaty Making in American Indian History* (New York: Oxford University Press, 2013), 91; James H. O'Donnell, *The Cherokees of North Carolina in the American Revolution* (Raleigh: Division of Archives and History, 1976), 7.

3. Colin G. Calloway, "Declaring Independence and Rebuilding a Nation: Dragging Canoe and the Chickamauga Revolution," in *Revolutionary Founders: Rebels, Radicals, and Reformers in the Making of the Nation*, ed. Alfred F. Young, Gary B. Nash, and Ray Raphael (New York: Knopf, 2011), 187; O'Donnell, *Cherokees of North Carolina*, 7.

4. Calloway, *Pen and Ink Witchcraft*, 91; Gregory Evans Dowd, *A Spirited Resistance: The North American Indian Struggle for Unity* (Baltimore: Johns Hopkins University Press, 1992), 48.

5. E. Lawrence Lee, *Indian Wars in North Carolina, 1663–1763* (Raleigh: North Carolina Division of Archives and History, 1997), 54; William Powell, *North Carolina through Four Centuries* (Chapel Hill: University of North Carolina Press, 1989), 24; James H. Merrell, "The Indians' New World: The Catawba Experience," in *American Encounters: Natives and Newcomers from European Contact to Indian Removal, 1500–1850*, ed. Peter C. Mancall and James H. Merrell (New York: Routledge, 2007), 38.

6. Lee, *Indian Wars*, 92; Theda Perdue and Christopher Arris Oakley, *Native Carolinians: The Indians of North Carolina* (Raleigh: North Carolina Department of Cultural Resources, 2010), 38; Ethan A. Schmidt, *Native Americans in the American Revolution: How the War Divided, Devastated, and Transformed the Early American Indian World* (Santa Barbara: Praeger, 2014), xv, xvi.

7. Quoted in James H. Merrell, *The Indians' New World: Catawbas and Their Neighbors from European Contact through the Era of Removal* (New York: W. W. Norton, 1989), 205.

8. Charles M. Hudson, *The Catawba Nation* (Athens: University of Georgia Press, 1970), 53; Douglas Summers Brown, *The Catawba Indians: The People of the River* (Columbia: University of South Carolina Press, 1966), 253; Merrell, "Indians' New World," 38–39.

9. Robert Ganyard, "Threat from the West: North Carolina and the Cherokee, 1776–1778," *North Carolina Historical Review* 45, no. 1 (1968): 48; John Grenier, *The First Way of War: American War Making on the Frontier* (Cambridge: Cambridge University Press, 2005), 151.

10. Daniel J. Tortura, *Carolina in Crisis: Cherokees, Colonists, and Slaves in the American Southeast, 1756–1763* (Chapel Hill: University of North Carolina Press, 2015), 188. The Cherokee position in the aftermath of the French and Indian War is chronicled well in his conclusion.

11. Armstrong Starkey, *European and Native American Warfare, 1675–1815* (Norman: University of Oklahoma Press, 1998), 113; Charles Patrick Neimeyer, *America Goes to War: A Social History of the Continental Army* (New York: New York University Press, 1996); Harry M. Ward, *The War for Independence and the Transformation of American Society* (London: UCL Press, 1999), 193.

12. Ward, *War for Independence*, 193; Starkey, *European and Native American Warfare*, 113; Colin G. Calloway, *The American Revolution in Indian Country: Crisis and Diversity in Native American Communities* (New York: Cambridge University Press, 1995), xiii, 24, 31.

13. Schmidt, *Native Americans in the American Revolution*, 88.

14. John Richard Alden, *The South in the American Revolution, 1763–1789* (Baton Rouge: Louisiana State University Press, 1957), 5.

15. Ibid., 12–13.

16. William Edwin Hemphill, ed., *Extracts from the Journals of the Provincial Congresses of South Carolina, 1775–1776* (Columbia: University of South Carolina Press, 1966), 56.

17. Henry Laurens to Joseph Kershaw, 25 July 1775, in *The Papers of Henry Laurens, Volume Ten: December 12, 1774–January 4, 1776*, ed. David R. Chesnutt (Columbia: University of South Carolina Press, 1985), 247n2.

18. William Moultrie, *Memoirs of the American Revolution*, 2 vols. (New York: David Longworth, 1802), 1:81.

19. Keith Krawczynski, *William Drayton: South Carolina Revolutionary Patriot* (Baton Rouge: Louisiana State University Press, 2001), 132; Brown, *Catawba Indians*, 256–57.

20. "Journal of the Council of Safety, for the Province of South Carolina, 1775," in South Carolina Historical Society, *Collections*, vol. 2 (Charleston: South Carolina Historical Society, 1858), 31–34.

21. Brown, *Catawba Indians*, 261; "Journal of the Council of Safety," 61.

22. "Journal of the Second Council of Safety, Appointed by the Provisional Congress, November 1775," in South Carolina Historical Society, *Collections*, vol. 3 (Charleston: South Carolina Historical Society, 1859), 88, 89, 253, 263–64.

23. C. L. Bragg, *Crescent Moon over Carolina: William Moultrie and American Liberty* (Columbia: University of South Carolina Press, 2013), 65.

24. John Buchanan, *The Road to Guilford Courthouse: The American Revolution in the Carolinas* (New York: John Wiley and Sons, 1997, 13); John Ferling, *Almost a Miracle: The American Victory in the War of Independence* (Oxford: Oxford University Press, 2007), 129; Christopher Ward, *The War of the Revolution*, ed. John Richard Alden (New York: Macmillan, 1952), 2:678.

25. Jack Sosin, *The Revolutionary Frontier, 1763–1783* (New York: Holt, Rinehart and Winston, 1967), 75, 90; Philip M. Hamer, "The Wataugans and the Cherokee Indians in 1776," *East Tennessee Historical Publications* 3, no. 3 (1931): 114.

26. Grace Steele Woodward, *The Cherokees* (Norman: University of Oklahoma Press, 1963), 92; Dowd, *Spirited Resistance*, 48.

27. O'Donnell, *Cherokees of North Carolina*, 16.

28. Calloway, "Declaring Independence," 191; Dowd, *Spirited Resistance*, 49.

29. Ganyard, "Threat from the West," 49; "Moravian Diary, April 13, 1776," in *Records of the Moravians in North Carolina*, ed. Adelaide L. Fries et al. (Raleigh: Division of Archives and History, 1922–69), 3:1061; Samuel Ashe, "Rutherford's Expedition against the Indians, 1776," *North Carolina Booklet* 14 (December 1904): 11.

30. Griffith Rutherford to the Council of Safety, 14 July 1776, in William L. Saunders, ed., *The Colonial Records of North Carolina* (Raleigh: Josephus Daniels, 1886–90), 10:669.

31. Council of Safety to Rutherford, 21 July 1776, in Walter Clark, ed., *The State Records of North Carolina* (Goldsboro, N.C.: Nash Brothers, 1895–1905), 11:318–19.

32. Thomas M. Hatley, *Dividing Paths: Cherokees and South Carolinians through the Era of Revolution* (New York: Oxford University Press, 1993), 193; North Carolina Delegates in the Continental Congress to the North Carolina Provincial Council, 7 August 1776, in Saunders, *Colonial Records of North Carolina*, 10:731.

33. Mary Elinor Lazenby, *Catawba Frontier, 1775–1781: Memoirs of Pensioners* (Washington, D.C.: Compiler, 1950), 81; Richard D. Blackmon, *Dark and Bloody Ground: The American Revolution along the Southern Frontier* (Yardley, Pa.: Westholme, 2012), 63.

34. Nadia Dean, *A Demand of Blood: The Cherokee War of 1776* (Cherokee, N.C.: Valley River Press, 2012), 145; Blackmon, *Dark and Bloody Ground*, 67–68; Maurice Moore, *Reminiscences of York* (Greenville, S.C.: A Press, 1981), 8–10.

35. "Fragment of a Diary Journal Kept by an Unidentified Officer Relating to the Cherokee Expedition of 1776, August–September 1776," transcribed and annotated by Will Graves, *Southern Campaigns of the American Revolution* 2 (October 2005): 34–35.

36. "Arthur Fairies' Journal of Expedition against the Cherokee Indians from July 18th, to October 11th, 1776," transcribed and annotated by Will Graves in ibid., 23; Dean, *Demand of Blood*, 155; Blackmon, *Dark and Bloody Ground*, 74.

37. Blackmon, *Dark and Bloody Ground*, 81; Frank G. Speck, "The Catawba Nation and Its Neighbors," *North Carolina Historical Review* 16, no. 4 (1939): 411.

38. Blackmon, *Dark and Bloody Ground*, 82–83; John Drayton, *Memoirs of the American Revolution as Relating to the State of South Carolina*, 2 vols. (Charleston: A. E. Miller, 1821; repr., New York: Arno Press, 1969), 1:357.

39. Ganyard, "Threat from the West," 50; Dean, *Demand of Blood*, 314.

40. Blackmon, *Dark and Bloody Ground*, 92.

41. David K. Wilson, *The Southern Strategy: Britain's Conquest of South Carolina and Georgia, 1775–1780* (Columbia: University of South Carolina Press, 2005), 62.

42. Colonel William Christian to Governor Patrick Henry, 14 October 1776, in Saunders, *Colonial Records of North Carolina*, 10:844; Dowd, *Spirited Resistance*, 54.

43. Calloway, *American Revolution in Indian Country*, 44; Dowd, *Spirited Resistance*, 55. In 1779 the separatist Cherokee moved to the Chickamauga Creek near Chattanooga. They can be considered Chickamauga as early as 1776 because they refused to sue for peace.

44. Hatley, *Dividing Paths*, 226–27; "Instructions to Charles McDowell, John Sevier, and Waightstill Avery Concerning a Treaty with the Cherokee Nation and the Chickamaugas," in Clark, *State Records of North Carolina*, 19:905–6; Calloway, *Pen and Ink Witchcraft*, 103.

45. O'Donnell, *Cherokees of North Carolina*, 34.

46. Peter N. Moore, *World of Toil and Strife: Community Transformation in Backcountry South Carolina, 1750–1805* (Columbia: University of South Carolina Press, 2007), 68–69.

47. Robert D. Bass, *Gamecock: The Life and Campaigns of General Thomas Sumter* (New York: Holt, Rinehart and Winston, 1961), 54–55.

48. The practice of bestowing honorary titles to Indian leaders dates from the late colonial period. Royal governors could issue the necessary documents to help certain loyal leaders maintain legitimacy and recruit warriors. William R. Reynolds, *Andrew Pickens: South Carolina Patriot in the Revolutionary War* (Jefferson, N.C.: McFarland, 2012), 156; Blackwell P. Robinson, ed., *The Revolutionary War Sketches of William R. Davie* (Raleigh: North Carolina Division of Archives and History, 1976), 8; Blackwell P. Robinson, *William R. Davie* (Chapel Hill: University of North Carolina Press, 1957), 45.

49. Alexia Jones Helsley, "The Catawba and American Liberty," *South Carolina Historical Magazine* 96, no. 3 (1995): 252–56; Merrell, *Indians' New World*, 150.

50. Helsley, "Catawba and American Liberty," 253–56; John Henry Logan, "Extracts from the Logan Manuscript [of the Upper South]," *Historical Collections of the Joseph Habersham Chapter*, Daughters of the American Revolution, vol. 3, (1910) 83; Merrell, *Indians' New World*, 216.

51. Michael C. Scoggins, *The Day It Rained Militia: Huck's Defeat and the Revolution in the South Carolina Backcountry, May–July 1780* (Charleston: History Press, 2005), 64; Merrell, *Indians' New World*, 216.

52. Nathanael Greene to Horatio Gates, 10 December 1780, in *The Papers of Nathanael Greene, Volume 6, 1 June 1780–25 December 1780*, ed. Richard K. Showman (Chapel Hill: University of North Carolina Press, 1991), 560 and note; Richard Winn, "General Richard Winn's Notes: 1780," *South Carolina Historical and Genealogical Magazine* 44, no. 1 (1943): 6–7.

53. A. S. Salley Jr., ed., *Journal of the Senate of South Carolina, January 8, 1782–February 26, 1782* (Columbia: Historical Commission of South Carolina, 1941), 44, 50; A. S. Salley Jr., ed., *Journal of the House of Representatives of South Carolina, January 8, 1782–February 26, 1782* (Columbia: Historical Commission of South Carolina, 1916), 59–60, 65, 102.

54. Theodora J. Thompson and Rosa S. Lumpkin, eds., *Journals of the House of Representatives, 1783–1784: The State Records of South Carolina* (Columbia: University of South Carolina Press, 1977), 472, 489, 491–92, 499.

55. Merrell, *Indians' New World*, 217. Quote from Merrell, "Indians' New World," 40.

56. Schmidt, *Native Americans in the American Revolution*, 166; Merrell, *Indians' New World*, 225.

57. Dowd, *Spirited Resistance*, 46.

58. Patrick Griffin, *America's Revolution* (New York: Oxford, 2013), 221; Gary B. Nash, *The Unknown American Revolution: The Unruly Birth of Democracy and the Struggle to Create America* (New York: Viking, 2005), 384.

59. Hatley, *Dividing Paths*, 228; Calloway, "Declaring Independence," 186.

60. Schmidt, *Native Americans in the American Revolution*, 158.

4

Our Common Country

John Sevier and the American Revolution

Michael Toomey

In the closing months of 1812, the United States was engaged in a war with Great Britain, and those old enough to do so quite naturally drew a parallel to an earlier war against the same enemy. One such person was John Sevier, who expressed his feelings in a carefully worded memorial to the North Carolina legislature. Any communication from John Sevier was something the legislators could not easily ignore. Not only had he once been a member of that same body, but he also was a veteran and a hero of the Revolution. He had later been commissioned as a brigadier general of militia in North Carolina and commissioned again at the same rank by none other than George Washington. In addition, the legislators knew that Sevier was currently serving as a member of the United States Congress from Tennessee and that he had previously served as governor of that state for six terms.

Sevier told the legislators that the current war against "our inveterate foe, the British nation," had "excited the same indignation and resentment in our breasts as was felt on a former occasion." Sevier was so incensed that he was willing, if called upon, to "cheerfully take up arms once more against the common enemy in the defense of our country." Sevier did admit that he was "considerably advanced in life," and it is doubtful that he expected anyone to take his offer of military service seriously, nor was that his primary purpose. Instead, he wrote to remind the legislators of a promise made by their predecessors more than three decades earlier in the aftermath of the Battle of King's Mountain. In a formal resolution, those earlier legislators had agreed that Sevier should be awarded "an Elegant sword and one pair of pistols." They had done this, Sevier pointed out, as a result of his "Conduct and Service . . . rendered the State, at the Most gloomy period of the Revolution." It was, he concluded, a "debt of honour of long Standing due for Services rendered our common country."[1]

The "common country" to which Sevier referred had changed considerably since that "gloomy period of the Revolution." Not only had the size of the country doubled, but the government itself had grown stronger and more active. Sevier's perception of that government, and indeed his allegiance to it, had likewise grown stronger since he first emerged as a leader in the frontier settlements of North Carolina's backcountry. Like so many others who moved there, Sevier was enticed by the prospect of owning land and gaining access to the economic, social, and political advantages that accompanied landownership in the late eighteenth century. He also believed that, in the pursuit of these advantages, he was at liberty to acquire whatever land he could. It was a notion of liberty that could ignore the contradictions of slavery and discount the claims of Native Americans, yet it could not survive without the larger resources offered by a common country. It was this need for a common country that shaped the political fortunes of John Sevier as he gained, lost, and then resurrected his place among the political elite.

Sevier first ventured into North Carolina's western lands sometime in 1771 or 1772, not long after the first settlers arrived there and established three separate communities generally referred to as the Watauga settlements. Only twenty-six years of age, Sevier had already been married for almost a decade and was the father of seven children. He had lived for most of his life in Augusta County, Virginia, where he achieved some success as a farmer, merchant, and land speculator. Sevier was also a veteran of frontier warfare, having seen service in Lord Dunmore's War, and he held a captain's commission in the Virginia militia. His arrival in the Watauga settlements, therefore, did not go unnoticed. Sevier's objective on that first visit to the Watauga settlements may have been business related, but it seems likely that he was also looking to move there, a decision that must have been encouraged by the Wataugans, who recognized that his presence would enhance the status of their new settlements. Sevier probably bought land on his first trip to Watauga or shortly thereafter, land that he and other residents of the Watauga community believed was located in Virginia.

A subsequent survey indicated that the Watauga settlements were instead beyond the Virginia border and situated on land included within North Carolina's colonial charter. That colony, however, recognized that most of its western claims, beginning on the western flank of the Appalachian Range, were clearly and legally under the control of the Cherokee. Unlike Virginia, which had negotiated a treaty with that tribe to encourage settlement in the lands "back of the mountains," North Carolina had no immediate plans to encourage settlement west of the Unaka range. The Wataugans were thus living beyond the authority of any colonial government and without any legal means to protect property, enforce law and order, or regulate the routine activities that take place in any community. Rather than abandon their settlements and retreat up the valley to Virginia, the Wataugans approached the Cherokee and negotiated a lease that allowed them to remain on their lands for ten years. To address the lack of government, the Wataugans created a temporary system of self-government. The "Articles of Association" that they established provided for a sheriff, a clerk, and other officials, who functioned under the direction of five elected justices, one of whom was John Sevier. These officers exercised authority over all aspects of community life, but most of their attention was apparently focused on land titles and routine law and order.

The Watauga Association, as it is commonly known, did not go unnoticed by colonial officials. The Earl of Dunmore, royal governor of Virginia, warned the British secretary of state for colonial affairs that the people on the Watauga River had, in effect, formed themselves into a "separate state." It was admittedly an inconsiderable state, but even so, "the consequences... may prove hereafter detrimental to the peace and security of the other colonies; it at least sets a dangerous example to the people of America."[2] Dunmore's fears notwithstanding, the Watauga Association was not an effort to defy the authority of any colonial government or the British Crown. Makeshift governments such as the Watauga Association did pose a threat to the orderly process of settlement and especially to relations with the Cherokee and other tribes. But the "separate state" that the Wataugans created was a state of necessity rather than defiance, designed simply to conduct the essential functions of a typical county court.[3]

The Watauga Association and its lease arrangement with the Cherokee were functioning well when Judge Richard Henderson arrived from North Carolina in 1775. Henderson was the leader of the Transylvania Land Company, a group of land speculators, which had arranged to meet with leaders of the Cherokee at Sycamore Shoals in the center of the Watauga community. Henderson's purpose was nothing less than the purchase of almost 20 million acres of land in Kentucky and along the Cumberland River. After four days of negotiations, the Cherokee agreed to surrender their claim to the region in exchange for 10,000 pounds of trade goods. The Wataugans were keen observers of these negotiations, and some, including John Sevier, were actively involved. Henderson himself was apparently a guest for several days at Sevier's home, and Sevier was selected by the Cherokee as one of two advocates to act on their behalf during the implementation of the agreement.[4]

Neither North Carolina nor Virginia sanctioned Hernderson's direct negotiations with the Cherokee for such a vast quantity of land, and the legality of the resulting agreement was highly questionable. Even so, there is no indication that Sevier or the other Watauga commissioners expressed any doubts or misgivings about the outcomes. Indeed, in the aftermath of Henderson's negotiations, the Wataugans moved quickly to convert their lease arrangement with the Cherokee into an outright purchase. But if Sevier was oblivious to the irregularities of the Transylvania purchase, he could not have failed to notice the factionalism among the Cherokee who attended at Sycamore Shoals. Members of a younger, militant party among the Cherokee were visibly angry at the willingness of their elders to part with so much land, and it was clear that their influence and their numbers were not insignificant. Nor would Sevier and other Wataugans have failed to recognize the implications of that militancy. In the event of open warfare between Great Britain and the American colonies, there was little doubt but that the Cherokee would ally with the British, their traditional trading partners, and seize on the opportunity to challenge not only the legitimacy of the Transylvania Purchase but the existence of the Watauga settlements as well. Emboldened by British support, the Cherokee were almost certain to attack the Wataugans should they refuse to abandon their settlements, and the Wataugans were ill prepared to withstand such an attack on their own. Even if open warfare was averted and the differences between the British and colonial governments were resolved, the Wataugans might yet be compelled to abandon their homes, for the British had sent clear signals through recent land policies that they intended to honor Native American land claims and strictly regulate backcountry settlement.

Henderson had been away from Watauga for no more than a month when news of the battles at Lexington and Concord arrived in the Watauga settlements. The Wataugans immediately formed a Committee of Safety and resolved "to adhere strictly to the rules and orders of the Continental Congress and in open committee acknowledged themselves indebted to the United Colonies their full proportion of the Continental expense."[5] Exactly what that proportion might be was impossible to determine, given the ambiguous status of the Watauga Association. Even so, the Wataugans organized and dispatched a platoon of riflemen for service in the defense of Charleston when the British targeted that city as an early objective. They were preparing to send additional troops when rumors of an impending attack began to filter out of the Cherokee towns. The extent to which the British were actively engaged in organizing such an attack is not clear, although the Wataugans needed little encouragement to believe that British agents were making every effort to encourage Cherokee hostilities. What is certain is that the militant faction among the Cherokee, recognizing the American Revolution for the opportunity it was, had gained the upper hand. In a meeting in West Florida in January 1776, the British formalized their alliance with the Cherokee and sent them home with an ample supply of powder and lead.[6]

These developments were not entirely unknown to the Wataugans or, for that matter, to the Continental Congress, which sent a delegation to meet with the Cherokee to dissuade them from allying with the British. The Cherokee were unreceptive to such overtures, however, and instead, through their British agents, demanded that the Watauga settlements be abandoned. The British agents apparently attempted to facilitate this demand by offering the Wataugans new lands in West Florida, but as Sevier later explained, the Wataugans were uninterested in such an offer; "their abhorrence of British tyranny," he claimed, "made them refuse."[7] They instead reorganized themselves as the Washington District and sent an appeal to Virginia for supplies, reinforcements, and annexation, pledging themselves at the same time to "readily embrace every opportunity of obeying any instructions or commands they may receive."[8]

With an attack now seemingly imminent, the Wataugans began to prepare. Sevier was given the responsibility of constructing a modest fort on the Nolichucky River and then taking command of the small garrison stationed there. In early July 1776, traders from the Cherokee towns brought word that the advance was finally underway. Alarmed by the numbers that the fleeing traders were reporting, the defenders of the outermost forts, including the small fort that Sevier commanded on the Nolichucky, retreated to Fort Caswell near Sycamore Shoals, not far from the site where, just the year before, Henderson had negotiated the Transylvania Purchase. Overall command of the fort fell to Charles Robertson, and Sevier's role as a junior officer was not prominent. As the Cherokee drew near, the defenders sallied out and engaged the Cherokee at Island Flats and then shut themselves inside the fort and awaited a relief column they knew was approaching from Virginia.[9]

The troops from Virginia numbered nearly 1,800 and were under the command of Colonel William Christian. As this column approached the besieged fort, the Cherokee had little choice but to retreat. Christian delayed for almost two months in the vicinity before departing on an invasion of the Cherokee homeland. There is no indication that John Sevier participated in this campaign, although it is possible that some members of his company did accompany Christian as scouts. Instead, Sevier took on the more pressing need to clarify the status of the Watauga settlements. Although Virginia had readily agreed to send supplies to the Wataugans and authorized Christian's campaign even before it was known that the Cherokee were on the move, the Virginia legislature was unwilling to annex the settlements.

Annexation by North Carolina therefore became critical, and it was this task to which Sevier addressed himself. Together with the other commissioners of their newly formed Washington District, Sevier prepared a petition to be presented to the North Carolina assembly meeting in Halifax. The "Watauga Petition" was read by the legislators and, after a "high and long debate," overwhelmingly approved. They agreed that the Washington District should elect five representatives to appear at the next session of the assembly.[10] When the legislators reconvened in November they voted overwhelmingly to annex the district, and three of the elected delegates immediately took their seats; Sevier arrived two weeks later and was likewise seated. Before that session was over, the legislature also voted to commission Sevier as lieutenant colonel of militia for the Washington District.[11]

Sevier's first extensive involvement with political procedures and intrigues began when he returned to the legislature the following year. He was not a natural politician, as later events revealed, but he was adept enough to create a career from the lessons he learned in 1777. In addition to introducing a bill that converted the Washington District into a county, Sevier supported legislation that stationed garrisons of militia to guard the frontier, approved the construction of a better road through the mountains, and guaranteed the legality of land titles conveyed through negotiations with the Cherokee.[12]

Sevier's legislative experience was interrupted in 1778, when he was elected clerk for the new Washington County. Much of his attention, however, was focused on an increasingly troublesome Loyalist population. Loyalists had made themselves known in 1776, when the Cherokee advance was approaching the settlements. Centered mostly on the Nolichucky River, these settlers had seemed poised to cooperate with the Cherokee. That alliance was averted when the Wataugans quickly identified almost a hundred suspected Loyalists and compelled them to take an oath of allegiance. But by the latter part of 1778, the number of Loyalists had grown considerably. Some were recent arrivals in the Watauga community, apparently driven to the frontier to escape persecution in the East, and were destitute enough to resort to begging for food. Others were established members of the community with substantial amounts of property, including slaves. None had ever figured prominently in the leadership of the Watauga community, but their numbers were now significant enough to pose a serious threat, and this, together with rumors that the British intended to renew their efforts in the southern colonies, seems to have encouraged Loyalist activity in Watauga. Unlike in 1776, however, when the Wataugan leadership could do little more than compel an oath of allegiance, the creation of Washington County provided them with the authority to confiscate the property of troublesome Loyalists. The county records indicate that some immediate confrontations did in fact take place in 1778, but tensions escalated dramatically in the following year.[13]

While some Loyalists apparently honored their earlier oaths of allegiance, the change in local authority encouraged others to form loose and irregular bands that harassed and often terrorized the community. The number of Loyalists is difficult to ascertain, but the records of the Washington County Court for the year 1779 alone contain numerous cases of treason or "being inimical to the common cause of liberty," as well as several other instances in which individuals were simply brought before the court and required to take an oath of allegiance. The charges against some suspected Loyalists were dismissed, and others were released on their good behavior. In some cases, however, the court sentenced Loyalists to jail or had them transported to military prisons, and in these instances their property could be confiscated by the county court.[14] By law, those confiscated lands became vacant lands and were open to entries by new claimants.

As an aspiring land speculator, Sevier was keenly interested in these cases. The population of Watauga had been increasing steadily since William Christian returned from his campaign against the Cherokee towns in 1776, and the value of any available land was likewise increasing. Improved lands, such as had been confiscated from the Loyalists, were especially desirable. In the summer of 1779 Sevier entered claims for what he later described as "a considerable quantity" of confiscated lands.[15] After news of what he had done circulated in the community, the Loyalist population became incensed, and the tensions that had been growing for the past year erupted into open violence. Some supporters of the county government were attacked and killed, generally by ambush, and known Loyalists were hunted down and often hanged on the spot. Sevier played an active role in patrolling the community and confronting the Loyalists. This, together with his earlier claims for confiscated lands, made him a focal point for retaliation. On at least one occasion Loyalists specifically targeted him for assassination. The plot was revealed at the last minute, and the perpetrators were themselves hunted down, cornered in a barn, and, after a brief fight, all killed.[16] Even so, Sevier remained vulnerable, and his followers decided to post a guard around him at all times. The tension of the summer of 1779 was still fresh more than twenty years later when Sevier was surveying lands on Tennessee's northern border and visited with David Hickey, who had been among those guards. "He well remembers," Sevier recorded, "my entering all the Tory lands and that they . . . threatened my life and that himself Martin Mary and Isaac Davis guarded me several nights."[17]

The Loyalists were never completely brought under control, but by the following summer the most troublesome of their number had been killed or driven out of the community. The Cherokee were likewise less threatening since the return of Christian's campaign in 1776 and the Treaty of Long Island the following year. The militant faction of the Cherokee—now known as the Chickamauga—had broken away and remained a concern, although most of their hostility was directed at the new settlements being established along the Cumberland River. The population in the Watauga settlements had continued to grow, so much so that in 1779 a new county, Sullivan, was carved out of Washington County. With the Loyalists and the Cherokee seemingly controlled, it did not seem likely that the North Carolina backcountry was to play a significant role in the Revolution, which continued to be fought for the most part well to the north.

The situation changed quickly in the summer of 1779 when the British launched a campaign to regain their southern colonies. The most important objective was the vital port city of Charleston. That city was under siege by early April of the following year, and one month later the city, with its garrison of more than 5,400 troops, was compelled to surrender. The British army, under the command of Charles Cornwallis, then turned north as American forces throughout the South, including militia from the North Carolina backcountry, scrambled to contest his advance. By August Cornwallis was at Camden, South Carolina, where he brushed aside an American army and prepared to continue his advance into North Carolina.

Guarding Cornwallis's western flank was a force of approximately 1,100 regulars and Loyalist militia under the command of Colonel Patrick Ferguson, an experienced officer with an impressive service record in Europe and America. He was aware that many of the patriot militia he had faced in the previous months were what he called "backwater men" who had come from settlements across the mountains and that a number had returned there in the aftermath of the disaster at Camden. Ferguson now boldly demanded that these backwater men lay down their arms immediately and swear allegiance to the Crown; otherwise he would "march his army over the mountains, hang their leaders, and lay the country waste with fire and sword."[18]

Ferguson's threat was relayed to these frontier leaders whose hangings had been threatened, and they recognized that the danger went well beyond their own necks. A British army in the Watauga settlements would certainly draw support from the bothersome Loyalist population and very likely from the Cherokee. Such a combined force would be impossible to resist, and the Watauga community might well be devastated. Much better, it was decided, to attack Ferguson before he crossed the mountains. Accordingly, a muster of militia was called, to be commanded by Isaac Shelby and John Sevier. Colonel William Campbell of Virginia was likewise informed of the threat and was persuaded to include his regiment. The "Overmountain Men" set out in late September in search of Ferguson. They were poorly trained in battlefield tactics and military protocol, but they were well armed and, after gathering reinforcements along the way, eventually numbered around 1,000 men.

Alerted to their approach, Ferguson posted his army on the summit of King's Mountain near the border between North Carolina and South Carolina to await the attack. Convinced that the superior training of his troops, particularly the regulars, would prove decisive, he felt confident as he waited atop his mountain stronghold. On 7 October the Overmountain Men located Ferguson and launched their attack in midafternoon. The weakness of Ferguson's position was immediately evident. With too little room to maneuver on the narrow crest of the ridge, Ferguson's men soon found themselves receiving fire from all sides. Nor did the superior training of the British force prove to be particularly advantageous on the wooded slopes of the mountain, where every tree and rock provided cover for the attackers. Ferguson ordered three bayonet charges to blunt the assault, and each proved effective. But as soon as the British returned to their hilltop positions, the attack was renewed. Within about an hour the battle was over; Ferguson and more than 200 of his men were dead, and the remainder of his army became prisoners.[19]

The victory of the Overmountain Men was decisive, but there was reason to believe that Cornwallis had already sent heavy reinforcements to assist Ferguson and that those troops might arrive at any moment. The Overmountain Men slept on the battlefield that night and began their return march the next morning, but encumbered by more than 600 prisoners their progress was slow. Five days later they arrived at Biggerstaff's Old Fields on the property of Aaron Biggerstaff in Rutherford County, North Carolina. By that time, some of the Overmountain troops had looked among their Loyalist prisoners and recognized former friends and neighbors who they claimed were guilty of robberies, murders, and other atrocities. By this point in the war, such claims were all too common in the backcountry among patriots and Loyalists alike, and neither side was hesitant to take revenge when the opportunity presented itself. But the Overmountain Men now found themselves in a unique position, with many of their most hated enemies standing helpless before them. Several officers presented Colonel William Campbell—nominally in command—with a petition demanding an immediate trial for those prisoners they claimed were guilty of the most notorious crimes. Before the day was over, somewhere between thirty-five and forty Loyalists had been tried, convicted, and sentenced to death. As darkness fell, the executions began, and nine of the most egregious offenders were hanged. At this point some of the colonels—including Sevier—intervened. Sevier was no stranger to the vicious nature of civil war in the Carolina backcountry, and his aggressive campaign during the previous summer against the Loyalists in Watauga demonstrated that he was not averse to summary trials and executions. But with the bodies of nine Loyalists hanging dead before him and at least two dozen more prisoners (including two deserters from his own command) awaiting the same fate, Sevier was compelled to reconsider. It is possible that he realized that the repercussions of such a mass execution were likely to be intense and brutal. In any event, the executions were halted and the march was resumed the next day. Some harassment of the prisoners occurred during the remainder of the march, but the tension decreased dramatically. Indeed, many of the prisoners discovered—and took advantage of—ample opportunities to escape. No more than 130 prisoners of the original 600 were still in custody when they were turned over to Continental authorities at Hillsborough.[20]

By that time, Sevier and his men had already separated from the main army and were on the way home. They took with them the knowledge that they had made an important contribution to the war effort, but they also carried a new sense of self-worth and importance. Their role in the Battle of King's Mountain gave them a unique status within their community that they retained for the remainder of their lives.[21] For John Sevier, as one of the battlefield commanders, this was especially true. His involvement with military affairs to that point had been noteworthy, to be sure, but his most visible service to his community had come in the North Carolina legislature. Likewise, his vigilance against the threat from Loyalist attacks had done much to earn the gratitude and loyalty of his neighbors. But the victory at King's Mountain catapulted Sevier into unimaginable heights of popularity and launched a military career that went far beyond any service Sevier had heretofore rendered. He had not, of course, been in command at the battle; the colonels of each regiment moved to their assigned positions and then exercised a virtual independent command. It was well understood, however, that John Sevier had played a key role in initiating and planning the campaign. Subsequent accounts of the battle claimed that Sevier's "bravery was well-attested" and "universally admitted."[22]

Sevier continued to pursue political office for the remainder of his life and was successful more often than not. But his leadership in politics was based to a significant degree on his success at King's Mountain and in subsequent military campaigns.

Immediately upon returning from King's Mountain, Sevier ordered a portion of the Washington County militia into the field in response to a renewed threat from the Cherokee. Although Sevier was aware that additional troops were marching from Virginia to participate in the campaign, he elected not to delay and instead led his troops down the valley. In December they encountered a body of Cherokee at Boyd's Creek, a tributary of the French Broad River, and after a sharp fight the Cherokee retreated. Sevier lacked the strength to launch a serious pursuit and was later criticized for the decision to push forward without enough troops to inflict a decisive defeat. Very little of that criticism came from the residents of Washington County, nor was this the last time that Sevier ordered his troops forward to engage the Cherokee at some point well beyond the borders of the settlements. Boldness to the point of rashness was to become a hallmark of his future campaigns, a tactic that was applauded by those whose homes he was charged with protecting. They were little concerned that many of Sevier's campaigns took place in response to isolated incidents and that very often his response far outweighed the threat to the community. For the next thirteen years, his aggressive and sometimes unauthorized campaigns into the Cherokee heartland earned him the enduring loyalty of the people he guarded and the dubious nickname "Scourge of the Cherokee." His actions were often frustrating to national policy makers attempting to frame a coherent Indian policy, but his forceful response to any semblance of a Cherokee threat, together with the memory of King's Mountain, became the foundation upon which his popularity was built and sustained.

Sevier led two more such campaigns against the Cherokee the following year, and in the late summer of 1781 he received a request from Nathanael Greene to provide reinforcements to his operations east of the mountains. Together with Isaac Shelby, commander of the Sullivan County militia, Sevier took approximately 200 men across the mountains and joined Francis Marion on the Santee River. The bulk of their service consisted of patrols and "annoying the British at every convenient opportunity." Many of the militia returned home at the end of their terms, but Sevier and most of his men remained for perhaps as long as four months before he went back to Plum Grove, his farm on the Nolichucky River in Washington County.[23]

Sevier's role in the Revolution thus came to an end after six years. His contributions were real, and his stature within the community had increased accordingly. The Watauga petition—which he had helped to write and then championed in the North Carolina legislature in 1776—expressed the desire of the Wataugans to be a part of the "glorious cause of liberty." Yet there is little in Sevier's writing to indicate his own feelings regarding that cause. Certainly the early historians of Tennessee, writing in the antiquarian tradition of the nineteenth century, had no difficulty in explaining Sevier's motives. J. G. M. Ramsey, writing at midcentury, claimed that the same Watauga petition "breathes the warmest patriotism; and is inspired with the spirit of justice and of liberty." Another such author wondered how Sevier's parents, gazing at their newborn child, might have reacted had they known that their son was destined to "smite the enemy of his country and make way for peace and civilization."[24]

A later generation of historians took quite a different approach. Thomas P. Abernethy claimed that "the serpent of greed and speculation" influenced many in the backcountry.[25] Sevier's biographer Carl Driver wrote that Sevier was largely motivated by the double threat of restrictive British land policies and the impending attack by the Cherokee. Beyond that, says Driver, Sevier and his fellow Wataugans probably "knew little and cared less about the struggles of the seaboard with the mother country to the east."[26]

Certainly the truth lies somewhere between these extremes. There can be no doubt that the Wataugans were very much aware of the rising tensions along the Atlantic Seaboard and that they were fully committed to the "glorious cause of liberty." But it was also likely that their commitment was influenced by a tenuous hold on their lands. Those lands had been acquired through an irregular process, one that the Cherokee contested and that both North Carolina and Virginia considered illegal. Yet it was a process that Sevier and his neighbors believed to be well within the bounds of legality, and in fact it conformed perfectly to their concept of liberty, which had at its heart the acquisition and protection of property as a means of participating in the political process. Securing that liberty required an alliance with either Virginia or North Carolina and, through that alliance, to the United Colonies.

Yet Sevier's conduct in the years immediately following independence suggests that his allegiance to the national government, functioning under the loose provisions of the Articles of Confederation, was, like his allegiance to the state of North Carolina, a recent development generated in large part by necessity. The situation changed dramatically in the spring of 1784, when North Carolina agreed to cede its western lands to the federal government. Congress had made similar requests to all states with western lands, but unlike those states, North Carolina's cession included established settlements with functioning county governments. The residents of those counties—Washington,

Sullivan, and Greene, a new county formed the previous year—were thus left once again outside the bounds of state government. They were waiting only for formal acceptance by Congress of North Carolina's cession, at which point they would be (or so they assumed) entitled to form their own state and apply for admission to the union. Accordingly, representatives from those counties met in Jonesborough and organized themselves as the independent state of Franklin, set a date for a constitutional convention, and prepared a request to Congress for admission as the fourteenth state.

What had seemed to be a logical progression of events suddenly became confused when the North Carolina legislature arbitrarily rescinded its act of cession and reasserted authority over its western counties. John Sevier's role in the movement for statehood had so far been comparatively subtle, and he now assumed, as did many others, that the movement should be abandoned. Much of his reasoning was based on the fact that North Carolina, in reasserting its authority, had also taken steps to address some of the administrative problems associated with governing the western counties, most notably the creation of a judicial district to serve the three counties. It is also possible that Sevier was willing to abandon the movement because the North Carolina legislature had appointed him as the brigadier general for this new district. But the proponents of the Franklin movement remained determined to push forward, and they believed that Sevier's leadership was the best means of securing regional support. Sevier remained reluctant, even going so far as to discourage elections for delegates to the upcoming constitutional convention. In the end, however, he joined the movement, or, as he later claimed, was "draged" into it, and when the convention met in March, Sevier was elected governor of the state of Franklin. Once elected, he embraced the movement wholeheartedly and without any further reservations.[27]

The state of Franklin movement itself has generally been ascribed to one of two possible motivations. In the first, the Franklin movement was a natural outgrowth of the Revolution. Poorly served by their government, situated too distant to receive fair representation, and held in generally low esteem by the eastern portion of the state, the Franklinites believed they were in a sort of quasi-colonial situation and thus within their rights in forming a new government that better served their needs. Alternately, the Franklin movement was a contest between rival groups of land speculators; one was centered in the east and included prominent businessmen and legislators, and the other was centered in the west and led by local speculators such as Sevier. Whether he accepted the governorship in response to a grassroots call for independence or in response to other landowners who looked to him to protect their titles from rival claimants, Sevier was responding as he had done during the Revolution to secure and protect his own property and that of his neighbors.

It was in many ways a similar situation to what Sevier had faced eight years earlier. Franklin, like Watauga, was politically and geographically isolated; if threatened its citizens seemed unlikely to survive indefinitely on their own resources. As had been true for Watauga in 1776, the solution for Franklin in 1784 was annexation into a larger community. A delegate was thus sent quickly to Congress with a petition requesting recognition of Franklin's independence. But the Confederation Congress was ill equipped to consider such a request; there was no precedent for admitting new states, and the refusal of North Carolina to honor its act of cession complicated the situation even more. Although the final vote was very close, the petition of the state of Franklin was rejected. Sevier was not yet prepared to admit defeat, and he remained in his role as governor in the hope that North Carolina or Congress or preferably both would relent and Franklin might yet be admitted to statehood.

Prospects for statehood would be vastly improved, Sevier believed, through increased immigration and settlement. Not only would a rapid influx of settlers create a core constituency of loyal proponents of statehood, but those new settlers would be difficult to remove once established. Their presence, he hoped, would leave North Carolina and Congress with little choice but to grant recognition. Such a plan required access to yet more lands, and the Cherokee had claimed most of the attractive lands south of the French Broad River. Sevier therefore extended an invitation to the Cherokee to meet with him in early June 1785 at Dumplin Creek on the French Broad River. The response to his invitation was disappointing, and the chiefs that did attend the negotiations did not constitute a full representation from the Cherokee. Even so, Sevier pressed forward and produced a treaty that created a new boundary, one that awarded to the state of Franklin all the lands between the French Broad and Tennessee (now the Little Tennessee) Rivers and was well to the south of the line the Cherokee had been compelled to accept several years earlier at the Treaty of Long Island. The legitimacy of the Dumplin Creek Treaty was doubtful, and in fact the Cherokee later claimed they had never agreed to such a cession and instead had only given permission for those few settlers already living in the region to remain there. Sevier and the Franklinites, however, viewed the treaty as an unconditional transfer of land, and within three years it was estimated that as many as 1,500 families were living south of the French Broad River.[28]

Despite such an increase in population, Franklin's prospects for statehood decreased sharply, and by 1788 Sevier was willing to consider other options.

The most intriguing of these options involved negotiations between Sevier and an agent of the Spanish governor at Pensacola who arrived in Franklin to discuss the prospects for annexing that government into the Spanish Empire. Sevier was receptive to the concept, and in a subsequent letter to the governor he stated that the "people of this country have come to realize truly upon what part of the world and upon which nation depend their future happiness and security." The citizens of Franklin, he claimed, now believed that their "interest and prosperity . . . depend entirely upon the protection and liberality of your government."[29] It was true that the Spanish did actually hold a tenuous claim to the southern half of the Ohio River valley and were actively exploring similar annexations throughout the region, most notably in Kentucky and among the struggling settlements on the Cumberland River. To all of these communities the Spanish could offer significant incentives, including navigation of the Mississippi River and access to the port of New Orleans. In addition, the Spanish could promise an end to Indian attacks by controlling trade with the southern tribes. For Sevier and the Franklinites, who were engaged in a serious war with the Cherokee, this last prospect was particularly attractive.

At the same time, Sevier's intentions in what has come to be known as the "Spanish Intrigue" are not altogether clear. By the autumn of 1788 the Franklin government had degenerated into factionalism and chaos. Sevier's term as governor had ended in February, and there was no successor. His own influence within the movement had decreased sharply, as evidenced by a recent pitched battle with an opposing faction that favored reconciliation with North Carolina, a battle in which Sevier's forces were soundly defeated. It is doubtful that he could have persuaded more than a few hundred of his most ardent followers to embrace Spanish annexation. As the leader of a sustained revolt against the authority of North Carolina, Sevier must have been concerned about the possible consequences for himself and those few Franklinites who remained around him. It is certainly possible that Sevier believed the benefits of Spanish annexation might reinvigorate the Franklin movement and reestablish his own leadership, but it is more likely that Sevier's intrigues with the Spanish were little more than an attempt to find a safe haven and a fresh start for himself, his family, and his closest followers.[30]

For a brief period in October it appeared as if Sevier's fear of political retaliation was not unfounded, as he was arrested and imprisoned. His imprisonment was short-lived, however, and it was quickly apparent that, aside from a few old enemies, there was little enthusiasm on either side of the mountains for retaliation against the hero of King's Mountain. In fact, Sevier was able to regain his regional leadership with remarkable speed. By the end of November, when the authority of North Carolina was reestablished in the western counties, Sevier's popularity was such that he was elected with ease to the North Carolina assembly, where he was promptly pardoned and reinstated as brigadier general of the Washington District. One year later he served as a delegate to North Carolina's second ratifying convention for the United States Constitution, where he voted in favor of ratification. Then in December he cast a vote that would prove to have a profound impact on his personal career when he supported the cession of North Carolina's western lands to the federal government.[31]

Before Congress acted on North Carolina's cession, the citizens of the Washington District, now entitled to a seat in Congress, elected John Sevier as their representative. He arrived in New York in June 1790 and took his seat, but his tenure as a U.S. congressman was brief. Congress had already accepted North Carolina's cession and created the "Territory of the United States South of the River Ohio." The new territory was to be governed under the basic outlines of the Northwest Ordinance. That document did not provide for congressional representation, which meant that as soon as the new government was in place, Sevier's seat in Congress would no longer exist. There was no guarantee that he would have a role in the territorial government, given that animosities still lingered among those who had opposed the Franklin movement. But President George Washington's decision to appoint William Blount as territorial governor was fortunate, for Blount understood better than most that the popularity of Sevier could become a real asset to his administration. Thus it was that Blount recommended Sevier as one of two brigadier generals of militia for the territory, and Washington approved the recommendation in February 1791.

Sevier served capably as brigadier general of militia, as might be expected given his background, yet much of his time was taken up by the thankless task of preventing the citizens of the territory from crossing the Cherokee border in search of land or, sometimes, in armed groups, of unauthorized raiders. He seems to have been restless with such duties and was eager for the transition to statehood. Sevier's popularity remained strong; he was confident that he could win any elective office to which he aspired in the new state government, and his aspiration was the office of governor. The first step toward statehood, however, was for William Blount, as territorial governor, to issue a call to hold elections for a territorial assembly, but this was something that Blount had shown little inclination to do. Instead, he had consistently and successfully diverted all calls for elections when they arose.[32]

By the early spring of 1793, however, those calls included the influential voice of John Sevier, who now began to question Blount's motives for refusing to move forward with elections. The two men had worked well together to this point, and Blount did not wish to risk losing the support of the popular general at such a critical juncture. In a personal letter to Sevier, Blount claimed that he had never been strictly opposed to an assembly. "On the contrary," he wrote, "if the people wished an Assembly I wished them to have it, and still wish it," and he reassured Sevier that "the question should be considered as yet open for their determination."[33] Two days later, still concerned that he had not adequately addressed Sevier's complaints, Blount wrote a second letter. "The present Bussle is very disagreeable to me," he said, and he offered to visit Sevier at his home on the Nolichucky River, where they could "talk all Things over."[34] At that meeting, Blount apparently convinced Sevier to postpone his demands for elections, at least for a while, as indicated in a subsequent letter to territorial secretary Daniel Smith. Blount wrote that he had "a very long Talk with the General, he ... may be depended on as a Friend to Government and its officers."[35]

By mid-October Blount was at last ready to authorize elections for the lower house of the territorial assembly.[36] Not surprisingly, Sevier was elected to the new assembly and subsequently nominated to serve on the Legislative Council, the upper body of the assembly. Sevier was an active member of the assembly, but his real objective was still statehood. Blount by this time had come to recognize the inevitability of statehood and had in fact become one of its strongest champions. Statehood would allow him to secure an appointment to the U.S. Senate and at the same time clear the way for the restless Sevier to be elected governor. In the early winter months of 1796, Blount spearheaded a movement that completed a new state constitution and held elections for the legislature and other state offices. On 29 March 1796, Sevier noted in his journal that he had been "duly elected Governor of the State of Tennessee."[37] Partisan differences in Congress temporarily delayed admission, but within two months a bill to admit the new state of Tennessee was before George Washington, and he signed it into law on the first day of June.

As governor, Sevier encouraged settlement and growth within the new state through internal improvements and maintaining peace with the Cherokee. He also spent a great deal of energy attempting to secure titles for families who, during the confusion associated with the Franklin movement, occupied land beyond the Cherokee border. Clarifying the process by which North Carolina awarded land warrants in its military reserve south of the Cumberland River proved challenging, and the appointment of officers in the state militia created some bitterness and hard feelings. Indeed, Sevier eventually found himself faced with serious political opposition as the growing population of the Cumberland settlements shifted political power away from Sevier's base of support in East Tennessee. Still, his popularity was such that he was able to survive a bitter campaign for reelection in 1803 that included embarrassing allegations of fraud and bribery. Sevier was reelected twice, and he continued to serve as governor until 1809. By that time it was obvious that Sevier could not contend with the powerful political energy centered in Nashville, and his dominant role in state politics came to a close.

At the same time, Sevier's popularity in his local community never diminished; he easily won a seat in Congress in 1811 and served there until his death in 1815. His influence on the floor and in committees was apparently not significant, but Sevier was a frequent visitor to the Executive Mansion and a pallbearer for two vice presidents. His support for war in 1812 was as strong then as it had been in 1776 when he and his fellow Wataugans declared their support for the "glorious cause of liberty." Sevier's concept of liberty was little changed during that period; it was one that guaranteed access to opportunity and protected personal property, but it was one that applied only to propertied white males. Sevier's concept of liberty therefore had little application among the Cherokee, for he, like most of his contemporaries, viewed them and all Native Americans as poor and unworthy stewards of the lands they held.

Sevier's concept of liberty was likewise unable to encompass the institution of slavery. Sevier left very few explicit references to slavery, but it is not likely that he ever contemplated the irony of his own fight in defense of the "glorious cause of liberty" and the conditions endured by his own slaves, whose lives were little affected by the Revolution. Perhaps his personal journal best reveals his views of slavery. Sevier began making entries in that journal in 1790 and continued to do so—with occasional lapses—until his death in 1815. Among the many subjects he recorded during that period was his management of the slaves who worked on his two farms. Those entries give no indication that Sevier ever questioned the morality of slavery; indeed, his casual comments regarding his slaves suggests that he viewed them as another component of the land that he had fought to protect.

Sevier's journal covers his last years at Plum Grove, his home on the Nolichucky River, and the years when he lived in Knox County as governor of Tennessee. In addition to a rented residence in Knoxville, Sevier owned Marble Springs, a 330-acre farm in south Knox County. The number of entries relating to slaves or slavery reveals that he relied heavily on slave labor at both Plum Grove and Marble Springs. At least ten slaves are indicated as working at one of the two locations, and one of those individuals sometimes moved between the two farms. In addition, Sevier lists seven slaves who seem to have been hired out. Another two individuals appear whose status is not definitive, but the context suggests that they too were slaves. Taken together, the total number of slaves owned by Sevier during this twenty-five-year period was perhaps as high as nineteen, although the number he owned at any one time was probably somewhat lower.

Among the slaves who emerge from the journal is Frank, who is mentioned five times. Frank ran away twice, although he returned voluntarily after the first escape and Sevier rewarded him with a pair of overalls. Another reference to Frank says he "blooded" a neighbor, which would indicate that Frank was not without some important skills. The last entry regarding Frank relates to the second escape, after which there is no indication that he returned.[38]

The slave who appears most often in the journal is Toby, who played an active role in managing Sevier's Plum Grove plantation and later at Marble Springs. Toby was by all accounts Sevier's personal slave and went with him on at least one official function as governor.[39] In addition, Toby made several unaccompanied trips away from both farms on errands (including the payment of debts) and on one occasion was sent off alone to find a strayed horse, which he returned with three days later.[40] Toby also owned some valuable personal property, as evidenced when Sevier dutifully noted in his journal, "Tobys sow piged last night and three [are] mine."[41]

Despite such extensive responsibilities, Toby was unquestionably and understandably dissatisfied with his status. He also ran away on at least one occasion, albeit under unique circumstances that were eventually resolved in the Pennsylvania Supreme Court. Sometime in the latter part of 1794, Sevier allowed his son John Sevier Jr. to take Toby to Philadelphia, where the younger Sevier was to wed Miss Rebecca Richards, who lived just across the river from Philadelphia in New Jersey. Four months later, when John Sevier Jr. was preparing to return home, it was discovered that Toby had run away. He was eventually found, at which point he claimed that he had received freedom papers, probably from the Philadelphia Abolition Society, and was therefore not bound to return to Tennessee. After conferring with Samuel Richards, his new brother-in-law, John Sevier Jr. devised a plan whereby Toby was to be apprehended and taken by force to New Jersey, a slave state, and from there to Tennessee. The plan was executed successfully, although Toby apparently resisted and his capture required "some severity." The Pennsylvania Abolition Society promptly filed suit against Samuel Richards, charging him with kidnapping with the intent to enslave. The ensuing trial proved conclusively that Toby was in fact not emancipated, and Richards was acquitted.[42] Toby returned to Tennessee, where he resumed his place on Sevier's farms with no apparent changes in his responsibilities.

Perhaps it should not be surprising that John Sevier found little connection between Toby's personal liberty and the liberty for which he himself had fought during the Revolution. In fact, despite the ideological rhetoric that surrounded the Revolution, it would be another half century before most Americans were able to make such a connection. Yet Sevier's concept of liberty was real—it was connected to the opportunity to acquire and use property, including slaves but most particularly land. It was a limited concept, to be sure, but it allowed him and others who embraced it to achieve economic prosperity and standing within the community. More important, it was what gave them the right to participate in the political process, a process that, like the common country that fostered and protected it, was destined to grow.

NOTES

1. Memorial from John Sevier and Isaac Shelby to the North Carolina legislature, December (?) 1812, John Sevier Papers, 1745–1815, David M. Rubenstein Rare Book and Manuscript Library, Duke University, Durham, N.C.

2. John Murray, Earl of Dunmore, to William Legge, Earl of Dartmouth, 16 May 1774, cited in Samuel Cole Williams, *Dawn of Tennessee Valley and Tennessee History* (Johnson City, Tenn.: Watauga Press, 1937), 371.

3. See John R. Finger, *Tennessee Frontiers: Three Regions in Transition* (Bloomington: Indiana University Press, 2001), 46–47.

4. Cora Bales Sevier and Nancy S. Madden, *Sevier Family History with the Letters of Gen. John Sevier* (privately published, 1961), 31.

5. "Petition from Inhabitants of the Washington District concerning the annexation of the district to North Carolina," in William L. Saunders, ed., *Colonial Records of North Carolina, 1622–1776* (Raleigh: P. M. Hale, 1886–90), 10:708–11. Accessed on Documenting the American South: Colonial and State Records of North Carolina, http://docsouth.unc.edu/csr/ (hereafter *CRNC*).

6. Samuel C. Williams, *Tennessee during the Revolutionary War* (1944; repr., Knoxville: University of Tennessee Press, 1974), 24, 32–33.

7. Cited in Samuel C. Williams, *History of the Lost State of Franklin* (Johnson City, Tenn.: Watauga Press, 1924), 157.

8. Cited in Williams, *Tennessee during the Revolutionary War*, 18.

9. Ibid., 32–33, 35–47.

10. "Minutes of the North Carolina Council of Safety, July 21, 1776–August 28, 1776," *CRNC*, 10:702–3; "Petition from the inhabitants of Washington District," *CRNC*, 10:708–11; Williams, *Lost State of Franklin*, 157.

11. "Minutes of the Provincial Congress of North Carolina, November 12, 1776–December 23, 1776," *CRNC*, 10:926, 951, 998. It is not clear if the fifth delegate, Jacob Womack, actually attended. Ramsey maintains that he did not. See J. G. M. Ramsey, *The Annals of Tennessee to the End of the Eighteenth Century* (1853; repr., Johnson City, Tenn.: Overmountain Press, 1999), 139.

12. "Minutes of the North Carolina House of Commons, November 15, 1777–December 24, 1777," in Walter Clark, ed., *State Records of North Carolina, 1776–1790* (Raleigh: P.M.,

1895–1903), 12:303–4, 334–35, 348, 407–8, 417–18. Accessed on Documenting the American South: Colonial and State Records of North Carolina, http://docsouth.unc.edu/csr/ (hereafter *SRNC*).

13. See "The Records of Washington County," *American Historical Magazine* 5 (October 1900): 326–81.

14. For example, see ibid., 351, 352, 355, 356, 357, 365, 366, 367–68, 369, 373.

15. John Sevier to James Glasgow, 1 June 1795, in Sevier and Madden, *Sevier Family History*, 119.

16. Microfilm edition, University of Tennessee Library, Knoxville, Tennessee; original in Draper Manuscript Collection (Madison: State Historical Society of Wisconsin, 1973), 11DD, 362–63.

17. "Journal of Honorable John Sevier from June 1790–September 1815," 30 August 1802, Claiborne (J. F. H.) Collection: Book D, Sevier Letters, Mississippi Department of Archives and History, Jackson (hereafter cited as Sevier Journal).

18. Cited in Lyman C. Draper, *King's Mountain and Its Heroes: History of the Battle of King's Mountain* (1881; repr., Baltimore: Genealogical Publishing Company, 1967), 169.

19. Draper's *King's Mountain and Its Heroes* is the most complete account of the battle. See also Ramsey, *Annals of Tennessee*, 222–49; and Finger, *Tennessee Frontiers*, 85–89.

20. Carl Driver, *John Sevier: Pioneer of the Old Southwest* (Chapel Hill: University of North Carolina Press, 1932), 57; Williams, *Tennessee during the Revolutionary War*, 159–60; Draper, *King's Mountain*, 330–60.

21. See, for example, Sarah J. Purcell, *Sealed with Blood: War, Sacrifice, and Memory in Revolutionary America* (Philadelphia: University of Pennsylvania Press, 2002), 79–81; and Michael Lynch, "Creating Regional Heroes: Traditional Interpretations of the Battle of King's Mountain," *Tennessee Historical Quarterly* 68, no. 3 (2009): 224–49. A general overview of the Tennessee backcountry before and during the Revolution is in Finger, *Tennessee Frontiers*, 23–98. An earlier source is Williams, *Tennessee during the Revolutionary War*.

22. See "Battle of King's Mountain" by Benjamin Sharp, from *The American Pioneer* (February 1843), reprinted in Draper, *King's Mountain*, 554–58; Col. John B. Campbell's letter, 30 July 1812, in ibid., 573–74; and Col. John Sawyer's letter, 16 February 1823, in ibid., 576–77.

23. James Sevier to Lyman Draper, 19 August 1839, reprinted in "A Memoir of John Sevier," *American Historical Magazine* 6 (January 1901): 40–46. James Sevier's Revolutionary Pension Declaration, cited in Sevier and Madden, *Sevier Family History*, 234–37.

24. Ramsey, *Annals of Tennessee*, 134; Francis Marion Turner, *Life of General John Sevier* (New York: Neale, 1910), 13.

25. Thomas P. Abernethy, *From Frontier to Plantation in Tennessee: A Study in Frontier Democracy* (Chapel Hill: University of North Carolina Press, 1932), 39.

26. Driver, *John Sevier*, 41.

27. John Sevier to Joseph Martin, 27 March 1788, in William P. Palmer, ed., *Calendar of Virginia State Papers and other Manuscripts* (Richmond, 1884), 4:416–17. Sevier's attempts to prevent elections are given in "Minutes of the North Carolina House of Commons," 30 November 1789, *SRNC*, 21:285–86. The best source of information on the Franklin movement is Keven Barksdale, *The Lost State of Franklin: America's First Secession* (Lexington: University Press of Kentucky, 2010). See also Williams, *Lost State of Franklin*.

28. "Hugh Williamson to the Indian Commissioners," 6 [?] September 1788, in Paul H. Smith et al., eds., *Letters of Delegates to Congress, 1774–1789*, 25 vols. (Washington, D.C.: Library of Congress, 1976–2000), 25:347–49, Library of Congress, accessed at http://memory.loc.gov/ammem/amlaw/lawhome.html. The first official census taken in 1791 shows a population of 3,619. See Clarence Carter, ed., *Territorial Papers of the United States* (Washington: Government Printing Office, 1936), 4:81.

29. John Sevier to Don Diego de Gardoqui, 12 September 1788, in Sevier and Madden, *Sevier Family History*, 95–96.

30. Sevier's negotiations with the Spanish are discussed in Finger, *Tennessee Frontiers*, 123–24; and Barksdale, *Lost State of Franklin*, 145–61. It is worth noting that Sevier was attempting to negotiate at the same time with several leaders of the Chickasaw Nation to rent or lease lands to a "great many good people." See John Sevier to William Glover, 15 December 1788, in Sevier and Madden, *Sevier Family History*, 103–4.

31. "Minutes of the North Carolina Senate, 5 November 1789–22 December 1789," *SRNC*, 21:584–85, 725–26; "Minutes of the North Carolina House of Commons, 2 November 1789–22 December 1789," ibid., 21:285–86, 426; "Minutes of the North Carolina Constitutional Convention at Fayetteville, 16 November 1789–22 November 1789," ibid., 22:36–51; "Acts of the North Carolina General Assembly, 7 November 1789–22 December 1789," ibid., 25:1–63. See also Driver, *John Sevier*, 99–110.

32. *Knoxville Gazette*, 14 July 1792. See also ibid., 17 December 1791 and 10 March 1792.

33. William Blount to John Sevier, 31 May 1793, in Carter, *Territorial Papers*, 4:264–66.

34. William Blount to John Sevier, 2 June 1793, in ibid., 4:267–68.

35. William Blount to Daniel Smith, 16 June 1793, in ibid., 4:272–73.

36. An Ordinance by Governor Blount, 19 October 1793, in ibid., 4:309.

37. Sevier Journal, 29 March 1796.

38. Ibid., 9 January 1794; 14 December 1794; 15 March 1795; 11 May 1795; 22 June 1795.

39. Ibid., 11 July 1798.

40. Ibid., 1 December 1794; 17 October 1796; 28 March 1797; 26 January 1799; 19 April 1800; 22 April 1800.

41. Ibid., 7 January 1794.

42. Respublica v. Richards, Supreme Court of Pennsylvania 2 U.S. (2 Dall.) 224; April Term, 1795. Accessed at https://supreme.justia.com/cases/federal/us/2/224/case.html.

III

The Federalists

5

Hugh Williamson

North Carolina Federalist

Jennifer Davis-Doyle

When one examines the lives of the framers of the U.S. Constitution, receiving less attention is one of North Carolina's delegates to the Constitutional Convention, Hugh Williamson. This oversight persists even though Williamson's varied accomplishments in science, philosophy, education, and politics rivaled those of Benjamin Franklin's, while his nationalist perspective on a future United States matched that of other prominent Federalists of his time. Georgia delegate William Pierce applauded him as "a gentleman of education and talents," and contemporary historians have called him "North Carolina's Benjamin Franklin."[1] Williamson not only was among the most influential of North Carolina's delegates at the Constitutional Convention's proceedings but also was among the most vocal of them, giving over seventy speeches and serving on five different committees.[2] Williamson was invaluable to his fellow colleagues as they sought to set a new course for the national government.

During heated debates at the 1787 convention in Philadelphia, Williamson was one of the first to suggest and unequivocally support the formation of a strong federal government to act as the supreme law of the land. This suggestion was a bold one given the political divisions among founders who had so recently fought a war against what they deemed oppressive centralized government. Yet when one studies Hugh Williamson's life, his support for a strong central government is unsurprising. Both admirers and critics accused Williamson of being an "aggressive nationalist" because of his insistence on the supreme sovereignty of the national government.[3] Other contemporaries noted the importance of his contributions at a critical period in early America. Thomas Jefferson observed that "he was a useful member, of an acute mind, attentive to business, and of an high degree of erudition" during his time as a member of the Continental Congress.[4] Benjamin Franklin once called Williamson a "detestable skunk" during a political disagreement, but he shared a close friendship with him.[5] Evidence illustrates that Williamson enjoyed the respect of his fellow founders and was an important part of the early American republic's founding. Historian Winthrop Jordan wrote that Williamson "brought to his work the assumptions of a Protestant Christian, a Pennsylvanian who lived in the South, a Jeffersonian intellectual, a gentlemanly go getter, and an American nationalist. It would be difficult to find a more representative man."[6]

It is fitting to reexamine the life of Hugh Williamson and his role as a founder of the United States. At a memorial to Williamson a few months after his death, a friend, David Hosack, suggested that among Williamson's endeavors in education, philosophy, medicine, and politics, his contributions to the nation's formation would be most remembered and appreciated. He predicted that Williamson's "name will be associated with those to whom we are most indebted for our country's independence, and the successful administration of that happy constitution of government which we now enjoy."[7]

Hugh Williamson was born in Chester County, Pennsylvania, on 5 December 1735. He was part of the first graduating class of the University of Philadelphia (now the University of Pennsylvania). There, he earned a bachelor's degree in mathematics, taught secondary courses in English and Latin, and studied astronomy and theology. Williamson continued to pursue varied interests in math, science, philosophy, medicine, and the ministry before ultimately earning a medical degree from Utrecht University in the Netherlands. Williamson later relied on his medical background as surgeon general of North Carolina in 1779.[8]

In addition to continued interests in medicine, Williamson, an eighteenth-century Renaissance man, was a member of the American Philosophical Society of Philadelphia, where he wrote essays and delivered speeches on such varied topics as "the transit of Venus over the Sun" and "some observations upon the change of climate that had been remarked to take place more particularly in the middle colonies of North America."[9] He also founded the Literary and Philosophical Society of New York and was active in the New York Historical Society.

Williamson advocated for the importance of education throughout his life. During his time in North Carolina (1777–93), he was instrumental in either founding or advising Dobbs Academy in Kinston, Pitt Academy in Greenville,

New Bern Academy, and Smith Academy in Edenton. Williamson's interest in forming schools in North Carolina is ironic, given that in 1793 he wrote a letter to George Washington complaining, "The State of the Climate [in North Carolina] proves unfavourable to the means of Learning."[10] Later that same year, Williamson chose to move to New York. He eventually served as a faculty member at what became Princeton University, the University of Delaware, and the University of Pennsylvania. He also served on the board of trustees for the University of North Carolina as both member and secretary from 1795 to 1798. Williamson considered education important for the betterment of individuals as well as necessary to liberty. Authoring a history textbook in 1812, Williamson explained, "Civil liberty has always been supported by learning . . . there never has been a nation who preserved the semblance of freedom without being enlightened by the rays of science."[11]

Perhaps the connection Williamson made between liberty and education explains how his diverse interests led him to a life in politics even though he initially lacked such aspirations. As a medical student and a fund-raiser for the University of Delaware, Williamson's travels took him throughout the American colonies as well as Europe. Perhaps his traveling also influenced him. Military historians Robert Wright Jr. and Morris MacGregor Jr. argue that these journeys not only served to make Williamson more well rounded but also encouraged his nationalist political views.[12] However much his travels affected his views, records show that Williamson moved extensively between the colonies and England just as conflict between them erupted into revolution and war.

Almost immediately after the signing of the American Declaration of Independence, Williamson returned to the colonies from England and made his home in Edenton, North Carolina, after finding it difficult to travel any farther north due to the British naval blockade. While living in Edenton, Williamson, in 1789, married Maria Apthorp, with whom he had two sons. Maria died soon after the birth of their second son. From North Carolina, Williamson served as surgeon general of the state and as a member of the North Carolina House of Commons. He also represented the state at the Continental Congress, the Annapolis convention (although he arrived late due to sickness after proceedings there had ended), the Constitutional Convention, and the U.S. Congress, all before retiring to New York in 1793. He remained in New York, still active in politics, philosophy, and education, until his death during a carriage ride at the age of eighty-three. He is buried in Trinity Churchyard, New York City, near political ally and fellow Federalist Alexander Hamilton. At Williamson's memorial, his friend David Hosack concluded, "Whatever may be the merits of Dr. Williamson, as a scholar, a physician, a statesman, or philosopher... he may be distinguished for his integrity, his benevolence, and those virtues which enter into the moral character of man."[13] To better understand Williamson's contributions to U.S. history as a statesman, one must look more closely at his activities during the Revolutionary era, particularly at the Constitutional Convention.

Williamson could be considered a political moderate in the years leading up to the American Revolution. He valued his connections with England; in fact, he was able to persuade the king of England to make a financial donation to the University of Delaware at a time when relations between the Crown and the colonies had all but collapsed. Even after the fighting at Lexington and Concord in 1775, Williamson, like some of his colleagues, was hesitant to advocate declaring independence. He believed that if England peacefully returned to its pre–French and Indian War policies, both the colonies and England would prosper. On the other hand, Williamson did not believe that colonists should endure oppressive leadership from the English, and he supported attempts by the colonists to drive this point home to the mother country using any means necessary, from petitions and boycotts to outright defiance.

An inveterate traveler, Williamson observed and supported colonial defiance firsthand in Boston, Massachusetts. During one visit, Williamson attended meetings of the Boston Sons of Liberty and witnessed the Boston Tea Party in 1773. Samuel Adams, a leader of the Sons of Liberty, noted that Williamson was present at their meetings and was involved in planning the rebellion.[14] Afterward, Williamson journeyed to England on his fund-raising campaign and there delivered the news of the Boston Tea Party to the king's officials. Williamson used this opportunity to plead for British leniency toward colonists he viewed as merely reacting to unfair treatment and to warn officials of potential civil war in the colonies. Parliament's leaders instead closed Boston's port until the city paid for the destroyed tea and then passed additional punitive legislation, which colonists referred to as the "Intolerable Acts."[15] In a 1775 essay addressed to Lord Mansfield, the king's chief justice, titled *Plea of the Colonies on the Charges Brought against Them by Lord Mansfield, and Others: In a Letter to His Lordship*, Williamson accused British officials of "erroneously" condemning colonists in Boston after the Tea Party.[16] He suggested that if English officials had investigated rebellious colonists' motivations rather than treated them as an "enemy," they might have seen that colonists were taking part in civil disobedience in response to legitimate grievances.[17] Williamson explained to Lord Mansfield in the essay that until the 1770s, colonists had "enjoyed as much liberty as was consistent with civil government" and were conscious of its "blessings."[18] It was only in light of these liberties being threatened that colonists rebelled, Williamson implied.

The messages in Williamson's *Plea of the Colonies* were widely disseminated, having been published in both London and Philadelphia. He wrote this essay in the years between the Boston Tea Party and his appointment as North Carolina's surgeon general during the Revolutionary War. During this time, Williamson transitioned from advocating for peace between the colonies and Britain to endorsing full American independence. Writing the preface to a reprinting of the essay in 1776, Williamson noted, in retrospect, that part of his objective in composing the piece had been "to prepare the public for an event that he thought could not be far distant—a declaration of independence."[19]

Initially, Williamson had hoped his essay would dispel an incorrect belief on the part of the British that the colonists were uninterested in peace with Great Britain and instead only desired independence. Williamson had hoped to appeal to Lord Mansfield—who had been quoted in the English press expressing the need to subdue the American colonists, violently if necessary—for more patience toward the colonies. By 1776, Williamson instead sought to convince British Whigs and other "friends to civil liberty" as to the justness of the colonists' cause, contrasted to the oppressive governing practices of the Crown.[20] He characterized American colonists as having been "patient" with the malpractices of British governing.[21] Yet, Williamson reminded readers, colonists could accept only so many threats to their liberties, particularly since "life and property were their sole concern."[22] Since British leaders had so mismanaged the colonies, Williamson contended, any hopes for an agreement concerning individual rights were abandoned by colonists left "to their own valour and to God they now trust for the preservation of their liberty."[23]

Since he believed that a defense of liberty included the protection of property, Williamson cited taxing policies and unfair treatment as a major cause of the Revolution. It was important to Williamson that Lord Mansfield realize the role poor leadership played in making independence more attractive to colonists than it otherwise might have been. He wrote, "Independence was foreign from their hearts but you will drive them" to such a goal with direction and reasoning that looked more "like children at play" than the guidance of "Christians."[24] He criticized the leadership of Mansfield and other British officials, writing, "I firmly believe that they [colonies] are already so far alienated, and their marginalization so perfectly roused by the late measures of government that you are in a fair way to lose them forever."[25] He concluded that "if human cares are the care of Providence, of which there can be no doubt, the

Americans in a cause of righteousness cannot possibly be subdued by men so unjust, perfidious, and cruel as their present enemies."[26]

Despite his early hesitancy, Williamson's *Plea of the Colonies* made clear his support of the independence movement as a last resort in defending liberty. He warned British officials of colonists' discovery that they "may the better be able to defend their liberties and lives" than anyone else, and he dedicated himself to the cause of independence.[27] When the Continental Congress declared independence in July 1776, Williamson was in England, still traveling in his capacity as fundraiser for the University of Delaware as well as a courier for Benjamin Franklin. However, Williamson made plans to return to Philadelphia once he heard about passage of the Declaration of Independence. Unfortunately for Williamson, he then found himself at odds with both the Americans and the British. He could not reach Philadelphia due to his inability to get past the British naval blockade without risking capture, and he was denied a position in the Continental army because he had been accused of being a traitor to the American cause.

This accusation of Williamson's betrayal came from Connecticut native and member of the Continental Congress Silas Deane, who had been sent to France in 1776. His primary purpose was to convince French officials of both the need and the advantage of an American-French alliance against Great Britain. During his time in Paris, Deane also acted as an American spy, noting the comings and goings of other diplomats, spies, and agents in Paris and London. He questioned how often Hugh Williamson traveled to London and spoke with influential leaders there. Williamson was trying to use his connections to help bring peace between the colonies and England, but Deane was suspicious. Ultimately, Deane took his concerns to General Washington and the Continental Congress, placing enough doubt on Williamson to prevent his attaining a national position in the Revolutionary effort. In a 1777 letter to a friend, future U.S. president John Adams acknowledged this suspicion: "The noted Dr. Williamson is arrived full of encouraging matter, but what confidence is to be put in him, or what dependence to be had on his intelligence I know not."[28]

Silas Deane was not the only official to initially question Williamson's true allegiances. In a confidential letter dated 9 October 1776 from British spy Lord Stormont, stationed in Paris, to Lord Weymouth in London, Stormont noted that Deane, on whom he had been spying, "was much displeased with Dr. Hugh Williamson, and among other Things reproached Him for the Visit he made me. I mention this the rather as thinking it possible that Williamson who I imagine is returned to London and who appeared to Me to be well enough calculated for being a double Spy might be of some use now that he finds himself Obnoxious to His Countrymen."[29]

In actuality, Williamson did not return to London and instead remained focused on returning to the colonies to join the fight for independence. As war continued, there appears to have been no more questioning of Williamson's loyalties. Given that he later shared leadership responsibilities and a friendship with George Washington, the commander who had been warned of his duplicity, Williamson must have been absolved of any doubts of his allegiance. Silas Deane was later accused, ironically, of treason, became embroiled in political disputes regarding his actions in Paris during the 1770s, spoke out against the new nation of the United States, and ultimately lived the rest of his days in Great Britain and the Dutch Republic. Writing a letter to a friend two years after Deane's accusations against him, Williamson expressed continued dismay that his own loyalties were ever questioned, claiming, "There was not in America a man who served it more faithfully or disinterestedly."[30] He was not alone in holding this opinion. Having apparently determined Williamson's true loyalties after his death, John Adams noted the character, intelligence, and "ardour" with which he pursued "the American cause."[31]

Although Deane's accusations kept Williamson from serving in the Continental army, Williamson found a way to aid in the Revolution. Once settled in Edenton, North Carolina, as a result of the British blockade, Williamson acted as surgeon general for North Carolina from 1779 to 1781. In caring for wounded soldiers, Williamson was among the first surgeons to press for inoculation of soldiers against smallpox "before they took the Field" as a way of preventing the spread of the disease, an extreme cause for concern among both the British and the American troops.[32] He even petitioned British general Lord Cornwallis, emphasizing the importance of both inoculation of soldiers against smallpox and quarantining infected soldiers. Cornwallis initially ignored him, and Williamson believed many soldiers died preventable deaths due to unnecessary exposure to "the seeds of the Small Pox."[33] Williamson lamented the death and disease he witnessed during the war, writing in a report to North Carolina's Speaker of the House, "I wish that I could say that our Loss after the Battle either by wounds or sickness was inconsiderable, but we labored under many difficulties."[34]

Conceivably, it was in his work with North Carolina's legislature that Williamson realized his desire to become a state legislator himself. By 1782, Williamson ran successfully for North Carolina's House of Commons, and later that year he was chosen as one of the state's representatives to the Continental Congress. Even as a state legislator, Williamson occasionally became involved in Revolutionary skirmishes. In a 1782 letter to North Carolina Whig and future U.S. Supreme Court judge James Iredell, Williamson noted an incident in which he became caught in the crossfire after a skirmish between Loyalist and patriot militias. He wrote, "Last night we lost some sleep . . . we were called to arms and paraded; for you are to note that we are all Soldiers." Williamson humorously concluded, "You see we are not without employment of different kinds," even while working as state legislators. He also shared his regret that he was unable to see more legislation passed in North Carolina since "the generous, public, comprehensive spirit of legislation is wanting among our other wants."[35]

Despite the pressure of being a legislator for a state at war, Williamson continued to work toward a stronger nation while simultaneously focusing on North Carolina's needs. He illustrated this concern, for example, when he made a speech to Congress in which he noted that North Carolina had been "zealously pressed" to send troops for the "immediate support" of the South. He explained that in light of the "critical and dangerous" nature of the military need, there were North Carolinians who had been quickly drafted before being able to join the national army. Because of this hastiness, Williamson was concerned that soldiers would not receive their "full pay," and he made a motion that the Continental Congress treat all soldiers the same regardless of how they joined the army.[36]

Once the Revolutionary War ended and the United States began operating under the Articles of Confederation, Williamson faced lawmaking decisions related to Indian affairs, expansion of the country into the West, and cession of western lands by existing states, including North Carolina. As he participated in these debates, Williamson became more aware of the need for a stronger national government as a means of promoting the United States' economic prosperity and overseeing westward expansion. In a letter informing North Carolina governor Alexander Martin about the debates in the Continental Congress over the Land Ordinance of 1784, Williamson endorsed Congress's "plan for laying off and settling the Western Territory." He had joined Thomas Jefferson and others in attempting to include a ban on slavery in new western areas, although this proposal did not pass. Yet Williamson supported it in its completed form, writing, "I think the plan proposed will prevent innumerable frauds and enable us to save millions." Williamson acknowledged his close involvement with the congressional plan to Governor Martin, writing, "As I happen to have suggested the plan to the Committee it is more than probable that I may have parental prejudices in its favour."[37]

Although evidence suggests Williamson desired a strong federal government, he also sought to protect the state government. Williamson encouraged North Carolina's leaders to proceed with caution as they decided how best to cede western lands to the national government in 1784. He was concerned that North Carolina was not fully protected in the state's proposed Cession Act. Although he supported the Northwest Ordinance, he was not entirely confident of the weak national government's ability to handle all the lands without certain protections in North Carolina's legislation. "I have not seen the act for making a cession of Western Territory but am told to my surprise that no provision is made for passing the Indian expeditions to the credit of the State in its account with the United States," Williamson wrote. He expressed hope that "when the State reconsiders this Subject and finds that no attention has been paid to the Southern Indians, and little done for securing the Western frontier, I presume they will at least suspend certain conditions in the Cession."[38]

Williamson remained in the Confederation Congress until the new federal Constitution took effect. Ultimately, North Carolina's voters rescinded the cession act of western lands because they distrusted the national legislature. It was not until 1790, under the new federal government, that North Carolina finally and completely ceded lands that became the state of Tennessee to the national government. Williamson had expressed doubt all along for the weak federal government under the Articles of Confederation. North Carolina's delay in ceding lands vindicated his feelings, and the concern for a stronger national government continued to motivate Williamson.

When Williamson accepted North Carolina governor Richard Caswell's request to attend the Annapolis convention in 1786, he explained that his acceptance was due to his "zealous desire to promote the Mercantile interests of this State," which was the proposed topic of the convention.[39] The fact that only five of thirteen states sent representatives, coupled with delegates' realization that the federal government needed to be significantly strengthened, prompted them to call for another conference. This rescheduling was good news for Williamson; he had arrived too late due to sickness. Still, Williamson's disappointment that nothing concrete resulted from the Annapolis convention was clear. He wrote to Governor Caswell, "I sincerely regret that nothing has been effected at the proposed meeting, and that while the United States are wasting by the most destructive Commerce no progress is made towards safety or system."[40] Due to Williamson's continued interests in American commerce and national politics, Governor Caswell asked Williamson to again serve as a delegate for North Carolina at the Philadelphia convention in 1787, filling a vacancy created by Willie Jones, who had refused the appointment. Williamson wrote to Governor Caswell that he was "extremely flattered" to join William Blount, William Richardson Davie, Alexander Martin, and Richard Dobbs Spaight Sr. in a task requiring "much political knowledge"—a task Williamson felt prepared for after devoting "many an hour to studying the true interest of this State and of the Union at large."[41] Williamson added that he had "a constant and sincere desire to serve the State and am very desirous in every case to fulfill the expectations of my friends."[42]

Once Williamson arrived at the convention, he joined others in realizing that the needs of the United States required a new constitution rather than a simple amending of the Articles of Confederation. Along with his fellow North Carolina representatives, he warned Governor Caswell, "Though we sit from day to day, Saturdays included, it is not possible for us to determine when the business before us can be finished." The reason for this lengthy process, they wrote, was that they were guiding the United States toward a path never before "trodden by the feet of Nations." They concluded that a "union of Sovereign states, preserving their Civil Liberties and connected together by such ties as to preserve permanent and effective governments is a system not described, it is a circumstance that has not occurred in the history of men; if we shall be so fortunate as to find this . . . our Time will have been well spent."[43] Later in the summer, Williamson assured Caswell that as far as he was concerned, "it will be sufficient for us if we have the satisfaction of believing that we have contributed to the happiness of millions."[44] Williamson believed this happiness was tied to the unprecedented creation of a new federal government.

In proceedings at the Constitutional Convention, Williamson pushed for a federal system consisting of a strong national government with protections for the powers of the state governments. He sided with more populous states in conflicts regarding representation between large and small states, stating that "proportional representation" was fair to all states and would serve the nation well.[45] It was important to Williamson that both power and responsibility be shared as fairly as possible among large and small states as well as future states "to the Westward" that might join the union.[46] He supported fellow delegate Oliver Ellsworth's proposal that state governments, rather than the federal government, be responsible for paying their national senators and representatives. Williamson feared that poorer states would become a financial burden to richer ones. Delegates rejected this proposal as well as a suggestion that all representation be proportional. Williamson eventually accepted the Connecticut Compromise, which created a lower house based on proportional representation and an upper house in which each state would have an equal vote.[47] This compromise was not the only one to which he agreed.

Williamson carefully considered regional differences and sought to maintain a balance of power between the North and the South. The need to promote southern influence in the new government led Williamson to speak in favor of the Three-Fifths Compromise, despite his personal opposition to slavery.[48] As a North Carolina representative, Williamson saw the institution as an unavoidable reality, and he supported a compromise that softened the impact on the South of a possible federal tax on slaves. Records that seek to reconstruct the debates using both the Constitutional Convention secretary's notes as well as James Madison's private notes reveal that "Mr. Williamson reminded Mr. Ghorum that if the Southern States contended for the inferiority of blacks to whites when taxation was in view, the Eastern States on the same occasion contended for their equality. He did not however either then or now, concur in either extreme, but approved of the ratio."[49] Later in the debate Williamson, a pragmatist, explained that he supported the compromise because of the reality that "the Southern states could not be members of the Union if the clause should be rejected."[50]

In regard to the power of the national Congress, Williamson supported six-year terms for senators, believing this was sufficient time to accomplish a good deal. Williamson feared that shorter terms might see less productivity. He also believed that the national Congress should have the power to negate state laws, although he stipulated that this power would be necessary only if state laws threatened to "encroach on the national government."[51] When Virginia's Edmund Randolph made a motion to add a clause preventing state governments from amending the Constitution to permit a monarchy, Williamson argued such a clause was unnecessary. Williamson predicted that even without it, the "union will become the law of the land," a goal he clearly supported.[52] He was one of the first delegates to so staunchly support the supreme sovereignty of the United States.

While he promoted national sovereignty, Williamson advocated checks on the federal government's authority. He suggested that all legislation require a two-thirds vote. While he supported a powerful federal government, he "professed himself a friend to such a system as would secure the existence of the state government" as well, since he believed "the happiness of the people depended on it."[53] He stressed a clear division of authority in which state governments had independence in "cases purely local" while the federal government was supreme in national matters.[54] He urged delegates not to give the federal government so much power that states would lose the authority to "regulate their internal police."[55] He preferred a smaller number of senators in the national congress, but he concluded that the "mutual check" of the branches in the federal government would suffice to avoid tyrannical leadership.[56] Williamson continued to strike a balance between protecting state governments and ensuring that the federal government would have enough power to be effective.

To further place a check on the national executive branch, Williamson made a motion that the Constitution authorize impeachment and removal from office upon a "conviction of mal-practice."[57] Revisions such as these gratified Williamson, who had compromised on issues like numbers of senators, length of executive terms, and more in order to produce a finished document. He warned fellow delegates of this need to compromise, acknowledging, "If we do not concede on both sides, our business must soon be at an end."[58]

In a letter to Governor Caswell, Williamson acknowledged that although he had not realized all of his goals at the convention, he was more or less satisfied with what had been accomplished.[59] As a result, he authored a series of letters, published in the national periodical *American Museum*, in which he campaigned for the new federal government by painting a picture of a fractured union in danger of internal revolt or external takeover in the absence of a stable, strong government. In evoking this image, Williamson addressed "freemen inhabitants of the United States," and he noted the problems of "scarcity of money" and the "present mode of taxation" and his opinion that "misfortune is general" in most of the country.[60] He observed that the promotion of American trade and manufacturing would address the economic troubles of the country, but he complained that the absence of strong government hindered this goal.

Williamson believed that a state's choice to ratify the Constitution or not was a choice between chaos and prosperity. "We are going to consider whether the administration of government, in these infant states, is to be a system of patchwork, and a series of expedients—whether a youthful empire is to be supported," Williamson wrote.[61] He tied the fate of the nation to independence itself. He explained, "We are going to consider whether we shall deserve to be a branch of the most poor, dishonest, and contemptible, or of the most flourishing, independent, and happy nation on the face of the earth."[62] Early divisions between those desiring ratification and those suspicious of such a strong central government led to political divisions between Federalists and Anti-Federalists. Williamson assuredly aligned himself with the Federalists, sharing Alexander Hamilton's views of a strong national government to promote economic growth and expansion. As a result, Williamson was at odds with some North Carolinians who had voted for him as a representative, since North Carolina was generally an Anti-Federalist state that leaned toward decentralized national government in favor of state and local government. Many North Carolinians feared the threat of a despotic federal government that could, either through the executive, legislative, or judicial branches, override state laws, courts, or authority. They dreaded the potential tyranny of a standing army, and they were ever concerned about the taxes that might be imposed by the federal government.

Williamson attempted to assuage North Carolinians' fears in a speech he delivered on the courthouse steps in Edenton. Addressing the "freemen of Edenton," he assured citizens that rather than being frightened of the changes made in the Constitution, they should celebrate that it was "well calculated to relieve grievances" currently endured under the Articles of Confederation.[63] Williamson implored his fellow citizens to place their trust in the new Constitution and the republic it sought to form because it was an experiment in self-government, liberty, and independence never before seen in the world. In noting the exceptionalism he believed was present in this new government, Williamson explained, "I should describe it as more free and more perfect than any form of any government that has ever been adopted by any nation."[64] Realizing that North Carolinians were especially concerned about individual rights, Williamson promised that "every right is reserved to the individual" in the Constitution. He specifically noted that there were "no restraints" on a free press in the document. Addressing concerns that a strong national government would ultimately swallow state governments, Williamson reminded his audience that the national government would not regulate domestic life in the states. He estimated, "Nine of ten state laws are domestic and not national" in nature, predicting that on most state legislative issues, leaders would barely notice any interference from the federal government.[65] In answer to those individuals concerned that national leaders would grow tyrannical, Williamson explained, "They do not yield a single power which is not absolutely necessary to the safety and prosperity of the nation."[66] Furthermore, Williamson assured his fellow citizens that, "protected and cherished by the small addition of power which you shall put into their hands, you may become a great and respectable nation."[67] He predicted that this unprecedented greatness, seen particularly in national sovereignty, economic prosperity, and broad personal liberties, would benefit both the nation and North Carolina.

Williamson's speech was published in North and South Carolina as well as in Pennsylvania and New York.[68] He focused on North Carolina, however, suggesting to fellow citizens that their state in particular would benefit economically from the new union, given that the state owed a heavy war debt that the national government would presumably absorb. Williamson expounded on his beliefs that the government created by the Constitution would assist North Carolina's economy; rather than being frightened by the federal Congress's power to regulate trade, North Carolinians should be encouraged to know that a central authority would attempt to ensure the economic health of the entire nation. This economic prosperity, Williamson reasoned, benefited North Carolina more than the absence of national regulation on trade would. In an article he authored anonymously, Williamson advocated for a federal government that encouraged American manufacturing and less dependence on foreign goods. He wrote, "Every empire under the sun is supposed to be independent of any other: that is to say, the subjects . . . are supposed to enjoy a natural as well as a political independence"—an independence Williamson believed was more secure in a strong federal government guiding the economy toward self-sufficiency.[69]

Lest the examples in his speech were not enough to convince North Carolinians that there was no need to fear the government created by the Constitution, Williamson appealed to their anxieties about the nation's safety and sovereignty. He suggested that the United States lived in a "state of dangerous weakness" and that the country was "not in a condition to resist the most contemptible enemy." The new republic, Williamson believed, would not have these weaknesses. He postulated that the "government, unless I am greatly mistaken, gives the fairest promise of being firm and honorable, safe from foreign invasion or domestic sedition."[70] When Williamson wrote to British officials of his concerns for colonists' liberties leading up to the Revolutionary War, he linked the importance of liberty and personal property. In promoting the new Constitution, Williamson remained consistent, telling North Carolina's citizens that the new government was "perfectly fitted for protecting liberty and property and for cherishing the good citizen and the honest man." He predicted that the citizens shared "utmost reason to rejoice in the prospect of better times," and he suggested that those who were opposed to the Constitution were actually "secret enemies, who have never been reconciled to our Independence."[71] Despite Williamson's efforts, North Carolinians, legislators and voters, hesitated to ratify the document. While Williamson remained in New York, still active as a member of the Confederation Congress, leaders at the Hillsborough convention in 1788 voted to neither accept nor reject the Constitution. Until November 1789, North Carolina remained apart from the new federal union, which had gone into effect in June 1788 after nine of thirteen states ratified the Constitution.

During this period of North Carolina's exclusion from the federal union, Williamson remained in New York, meeting with members of Congress and generally acting as ambassador for the state. Williamson was convinced, as he assured leaders of Congress, that North Carolina would ultimately ratify the federal Constitution. He urged national leaders to have patience with the state while Federalists worked to persuade North Carolina voters of the need for ratification. Although Williamson was certain his state would eventually join the union, he worried that North Carolina was missing opportunities to influence the new government in the meantime. He warned Governor Samuel Johnston in July 1788, "Gentlemen in congress are extremely desirous to fix the time and place where and when proceedings shall commence under the new government." Along with colleague John Swann, he noted that "hitherto they have been restrained, partly as we conceive from a regard to the feelings of our State," but Williamson added that "we [North Carolinians] flatter ourselves" to think that the federal government would wait indefinitely on North Carolina's cooperation.[72] While in New York as a representative from a state not officially in the United States, he later assured Governor Johnston, "I do not eat the bread of idleness."[73] Instead, Williamson continued to express his opinions on Indian policy, national banking policies, trade laws, and foreign policy. He advocated for a federal government strong enough to provide security for its citizens while still protecting their liberty, property, and individual rights. Williamson unwaveringly reminded leaders in North Carolina that "many things continue to engross the Attention of Congress which are of considerable national importance." He wrote to the governor, "Whether North Carolina shall be confederated or not, she is equally interested with other states in those measures" being considered by Congress.[74]

Williamson remained dedicated to the new federal government as well as to North Carolina's future involvement in it. He expressed disappointment as time passed without his state joining the union. Writing to Governor Johnston, he opined, "You will observe that the members of the new congress hitherto arrived, are chiefly from the Eastward, and I presume that a house will be formed and several officers chosen before the Southern members arrive. This may be the first of the distorted effects to be expected from the seat of congress being far distant from the center of the union."[75] Williamson implied such a distortion of power between the Northeast and the South might have been avoided had North Carolina joined the federal union. He remained faithful to the cause of convincing North Carolinians to trust that the new government would have their best interests at heart.

By November 1789, Williamson returned to North Carolina and attended the Fayetteville convention; there he joined colleagues in voting to ratify the U.S. Constitution. By March 1790, Williamson resumed his role as legislator, serving as North Carolina's representative in Congress where he remained until he left North Carolina for retirement in New York in 1793. During his eventful and diverse career, Williamson studied and published on subjects ranging from electricity, science, medicine, and theology to politics. He worked as physician, minister, professor, and politician. Throughout these many endeavors, Williamson, ever the Renaissance man, remained steadfast in his beliefs about the United States, liberty, and government. Whether defending the colonies against British officials or promoting the Constitution to North Carolina's citizens, Williamson expressed his belief that people have the right to liberty and property. This belief led Williamson to support individual rights, especially as they were expressed in the Bill of Rights, as well as national economic policy meant to promote fair taxes and trade. In one speech to the Continental Congress, he highlighted the travails of the average North Carolina farmer as he advocated for American manufacturing as well as an excise tax that he believed would be more fair than an extremely high land tax.[76] This example is one of many that illustrates Williamson's consistency in his advocacy for the state he represented as well as his dedication to the nation that he helped to found. Once Williamson was satisfied that the document he and his colleagues authored in Philadelphia that summer of 1787 was the best option the United States had for a more stable, secure government, he did all he could to support it. He believed that the United States was on a course never before charted by other nations, in that Americans wanted a powerful government deriving its authority from the people, whose liberty and individual rights were protected.

As Williamson's health began to fail during his early eighties, he understood that his time influencing and guiding the nation was nearing an end. In a letter to his nephew a few months before his death, Williamson wrote, "I have, I think, nearly finished my course."[77] He was proud of his contributions to the United States. Although some sources mention little about Williamson's influences in early America, he was well known enough for an artist to request his permission to sculpt a bust of him. A good-humored Williamson informed the artist that he did not anticipate that future generations would concern themselves with his appearance. He did, however, desire to leave behind a legacy for them to remember. Williamson wrote, "He hopes, nevertheless, for the sake of his children, that posterity will do him the justice to believe, that his conduct was upright, and that he was uniformly influenced by a regard to the happiness of his fellow citizens, and those who shall come after them."[78]

NOTES

1. See Gordon Lloyd, "The Constitutional Convention: Hugh Williamson," Teaching American History, accessed 10 September 2015, http://teachingamericanhistory.org/static/convention/delegates/williamson.html; Louis W. Potts, "Hugh Williamson: The Poor Man's Franklin and the National Domain," *North Carolina Historical Review* 64, no. 4 (1987): 371; and "Hugh Williamson: North Carolina's Ben Franklin," This Day in North

Carolina History, accessed 11 September 2015, https://nchistorytoday.wordpress.com/2013/03/14/hugh-williamson-north-carolinas-ben-franklin/.

2. "Hugh Williamson," North Carolina History Project, accessed 12 May 2013, http://www.northcarolinahistory.org/commentary/392/entry.

3. George F. Sheldon, *Hugh Williamson: Physician, Patriot, and Founding Father* (Amherst, N.Y.: Humanity Books, 2010), 240.

4. Quoted in ibid., 247.

5. Quoted in ibid., 37.

6. Winthrop Jordan quoted in Potts, "Hugh Williamson," 373.

7. David Hosack, *A Biographical Memoir of Hugh Williamson: Delivered on the First Day of November, 1819, at the Request of the New York Historical Society* (New York: C. S. Van Winkle, 1820), 90, http://archive.org/details/biographicalmem01820hosa.

8. Ibid., 45.

9. Ibid., 20–22, 25.

10. Hugh Williamson to George Washington, 9 December 1793, Washington Papers, Founders Online, http://founders.archives.gov.

11. Hugh Williamson, *The History of North Carolina*, 2 vols. (Philadelphia: Thomas Dobson, 1812), 2:83.

12. Robert K. Wright Jr. and Morris J. MacGregor Jr., *Soldier-Statesmen of the Constitution* (Washington, D.C.: Center of Military History, 1987), http://www.history.army.mil/books/RevWar/ss/wiliamson.htm.

13. Quoted in Sheldon, *Hugh Williamson*, 88.

14. Ibid., 59.

15. Kenneth Penegar, *The Political Trial of Benjamin Franklin* (New York: Angora Publishing, 2011).

16. Hugh Williamson, *The Plea of the Colonies on the Charges Brought against Them by Lord Mansfield, and Others: In a Letter to His Lordship* (Philadelphia: Robert Bell, 1775), 11.

17. Ibid., 13.

18. Ibid.

19. Ibid., ii.

20. Ibid., 6.

21. Ibid., 8.

22. Ibid., 9.

23. Ibid., 7.

24. Ibid., 28.

25. Ibid.

26. Ibid., ii.

27. Ibid., 38.

28. John Adams to James Warren, 18 March 1777, Adams Papers, Founders Online, http://founders.archives.gov.

29. *Naval Documents of the American Revolution, Volume 7* (Bolton Landing, N.Y.: American Naval Records Society, 2012), 684.

30. Quoted in Sheldon, *Hugh Williamson*, 99.

31. John Adams to David Hosack, 28 January 1820, Adams Papers, http://founders.archives.gov/documents/Adams/99-02-02-7301, 1.

32. Hugh Williamson to Thomas Benbury, 1 December 1780, *Colonial and State Records of North Carolina*, Documenting the American South, http://docsouth.unc.edu, 532.

33. Ibid.

34. Ibid., 530.

35. Hugh Williamson to James Iredell, 1 May 1782, ibid., 613.

36. *Journals of the Continental Congress of the United States, 1774–1789*, ed. Worthington C. Ford et al. (Washington, D.C.: Government Printing Office, 1914), 23:710.

37. Hugh Williamson to Alexander Martin, 5 July 1784, *Colonial and State Records of North Carolina*, 81.

38. Ibid.

39. Hugh Williamson to Richard Caswell, 27 October 1786, *Colonial and State Records of North Carolina*, 772.

40. Ibid.

41. Hugh Williamson to Richard Caswell, 19 March 1787, ibid., 643.

42. Ibid.

43. Hugh Williamson, Alexander Martin, Richard Dobbs Spaight, and William Richardson Davie to Richard Caswell, 14 June 1787, ibid., 724.

44. Hugh Williamson to Richard Caswell, 20 August 1787, ibid., 766.

45. Max Farrand, ed., *The Records of the Federal Convention of 1787* (New Haven: Yale University Press, 1911), http://oll.libertyfund.org/title/1057/95917/2145086, 146.

46. Ibid., 287.

47. Forrest McDonald, *Novus Ordo Seclorum: The Intellectual Origins of the Constitution* (Lawrence: University Press of Kansas, 1985), 237.

48. Burton Craige, *The Federal Convention of 1787* (Richmond: Expert Graphics, 1987), 131; "Hugh Williamson," Penn Biographies, Penn University Archives and Records Center, accessed 4 February 2015, http://www.archives.upenn.edu/people/1700s/williamson_hugh.html.

49. Farrand, *Records of the Federal Convention*, 442.

50. "The Constitutional Convention Debates and the Anti-Federalist Papers: Slavery and the Constitution," From Revolution to Reconstruction and Beyond, accessed 4 February 2015, http://www.let.rug.nl/usa/documents/1786–1800/the-anti-federalist-papers/slavery-and-constitution-(august-21–22).php.

51. Farrand, *Records of the Federal Convention*, 138.

52. Ibid., 168.

53. Ibid., 313.

54. Ibid., 140.

55. Ibid., 135.

56. Ibid., 125.

57. Ibid., 74.

58. Ibid., 389.

59. Hugh Williamson to Richard Caswell, 20 August 1787, *Colonial and State Records of North Carolina*, 766.

60. Hugh Williamson, "Letters to Sylvius," in *Historical Papers, Series XI*, ed. William K. Boyd (Durham, N.C.: Trinity College Historical Society, 1915), 5–47 (quotes on 5).

61. Ibid., 6.

62. Ibid.

63. Hugh Williamson, "Remarks on the Proposed System of Federal Government Delivered in an Address to the Freemen of Edenton and the County of Chowan, NC," *American Museum*, 1788, 547.

64. Ibid., 550.
65. Ibid.
66. Ibid., 551.
67. Ibid.
68. "A Speech at Edenton," North Carolina History Project, accessed 12 May 2013, http://www.northcarolinahistory.org/commentary/392/entry.
69. [Hugh Williamson], "Essay on Paper Money," *American Museum*, 1787, 116.
70. Williamson, "Remarks on the Proposed System of Federal Government," 560.
71. Ibid.
72. Hugh Williamson and John Swann to Samuel Johnston, 29 July 1788, *Colonial and State Records of North Carolina*, 486.
73. Hugh Williamson to Samuel Johnston, 1 September 1788, ibid., 495.
74. Ibid.
75. Hugh Williamson to Samuel Johnston, 23 March 1789, ibid., 539.
76. *Journals of the Continental Congress of the United States*, 23:710.
77. Hosack, *Biographical Memoir*, 90.
78. Ibid., 87.

An Ordinary Founder

Richard Dobbs Spaight Sr.

Karl Rodabaugh

Probably no North Carolinian is more deserving of the title "founder" than Richard Dobbs Spaight Sr. of New Bern. Soon after he turned thirty in 1788, Spaight had compiled an estimable record while serving (often alongside many other "founders") in a variety of important roles. He was a militia officer during the Revolution; a well-connected state legislator (including a term as House Speaker); a delegate to the Confederation Congress; a member of the Philadelphia convention of 1787; and a delegate to North Carolina's 1788 Hillsborough convention. Despite his efforts as a leading Federalist at Hillsborough, the huge Anti-Federalist majority refused to ratify the new Constitution.[1]

Most historical works on the founding era have given him scant attention, focusing instead on such well-recognized figures as George Washington, Benjamin Franklin, John Adams, Alexander Hamilton, Thomas Jefferson, John Jay, and James Madison. During the past thirty years, moreover, some fellow founders from North Carolina—including Hugh Williamson and James Iredell—have received considerably more attention than Spaight.[2] And when Spaight has been mentioned in works of a general nature (usually only in passing), he has not been rated all that highly. Winton Solberg's assessment is typical: Spaight "favored a stronger government," but he "lacked aptitude for debate, and although he attended faithfully, his influence in the [Philadelphia] Convention was negligible." Indeed, Spaight, heretofore, has been evaluated at best by most historians as an ordinary founder.[3]

What was so ordinary about Spaight's contribution to the founding? He was a member of the Philadelphia convention of 1787, where he attended every session and contributed several consequential measures. During the deliberations, he favored a constitutional system that would not be overly democratic, with an upper house chosen by the state legislatures and an electoral college for selecting a president. He joined other North Carolina Federalists in advocating and campaigning for their state's eventual ratification of the Constitution.

Could Spaight's thinking on the idea of American exceptionalism be described as commonplace? Apparently, whether or not one subscribes to Michal Rozbicki's views on what he describes as "the now outdated theories of American exceptionalism,"[4] no surviving evidence clarifies Spaight's precise thoughts on the matter. Yet Spaight's overall record suggests almost certainly that he would have agreed with Rozbicki's contention that four factors made America uniquely susceptible to the expansion of political liberty: a denominational system that made religious freedom almost inevitable, a long-standing respect for the rule of law and for constitutional principles, the important role of deeply rooted local governmental structures, and a widespread veneration of the British concept of liberty.[5]

Was Spaight's definition of a just and free political society unusual for the time in which he lived? Apparently, Spaight shared a vision of a political order with other elite North Carolina slaveholders. To him, "liberty" and "freedom" were preserved for those whose station in life (secured primarily through education and social status based on wealth in land and slaves) permitted them to serve virtuously in various high offices. These disinterested elites were selected by deferential white freeholders.

Was Spaight's functional outlook on liberty and freedom out of the ordinary? Spaight's thinking apparently was typical of elite slaveholders whose self-proclaimed public virtue entitled them to enjoy the pinnacle of liberty and freedom despite the fact that their status rested on slave labor. Liberty and freedom were applicable not only to Spaight's equals but also to the common freeholders, who were deserving of inclusion though only to a lesser degree. Spaight's political principles seemingly were rather straightforward: political and legal systems should be based upon a written constitution; political institutions should be dominated by men who exhibit a disinterested public virtue; and the central government—and also in similar fashion the state and local governments—should provide military protection against external and internal threats, promote economic growth and commerce, guarantee such basic rights as religious freedom and trial by jury, and enforce the laws through a well-ordered judiciary, though he opposed vehemently the still-controversial notion of judicial review.

After close examination, Richard Dobbs Spaight certainly does not stand out among the founders as a unique or remarkable figure, except that both he and Alexander Hamilton were mortally wounded in duels with political rivals. Yet even as an ordinary founder, Spaight played a consequential role during the founding era. As a member of the Philadelphia convention, for example, Spaight offered one often-overlooked procedural recommendation that had profound implications. After the convention had rejected the formal recording of votes, thus making it easier for the delegates to reach a consensus, Spaight "went even further, suggesting that any member of the Convention be allowed to request reconsideration of any motion previously discussed and voted upon." Apparently, despite Spaight's comparative youth (he was the second-youngest delegate to sign the Constitution), he had gained enough meaningful legislative experience to understand the "far-reaching consequences" of his proposal. Indeed, Spaight's simple measure allowed the convention "to function not like a legislative body, with strict rules for the recording of votes and the bringing of business to the floor, but rather as an informal 'committee of the whole.'" This practice provided the delegates with the chance "to take 'straw votes'—to measure the relative strength of opposing opinions on particularly contentious issues and, when appropriate, to change their minds as they groped their way toward compromise and consensus."[6] Furthermore, as the results later revealed, Spaight's proposal actually would "reduce the risk of a fatal rupture in the harmony of the Convention early in the game, for it would allow those delegates who had grave misgivings about the plans presented by [Edmund] Randolph and [Charles] Pinckney to feel some assurance that they would have ample opportunity to voice their objections and to offer alternative proposals."[7] Through such unspectacular yet still noteworthy contributions, Spaight and many other lesser figures played "ordinary" roles in shaping the constitutional foundation that ultimately became the basis for a more inclusive American society.

Richard Dobbs Spaight was born in New Bern on 25 March 1758, the son of Elizabeth Wilson Spaight and Richard Spaight. He was noted to be "a very sprightly and gay young man."[8] At the time of young Richard's birth, his father was a member of the Royal Council and also the secretary and treasurer of the colony. In 1754, Richard Spaight had come from Ireland to North Carolina in company with Arthur Dobbs, his great-uncle, who recently had been appointed as the royal governor of the colony. In remarkably quick succession, Dobbs had placed the elder Spaight in several rather lucrative but previously vacant government positions.[9] Richard Spaight soon had amassed considerable wealth in land and slaves, some as part of his wife's dowry, including extensive landholdings in Craven County.[10] Indeed, such marriages among North Carolina's leading families played a major role in securing and expanding both their influence and their wealth.[11] No matter how his parents acquired their wealth, however, by the time of his birth young Spaight's family owned or controlled extensive properties in the agricultural and mercantile region of the Neuse-Pamlico near New Bern. And the elder Spaight had become a prominent member of the colonial aristocracy of planters and slaveholders.[12]

During the 1760s, New Bern was rapidly becoming one of the colony's most important commercial and governmental centers.[13] A relatively small group of families dominated the local scene where Tryon Palace soon would be erected (on land owned by the Spaight family)[14] to serve as the new seat of the royal government. Over the years, the leaders of the New Bern elite had formed relationships with other prominent groups beyond the local area, and their combined power had rapidly transformed them into a colonial aristocracy.[15] Later, at the time of the Revolution, many prominent Newbernians, including Richard Dobbs Spaight (and other men with close connections to the borough town), often were descendants of prominent figures like Spaight's father who had come to the area with valuable resources (especially political influence and perhaps some money).[16]

The younger Spaight was orphaned at no later than age six. His well-being soon was entrusted to Frederick Gregg and Governor Dobbs, two of the colony's most prominent men.[17] Young Spaight's considerable inheritance certainly must have included some of the bondmen who had been owned by his slaveholding father. For whatever reasons, the young orphan's background seems to have fostered an uncritical acceptance of slavery. Considering the large number of slaves Spaight would own after 1790, his family may have belonged even earlier to the exclusive group of large slaveholders, or he may have gained a sizable number of his slaves through marriage.[18] Later in life, young Spaight's fortune in land and slaves allowed him to enjoy an aristocratic lifestyle.[19] And Spaight benefited personally from participating in several of the transformative events of the early national period. The results of the American Revolution and Philadelphia convention left the slave system almost completely intact. In fact, the adoption of the Constitution, with its numerous provisions protecting slavery, may actually have improved Spaight's chances for maintaining a prosperous lifestyle as a wealthy member of North Carolina's planter-slaveholding elite.[20]

To many prominent Englishmen, perhaps including Spaight's family, "order" was more important than "liberty" or "freedom."[21] This outlook was consistent with the basic features of Britain's hierarchical society of masters and laborers. Throughout the eighteenth century, among British men at the top of the hierarchy, the main concern was not how to explain unequal treatment of the "meaner sort" and slaves in light of abstract concepts. Rather, it was entirely the opposite: the hierarchical vision of a social order was fundamental. "Liberty," even though proclaimed as "an abstract and universal concept," was "a privilege applicable in full only to a group entitled to it by property, reason, and virtue."[22] And under such circumstances, slavery was viewed (especially by slaveholders) as a justifiable and understandable lack of "freedom" for some subordinates within the hierarchical order. Apparently, in keeping with this outlook, young Spaight later would look downward from his inherited perch atop North Carolina's social, economic, and political hierarchy, and he would accept (or at least he left no sign he ever questioned) that his elevated station in life was in large measure dependent upon human slavery.[23]

At an appropriate age (perhaps eight or nine), Spaight's guardians sent him to Ireland (the homeland of his father and great-great-uncle), where among his Anglo-Irish relatives he could be educated and reach maturity as a worthy young gentleman. In due course, Spaight seems to have received a fine preparatory education. And although incomplete records prevent verification of his attendance, he may even have graduated from the University of Glasgow.[24]

Spaight's basic social and political philosophies most likely were shaped during his formative years, the bulk of which were spent far from North Carolina. During a time when Americans increasingly resisted British encroachment on the powers of their colonial assemblies, most of Spaight's Anglo-Irish relatives probably would have applauded a strong stand against any perceived efforts to curtail the rights and liberties of Englishmen. At the University of Glasgow, Spaight might even have been thrust into the intellectual ferment swirling around such Enlightenment philosophers as Francis Hutcheson, a teacher of Adam Smith. Hutcheson and others were proclaiming that government was a social contract between the people and their sovereign, with each party possessing certain inalienable rights. Typically, the elite interpreted "the people" to mean themselves, along with some other worthy landholders or property holders, and they restricted eligibility to serve as leaders even at the local level to those men whose education and property would guarantee the requisite level of disinterest essential to public virtue. This thinking enabled those holding power to focus on the common good. And while public virtue was seen as a requirement for worthy gentlemen who deserved the fullest measure of liberty and freedom, the lowest among the population were not considered to possess the basic requirements for freedom from their rightful masters, much less for full citizenship. According to Hutcheson, "liberty" and "freedom" should be reserved only for those who exhibited "virtue, distinction, wit, and kindness."[25] As a well-educated young British gentleman possessing a sizable fortune and a sterling pedigree, Richard Dobbs Spaight certainly would have met Hutcheson's requirements.

In 1778, at age twenty, Spaight finally returned to North Carolina. After arriving back in his birthplace, he apparently wasted no time in offering his services to Governor Richard Caswell. Despite the egalitarian and democratic tendencies unleashed during the Revolutionary era, family status and wealth still counted for much in the social, economic, and political life of North Carolina's coastal region. Governor Caswell, who also served as commander in chief of the militia, promptly appointed the wealthy, well-educated young patriot as his aide-de-camp.[26] In this capacity, Spaight seems to have played some role in the mobilization of North Carolina's militia under Caswell's command. Earlier, at the Battle of Moore's Creek Bridge in 1776, Caswell had commanded the patriot forces that had been victorious over the Loyalists. Caswell's military success had "established the permanent ascendancy of Patriot military and political power in North Carolina."[27] Soon thereafter, patriot success had resulted not only in numerous arrests of Loyalists but also frequent confiscation of their lands.[28] Consequently, had Spaight even remotely harbored any Loyalist sentiments in 1778, he would have found it well-nigh impossible in New Bern (or at least risky and costly) to choose other than the patriot banner.

Spaight's pedigree—not to mention his adherence to the patriot cause—appears to have opened up for him immediately a place among the leading families of New Bern and the surrounding area. He joined an elite group whose members dominated society through their control over the essential "factors of production: capital, labor, and land."[29] Spaight soon would be known not only as a gentleman with a taste for "the best madeira" and the "best Claret" but also as someone with an eye for horses "of the first quality."[30] During the period, the advantages of family status, education, and wealth typically generated among others a traditional deference. By 1780, the freeholders of New Bern chose Spaight to represent their town in the state legislature. There he served off and on for nearly a decade, including one term as Speaker.[31]

Spaight's service in the North Carolina assembly began amid some initial controversy. In 1779, William Blount, another member of the local elite, successfully challenged Spaight's election on the grounds of voting irregularities.[32] Soon, however, Blount and Spaight became conservative allies on most political issues, and later they served together in the Continental Congress and at the Philadelphia convention of 1787.

By the early 1780s, Spaight devoted much time representing New Bern or Craven County.[33] His role as a legislator brought him into frequent contact with a long list of prominent North Carolinians who often exhibited different perspectives. Among those aligned generally with the conservative or establishment group (who later became Federalists) were Samuel Johnston, William Blount, John Gray Blount, Archibald Maclaine, Hugh Williamson, William Davie, and John Sitgreaves. Among those associated loosely with the "liberal" or antiestablishment or western group (who later became Anti-Federalists) were Thomas Person, Samuel Spencer, Willie Jones, Timothy Bloodworth, and Richard Nixon (or Nixson). From the beginning, Spaight supported and promoted not only the coastal region generally and mercantile interests particularly but also the conservative position on the following issues: public finances—including whether to end the use of paper currency; the adoption of a scale of depreciation; the duties and responsibilities of "Public Treasurers"; and the annual tax levy.[34] In 1781 Spaight was appointed to the joint committee charged with overseeing the assembly's balloting for governor.[35] In July of that year, he and Thomas Person served on the committee charged with considering the governor's call for additional troops to bolster Nathanael Greene's forces (with impressment being an option if necessary).[36] During the early 1780s, Spaight and Person were often found on opposite sides of many divisive questions. Examples include vesting permanent titles for confiscated lands and slaves, appropriating funds to defray expenses incurred by certain parties during the Revolution, and compelling attendance by members of the General Assembly. Generally, Person was less than supportive of the government and its leaders, while Spaight was more likely to back those in positions of authority.[37]

By 1783, Spaight was fully engaged—often as chair—on numerous committees handling a host of matters ranging from the mundane to the controversial. As a key member of the select joint committee charged with reporting "such Bills of a public nature as are necessary to be passed into Laws this Session," he dealt with some heated issues that foreshadowed future divisions between Federalists and Anti-Federalists.[38] Spaight supported those gentlemen who wanted to honor state debts at face value, which favored speculators, and simultaneously he backed a depreciation scale favored by such like-minded conservatives as Governor Richard Caswell. Yet Spaight wound up on the losing side in a closely contested vote won by Anti-Federalists in the House who advocated a bill "to prevent the selling of Goods, Wares or Merchandise, for hard Money only, and to prevent the depreciation of the paper currency."[39]

In 1785, upon Spaight's return from Congress, Hugh Williamson nominated him for the House speakership, whereupon he "was unanimously chosen."⁴⁰ During his term as Speaker, the legislature was focused, as in prior years, on some issues held over from the Revolution—including disqualification of Loyalists to vote or hold office as well as disputes arising from the confiscation of Loyalists' lands and slaves.⁴¹ The legislature also voted (as on previous occasions) to reject a bill introduced by Archibald Maclaine "for permitting the emancipation of Slaves under certain restrictions."⁴² And in 1785, the General Assembly passed a law requiring that free blacks wear badges to distinguish them from slaves; the badges had to exhibit in capital letters the word "FREE."⁴³

During Spaight's speakership, the lines of division separating future Federalists and Anti-Federalists were increasingly visible. In a close vote, Thomas Person and his colleagues opposed the tax increase proposed by Spaight ally John Gray Blount; Person also supported the "further emission of Paper Currency," but Abner Nash and Blount led those conservatives "praying against" such a measure.⁴⁴ The two main factions divided closely over whether to adopt laws for the suppression of such "vice and immorality" as "excessive Gaming" and for "the better observation of" the Sabbath.⁴⁵ The House also was split almost evenly along the same lines when it passed a bill to permit the incorporation of "religious Societies" and another "for incorporating the Protestant Presbyterian Church of Wilmington."⁴⁶ On the question of court reform, Person and his followers tried unsuccessfully to establish certain limits on the activities of attorneys—including the setting of maximum fees.⁴⁷ There was general agreement, however, on such matters as enforcement of the act barring dual officeholding, the adoption of clear procedures for the House, and the urgent need "to quiet the inhabitants of certain Western Counties," many of whom had clamored recently for establishment of the "State of Franklin."⁴⁸ To work toward a solution of one generally recognized problem related to the western settlements, William Blount was appointed as the commissioner charged with securing a treaty with the Cherokee Indians.⁴⁹ At the end of Spaight's speakership, however, the fault lines appeared once again over whether to select Hillsborough as the site for the next legislative session.⁵⁰ The young planter-slaveholder presided over the House during a time when the speakership certainly must have required the proper decorum to maintain order during the consideration of many divisive questions. Notwithstanding his relative youth, Spaight's experience as Speaker could only have helped prepare him for future roles befitting a gentleman of his station.

By the time of the Philadelphia convention, Spaight was clearly one of the principal leaders in the House. Once again his election was challenged—this time, however, unsuccessfully by some members who stood on the other side of most major questions. He was closely associated with the conservative side in virtually all House business. And he introduced bills regularly on such weighty matters as state finances, annual taxes, court reforms, and elections. He also proposed a sweeping reorganization of important House committees to improve consideration of such key matters as "Revenues & Taxes," "the nature and amount of [Revolutionary War] Debts," "Tobacco," state contracts, confiscated lands, and western lands and settlements.[51] Moreover, Spaight often was able to sponsor special legislation benefiting the common freeholders who made up his local constituency.[52] And shortly before his selection as a delegate to the Philadelphia convention, where he would play a role in reshaping the national polity, Spaight could be found toiling diligently in an attempt to prevent annexation of part of Craven County by Pitt County, a struggle he lost in a 60 to 4 vote.[53]

In May 1783, Spaight was selected as one of North Carolina's delegates to the Confederation Congress scheduled to meet in Annapolis, Maryland—although he did not attend for the first time until 13 December 1783[54]—and he remained a member of that body until the summer of 1785.[55] He plunged earnestly into the role by attending faithfully and participating meaningfully—if not always graciously—in the business at hand. Generally, he seems to have considered the issues with a sincere concern for both the interests of North Carolina and the well-being of the new nation. Serving in Congress involved some hardship and expense, but outwardly he seems to have approached his new role by maintaining an aura of disinterested public virtue. After Spaight's first year in Congress, Archibald Maclaine suggested that he had become somewhat aloof, "confident of his own abilities" and "so elated with his present dignity that he chooses to be courted to communicate the important matters with which he is intrusted."[56]

For several years as a delegate, Spaight had frequent—sometimes almost daily—interactions with such leading founders as Thomas Jefferson and James Monroe. At times he was closely involved with them on a variety of committees. Those personal connections may have been a factor in Spaight's nomination of James Monroe for "Minister to the Court of Madrid" (which later was withdrawn).[57] And as might be expected for a group whose total number usually did not exceed two dozen, Jefferson soon knew Spaight's personal activities well enough to inform James Madison that Spaight was among a small number of delegates who recently had missed sessions due to a touch of "gout."[58] Predictably, as when Spaight seconded Jefferson's motion requiring "an injunction of secrecy" for all diplomatic correspondence, his name soon appeared frequently in the record alongside those of Jefferson and others of similar repute.[59]

Jefferson had become convinced that service in Congress for "young statesmen" such as Spaight would prove instrumental in shaping a national outlook. Because they "see the affairs of the Confederacy from a high ground," claimed Jefferson, "they learn the importance of the Union & befriend federal measures when they return."[60] Jefferson's expectations generally proved true with regard to Spaight. He supported a stronger national government in such matters as commerce, foreign affairs, and the military.[61]

On the other hand, he displayed a decidedly sectional outlook on the question of slavery and the western territories. His overt sectional tendencies motivated the rash actions that caused Jefferson to privately denounce Spaight as "a young fool." Spaight gained a reputation for foolhardiness in late April 1784, when he challenged a northern delegate, David Howell of Rhode Island, to a duel.[62] Howell soon reported that he also had received a similar challenge from Spaight's friend John Francis Mercer of Virginia.[63] Before their confrontation, Spaight and Howell had worked together in Congress on many occasions.[64] Yet suddenly Spaight had denounced Howell as a "Scoundrel" (one of the accusations most likely to result in a duel), and he had demanded "the satisfaction of a Gentleman" by meeting him "with a case of pistols."[65] Howell responded by bringing Spaight's letter of challenge to the attention of the entire Congress to embarrass the "young hothead," noting with dramatic restraint that he had received a "very extraordinary Letter" from the North Carolinian.[66]

A variety of possible reasons have been suggested for the conflict: southern interests versus New England interests related especially to the cession of western lands; "frustration over Rhode Island's hostility to the impost amendment"; disagreements over the appointment of foreign ministers and the negotiation of foreign treaties; and exasperation over the obstructionist tactics resorted to frequently by Howell and William Ellery, his colleague from Rhode Island.[67] Although those causes probably factored into the equation, the precise reasons may never be known with certainty. Yet undoubtedly Spaight harbored a sectional outlook in his support for slavery, and Howell believed that nonslaveholding whites would settle the northern tier of western territories. Recently, Jefferson and Howell, along with Jeremiah Chase, had served on the committee chaired by Jefferson "to prepare a plan for temporary government of western territory."[68] The plan as brought forth originally included a provision prohibiting slavery. The committee's report had been presented only a short while before Spaight issued his challenge to Howell, who earlier seems to have supported the 1783 "Appeal of the Quakers" for congressional action to end the slave trade.[69] Moreover, Howell and Ellery certainly had employed (and would continue to employ) a variety of obstructionist tactics against measures supported by Spaight and other delegates.[70] In any case, the enmity continued unabated for some time, even after it had become apparent that there would be no duel.

Soon John Mercer, supported by Spaight, tried to bring about the expulsion of Howell and Ellery. The question ultimately was decided in favor of the Rhode Islanders on a largely sectional vote, but not before some acrimonious deliberations.[71] Behind the scenes, Monroe and Jefferson and others discussed at length whether Congress should or could determine the answer.[72] And publicly for at least several weeks before the final resolution, Spaight and Mercer were aligned against Howell and Ellery in a bitter controversy with sectional implications. Francis Dana offered a decidedly northern outlook on the matter, especially with regard to the challenge to a duel. He also declared that Spaight and Howell had committed "indecencies" that were "highly derogatory" to the "honour" of Congress; that the pair deserved the "most pointed censures"; and that he was pleased once they had been "greatly reprobated."[73] Even a southerner like Monroe told Jefferson that, during the debates over Howell's and Ellery's seats, he had never seen "more indecent conduct in any assembly before."[74] Jefferson, writing to Madison, reported that Mercer, his former law student, had been "acting a very extraordinary part," relying heavily on Spaight and a few others, notably George Read of Delaware, a fellow slaveholder, "to obstruct business inconceivably."[75] Apparently with little regard for the opprobrium and scorn of some older and more temperate delegates, the brash young planter-slaveholders had made it difficult for Congress to ignore completely the unpleasant sectional implications of their dispute with the Rhode Islanders. Jefferson responded privately by describing Spaight as "a young fool from North Carolina" who is "no[t] otherwise of consequence than as by his vote according[ly] can divide his state."[76]

On at least one important question with sectional implications, Spaight indeed did divide the vote of North Carolina. Hugh Williamson, who owned no slaves, had informed Madison in 1783 that he was against slavery, an institution he deemed burdensome to society. In the voting in 1784 concerning whether to exclude slavery in the new western territories ceded by the states to the Confederation government, Williamson had been the only southern delegate who voted with Thomas Jefferson for exclusion.[77] Spaight, on the other hand, appears consistently to have opposed any barriers to the extension of slavery. Spaight has even been credited with making the motion to strike the antislavery clause Jefferson had inserted in the 1784 version of the ordinance.[78]

During the early years of the republic, Americans such as Richard Dobbs Spaight "could have no way of knowing that promoting or defending local and regional interests would ultimately lead to a crisis of union and national identity."[79] Yet on more than one occasion Spaight made clear that he expected several distinct regional issues before Congress to result in "a little dust kicked up" or to ignite "the flames of Civil War."[80] And whether Spaight or other early Americans saw those on the opposite side as "sectionalists," they did not easily "recognize particularistic impulses in themselves." Indeed, Americans had been "taught to believe that the genius of republican government was to secure the rights and interests of localities as well as of people."[81] Thus, while Spaight expected the national government to serve the common interests of the nation, he also looked upon specific measures from a regional or even a local perspective. In this vein, Spaight spoke in 1784 of the possibility of "a dissolution of the Confederacy" and "Civil War" if "the Eastern Delegates" did not soon begin showing more concern for "the general good of the whole, uncrampt by the policy and interest of particular States."[82]

During the summer of 1784, while Congress was in recess, Spaight remained in Annapolis representing North Carolina on the Committee of the States, for that body attempted to manage the affairs of the Confederation government.[83] Any number of such activities would have made him acutely aware of the weaknesses of the Confederation. He saw firsthand the difficulty that Congress faced not only in maintaining quorums but also in securing the votes of enough states to pass worthwhile or even urgent bills. And he knew that it was altogether another matter for states to comply with those measures that Congress actually passed. Indeed, when he backed a motion to request that New Hampshire and Massachusetts send delegates so that Congress could respond to the likely British failure to evacuate western posts, New Hampshire simply withdrew from Congress, thus stymying any action.[84] At that approximate time, Spaight had told Governor Alexander Martin that he believed the British still harbored the hope of reversing the success of the American Revolution.[85] Later, Spaight would display a martial spirit toward Britain, whose "hostile" disposition "against America," he said, was cause enough to "be prepared for any [thing] that might happen."[86]

Spaight's frequent service on the Committee of the States may have shaped his outlook on the role of a national executive. The committee, in the absence of a chief executive or an executive branch of government, sat during recesses "for transacting the business of the United States," though with clear limits on its power.[87] Perhaps Spaight's experiences had the effect of highlighting especially the difficulties of transacting certain kinds of business under the Confederation. Without explaining for posterity his reasons, Spaight vaguely mentioned having an interest in some sort of changes that might have created a stronger, or at least more effective, executive power. Late in 1784, Spaight and John Francis Mercer discussed the Congress's current practice of maintaining a rotating presidency that each year was expected to be handed off to someone else, until each of the thirteen states had had its turn. In this context, Spaight expressed admiration for his good friend's recommendation that, as Spaight put it, the presidency be placed "upon a different footing such as the mode you propose, or some other which would materially alter it."[88] Yet soon thereafter, in June 1785, Spaight left the Confederation Congress. And once back in North Carolina he wrote Governor Caswell, in office again, asking his permission "to resign my Appointment for the residue of the year" and declining to accept another appointment for the following year on the grounds that he had "long neglected" his "private business."[89]

By the time the Constitutional Convention convened in Philadelphia only a few years later, Spaight had accepted once again a call to serve at the national level. He was the first delegate from North Carolina to arrive in the City of Brotherly Love, perhaps because he had traveled by water.[90] He would attend every session, make a few notable if relatively unspectacular recommendations, and sign the completed document; afterward he supported its ratification in North Carolina. Fellow North Carolinians Hugh Williamson, William Davie, and Alexander Martin joined Spaight for the convention's opening day. William Blount arrived later.[91] Also present were John Francis Mercer and George Read.[92] At the 1787 convention, however, Spaight, Mercer, and Read refrained from any actions similar to the "indecent conduct" Monroe and Jefferson had condemned a few years earlier.[93] In Philadelphia, moreover, the elites' staunch belief that "they were one upper class" was "clearly discernible" inasmuch as the "decorum, language, and style were all taken from the gentry playbook."[94] Throughout the proceedings, Spaight conducted himself as a gentleman, though he was singularly intransigent about one of the most important matters before the body: at every turn he opposed the Great Compromise, whereby the delegates agreed to establish equal representation of the states in the Senate. He was adamantly against granting an equal voice to such small eastern states as Rhode Island. And ultimately he stood alone on that question among the North Carolinians by voting "no" during the crucial vote that—no thanks to Spaight—allowed the convention to break the stalemate and move forward.[95]

Spaight's substantive contributions to the convention's proceedings were limited but noteworthy. He not only proposed one of the convention's most important procedural decisions (to allow reconsideration and thus promote less formality) but also introduced several motions that closely resembled three of the Constitution's final provisions: the term of senators, the selection of senators by the state legislatures, and the president's power to make recess appointments.[96] Apparently, Spaight also helped frame the provision that prohibited members of Congress from holding any other federal offices during their terms. When he joined with Williamson to propose that any treaties affecting territorial rights must receive a two-thirds vote of approval in the Senate, Spaight most likely was responding to North Carolina's concerns over a possible treaty with Spain. And Spaight might have been influenced by Williamson to support "stringent requirements to admit western states to the Union," although he may just as likely have been acting on his own convictions shaped by his outlook on the cession of western territories and the "State of Franklin."[97] Whatever the case, Spaight also supported Williamson's recommendation that "equality of representation" be denied to new states until they were roughly equivalent in population and wealth to existing states. And perhaps for reasons arising from his earlier discussions with Mercer regarding a stronger executive, Spaight did not support Williamson's call for a national triumvirate that would have granted "the northern, middle, and southern interests equal powers."[98] At one point, moreover, Spaight joined with John Rutledge of South Carolina to propose that the Senate choose the president from a list of thirteen rather than five provided by the electors, but he shifted quickly to recommend that, if no one got a majority, the electors should choose the president rather than the Senate.[99]

To prevent "intemperate and unjust proceedings of the legislature," Spaight believed that some constitutional "check" should be devised other than frequent elections. Yet he refused to acknowledge that judicial review might be the answer. During the convention, Spaight clarified his views in a biting letter to James Iredell of North Carolina, a notable advocate for the principle of judicial review (and a future associate justice of the Supreme Court). Spaight denounced the concept of judicial review as "despotic" and "absurd," and he proclaimed that its recent application in North Carolina in *Bayard v. Singleton* (1787) was "alarming" and "destructive" to the balance of power.[100] Perhaps he thought that the proposed "upper house" or Senate would serve as a check on intemperance by acting in a more reasonable and balanced manner. For whatever reason, Spaight took the lead in proposing a relatively lengthy term for senators, even though his home state limited most terms of office to one year.[101] Be that as it may, the record shows clearly that Spaight was more concerned in Philadelphia with guarding against potential excesses of the central government than of the state legislatures. Consequently, he hoped to settle on "some means by which the state legislatures, rather than the lower house of Congress, would select members of the upper house." According to Richard

Beeman, Spaight was among those delegates who were "beginning to feel some uneasiness about the 'national' character of the new government, and by giving each state legislature the right to select senators, they hoped to return at least some measure of power to the states."[102]

Gouverneur Morris of Pennsylvania chided Spaight for expressing "such a distrust" when he claimed to be fearful that New York City soon might become the nation's permanent capital "especially if the Presidt. should be [a] Northern Man."[103] Despite Spaight's sectional proclivities, however, he had supported most of the key measures designed to increase the power of the central government. Toward the end of the convention, moreover, Spaight shared with James Iredell his hopes for the ultimate outcome of the new experiment: "It is not probable that the United States will in future be so ideal as to risk their happiness upon the unanimity of the whole; and thereby put it in the power of one or two States to defeat the most salutary propositions, and prevent the Union from rising out of that contemptible situation to which it is at present reduced. There is no man of reflection, who has maturely considered what end must and will result from the weakness of our present Federal Government, and the tyrannical and unjust proceedings of most of the State governments, if longer persevered in, but must sincerely wish for a strong and efficient National Government."[104]

Opposition to ratification of the Constitution was intense in North Carolina. According to Pauline Maier, "memories of the Regulation—or, more exactly, the grievances that prompted it—made many North Carolinians acutely conscious" of a variety of threats posed by distant governments. Proponents of the Constitution, she has concluded, "too often ran up against those sensitivities."[105] Thus, even though North Carolina's delegates in Philadelphia, including Spaight, "had been moderately sympathetic to the nationalist vision of the Constitution," the average citizen of North Carolina was "far more concerned by the threat of consolidation posed by the new government."[106]

The General Assembly had authorized the Hillsborough convention to meet in late July 1788.[107] Ultimately, over 260 delegates were elected to consider whether the proposed Constitution should be approved. As the election of delegates proceeded, Archibald Maclaine, a Federalist, expressed concern because so many of his group had gone down to defeat. "We have," he wrote, "a set of fools and knaves in every part of the State, who seem to act as by concert; and they are uniformly against any man of abilities and virtue."[108] Once the convention had assembled, the delegates began debating the Constitution clause by clause. The Anti-Federalists usually said relatively little during the process, while Iredell, Davie, Maclaine, and Spaight spoke at length. "The Constitution's critics were sometimes informed by their more learned colleagues who supported ratification," says Maier, "but they were never convinced that the Constitution was safe in its current form."[109]

Spaight was prominent among the Federalists who tried to convince their colleagues in Hillsborough that they should ratify the new plan of government. Although usually he did not respond in kind to the snide comments or personal attacks made by some Anti-Federalists, he did take advantage of the chance to condemn the "very refractory conduct of Rhode Island" under the Confederation "in opposing" the common good. Such practices, he proclaimed, had made it necessary to fashion a more effective government.[110] Although he was quite taken aback by objections to the president serving as commander in chief, Spaight reminded the delegates that Congress controlled the raising of armies, that Congress could impeach the president, and that if Congress had not vested control of the military in one man during the Revolution, then "perhaps the independence of America would not have been established."[111] He also defended the power of the president to make treaties as a much better arrangement than under the Confederation—even though he admitted that northern influence might cause southern interests to suffer as a result.[112]

Spaight's support for the Constitution often pitted him against earlier opponents in the political arena who now were Anti-Federalists. In response to Samuel Spencer's claim that the federal tax power might "destroy" the people and "produce insurrections," Spaight countered that "it was thought absolutely necessary for the support of the general government to give it power to raise taxes"; that requisitions had been a failure; and that the notion of paying taxes in produce would not be efficient.[113] When Timothy Bloodworth claimed that the "supreme law" clause might "produce an abolition of the state governments," Spaight left the counterattack to Iredell, Maclaine, and Davie. Yet Spaight vigorously defended the provisions for a federal judiciary as being necessary to enable the new government to enforce its laws. Congress could be expected to establish "inferior tribunals" in each state, he said, yet the framers "unanimously" had sought "to keep separate and distinct the objects of the jurisdiction of the federal from that of the state judiciary."[114] And Spaight reminded the delegates that trial by jury still would remain "in full force in the state courts," though he acknowledged that Congress could determine the extent of jury trials in federal matters.[115]

Spaight's principal speech in Hillsborough was primarily an extended rebuttal of William Lenoir's claims not only that the delegates at Philadelphia had exceeded their authority but also that the Constitution "may be very oppressive on this state, and all the Southern States."[116] "The gentleman says, we exceeded our powers," began Spaight. "I deny the charge," he continued, for "what the Convention has done is a mere proposal. It was found impossible to improve the old system without changing its very form; for by that system the three great branches of government are blended together. All will agree that the concession of a power to a government so constructed is dangerous." Further, he noted, "The gentleman has insinuated that this Constitution, instead of securing our liberties, is a scheme to enslave us. He has produced no proof, but rests it on his bare assertion—an assertion which I am astonished to hear, after the ability with which every objection has been fully and clearly refuted in the course of our debates. I am, for my part," he proclaimed, "conscious of having had nothing in view but the liberty and happiness of my country; and I believe every member of that Convention was actuated by motives equally sincere and patriotic." The gentleman "says that it will tend to aristocracy," but "where is the aristocratical part of it?" he asked. "I always thought that an aristocracy was that government where the few governed the many, or where the rulers were hereditary. This is a very different government from that." After Spaight next characterized the new government as "democratical" because the "privilege of representation is secured," he then asserted that "trial by jury" and "liberty of the press" had been preserved rather than threatened. And regarding religion, he proclaimed, "No power is given to the general government to interfere with it at all." "No sect is preferred to another." "No test is required." He also pointed out that treason was narrowly defined as "levying war" against the United States. And finally, in rebutting the claim that the powers of the general government were too vague, he declared that the powers of the central government "are better defined than the powers of any government."[117] Given their reasoned responses to a litany of fears, Spaight and the other Federalists must have been frustrated—though certainly not surprised—when the overwhelming majority of Anti-Federalists finally voted 184 to 83 neither to ratify nor to reject the Constitution and submitted a list of proposed amendments for consideration by Congress and the states.[118]

After declining to ratify the Constitution, North Carolina remained officially outside the new nation for nearly sixteen months. In the meantime, however, supporters of the Constitution were able to gain authorization for a second convention to meet in Fayetteville in November 1789. By that time, George Washington had been elected as the first president, and the expected adoption of the Bill of Rights seemed likely to implement many of the provisions recommended earlier by North Carolina. In large measure due to those circumstances, the Fayetteville convention proved to be almost completely the opposite of the previous gathering. Federalists then made up a large majority of the delegates. Many Anti-Federalists had resigned themselves to the inevitable, and therefore the Constitution was ratified with almost no debate.[119] Richard Dobbs Spaight did not attend the Fayetteville convention. Recently, he had wedded Mary Leech, daughter of Colonel Joseph Leech of New Bern; she was described as an "amiable" and "beautiful" young lady with "an extensive fortune."[120] For a short time, personal matters diverted his attention away from the political arena.

Although Spaight remained out of the limelight for several years, he soon returned to politics and served consecutively as governor, congressman, and state senator. Prior to his selection as governor in 1792, however, Spaight had been suffering from health problems, family matters, and other concerns common to wealthy planter-slaveholders.[121] From 1792 to 1795, while still a Federalist, he served as North Carolina's first native-born governor.[122] By the late 1790s, however, he had become a Democratic-Republican (if not exactly a "Jeffersonian") for reasons that probably cannot be discerned today with much certainty. Yet by then the Federalists' influence was declining in North Carolina, and the emerging Democratic-Republicans were gaining strength as they embraced an outlook in keeping with the views of many prominent southern slaveholders—especially nascent sectionalists like Richard Dobbs Spaight.[123]

As a professed Democratic-Republican congressman elected in 1798, Spaight ultimately supported that party's position on most key matters before the House—but not altogether until 1800.[124] For several years, he had eschewed close identification with either party. "I can only say," he confessed early in 1800 to his friend John Gray Blount, "that last Session I was a mere observer, endeavoring to find out the views of both parties, but not to be of any party myself."[125] Yet the election of 1800 seems finally to have induced Spaight's metamorphosis into a full-fledged Democratic-Republican, at least on the floor of Congress, for he certainly voted with that party there amid the heated contest between Adams and Jefferson. Indeed, during the months before the presidential election was thrown into the House, Spaight voted against the Federalists on virtually every issue: the Sedition Act, the Judiciary Act, the Uniform Bankruptcy Act, and the proposed commercial intercourse treaty with France.[126]

Perhaps most telling was Spaight's rejection of the Federalists' efforts "to sanctify" George Washington after his death in 1799 by appropriating funds for a mausoleum. Until the late 1790s, sectional impulses had been controlled, more or less, as a consequence of Washington's leadership and the national consensus that had been reached at Philadelphia in 1787.[127] When Spaight joined with the Democratic-Republicans to reject the proposed mausoleum, he was not only rejecting the Federalists' reinterpretation of the national consensus but also embracing firmly the sectional outlook he had displayed earlier. And by the time the House began deliberating on the final outcome of the election of 1800, Spaight had taken to describing the "Anglo-Federalists" or "Essex Junto" as "Malignant," "Diabolical" schemers who should be consigned "to eternal infamy here, & Damnation in the World to Come."[128]

Despite Spaight's caustically partisan rhetoric and his partisan voting record, which included unwavering support for Thomas Jefferson during the House's balloting on the presidency in 1801,[129] some observers doubted his commitment to the Democratic-Republican vision. During the election, the *New York Gazette*, though apparently uncertain as to how to categorize Spaight, had described him as "a spurious federalist."[130] Yet, clearly, Spaight still retained much of the conservative outlook common among those aristocratic southern slaveholders who had taken part in the establishment of a national polity designed to preserve their eighteenth-century British American conceptions of "liberty" and "freedom." In fact, Spaight soon demonstrated—unequivocally yet tragically—his deep-seated personal devotion to the conservative tenets of a society led by elite gentlemen distinguished by a disinterested public virtue.

When the Federalist John Stanly of New Bern openly made accusations casting aspersions on Spaight's public virtue, the affront to Spaight's honor caused him to respond in a manner clearly intended to result in Stanly's challenge to a duel. In 1800, Stanly had soundly defeated Spaight's bid for reelection to Congress.[131] Subsequently, especially during and after Spaight's successful 1802 campaign for the state senate, the two gentlemen often traded sharp oral and written assaults. Their biting accusations finally reached the point where a defense of honor was deemed to be a necessity. On 5 September 1802, Stanly and Spaight, who was accompanied by his second, Edward Pasteur, publisher of New Bern's *North Carolina Gazette*, met on the outskirts of New Bern, where they exchanged shots with pistols. Spaight was mortally wounded during the fourth exchange, and he died the following day.[132]

Spaight's place in history among the founders is based primarily on his modest record as a delegate to the Philadelphia convention. Had he failed to attend that gathering, historians most certainly would have accorded him even less attention, despite his prominent role in the Hillsborough convention of 1788 and his later service as governor of North Carolina. Yet even if Spaight—as an ordinary founder—cannot be credited with more than a few substantive contributions, he stood nevertheless among those elite gentlemen who framed a national polity based ultimately on evolving visions of "liberty" and "freedom." Indeed, it is profoundly significant that those principles were not presented at the time as being limited clearly "to a particular status but general to all humans."[133] The "liberty" and "freedom" advocated at the time by Spaight and most other founders, however, did not extend to slaves or Native Americans, or even to free women of any color. As one historian has said, though, the founders did not need to instantly create a "literal, modern, egalitarian liberty" to be appreciated. Rather, they should be regarded as neither "intentional creators of full modernity nor its betrayers, but as remarkably resourceful originators of progressive change."[134] On the other hand, Spaight and his elite counterparts probably could not have imagined that their republican experiment would foster the evolution of such a profoundly egalitarian political system when compared with the political traditions of their era.

NOTES

1. For general information (despite some discrepancies) on Spaight's life and career, the most helpful secondary sources are Alan Watson, *Richard Dobbs Spaight* (New Bern, N.C.: Griffin and Tilghman, 1987); Alexander Andrews, "Richard Dobbs Spaight," *North Carolina Historical Review* 1, no. 2 (1924): 95–120; Burton Craige, *The Federal Convention of 1787: North Carolina in the Great Crisis* (Richmond: Expert Graphics, 1987), especially "Richard Spaight," 105–30; R. C. Lawrence, "The Unique Career of Richard Dobbs Spaight," *The State* 12, no. 32 (1945), 7, 16–17; and Louise Irby Trenholme, *The Ratification of the Federal Constitution in North Carolina* (New York: Columbia University Press, 1932), especially chapters 2–4.

2. See, for example, George Sheldon, *Hugh Williamson: Physician, Patriot, and Founding Father* (Amherst, N.Y.: Humanity Books, 1987); and *The Papers of James Iredell*, ed. Don Higginbotham et al., 3 vols. (1976; repr., Raleigh: Office of Archives and History, 2003).

3. Winton Solberg, ed., *The Constitutional Convention and the Formation of the Union*, 2nd ed. (Urbana: University of Illinois Press, 1987), 406.

4. Michal Rozbicki, *Culture and Liberty in the Age of the American Revolution* (Charlottesville: University of Virginia Press, 2011), 224.

5. Rozbicki finds the concept of American exceptionalism to be outdated, yet he promotes the view that unique circumstances in America helped foster a more expansive definition of liberty; see *Culture and Liberty*, 224–25.

6. Richard Beeman, *Plain, Honest Men: The Making of the American Constitution* (New York: Random House, 2009), all preceding quotations, 82. Beeman does not include Spaight among those on his lists of "The Indispensable Men of the Convention," "Men Who Helped Shape the Constitution," or "Influential Characters." See xix–xxii.

7. Ibid., 99.

8. Rev. McDowell to Secretary of the Society for the Propagation of the Gospel, 26 March 1763, in William L. Saunders and Walter Clark, eds., *Colonial and State Records of North Carolina* (Raleigh: State of North Carolina, 1896–), 6:978 (hereafter *CSRNC*).

9. Watson, *Spaight*, 2. See also "Commission to appoint Richard Spaight," 2 October 1755, *CSRNC*, 5:442.

10. Upon their marriage in 1756, Richard Spaight took possession of his wife's dowry consisting of a "very valuable" estate comprising not only extensive landholdings but

also "Negroes & goods amounting to £6,000 sterling Great Britain money." A. B. Pruitt, *Abstracts of Deeds, Craven County, NC, 1750–1758* (North Carolina[?]: A. P. Pruitt, 2004), 125–26. In 1760, Richard Spaight was part-owner of a "tanyard" in New Bern; see Stephen Bradley Jr., *Abstracts of Wills, Craven County, NC, Vol. 3, 1801–1812* (Lawrenceville, Va.: Stephen Bradley Jr., 2001), 11.

11. According to one historian, elite marriages before 1760 promoted a degree of unity but only among the leading local families because such unions usually did not merge families from different regions of North Carolina. A. Roger Ekirch, *"Poor Carolina": Politics and Society in Colonial North Carolina, 1729–1776* (Chapel Hill: University of North Carolina Press, 1981), 37–38.

12. "It would be a mistake to conclude that a wealthy plantation class had emerged in eastern North Carolina by the 1760s," says Ekirch in *"Poor Carolina,"* 23. Yet Kay and Cary have concluded that, as early as the 1750s, large-scale plantation slavery had taken hold in the coastal regions; see Michael Kay and Lorin Cary, *Slavery in North Carolina, 1748–1775* (Chapel Hill: University of North Carolina Press, 1995), 22–24. At the very least, the evidence suggests that the Spaight family should be listed among the more notable exceptions to Ekirch's general rule. "Madame" Mary Moore, one of North Carolina's wealthiest and most socially prominent women (and Richard Dobbs Spaight's grandmother), left her daughter Elizabeth not only fine clothing, valuable furniture, silverware, and gold and diamond-studded jewelry but also "first choice" of some of her "negroes"; see "The Will of Madame Moore," in Elizabeth Moore, *Records of Craven County, NC, Vol. 1* (Bladensburg, Md.: Genealogical Recorder, 1960), 72–74. In 1762, the elder Spaight was able to secure £60 in compensation for his slave named Cato, who had been outlawed and killed; see "Report of the Committee concerning Public Claims," General Assembly, 29 April 1762, *CSRNC*, 22:833. According to one source, the younger Spaight inherited not only the brick mansion at Clermont plantation (owned formerly by his mother's family), located a few miles up the Trent River from New Bern, but also approximately 100,000 acres in Craven County extending from the Trent River to Carteret County; see a commemorative plaque (dated 1934) at gravesite of Richard Dobbs Spaight, Craven County, N.C. According to another source, in 1779 the younger Spaight took control of property in Craven County assessed at £65,000—"the most valuable estate in the county"; see Watson, *Spaight*, 4. Within a few decades, Richard Dobbs Spaight would own nearly 90 slaves; see Watson, *Spaight*, 23.

13. See Ekirch, *"Poor Carolina,"* 151–52.

14. *Minutes of the Senate*, 8 December 1787, *CSRNC*, 20:204.

15. William Powell, *North Carolina through Four Centuries* (Chapel Hill: University of North Carolina Press, 1989), 145–48; Ekirch, *"Poor Carolina,"* especially chapters 2–4, though Ekirch concludes that in North Carolina the elite lacked the wealth, cohesiveness, and authority of neighboring colonial aristocracies.

16. The list includes Richard Caswell (governor), Abner Nash (governor, who married the widow of Governor Arthur Dobbs), William Blount (U.S. senator), John Sitgreaves (federal judge), and Abner Neale (clerk of the federal court). For information on the lesser-known pair of Sitgreaves and Neale, see *North Carolina Gazette* (New Bern), 2 July 1791.

17. "Bond from Dobbs & Gregg," 25 April 1764, *Records of the Office of the Secretary of State, CSRNC*, 6:1042–43. The bond qualified the pair to serve as guardians of "Richard Spaight an Orphan Son of the late Richard Spaight, Esqr. deceased." Apparently, Elizabeth

Spaight, young Richard's mother, did not survive her husband for even one year, though she was recognized as "admx. of Richard Spaight Esquire decd" in July 1763; see Craven County Court, *Minutes*, book 5, July 1763, 684.

18. Watson, *Spaight*, 23; "Craven County Census of 1790," *CSRNC*, 26:411.

19. Bradley, *Abstracts*, 11; Watson, *Spaight*, 4, 28; *Columbian Magazine* (Philadelphia), October 1788, cited in Andrews, "Spaight," 112; *The Annual Register, or a View of the History, Politics, and Literature for the Year 1770* (London: J. Dodsley, 1771), bearing the inscription "Taken from Claremont, the residence of Governor Spaight, Newbern, N.C. 1862," Kellenberger Room, New Bern–Craven County Public Library; "Clermont Plantation," broadside dated 26 November [1920], Broadsides and Ephemera Collection, Duke University, Durham, N.C.

20. See George Van Cleve, *A Slaveholders' Union: Slavery, Politics, and the Constitution in the Early American Republic* (Chicago: University of Chicago Press, 2010); Don Fehrenbacher, *The Slaveholding Republic: An Account of the United States Government's Relations to Slavery* (New York: Oxford University Press, 2001); and Paul Finkleman, *Slavery and the Founders: Race and Liberty in the Age of Jefferson*, 2nd ed. (Armonk, N.Y.: Routledge, 2001), especially chapters 1, 2, 5, and 6.

21. Rozbicki, *Culture and Liberty*, 52–53. In 1760, Royal Governor Arthur Dobbs, Spaight's great-great-uncle, had indicated his support for the primacy of "order" and decried the "republican spirit of Independency" displayed by members of the lower house of the General Assembly; see Dobbs to Board of Trade, 3 August 1760, cited in Ekirch, "Poor Carolina," 153.

22. Rozbicki, *Culture and Liberty*, 52.

23. Spaight consistently opposed legislation that would have made it easier for North Carolina masters to free their slaves, and he followed the established procedure in 1786 for obtaining the General Assembly's permission "to set free a certain mulatto girl now his property, called or known by the name of Mary Long." See House of Commons, *Minutes*, 13 December 1786, *CSRNC*, 18:317; and *Acts of the North Carolina General Assembly*, *CSRNC*, 24:930. Jeffrey Crow has noted not only that North Carolina's lawmakers denounced manumission as a dangerous practice but also that by 1790, "North Carolina was the only southern state in which manumission was not the prerogative of the slave owner." Crow, "Slave Rebelliousness and Social Conflict in North Carolina, 1775–1802," *William and Mary Quarterly* 36, no. 1 (1980): 91–92.

24. Andrews, "Spaight," 96–97; Watson, *Spaight*, 3.

25. Quoted in Rozbicki, *Culture and Liberty*, 48–49, 76, 51.

26. Andrews, "Spaight," 98; Watson, *Spaight*, 4.

27. David Wilson, *The Southern Strategy: Britain's Conquest of South Carolina and Georgia, 1775–1780* (Columbia: University of South Carolina Press, 2005), 33.

28. Ibid., 32.

29. Woody Holton, *Forced Founders: Indians, Debtors and Slaves in the Making of the American Revolution in Virginia* (Chapel Hill: University of North Carolina Press, 1999), xix.

30. See Spaight to Mark Pringle [a Baltimore merchant], 5 and 12 July 1784, in Paul Smith et al., eds., *Letters of Delegates to Congress, 1774–1789* (hereafter *LDC*), 25 vols. (Washington, D.C.: Library of Congress, 1976–2000), 22:717; Hugh Williamson to William Blount, 28 November 1783, *LDC*, 22:166–68.

31. Craige, *Federal Convention*, 123.

32. House of Commons, *Minutes*, 18 and 21 October 1779, *CSRNC*, 13:914, 928–29.

33. House of Commons, *Minutes*, 23 June 1781, *CSRNC*, 17:877–79, and 16 and 19 April 1782, *CSRNC*, 16:1–2, 29. Spaight had not given up on the possibility of serving again in the militia; he allowed his name to be placed in nomination for second major of the unit authorized in 1781 by the General Assembly to be formed under the command of Benjamin Hawkins, but the legislature selected Bennett Crofton over Spaight after several rounds of balloting. See House of Commons, *Minutes*, 10–11 July 1781 and 13 July 1781, *CSRNC*, 17:951–52, 957, 964.

34. See, for example, ibid., 28 June 1781, 17:906; and 23 April, 3 May, 8 May, and 9 May 1782, 19:18, 87, 90, 130.

35. Ibid., 24 June 1781, 17:896.

36. Ibid., 19 July 1781, 17:948.

37. Ibid., 6, 8–11, and 13 July 1781, 17:936, 944, 948, 952–53, 963; 2 May 1783, 19:294–95.

38. Ibid., 19 April 1783, 19:135.

39. Ibid., 22 December 1786, 18:361–62.

40. Ibid., 19 November 1785, 17:266.

41. See ibid., 1–23 December 1785, 17:264–392, especially 21 and 28 December 1785, 414, 418–19.

42. Ibid., 3 December 1785, 17:312.

43. Crow, "Slave Rebelliousness," 93. Earlier, while serving as a delegate to Congress, Spaight had joined with fellow Newbernian John Sitgreaves to propose that the nation's diplomatic goals include a demand for "compensation for the negroes that were carried away [by the British] in open violation of the Definitive Treaty of Peace." See Spaight and Sitgreaves to Alexander Martin, 1 March 1785, *CSRNC*, 17:606–7.

44. House of Commons, *Minutes*, 14, 15, 19 (printed incorrectly as 14), and 24 December 1785, *CSRNC*, 17:349, 351, 364–66, 394–95, 398.

45. Ibid., 7 and 10 December 1785, 17:319, 332.

46. Ibid., 2 and 17 December 1785, 17:304, 359.

47. Ibid., 7 and 20 December 1785, 17:323–25, 368–69.

48. Ibid., 29 November, 6 and 17 December 1785, 17:296, 316, 361.

49. Ibid., 21 November 1785, 17:269–72.

50. Ibid., 16 December 1785, 17:354.

51. "Preface," *CSRNC*, 18:iv; House of Commons, *Minutes*, 18 November, 4–5 December 1786, ibid., 18:226, 269–70, 276; 1–2 January 1787, 18:425, 428.

52. House of Commons, *Minutes*, 4–5 December 1786, ibid., 18:271, 276.

53. Ibid., 6 December 1786, 18:284.

54. Spaight to William Blount, 26 December 1783, *LDC*, 26:235–36.

55. *Journals of the Continental Congress, 1774–1789* (hereinafter *JCC*), ed. Worthington C. Ford et al., 34 vols. (Washington, D.C.: Government Printing Office, 1904–37), 14 May 1783, 26:341; Spaight to Richard Caswell, 10 August 1785, cited in "Notes" for Spaight to Caswell, 5 June 1785, *LDC*, 23:434–37; House of Commons, *Minutes*, 10 May 1783, *CSRNC*, 19:333.

56. Ibid.; Spaight to John Gray Blount, 8 April 1784, ibid., 27:499; A. Maclaine to George Hooper, 28 September 1784, *CSRNC*, 17:169.

57. See, for example, *JCC*, 5–12 and 21 January 1784, 27:38–41, 714–15; Monroe to John Francis Mercer, 29 January 1785, *LDC*, 22:152–53; *JCC*, 11 February 1785, 2 February 1785 (printed incorrectly as 31 January 1785), 29:56, 25.

58. Jefferson to James Madison, 20 February 1784, *LDC*, 21:367.

59. See, for example, *JCC*, 3 May 1784, 27:331.

60. Jefferson to Madison, 20 February 1784, *LDC*, 21:369.

61. See the following in *LDC*: Spaight to Alexander Martin, 24 February 1784, 17:17–19; Spaight to Martin, 12 March 1784 and 23 July 1784, 21:430, 754; Spaight to Martin, 6 December 1784, 22:53; Richard Beresford to Certain States, 30 March 1784, 21:465–66; Spaight to James Iredell, 9 March 1785, 22:266; Spaight to William Blount, 27 March 1785, 22:287.

62. Spaight to David Howell, 29 April 1784, ibid., 21:557–58, including "Notes." At the time, heated debates in Congress "apparently concerned the cession of western lands." See Jefferson to Madison, 25 April 1784, ibid., 21:545–48; and Charles Thomson to Jefferson, 19 May 1784, ibid., 21:630–32, including "Notes."

63. Howell to Jabez Bowen, 22 May 1784, ibid., 21:639.

64. See, for example, *JCC*, 3 June 1783, 26:380, and 23 January and 25 March 1784, 27:49, 167–68; Jefferson to Benjamin Harrison, 3 March 1784, in *The Papers of Thomas Jefferson*, ed. Julian Boyd (Princeton, N.J.: Princeton University Press, 1953), 7:4–7, including "Note." Later, Spaight and Howell would work together in Congress without displaying any outward signs of lingering bitterness; yet Spaight still referred privately to Howell as one of the "Dealers in troubled Waters" who, he declared, "will prove an eternal plague to us." See *JCC*, 1 March 1785, 29:112–13; and Spaight to Edward Hand, 28 December 1784, *LDC*, 22:94.

65. Spaight to Howell, 29 April 1784, *LDC*, 21:558.

66. Howell to Bowen, 22 May 1784, ibid., 21:639; Howell to Thomas Mifflin, 30 April 1784, ibid., 21:563.

67. Thomson to Jefferson, 19 May 1784, ibid., 21, "Notes," 632; Jefferson to Madison, 25 April 1784, ibid., 21, "Notes," 548.

68. Howell to William Greene, 23 August 1785, ibid., 22:587–88; *JCC*, 22 March 1784, 27, "Bibliographical Notes," 719. See also William Merkel, "Jefferson's Failed Anti-slavery Proviso of 1784 and the Nascence of Free Soil Constitutionalism," *Seton Hall Law Review* 38, no. 2 (2008): 555–603. Merkel argues that most historians (including Paul Finkelman and Peter Onuf) have overlooked the enormous consequences of the defeat of Jefferson's antislavery proviso.

69. *JCC*, 8 January 1784, 27:13–14.

70. See, for example, ibid., 5 May 1784, 27: 341–48.

71. Ibid., 18–20 May 1784, 27:408–9, 411–18.

72. See Monroe to Jefferson, 20 and 25 May 1784, *LDC*, 21:633, 644–45.

73. Dana to Elbridge Gerry, 17 June 1784 (misdated as 1782), ibid., 21:688–89.

74. Monroe to Jefferson, 25 May 1784, ibid., 21:644–45.

75. Jefferson to Madison, 25 April 1784, ibid., 22:546.

76. Ibid.

77. Sheldon, *Williamson*, 152; Potts, "Hugh Williamson," 382.

78. Craige, *Federal Convention*, 127. See also Jefferson to Madison, 25 April 1784, *LDC*, "Notes," 22:547–48.

79. Peter Onuf, "Federalism, Republicanism, and the Origins of American Sectionalism," in *All Over the Map: Rethinking American Regions*, ed. Edward Ayers et al. (Baltimore: Johns Hopkins University Press, 1996), 36–37.

80. Spaight to Martin, 23 July 1784, *LDC*, 21:740; Spaight to Martin, 30 April 1784, *CSRNC*, 17:66.

81. Onuf, "Federalism," 36.

82. Spaight to Martin, 16 October 1784, *CSRNC*, 17:172–74.

83. *JCC*, 4 June 1784, 28:561–64. See also "Standing Committees," ibid., 28:713. During the same year, Spaight also served frequently on the Committee of the Week, ibid., 714–15.

84. Ibid., 9 August 1784, 28:634–45.

85. Spaight to Martin, 12 March 1784, *LDC*, 22:430.

86. Spaight to Iredell, 10 March 1785, ibid., 23:266. See also Spaight to Martin, 18 December 1784, *CSRNC*, 17:187.

87. *JCC*, 4 June 1784, 28:561–67.

88. Spaight to John Francis Mercer, 6 November 1784, quoted in "Notes" for Monroe to Madison, 15 November 1784, *LDC*, 22:21. Spaight's views may have been shaped in part by the "concerted scheme" of "Eastern Delegates" to "weaken the power of the union" by causing "the dissolution of the Committee of the States." See Spaight to Martin, 16 October 1784, *CSRNC*, 17:172–74.

89. Spaight to Caswell, 10 August 1785, cited in "Notes" for Spaight to Caswell, 5 June 1785, *LDC*, 23:437.

90. Caswell to William Davie, 1 March 1787, *CSRNC*, 20:627–28.

91. Beeman, *Plain, Honest Men*, 82, 59; Craige, *Federal Convention*, 105–30; Trenholme, *Ratification*, 147–58; Max Farrand, ed., *The Records of the Federal Convention of 1787* (hereafter *Records*), rev. ed., 3 vols. (New Haven: Yale University Press, 1937), 1:5, 3:590, 588; William Blount to John Gray Blount, 30 May 1787, in James H. Hutson, ed., *Supplement to Max Farrand's "The Records of the Federal Convention of 1787"* (New Haven: Yale University Press, 1987), 34.

92. Beeman, *Plain, Honest Men*, 52, 278, 291; Farrand, *Records*, 3:589–90.

93. Although Mercer attended the convention only briefly, he did manage to stir up some controversy over a list he had compiled during the proceedings for some unknown purpose. According to James McHenry, Mercer claimed that the list contained the names of about twenty delegates who favored the establishment of a monarchy, but most likely Mercer was just diddling McHenry. See Daniel Carroll to James Madison, 28 May 1788, in Farrand, *Records*, 3:305–6.

94. Rozbicki, *Culture and Liberty*, 203.

95. Craige, *Federal Convention*, 105. Shortly after the convention opened, Spaight seconded Alexander Hamilton's motion that would have made a free population the basis for each state's representation; Spaight never wavered from his original position on that issue.

96. Beeman, *Plain, Honest Men*, 82; Craige, *Federal Convention*, 105–7; Farrand, *Records*, 1:36, 2:540.

97. Craige, *Federal Convention*, 106–7; Farrand, *Records*, 1:390; Sheldon, *Williamson*, 59, 183.

98. Sheldon, *Willamson*, 183, 175.

99. Farrand, *Records*, 2:515, 526.

100. Spaight to Iredell, 12 August 1787, cited in Craige, *Federal Convention*, 188–89.

101. Farrand, *Records*, 1:218.

102. Beeman, *Plain, Honest Men*, 119.

103. Farrand, *Records*, 2:261.

104. Spaight to Iredell, 12 August 1787, cited in Craige, *Federal Convention*, 188–89.

105. Pauline Maier, *Ratification: The People Debate the Constitution, 1787–1788* (New York: Simon and Schuster, 2010), 406. Commentaries for and against the proposed constitution appeared in the *North Carolina Gazette*, 19 December 1787.

106. Beeman, *Plain, Honest Men*, 403.
107. Trenholme, *Ratification*, 104.
108. Quoted in ibid., 102.
109. Maier, *Ratification*, 420.
110. Jonathan Elliot, ed., *The Debates in the Several State Conventions on the Adoption of the Federal Constitution*, 5 vols. (Philadelphia and Washington, published by the editor, 1836–59), 4:207.
111. Ibid., 114–15.
112. Ibid., 115, 124.
113. Ibid., 81–82.
114. Ibid., 179–83, 139.
115. Ibid., 144.
116. Ibid., 205.
117. Ibid., 206–10.
118. Ibid., 251.
119. Powell, *North Carolina*, 228–29.
120. *Columbian Magazine* (Philadelphia), October 1788, cited in Andrews, "Spaight," 112; Frances Ingmire, *Craven County, C, Marriage Records, 1780–1867* (St. Louis: published by author, 1984), 106. Mary Leech's father served as a Federalist delegate to the Hillsborough convention of 1788. See Elliot, *Debates*, 4:250.
121. See, for example, Spaight to John Gray Blount, 20 August 1792, 11 June 1793, in *The John Gray Blount Papers*, ed. Alice Keith (Raleigh: Division of Archives and History, 1959), 2:210, 269–70.
122. Craige, *Federal Convention*, 128–29; Andrews, "Spaight," 114–15.
123. *North Carolina Gazette*, 1 September 1798; Watson, *Spaight*, 18–20; Powell, *North Carolina*, 234–38. See also Delbert Gilpatrick, *Jeffersonian Democracy in North Carolina, 1789–1816* (New York: Octagon Books, 1967); and David Fischer, *The Revolution of American Conservatism: The Federalist Party in the Era of Jeffersonian Democracy* (New York: Harper and Row, 1965).
124. On Spaight's inconsistent voting record (at least in terms of party affiliation), see U.S. Congress, *Journal of the House of Representatives of the United States* (Washington, D.C.: Gales & Seaton, 1789–), 5th Cong., 3rd sess., 10 December, 28 December 1798, 404, 421–22; 6th Cong., 1st sess., 9 January, 17 January, 25 January, 30 January 1799, 19 February 1800, 427–29, 439–40, 446–47, 456–57; 6th Cong., 2nd sess., 1 January, 10 February 1801, 749–50, 793–94.
125. Spaight to Blount, 28 May 1800, in *The John Gray Blount Papers*, ed. William Masterson (Raleigh: Division of Archives and History, 1965), 3:355.
126. The Federalists' agenda is presented succinctly in James Broussard, *The Southern Federalists, 1800–1816* (Baton Rouge: Louisiana State University Press, 1978), 35–38. For Spaight's voting record in 1801, see *House Journal*, 6th Cong., 2nd sess., 1 January, 2 January, 12 January, 13 January, 19 February, 21 February, 27 February, 28 February 1801, 749–52, 757–61, 771, 808–9, 816–17, 832–34.
127. See Dorothy Twohig, "'That Species of Property': Washington's Role in the Controversy over Slavery," in *George Washington Reconsidered*, ed. Don Higginbotham (Charlottesville: University of Virginia Press, 2001), 114–39.
128. See Spaight to John Gray Blount, *Blount Papers*, 13 January 1801, 18 December 1800, 22 December 1800, 3:471–72, 462, 464.

129. Watson, *Spaight*, 18–20.

130. *New York Gazette*, 11 September 1800.

131. Watson, *Spaight*, 20. Stanly defeated Spaight, 2,555 votes to 1,699; Spaight carried only Carteret and Craven Counties.

132. Lawrence, "Unique Career," 17; Diana Bell-Kite, "The Stanly-Spaight Duel and Honor Culture in the Antebellum South," *The Palace* 7 (Summer 2007): 3–4; Mrs. Max Abernethy, "The Spaight-Stanly Duel," *The State*, 18 (3 February 1951), 11, 17. See also Joanne Freeman, *Affairs of Honor: National Politics in the New Republic* (New Haven, Conn.: Yale University Press, 2001), especially chapter 4, "Dueling as Politics," 159–98.

133. Oscar and Lilian Handlin, *Liberty and Power, 1600–1760* (New York: Harper and Row, 1986), 233.

134. Rozbicki, *Culture and Liberty*, 232–33.

7

The Political Views of Richard Caswell and the Founding of the New Nation

Lloyd Johnson

Richard Caswell was the first and fifth governor of North Carolina, and he played a major role in the success of the Revolution in the state. With over twenty years of experience in the state assembly, he was popular among the citizens and became known as an advocate for the people. Caswell served as a delegate to the First and Second Continental Congresses held in Philadelphia. He coauthored the state's constitution in 1776, championed popular sovereignty, and was an early advocate of public schools and the establishment of a state university. As governor, he strengthened North Carolina's ties to the federal government. He supported revising the Articles of Confederation and became a proponent of the creation of a strong United States Constitution with separate executive, legislative, and judicial branches.

Richard Caswell was born in Baltimore County in the tiny seaport town of Joppa, Maryland, on 3 August 1729. The son of Richard Caswell and Christian Dallam, he was educated at an Anglican parish school in Maryland and worked in his father's mercantile business. At sixteen his family migrated from Maryland to eastern North Carolina, settling in a section of Johnston County that later became Dobbs County and is today Lenoir County. After he arrived in North Carolina, Caswell received his first government position, an apprentice to the surveyor general, and two years later he became a deputy surveyor general. In 1748 Caswell served as the deputy clerk of Johnston County, and a year later he was the clerk of court. In 1753 he became the sheriff of Johnston County, and soon after he began to read law under William Herritage, a prominent attorney and a member of the North Carolina assembly. Caswell's first wife was Mary Mackilwean, the daughter of James Mackilwean, the surveyor general. They had one son, William. Mary died in 1757, and Caswell married Sarah Herritage, the daughter of William Herritage, on 20 June 1758. Together they had eight children. Caswell accumulated over 9,000 acres of land, mostly situated in Dobbs County, but his holdings included land in Johnston, Orange, Cumberland, Tryon, Carteret, Washington, and Greene Counties and some western land in what later became Tennessee.[1]

Caswell's residence was "Red House," located near Stringer's Ferry on the Neuse River about a mile west of present-day Kinston. He was elected to the assembly, at the age of twenty-five, to represent Johnston County in 1754. That same year he also served as a militia officer and soon rose to the rank of lieutenant and later captain, a position he held for nearly ten years. He served in the assembly for over twenty years, and his first committee assignments dealt with revising the laws governing surplus lands. This subject created some tension among the settlers and the land agents. According to one biographer, "The quarrels over the fees, quit rents, and fraudulent practices of the land agents finally produced the Enfield Riots in 1759." A few years later Caswell was one of the commissioners who surveyed the boundary between Johnston and Pitt Counties.[2]

His twenty-year legislative career was extensive, and his activities in the assembly have been classified by one historian under four categories: "(1) trade and industry; (2) reforms of the court system and of its officials; (3) provisions for better finances and public defense; (4) humanitarian policies." Among his fellow members he was regarded as a leader when it came to these subjects.[3]

Caswell proposed bills to establish ferries and also worked to designate commissioners to make roads. In 1758, he proposed a bill that cut off Dobbs County from Johnston County. He also sponsored a bill requiring the justices to appoint commissioners to build four warehouses on the Neuse. Caswell promoted shipping through a bill that exempted shipbuilders from paying import and export duties on lead used for making gunpowder. Additionally, he sponsored a law to prevent the sale of trashy tobacco that required farmers to transport their tobacco in hogsheads, which would be inspected at tobacco warehouses. That same year he also presented a bill to make Tower Hill, later Kinston, the center of government in the colony by building a governor's house and public offices. This bill angered the assembly members from the Albemarle region, and years later it would be Governor William Tryon who made New Bern the seat of government for the province.[4]

In 1770, Caswell was elected the Speaker of the assembly, a position that made him the principal representative of popular opinion within the colonial government. While he actively promoted trade, he also had a concern for the health and welfare of the citizens of North Carolina. In 1773, he supported legislation that prohibited people infected with smallpox from traveling into the province. He hoped it would protect the colony's commercial interests. He also proposed bills to encourage the production of silkworms, but due to the cold climate silk production failed. Other bills of his promoted iron production in Chatham County, but this industry did not flourish until 1777, when the Revolutionary War increased the demand for iron.[5]

Although Caswell had no active role in the French and Indian War, he did work in the assembly to provide funding for the troops and for building and equipping forts. He recommended that the government issue treasury notes that bore interest, "guaranteed by a poll tax of two shillings on each taxable," and promoted taxes on "liquors and other consumption goods." He also served on a committee to see that the money was properly spent. He traveled to Fort Dobbs, a fort near modern-day Statesville that had been built to defend the settlers west of Salisbury. He and his committee members reported that the fort was not adequate to defend the western settlers and recommended that a stockade be constructed to protect the friendly Catawba Indians. He also found that the conditions at the fort at Topsail Inlet were inadequate because it had few "guns, powder or ball."[6]

In 1758, Caswell introduced a bill in the assembly to secure £50,000 from Parliament to reimburse the southern colonies for their costs incurred in the French and Indian War. Of that amount allocated by Parliament, North Carolina received only £7,789, even though the colony had spent over £66,000 in appropriations for the war. Half of the funds disbursed by Parliament went to the other colonies that did not contribute to the war effort.[7]

Following the French and Indian War, Caswell quarreled with Governor Arthur Dobbs over the auditing of public accounts, one of Caswell's duties as a member of the assembly. Caswell's committee recommended that the governor's accounts be examined by an auditor general and that copies of the audit be sent to England. The assembly, moreover, "ordered the treasurer to pay out no money by order of the governor and council without the approval of the house." The House responded by censuring the governor "for not laying before the house the accounts of monies paid out by his order and for failing to show for what purposes sums were drawn from the treasury."[8]

In 1765, Caswell was nominated by the House to replace John Starkey, the treasurer of the southern district, who had died in office. The Governor's

Council, jealous of the power the House had in financial affairs, nominated Lewis De Rossett for the position instead. The House warmly insisted on Caswell as its choice, yet the council refused to yield, and no treasurer was selected during that session. In 1773, Caswell was again appointed by the House as treasurer for the southern district. As one of his first duties, "he gave bond for £50,000 for the diligent and faithful collection of taxes from the sheriffs of the several counties to be paid to the assembly by him." This was an important and desirable office, and Governor Josiah Martin wrote a letter on 1 September 1774 to the Earl of Dartmouth attesting to Richard Caswell's character. He described Caswell as being "a man of the fairest and most unblemished character in the whole country, who has acted as the commissioner of the court of oyer and terminer to the universal satisfaction and contentment of all the people." Martin discussed the politics surrounding Caswell's appointment and noted that "the leaders of the faction hurried for the time the current of popularity against Mr. Caswell." Martin explained that this "was the true cause of opposition to these measures and that the courts of oyer and terminer would never have been brought into question if Mr. Caswell, the fittest man in the country, had not acted as judge in them."[9]

Caswell made significant reforms when it came to improving the court system in North Carolina, including those concerning the relief of insolvent debtors in prison and securing speedy hearings for those imprisoned for debt. He also became an advocate for the orphans of the province, helping craft a comprehensive law providing a special court session for orphans instead of relying on the court of pleas and quarter sessions and recommending that grand juries perform the work that was formerly left to the church wardens. Although his proposal was never enacted by the assembly, Caswell was also an early advocate for public education and proposed a small tax on land for the building of public schools. This became an important "step toward the colony's regarding it as its duty to care for the poor and the education of the young."[10]

Caswell considered reforming the court system as his best work in the assembly in the twenty years that he served. He introduced bills to better regulate the county clerks, whom he wanted to be honest and competent and who would swear they had not paid a bribe to secure their appointments. The clerks were to keep wills and letters of administration in books for that purpose, and they were also required to make annual reports to the secretary of the province. The Court Bill of 1762, primarily authored by Caswell, passed with few modifications. The situation changed when Governor Josiah Martin took office in 1771; he came with instructions from the Crown "to disallow the court laws unless the attachment clause were omitted." The attachment clause allowed the garnishment of property of nonresidents in certain cases of debt. In 1773, the struggle with the royal governor over the court laws continued. The assembly drew up a petition to the Crown "averring that the right of attaching estates of foreign debtors had long been exercised in the province as well as others." Caswell served on the committee to draw up the court bills while also functioning as one of three judges on the court of oyer and terminer. Caswell was regarded by the people as one of the advocates of their rights. Governor Martin strongly recommended that the assembly pass a court bill without the attachment clause. The assembly responded to Governor Martin, stating that "they could not agree with his mode of issuing attachments, but that the assembly would pass laws regulating the criminal justice of the province." This controversy came to a deadlock, evidenced by the fact that no courts were held in North Carolina from 6 March 1773 to 24 December 1774. Thus the origins of the Revolution had begun in North Carolina with the Committees of Safety taking over the functions needed to maintain good order.[11]

When the First Provincial Congress met at New Bern on 25 August 1774, Caswell was elected, along with Joseph Hewes and William Hooper, to attend the First Continental Congress to be held at Carpenter's Hall in Philadelphia. All three of these men were members of the Committee of Correspondence, which actively supported Boston's opposition to the Intolerable Acts. They also favored cooperation among the colonies in their resistance to Parliament.[12] However, it is not known what was discussed by the delegates at Carpenter's Hall, since the meeting was held in secret behind locked doors.

Governor Martin expressed his views of Caswell in a letter he wrote to the Earl of Dartmouth on 28 August 1775: "At his going to the first Congress and after his return, Caswell appeared to me to have embarked on the cause with reluctance that much extenuated his guilt. In my estimation he now shows himself to be the most active tool of sedition, although his professions still are averse to his ostensible conduct, and character which at the crisis of affairs serve but to aggravate his guilt and infamy."[13]

The Second Provincial Congress was held in New Bern on 5 April 1775. Caswell attended and presented the Continental Association's plans to the North Carolina delegates. The plan continued the boycott of British goods that had been begun by the local committees. It was hoped that this boycott would force Britain to repeal the Townshend Duties as a means of restoring the trade of British merchants. Hewes, Caswell, and John Penn were elected as delegates to the Second Continental Congress to be held in Philadelphia. Governor Martin retaliated by dissolving the assembly on 8 April 1775. This was the last time that the assembly met under royal authority.[14]

On their return from the Second Continental Congress, Caswell and the other North Carolina delegates encouraged public support for the Revolutionary War in an address they gave to the Committees of Safety on 19 June 1775. They said in part, "North Carolina alone remains an inactive spectator of this general defensive armament, supine and careless of her duty, it seems. Why have you been exempt from the act of Parliament restarting trade? Obviously, because Britain cannot keep up her naval force without you. . . . Preserve the small quantity of gunpowder among you. It will be the last resource when every other means of safety fails you. Great Britain has cut you off from further supplies. He betrays his country who sports it away. The crisis of America is not at a great distance."[15]

Caswell's actions infuriated Governor Martin, who decided to flee North Carolina. While he was aboard a Royal Navy ship anchored off the coast, he wrote a letter condemning Caswell, who had recently returned from Philadelphia: "Richard Caswell, who most of all had promoted sedition in the present convention with all his might, . . . remains here to superintend his movements and no doubt to inflame it with the extravagant spirit of that daring assembly in Philadelphia. I am credibly informed that at New Bern he had the insolence to reprehend the committee of safety for suffering me to remove from thence."[16]

The Third Provincial Congress met in North Carolina and gave unanimous approval for the acts and resolutions of the Continental Congress. Caswell was so busy serving as a treasurer and as a militia captain and paymaster of the troops that he had to give up his position as a member of the Second Continental Congress. His replacement was John Penn. Caswell accepted an appointment as commander of the minutemen in the New Bern District. He also served on a committee to secure the necessary sums of money for arms and ammunition and was appointed to a committee that examined how to pacify the former Regulators who had been defeated at the Battle of Alamance and who may have been reluctant to support the Revolution because they had been required in 1771 to take an oath of allegiance to the Crown following the defeat of the Regulator movement.[17]

His victory over the Highlanders at Moore's Creek Bridge, seventeen miles north of Wilmington, made Caswell a hero, along with fellow officer Alexander Lillington. Caswell expressed his zeal for the Revolution in a letter dated 8 February 1776 to his son William, who was serving with the Second Continental Regiment: "If other officers are dissatisfied with the service, it is no rule you should be. I hope my dear child, the virtuous cause you are engaged in and the hope you have of giving the little assistance in your power to the relief of your country will stimulate you to put up with hardships, fatigue and other inconveniences which others may shudder at, to ward off that slavery under which it is attempted to put the present and future generations in this once happy land."[18]

When the Fifth Provincial Congress met at Halifax on 12 November 1776, the popularity won at Moore's Creek Bridge enabled Caswell to secure the necessary assembly votes to become the first governor of the newly independent state. He was also president of congress and served on a committee to write the state's first constitution and a bill of rights that became known as the "Declaration of Rights." The constitution embraced popular sovereignty and was very similar to Virginia's Declaration of Rights. There were strict limitations placed on the power of the governor. He was to be elected annually by the General Assembly, and he could serve for only three consecutive years. He also could not transact important executive business without the approval of the executive council. The governor had no veto power, and he had no authority to dissolve the assembly, as the previous royal governors had done. The constitution also had a clause for establishing public schools as well as a state university.[19]

In February 1777, Caswell took the oath of office in front of Tryon's Palace in New Bern. As governor, three problems required his constant attention during the Revolution: disturbances by the Indians on the frontier, the periodic coastal raids of the British, and the intrigues of the numerous Loyalists throughout the state. Caswell's duties were further compounded by problems maintaining a standing army in the state militia and also by the Continental army, a limited treasury, the lack of manufacturing, "the scarcity of ships in which to import supplies from abroad," and "the dearth of officers with technical training in military affairs."[20]

In August 1777, Caswell made a treaty with the Cherokee Indians to prevent a possible Indian war in the western counties. Caswell "tried to reconcile Savanuca, the Raven of Chota, by assuring him that he had issued a proclamation forbidding trespassing" on Indian lands "in the future on pain of punishment." He also gave notice that the last assembly had voided all entries of Indian lands with the requirement that all money paid for the lands be returned to the state. This treaty produced lasting results in Indian and white relations, and during Caswell's administration many of the Cherokees remained at peace with the settlers of North Carolina "and carefully observed their promises made in the treaty although the extensive encroachments of the white men on the Indian lands stirred up bitter resentment."[21]

Caswell also worked to improve the state's coastal defenses against British raids, a concern that was a low priority for western assembly members. In 1778, Caswell told the assembly that "our coast is much infested with the enemy constantly landing men and plundering." In 1779, legislators finally approved of resolutions to defend Ocracoke. They likewise commissioned a ship named for Governor Caswell to help defend the coast. Yet shortly after the ship went into service it ran aground in Bogue Sound. Caswell ordered the commissioning of other ships to protect the coast, but many of these attempts proved to be disappointing. Privateering was more successful in the state, and Caswell authorized a number of privateers who went on daring adventures and "made large profits by capturing prizes and selling their cargoes in the ports where supplies were in great demand." By contrast, the state treasury was depleted during the Revolution with no funds to repair forts around New Bern or Wilmington, and in 1781 these towns were easily taken by the British.[22]

Despite the fact that the Highlanders met defeat at Moore's Creek Bridge, the Loyalists continued to create havoc in the state. They had a demoralizing effect on the citizens because they tried to prevent enlistments. In February 1777, 150 men were called into service of the militia to prevent Loyalist uprisings in the western counties of Tryon, Surry, and Rowan. By April 1777, the assembly passed a law that gave all who refused to take an oath of allegiance to the state sixty days to leave North Carolina. Many departed by ship in July and October of that year.[23]

Throughout the war Caswell had to deal with a depleted treasury, but he also had to secure supplies like salt, deerskins, clothes, and food for the troops. While many North Carolina troops were at Valley Forge during the winter of 1777, some of them were sick or barefoot and lacked adequate supplies to participate in drills. Aware of this situation, Caswell complained, "Were I to exert every nerve and influence in my power (and no man is more willing than myself), it would be to very little purpose until the Assembly meets." He then described his varied activities: "I am busy daily buying clothes, leather skins, salt, pork and provisions, setting manufactures to work and procuring wagons and boats to send goods on to Pennsylvania." Sometimes he even used his own credit to obtain these goods for the troops.[24]

As a wartime governor, Caswell also worked to encourage manufacturing. North Carolina was known for being an exporter of deerskins, and in November 1777 Congress approved a resolution requesting that Caswell provide as many deerskins as possible for the army. He was also responsible for getting purchasing agents across the state to secure provisions for the military. Men in various parts of the state packed pork and collected deerskins and other supplies for the troops. Caswell also worked to get iron extracted from the ironworks owned by John Wilcox in Chatham County to be used in munitions and other iron products for the war effort. On 8 January 1778, he wrote William

Aylett, "I think no labor or trouble too great to be performed in these necessary matters for the public. I hope you will ask anything you think in my power without apologizing. It is a duty I owe the country I wish to save."[25]

Caswell also had to contend with morale issues and the recruiting and enlisting of troops for the state. Caswell was required by "Congress to raise nine of eighty-eight battalions apportioned among the several states according to their population." He dealt with draft riots occurring in some counties. Moreover, as time passed, he faced a decline in enthusiasm for the war among the general population. He also coped with reluctant officers who had not properly trained new recruits to fight against the British army. In a letter to Thomas Burke, who represented the state in Congress, Caswell complained that many officers, "nay, the greatest number of them were far from using the diligence I could wish. Their indolence seems such as to do no honor to their country or to themselves."[26]

Caswell's greatest difficulty during the war was summed up in letters written in May 1779 by Brigadier General William Bryan and General Benjamin Lincoln in May 1780 to Caswell in which they expressed their disgust with the militia system. Bryan's revulsion to the system caused him to resign his position. He summed up the situation: "I cannot therefore help saying it is my opinion that armies thus raised, officered, armed, and supplied must eventually bring dishonor on the command, as it would be very difficult for the best and most experienced commander to arrange them in such order as to insure any degree of success when opposed by a Regular, disciplined force."[27]

Being even more candid than Bryan, Benjamin Lincoln criticized the militia and presented many arguments to Caswell "against depending on it for defense." He indicated that the British had landed on James Island and were preparing to take Charleston. He revealed that the North Carolina militia would not stay any longer in South Carolina, "though Governor Edward Rutledge of South Carolina offered them a bounty of $300 and a suit of clothes if they would remain three months." But after the siege of Charleston had begun, Lincoln had not heard from North Carolina regarding his appeal that the assembly approve 3,000 additional troops to help in the defense of South Carolina: "He had requested the officer in charge of the other 2,000 militia in North Carolina to assemble the men on the border so as to be ready for marching to the relief of Charleston on short notice."[28]

In 1780 Caswell's third term as governor of the state expired, and in May of that year he was appointed major general of the state militia. The assembly also appointed Caswell to head a militia of 4,000 troops to march into South Carolina with the goal of defeating British general Charles Cornwallis's troops that were now moving into the backcountry after Charleston fell to the British in May 1780. Caswell saw action in the Battle of Camden in mid-August 1780; it included Continentals from Virginia, Maryland, Delaware, North Carolina, and South Carolina. The battle commenced when "Cornwallis ordered Colonel James Webster to begin the attack and concentrated on the two Maryland brigades. As the British came on firing and huzzing, the Virginia militia broke" and dispersed in a panic. This exposed "Caswell's militia to attack both on the flank and in the front. They immediately gave way without firing and threw away their arms in their terror." Caswell did all he could to restore order among his panic-stricken militia. The Americans found themselves outnumbered, 1,300 British troops to 1,000 Continentals, and they could not stop the flanking movements of the British. "The fighting lasted about an hour, during which about 300 Continentals were killed"; in contrast, there were very few casualties among the militia "as they had fled without firing a shot, escaping into the woods and swamps."[29]

Following Caswell's defeat at Camden, the assembly, meeting at Halifax in September, replaced Caswell with Brigadier General William Smallwood of Maryland, who became the major general of the state. Caswell also resigned his position in the militia, but he remained in good standing in North Carolina. The assembly expressed its appreciation and high regard for Caswell's service to the state and recognized "the merits of General Caswell and of his singular services of the state." Caswell's military performance during the Revolution has been evaluated by Caswell's mid-twentieth-century biographer, Clayton Brown Alexander: "It may be said that he was not pre-eminent as commander, for he did not plan or execute independently any military operations of major importance, and he showed no such remarkable skill in handling men on the field of battle as he did in civil affairs or political life. Yet, on the other hand, he did not deserve to be blamed for the failure of the militia to stand their ground at Camden."[30]

Following his military service in the Revolution, Caswell was again elected to the senate to represent Dobbs County, and on 2 February 1781 he presented a bill approved by the assembly "substituting for the Board of War a council extraordinary to advise the governor." Caswell also went on a trip to the frontier settlements to speculate in the purchase of land in Sullivan and Washington Counties, to attempt to pacify the Indians, and to improve his health. For several months, he had been on the verge of a breakdown, and he often complained of "giddiness in the head." Although not known at the time, he perhaps suffered from high blood pressure.[31]

In May 1782, Caswell was named comptroller general of the state, a position he held until May 1785. He was again elected governor of the state and served from 1785 to 1788. He had been a candidate for governor in 1784, but he lost to Alexander Martin, who received sixty-six votes in the assembly to Caswell's forty-nine. In the next election for governor, Caswell received large majorities in both houses of the assembly. In his remaining years as governor, his administration primarily dealt with three major issues: "(1) the insurrection of the state of Franklin; (2) the menace of the Indian attacks; and (3) relations with the federal government."[32]

The desire of the inhabitants of the western counties to set up an independent government separate from North Carolina was a problem that had not been resolved in Governor Martin's administration. John Sevier, the spokesman for the western settlers, "reminded Caswell how pressingly Congress had requested the cession of the western territory ever since the year 1780." He continued that there was a "necessity of protecting themselves from the common enemy that always infested that part of the world and had compelled the people of Franklin to act as they had done." On 14 May 1785, Caswell responded to Sevier's concerns and indicated that goods would be supplied to the Indians. He helped negotiate a treaty through the efforts of William Blount, who was named as a commissioner to the Indians at Fort Rutledge, South Carolina. The treaty with the Cherokees improved conditions in the west, and Caswell hoped that the settlers would return their allegiance to North Carolina. A year after the assembly approved the treaty, Sevier advised Caswell that its terms had been accepted by the western settlers. The legislature of North Carolina pardoned the settlers in January 1787 provided they would return as loyal citizens and pay taxes to the state. Nevertheless, by the spring and summer of 1788, the situation among the western inhabitants had deteriorated, and "the assembly of the state of Franklin threatened to imprison or fine any officers who accepted commissions from North Carolina."[33]

On 1 May 1788, Caswell responded to the worsening conditions in the west caused by fears that the Indians were going to be supplied by European powers to attack the settlers. In an address Caswell made to the western inhabitants, he said, "I have received information that the former Contention between the Citizens of those Counties respecting the severing such Counties from the State & erecting them into a separate & Free and Independent Government" had been revived. Caswell hoped that further reflection on the issues without violence or bloodshed would bring about "the necessity of Mutual Friendship and the Ties of Brotherly love being strongly cemented among you." Caswell wanted to prevent a civil war between the settlers and the Indians, and he warned, "If such an event should take place, that Government will supinely look on and see you Cutting each other's throats without interfering and exerting her powers to reduce the disobedient."[34]

North Carolina sent troops to the Cumberland in February 1788, but before they had engaged with the Indians, Indian attacks on the settlers appear to have subsided. Shortly thereafter the state of Franklin collapsed, and "the General Assembly of North Carolina passed an act of oblivion and pardon for all, and accepted Sevier as a member of the senate." Moreover, Caswell, through his diplomacy, "first-hand knowledge of the country beyond the mountains and . . . kindly sympathy and understanding of the frontiersman made reconciliation possible."[35]

During Caswell's final years as governor he worked diligently to strengthen the state's relations with the federal government. He had a profound influence on the founding of the new nation. "The amendments to the Articles of Confederation proposed by Robert Morris were supported by North Carolina, but failed to get approval from the other states," noted Alexander. Caswell supported Congress in the peace treaty that ended the war between the United States and Great Britain. He also supported the federal government's decision to send troops to the Great Lakes region to defend American forts in that area. Caswell endorsed the request of John Jay, the secretary for foreign affairs, "that retaliatory duties should be imposed by the state on British vessels." In response the assembly "levied a duty of five shillings a ton on vessels from countries refusing to make treaties of commerce with the United States."[36]

With regard to the central government, Caswell in 1786 favored amending the Articles of Confederation. In a letter to James Boudin, the governor of Massachusetts, on 24 June, Caswell expressed his approval of "the proposal of Virginia for holding at Annapolis, Maryland a Convention of Delegates from the several states in the Union for the purpose of considering trade with the United States." He then appointed five delegates to the Annapolis convention. But the only one who attended was Hugh Williamson, who reached Annapolis the day the convention ended.[37]

Charles Thomason, the secretary to Congress, sent a circular letter to the governors on 11 February 1787: "It is expedient that on the second Monday in May next a Convention of Delegates who shall have been appointed by the several States, be held at Philadelphia, for the sole and express purpose of revising the Articles of Confederation." The recommendation for a general convention to be held at Philadelphia the following May to revise the Articles of Confederation was accepted by the General Assembly, and five more delegates were appointed.[38]

Caswell was elected one of the original five delegates to attend the Constitutional Convention, but shortly after his appointment he wrote the North Carolina Council of State and declined for health reasons. He appointed William Blount in his stead. In a letter to Blount dated 24 April 1787, Caswell said, "Believe me it gives me pleasure that my place will be so well supplied not only on my own account but for the dignity and honor of the state." Willie Jones, who refused to serve, was replaced by Hugh Williamson. In a letter to Williamson, Caswell wrote, "Mr. Willie Jones has declined his appointment, I have done myself the honor of naming you to fill the vacancy." Caswell further noted that the Council of State agreed unanimously. Both Blount and Williamson favored replacing the Articles of Confederation with a stronger constitution. Only Alexander Martin opposed changes to the Articles of Confederation. William R. Davie and Richard Dobbs Spaight were also strong believers in strengthening the national government.[39]

Caswell frequently corresponded with the delegates, and oftentimes he supplied them with sympathetic and encouraging letters. After Davie agreed to serve as a delegate to the convention, Caswell wrote, "Your favor from Warrenton I received by my son Winston and am very glad you accept appointment of deputy to the Convention." Caswell had a concern that the delegates receive adequate compensation for their service to Congress, "especially if their attendance should be longer than first it was apprehended might be necessary, and as they are to account it has been judged proper to grant them warrants for another month's allowance." Thus the delegates were provided sixty-four pounds per month to cover their living expenses in Philadelphia. The delegates to the convention were also granted the same franking privileges as the members of Congress.[40]

In a letter to the delegates Caswell wrote on 1 July 1787, he expressed his strong support for their work at the convention: "Your Task is arduous, your undertaking is of such magnitude as to require Time for Deliberations and Consideration, and altho' I know each Gentleman must sensibly feel for his own private concerns in being so long absent from them . . . I am convinced your wishes to promote that happiness to your Country are such as to induce you to attend to the completing this business if possible. Anything I can do which may tend towards making your stay agreeable shall be most cheerfully attended to & I shall be most happy at all times in rendering you service or receiving any communications or advice from you."[41]

In late May 1787, William Blount informed Caswell that "on the 24th Inst. . . . only six states had appeared" at the Continental Congress and that "North Carolina four Members present had." He added, "For some days past not more than five States have appeared on the floor of Congress Chamber, it is generally believed that there will not appear a Sufficient Number to form a Congress until the Convention rises." By the end of the month, Caswell noted that he had "not learned that a Convention had formed," and only the state of Virginia was fully represented. "Only Colo. Spaight of our Deputies was arrived at Philadelphia then Govr. Martin & Colo. Davie are gone on. Mr. Jones has resigned and Dr. Williamson appointed in his stead and gone forward." He added, "Mr. Blount is appointed in my stead"; he was to leave Congress in May when his six months' "tour of duty would end and I have reason to believe he is before this attending the Convention." William Blount, writing from New York to Caswell on 10 July 1787, expressed his intention to leave the convention and return to Congress: "I conceived it more for the benefit and honor of the State, in which Opinion my Colleagues in the Convention agreed, that I return with Mr. Hawkins and represent the State in Congress than to continue in the Convention." In late August, Blount wrote Caswell from Philadelphia explaining why he did not attend every session of the convention: "I was not present all the time the Convention were debating and fixing the principles of the Government. I have been and mean to continue to be present while the detail is under Consideration that is until the Business of the Convention is completed."[42]

As the debates in Philadelphia continued throughout the summer months, Caswell, in a letter written from his home in Kinston to Richard Dobbs Spaight, made clear his support for a strong centralized federal government: "The Convention in my judgement have done wisely in enjoining secrecy in their Members, was the case otherwise it would give more room to Bablers & Scriblers to exercise their powers than they can be at liberty to take in their present case." Caswell expressed his belief that "a National Parliament and Supreme Executive with adequate powers to the Government of the Union will be more suitable to our situation & circumstances than any other." Moreover, Caswell wanted "an independent Judicial department to decide any contest that may happen between the United States and individual States & between one state and another." He closed his letter by recommending that the convention persevere to the end.[43]

In a letter dated 14 June 1787, the delegates described to Richard Caswell how they "sit from day to day. Saturdays included, it is not possible for us to determine when the business before us can be finished." They continued, "Several members of the Convention have their wives here and other Gentlemen have sent for theirs." They went on to complain how the North Carolina currency "is subject to considerable Decrements when reduced to Current Coin." In a brief letter to Caswell written from Philadelphia on 19 June, Davie told Caswell,

"We move slowly in our business; it is indeed a work of great delicacy and difficulty, impeded at every step by jealousy and jarring interests." On 3 July, Richard Dobbs Spaight told a friend that "the Convention has made, as yet but little progress in the Business they have met on, and it is a matter of uncertainty when they will finish. Secrecy being enjoined I can make no communications on that head." Toward the end of July Alexander Martin sent Caswell another report on the federal convention. He informed him about the secrecy of their deliberations, stating that "this Caution was thought prudent, least unfavorable Representations might be made by imprudent printers of the many crude matters & things daily uttered and produced in this Body, which are unavoidable." He told Caswell that he was not sure when the nation's business would be completed among the thirteen independent states. He concluded, "United America must have one general Interest to be a Nation, at the same time preserving the particular Interest of the Individual States." On 20 August, Alexander Martin told Caswell that "much time has been employed in drawing the outlines of the Subjects of their Deliberations in which as much unanimity has prevailed as could be well expected from so many Sentiments Arising in twelve independent Sovereign Bodies." He noted that Rhode Island had boycotted the convention and that progress was slow and tedious. He believed, though, that the work of the convention would be finished by the middle of September. Although he could not tell Caswell what the delegates at the convention had done, "I can tell you negatively what they have not done. They are not about to create a King as hath been represented unfavorably in some of the eastern States, so that you are not to expect the Bishop Oznaburg or any prince or great man of the World to rule this Country."[44]

The delegates also gave an appraisal of their deliberations in Congress during the summer. Writing from Philadelphia, they informed Caswell of their work: "The Convention having on the 26th of last Month finished the outline of the Amendments proposed to the Federal system, the business was of course Committed for detail" and they had "the pleasure to inform your excellency that the report was received on yesterday." After three months, the convention was ready to submit its proposal to the states for approval.[45]

The delegates from North Carolina did finish their work at the Constitutional Convention on 18 September 1787. In their letter to Richard Caswell they said that they had "many things to hope from a National Government and the chief thing we had to fear from such a Government was the Risque of unequal or heavy Taxation." They further hoped "that the Southern States in general and North Carolina in particular are well secured on that head by the proposed system." With regard to the Three-Fifths Compromise they noted that "five blacks are only counted as three" and "a navigation Act or the power to regulate Commerce in the Hands of the National Government by which American ships and Seaman may be fully employed" was a reasonable concession. "North Carolina does not appear to us to have given up *anything*," because North Carolina was an independent state likely to take the lead in shipbuilding. They closed their letter by indicating that "there are other Considerations of great Magnitude involved in the system, but we cannot exercise your patience with a further detail, but submit it with the utmost deference."[46]

With the work of the convention completed, Caswell submitted the Constitution to the General Assembly on 2 November 1787, accompanied with a letter of support from the state's deputies. The Constitution stipulated that the voters of the states had the responsibility to select a convention to consider ratifying the document. The General Assembly approved such a convention to be held at Hillsborough.[47]

According to an anonymous writer to the *New York Daily Advertiser* on 20 June 1788, representing Dobbs County on the Federalist ticket were "Richard Caswell and his son, Winston; his brother-in-law, John Herritage; James Glasgow, then secretary of state; and Benjamin Sheppard." These were well-known men, experienced in public affairs, who were opposed by five less-distinguished individuals who made up the Anti-Federalist ticket. When the election returns were tabulated on Saturday night, "the intense feeling grew to consternation as the count went on. The total number of votes cast at Kinston was 372," and the tabulation of the first 282 ballots showed that the Anti-Federalists were leading by nearly forty votes over the Federalist candidates. Fearful that "Dobbs County would be disgraced by putting 'preacher Baker before Governor Caswell,' the Federalists decided on a daring plan to prevent further counting of the votes." Candles were extinguished, "and in the darkness the ballot box was forcibly taken from Sheriff Benjamin Caswell, who had been knocked down." The next day "the box was found near the jail broken open and the ballots scattered. Both sides picked up ballots and claimed favorable results."[48]

When the convention met in Hillsborough, the five Federalists took their seats, but they were met with strong protests. The Anti-Federalists from Dobbs County who were refused seats at the convention objected, as did their allies from elsewhere in the state. Despite all the efforts of the Federalists, "there were only two delegates in the convention from the counties west of the mountains who voted for ratification of the Constitution." Opposition from the Anti-Federalists was so intense that it was almost a year before the assembly approved another convention to be held in Fayetteville in the fall of 1789. Caswell was no longer the governor, but he was again elected to the senate to represent Dobbs County.[49]

It was Caswell, as Speaker of the state senate, who made the motion in the assembly for a convention to be held in Fayetteville on 16 November 1789. Recent scholarship suggests that North Carolina's reasons for not joining the union are complex. J. Edwin Hendricks noted that North Carolina's hesitancy "belied its reluctance in approving the Constitution." The state remained out of the union to weave individual and state rights "more firmly into the fabric of the new order."[50] By that time a bill of rights had been introduced in Congress, its introduction swayed many Anti-Federalists in North Carolina to support the Constitution.

Caswell was in Fayetteville as a delegate to the convention that later approved in December 1789 the charter to establish the University of North Carolina. Caswell died at the age of sixty on 10 November 1789, a month before the assembly chartered the university and six days before the Constitution was to be ratified by the state. Caswell's old friend William Blount was put in charge of his funeral arrangements. The funeral procession made its way to Market Square, where outdoor eulogies were read. Caswell's body was taken back to Kinston, and he was buried in the family cemetery at Tower Hill.

Caswell's public service began in 1754 and ended in 1789. Throughout his long political career, he was a member of the assembly, elected twice to serve in the Continental Congress, "and four times a member of the provincial congress, presiding over the last one, which drew up the first constitution of this state." He was a true patriot "who sacrificed his own personal gains for the good of the state."[51] With over thirty years of public service, he was popular among the people. He believed in popular sovereignty and was an advocate for the creation of public schools and the establishment of a state university. He believed in a strong centralized federal government, and as a Federalist he strongly encouraged North Carolina to adopt the United States Constitution.

NOTES

1. Lindley S. Butler, "Caswell, Richard," in *American National Biography*, ed. John A. Garraty and Mark C. Carnes (New York: Oxford University Press, 1999), 4:566–67; Eugene C. Brooks, "Richard Caswell," in *Biographical History of North Carolina: From Colonial Times to the Present*, ed. Samuel A. Ashe (Greensboro, N.C.: Charles L. Van Noppen, 1905), 3:65–79; Charles L. Holloman, "Caswell, Richard," in *Dictionary of North Carolina Biography*, ed. William S. Powell (Chapel Hill: University of North Carolina Press, 1979), 1:343–44; Michael Hill, ed., *The Governors of North Carolina* (Raleigh: Office of Archives and History, 2007), 25–26; Kellie Slappey, "Richard Caswell," North Carolina History Project, accessed 12 September 2015, http://www.northcarolinahistory.org/encyclopedia/476/entry; Clayton Brown Alexander, "The Training of Richard Caswell," *North Carolina Historical Review* 23, no. 1 (1946): 13–31; W. Keats Sparrow, ed., "The First

of Patriots and Best of Men": Richard Caswell in Public Life (Kinston, N.C.: Lenoir County Colonial Commission, 2007). Material on Caswell can also be found in William L. Saunders, ed., *Colonial Records of North Carolina*, 10 vols. (Raleigh, N.C.: P. M. Hale, 1886–90); Walter Clark, ed., *The State Records of North Carolina*, 20 vols. (Goldsboro, N.C.: Nash Brothers, 1895–1911); Richard Caswell Papers, Southern Historical Collection, the Wilson Library, University of North Carolina at Chapel Hill (hereafter SHC); Richard Caswell Papers, North Carolina Division of Archives and History, Raleigh; and Clayton Brown Alexander, "The Public Career of Richard Caswell" (Ph.D. diss., University of North Carolina, 1930).

2. Alexander, "Training of Richard Caswell," 21.
3. Ibid., 23.
4. Ibid., 22–23.
5. Ibid., 24.
6. Ibid., 25.
7. Ibid.
8. Ibid., 26.
9. Ibid., 26–27; Saunders, *Colonial Records*, 9:1052.
10. Alexander, "Training of Richard Caswell," 28.
11. Ibid., 29–31.
12. Clayton Brown Alexander, "Richard Caswell, Versatile Leader of the Revolution," *North Carolina Historical Review* 22, no. 2 (1946): 119–21.
13. Ibid., 119; Saunders, *Colonial Records*, 10:232; Vernon O. Stumpf, *Josiah Martin: The Last Royal Governor of North Carolina* (Durham, N.C.: Carolina Academic Press, 1986), 85.
14. Alexander, "Richard Caswell, Versatile Leader," 121.
15. Ibid., 123; Saunders, *Colonial Records*, 10:26.
16. Quoted in Alexander, "Richard Caswell, Versatile Leader," 123.
17. Ibid., 124.
18. Quoted in ibid., 125.
19. Ibid., 128. For a discussion on state constitution-making in the Revolutionary period, see Marc W. Kruman, *Between Authority and Liberty: State Constitution Making in Revolutionary America* (Chapel Hill: University of North Carolina Press, 1997), 145–50.
20. Alexander, "Richard Caswell, Versatile Leader," 129–30.
21. Ibid., 130–31.
22. Ibid., 132–33.
23. Ibid., 133.
24. Ibid., 136; Clark, *State Records*, 13:42.
25. Quoted in Alexander, "Richard Caswell, Versatile Leader," 138.
26. Quoted in ibid., 139.
27. Quoted in ibid., 140.
28. Ibid., 140–41.
29. Clayton Brown Alexander, "Richard Caswell's Military and Later Public Services," *North Carolina Historical Review* 23, no. 3 (1946): 295.
30. Ibid., 297–98.
31. Ibid., 259.
32. Ibid., 302.
33. Ibid., 303.
34. Ibid., 304–5; Clark, *State Records*, 20:305.

35. Alexander, "Richard Caswell's Military and Later Public Services," 306.

36. Ibid., 308–9.

37. Richard Caswell to James Boudoin, 24 June 1786, Richard Caswell Papers, North Carolina Division of Archives and History; Alexander, "Richard Caswell's Military and Later Public Services," 309.

38. Circular letter from Charles Thomson to the state governors, 11 February 1787, SHC; Richard Caswell to William Richardson Davie, 7 January 1787, SHC.

39. Richard Caswell to William Blount, 24 April 1787, SHC; Richard Caswell to the North Carolina Council of State, 14 March 1787, ibid.; Richard Caswell to Hugh Williamson, 14 March 1787, ibid.; Alexander, "Richard Caswell's Military and Later Public Services," 309.

40. Alexander, "Richard Caswell's Military and Later Public Services," 309; Richard Caswell to William Richardson Davie, 15 April 1787, SHC.

41. Richard Caswell to William Richardson Davie et al., 1 July 1787, SHC; Resolves of Congress, 23 April 1787, SHC.

42. William Blount to Richard Caswell, 28 May 1787, SHC; Richard Caswell to Anthony Bledsoe, 31 May 1787, ibid.; William Blount to Richard Caswell, 10 July 1787, ibid.; William Blount to Richard Caswell, 20 August 1787, ibid.

43. Richard Caswell to Richard Dobbs Spaight, 26 July 1787, ibid.

44. Alexander Martin et al. to Richard Caswell, 14 June 1787, ibid.; William Richardson Davie to Richard Caswell, 19 June 1787, in James H. Hutson, ed., *Supplement to Max Farrand's "The Records of the Federal Convention of 1787"* (New Haven: Yale University Press, 1987), 97; Richard Dobbs Spaight to James Iredell, 3 July 1787, in Max Farrand, ed., *The Records of the Federal Convention of 1787*, 4 vols. (New Haven: Yale University Press, 1937), 3:54; Alexander Martin to Richard Caswell, 27 July 1787, SHC; Alexander Martin to Richard Caswell, 20 August 1787, SHC.

45. Alexander Martin et al. to Richard Caswell, 7 July 1787, SHC.

46. William Blount, Richard Dobbs Spaight, and Hugh Williamson to Richard Caswell, 18 September 1787, ibid.

47. Alexander, "Richard Caswell's Military and Later Public Services," 310.

48. Ibid.; Louise Irby Trenholme, *The Ratification of the Federal Constitution in North Carolina* (New York: Columbia University Press, 1932), 111–13. The campaign and election have also been described by Pauline Maier in *Ratification: The People Debate the Constitution, 1787–1788* (New York: Simon and Schuster, 2010), 403–408.

49. Trenholme, *Ratification*, 114–15.

50. J. Edwin Hendricks, "Joining the Federal Union," in *The North Carolina Experience: An Interpretive and Documentary History*, ed. Lindley S. Butler and Alan D. Watson (Chapel Hill: University of North Carolina Press, 1984), 147–70, 157. See also Richard Beeman, *Plain, Honest Men: The Making of the American Constitution* (New York: Random House, 2009), 403–5; and Elisha P. Douglass, *Rebels and Democrats: The Struggle for Equal Political Rights and Majority Rule during the American Revolution* (Chicago: Quadrangle Books, 1965), 130–35.

51. John C. Cavanagh, *Decision at Fayetteville: The North Carolina Ratification Convention and General Assembly of 1789* (Raleigh: Division of Archives and History, 1989), 22–23; Alexander, "Richard Caswell's Military and Later Public Services," 311–12.

James Iredell

Revolutionist, Constitutionalist, Jurist

Willis P. Whichard

North Carolina's contributions to the establishment of the United States were, in no small degree, coterminous with those of James Iredell. He was a leading essayist for American independence, an intellectual and political leader in creating a new government, and a judicial defender and promoter of the government created. Indeed, unlike many of his Revolutionary era contemporaries, Iredell made some of his most important contributions after the Revolution and after the Constitution was adopted.

Iredell's origins made him improbable for these roles. Family poverty had impelled his voyage to America to assume a customs post in the North Carolina village of Edenton.[1] The timing was propitious for the roles he would assume for his new country.

Iredell's wealthy bachelor uncle counseled him, "The less you meddle with politics the better. As you are a King's officer, stand neuter at least." Had Iredell heeded this advice, he would have been lost to history. He instead took "an open and eager part in rebellion," making significant contributions to the political debate of the period and earning descriptions such as "one of the ablest of the Founders" and "the letter writer of the war . . . [with] no equal amongst his contemporaries."[2]

Friction between Britain and the colonies was extensive, and by the 1760s Iredell's friends predicted a break with England if the trend continued.[3] Nevertheless, Iredell came to the Revolutionary cause reluctantly. As late as June 1776, he wrote publicly that despite great provocations, a continuing connection to

Great Britain remained preferable. He might assent to independence, however, if it was necessary for America's safety.[4]

For some time Iredell had been writing letters to further the American cause. The first, published in September 1773, responded to the royal governor's rejection of laws allowing provincial courts to attach property of defaulting debtors residing in England. Acting under royal directives, the governor established courts like the harsh prerogative tribunals of earlier English history. Writing as "A Planter," Iredell began to etch his political essays across the pages of history by attacking the clandestine rules of the new courts as "inconsistent with the very idea of civil liberty."[5] "The law of discretion," he concluded, "is the law of tyrants, and can never be admitted in any free state."[6]

In September 1774, a second major polemic assailed the concept of parliamentary sovereignty over America. If Parliament had absolute dominion, Iredell posited, the colonists had no liberty. Such a state was "the very definition of slavery," and the Crown would be "fatally deceived" if it thought the colonies would "patiently bear" these hardships. Americans were not, he concluded, "conquered subjects."[7]

Iredell's next offering, "The Principles of an American Whig," was written early in the Revolution and bears unmistakable traces of consanguinity with the Declaration of Independence. Because it appears to predate the latter document, it is easy to believe Jefferson was familiar with it and drew upon it. Language from the two discourses is illustrative.

The Declaration affirms a divinely granted right to the pursuit of happiness. "Principles" declaims "that mankind were intended to be happy, at least that God Almighty gave them the power of being so, if they would properly exert the means . . . bestowed upon them."

The Declaration avers that governments are instituted to secure rights to life, liberty, and the pursuit of happiness and that when government becomes destructive of these ends, the people may alter or abolish it. "Principles" proclaims that when government deviates from these ends, and freedom and happiness are thereby endangered, government is no longer entitled to allegiance.

Prudence dictates that governments should not be changed "for light and transient causes," the Declaration attests, but when "abuses and usurpations" evince a design for absolute despotism, a duty arises to establish a new government. "Principles" maintains that subjects of government should long forbear before arriving at "the last stage of opposition," but not beyond the point at which government "proceeds so far as to interfere with the great law of common happiness nature has ordained for all mankind."

Finally, like the Declaration, "Principles" recites British abuses against the colonies, including the Stamp Act, other duties and taxation, and the dispatch of troops to Massachusetts.[8]

In "Causes of the American Revolution," another wartime essay, Iredell chronicled events since the Stamp Act that had brought the empire to the verge of dissolution. The only American crime, he wrote, was "*an ardent love of liberty,*" while different principles motivated the enemy. Only slaves, he said, would have submitted to the British indignities. Parliament's revenue measures exposed the colonies to ruin and were inconsistent with liberty.

Iredell selected from the Coercive Acts for special criticism the bill for the "Impartial Administration of Justice." He found its provisions for trials in England particularly inconsistent with liberty. Trials by juries in the colonies were crucial to secure witnesses and fact finders who knew their character.

Liberty was the only goal of American exertions, Iredell claimed. It was "the right of every human creature," and no rule "totally destructive of this universal right" could be just. Had God intended men to be slaves, "he would surely have distinguished them with some mark suited to the abject character." Iredell remained a reluctant dissolutionist, but if independence became necessary to America's safety, it would have his assent.[9]

While Iredell was addressing political slavery of the American colonies to Great Britain, application of the thoughts to individual human bondage could hardly have escaped him. A decade later, in advocating ratification of the Constitution, practical necessity dictated that he defend the clause allowing continuance of the slave trade. In doing so, however, he articulated his opposition to the institution of human slavery clearly. Its complete abolition, he said, would be "pleasing to every generous mind, and every friend of human nature." "Though at a distant period," he stated, the provision for eventual abolition of the slave trade would "set an example of humanity."[10]

These humane pronouncements notwithstanding, Iredell shared with other leaders of his time participation in the haunting moral contradiction of abhorrence to slavery in principle while personally owning slaves. He used slaves in his work and in personal matters. While he manumitted some, he still owned others at his death.[11] As a lawyer he handled the sales of slaves for clients.[12]

Following adoption of the Declaration of Independence, Iredell continued to excoriate the British government for "mismanagement, villa[i]ny, and perfidious ambition," which were the "effects of tyrannical temper, selfish infatuation, and weak ungovernable pride."[13] While the new nation focused on securing its freedom, Iredell was not among the men-at-arms. He engaged a substitute to serve in his stead. He promoted the effort by other means, however, becoming a clearinghouse for correspondents on the progress of hostilities and continuing to justify the cleavage, postulating that it emanated from the king's adoption of measures that free men could not support. Submitting to such tyranny, he said, would have made Americans "the most despicable slaves on earth."[14]

In his February 1777 essay, "To His Majesty George the Third, King of Great Britain, &c," Iredell produced facts and arguments vindicating the Revolution. The allegiance of Americans to the king was that of a free people, not that of "despicable slaves" to a tyrant. Americans demanded only the liberties they had previously enjoyed but found astounding the "stupendous claims" of a right to bind them "in all cases whatsoever." Such encroachments on privilege violated both the constitution and the concept of justice. The royal concept of freedom—the "liberty" to be governed by distant tyrants ignorant of the locals' situation, unconnected with their interests, uninfluenced by their opinions, and with multiple ignoble motives to oppress and injure them—was unacceptable.[15]

When North Carolina required an oath of allegiance to the state, Iredell was among the first to subscribe. Following English legal tradition, he, as one of the state's first judges, charged grand juries with assertions of patriotism containing expressions of devotion to America. An instruction in Edenton, the grand jury resolved, vindicated independence by arguments from "unalienable rights" and "incontestable facts."[16] As a judge, Iredell presided over trials of Tories that produced declamations promoting patriotism. He also criticized the Carlisle Commission, through which England sought reconciliation with its former subjects, signing as "A Man Who Despises Your Pardons."[17]

Peace—to Iredell a "most glorious affair"—did not end his service to the Revolution and the task of nation building. He submitted resolutions to the citizens of Edenton calling for fulfillment of the terms of the peace treaty, support of public credit, and redemption of public debts. He drafted instructions from these citizens to their state legislators designed to promote national unity, particularly endorsing George Washington's appeal on the eve of victory not to lose the peace.[18]

Personal consequences, too, endured. While his American stay had brought other success, financial stability had eluded him. Now, a golden opportunity to attain it evaporated. His uncle, who had advised against meddling with politics, rejected his attempts to explicate his pro-American conduct and disinherited him for adhering to his convictions in the caldron of imperial disintegration.[19]

Having won independence, the former English subjects confronted the necessity of establishing a government. Their initial effort, the Articles of Confederation, proved inadequate. Iredell was among those leaders who were dissatisfied with the Articles and receptive to major reform. Years later he summarized the problems. The Articles sufficed when war with a common enemy engendered national unity but not when "selfish and contending interests" imperiled the gains of war. The consequences were ruinous: public debts unpaid and unprovided for, commerce languishing, agriculture discouraged, disunion and jealousy prevailing, dissolution and anarchy threatening. The magnitude of the danger "alarmed all considerate men."[20]

Consequently, "considerate men" convened in Philadelphia in 1787, ostensibly to revise the Articles but ultimately to adopt a new constitution. Iredell's poverty precluded his attendance; however, North Carolina's delegates communicated with him regularly. William R. Davie soon solicited Iredell's views; he would trouble Iredell frequently, he warned, and expected the jurist's opinion "without reserve." Indeed, until forbidden by rules imposing secrecy, Davie had expected to seek Iredell's perspective on all important questions. Richard Dobbs Spaight exchanged missives with Iredell on the nascent doctrine of judicial review. Hugh Williamson also wrote Iredell, noting the slow progress of the convention and encouraging Samuel Johnston's membership in the next General Assembly to promote the convention's measures.[21]

Iredell refused to campaign for the General Assembly that would confront these measures. He was nominated without his consent, and he lost the election to another Federalist. Although a delegate neither to the convention that proposed the Constitution nor to the state assembly that called the ratification convention, Iredell rendered perhaps the most outstanding of his patriotic services in the ratification effort. He thrust himself vigorously into the debate, earning posthumous tribute as "the ablest defender of the Constitution."[22]

Iredell appears to have inaugurated the first movement in North Carolina in favor of the Constitution. He drafted the preamble and resolutions for citizens who convened at Edenton to instruct legislators to call a ratification convention and to urge approval of the document. He penned an address extolling the Constitution and urging appointment of a convention for its early consideration.[23]

Indeed, Iredell's pen was seldom idle in these days of birthing the new government. Anti-Federalists focused ire on the absence of a bill of rights. As a Virginia delegate to Philadelphia, George Mason had refused to sign the proposed document and had published eleven objections to it. Anti-Federalists rallied around his first sentence—"There is no Declaration of Rights"—as they decried the pace at which Federalists were "hustling" ratification.[24]

Iredell responded to Mason's demurrers. Mason had forecast an evolution under the Constitution from a moderate aristocracy to a monarchy or a corrupt, oppressive aristocracy. A very different entity would emerge, Iredell prophesied, if his answers to Mason were "in general solid." The new government's strength and its subjects' liberty would be novelties in world history. The country could not expect to move from convention to convention until all possible objections were removed; it was in a critical period that could not be neglected with impunity. The proposed system could withstand scrutiny. Flaws could be corrected at leisure, while advantages were simultaneously enjoyed. Justice, order, and dignity would supplant "anarchical confusion," and industrious exertions would generate recovery from war and produce an "independent, great, and prosperous people." The alternative was grim. If his countrymen continued wrangling over trifles, listening to a small minority rather than to the country's "first men," they would cause exultation for their enemies and dejection for their friends. The honor, glory, and prosperity within easy reach would be gone forever.[25]

A Norfolk printer soon informed Iredell of plans to publish his "Answers to Mason's Objections." The *State Gazette of North Carolina* advertised the publication "To All Friends of the Federal Constitution." The document, dated January 1788, preceded the majority of *The Federalist Papers* and thus attracted national attention.[26]

As Iredell penned his "Answers," North Carolina moved toward a ratification convention. Iredell was a delegate from Edenton. He thanked supporters and pledged to serve zealously and faithfully. Over modestly pleading abilities incommensurate with his ambition to serve, he reiterated his support for the Constitution. The "security of everything dear," he said, hung on its approval. His sentiments were not universally shared, however. Battle lines were forming, as Thomas Person, a leading Anti-Federalist delegate, denounced George Washington as "a damned rascal and traitor to his country, for putting his hand to such an infamous paper as the new Constitution."[27]

Iredell continued his literary efforts, preparing with William R. Davie a "collection on the subject of the Federal Government." He communicated with Federalist leaders regarding the ratification effort in other states and joined them in sharing information on the debates in other states and philosophical writings on the subject. For example, Davie congratulated Iredell when Maryland ratified and hoped South Carolina and Virginia would follow. Archibald Maclaine soon conveyed the "pleasing intelligence" that South Carolina had ratified; and Hugh Williamson advised that Virginia too had "confederated." Iredell sent Davie the Pennsylvania debates and "the second balance of the Federalist." When Davie thanked him, he happily told his friend that New Hampshire had ratified.[28]

On 21 July 1788, the North Carolina ratification convention became the focal point of this debate, and the proceedings there "resonated with... historical differences." The convention appointed Iredell to a rules committee, and the body approved all but one of the committee's recommendations, many of which were undoubtedly the product of Iredell's work. A day later the committee on privileges and elections, on which Iredell also served, recommended that the election from Dobbs County, characterized by riots and violence, be voided and that its members vacate their seats.[29]

With these formalities settled, the delegates broached the serious business of the convention. In response to a motion for clause-by-clause discussion, Anti-Federalist Willie Jones moved that the question on the Constitution itself be "immediately put." Surely, he contended, in light of ample opportunity for consideration, every member was prepared to vote; prudence and frugality recommended instant action. Thomas Person seconded Jones's motion.

This furnished Iredell his initial occasion to establish himself as "outstanding in debate" and the "acknowledged leader for ratification." He objected to deciding "without the least deliberation" perhaps the greatest question ever presented to such an assemblage. Even trivial statutes of short duration were properly subjected to debate, he argued; surely the body would not decide "without a moment's consideration" so important a question. The proposal was the product of extensive deliberation sanctioned by men of probity and understanding and ratified by ten of the states. Such a document should be neither adopted nor rejected hastily. Additional expense, though unappealing, was necessary on a question involving "the safety or ruin of our country." Responding to Person, Iredell said he would not want his own position to be predetermined either way. While favorably predisposed, he dubiously denied having resolved to vote for ratification "at all events." All, including him, should be there for information.

This initial skirmish went to Iredell and the Federalists. Jones deferentially conceded that if gentlemen differed with him, he would yield. Considerations of frugality, he acknowledged, did not rival the magnitude of the subject.[30]

Iredell was fully prepared to answer objections. To him, "this [was] a very awful moment." "On a right decision of this question," he said, "may possibly depend the peace and happiness of our country for ages." Thus motivated, he vigorously defended the document over thirteen days of Anti-Federalist assaults. Yet the effort failed; Iredell's eloquent words, as one Anti-Federalist delegate stated, went "in at one ear, and out at the other."[31]

Iredell gained friends and benefited from his role in the convention. A new North Carolina county was soon named for him,[32] and warm encomiums reflected national recognition for his dialectical prowess.[33]

He barely paused to savor this acclaim. Even in his gratitude over the christening of Iredell County, he did not cease to promote the Constitution. His note of thanks to the representative primarily responsible for the designation concluded by touting support for the proposed charter as the surest proof of devotion to the public interest and the sole lifeline from the swamp of anarchy.[34]

Absence of a bill of rights was the foremost reason for rejection of the Constitution. For urging that all constitutions should so commence, the Anti-Federalists deserve much credit for ultimate adoption of the Bill of Rights. Momentarily, however, their rigidity had placed North Carolina in a difficult position and left the acknowledged leader of the ratification movement distraught. "We are . . . for the present out of the Union," Iredell wrote privately, "and God knows when we shall join it again."[35]

North Carolina was now a foreign state. It could have no part in selecting the first president, no role in devising the amendments on which the convention majority had insisted, and no participation if a second constitutional convention were called. Formative national laws would be enacted without its voice and would not apply to it. The Judiciary Act of 1789, for instance, would cease to operate at its borders. The state could not aid in securing a more advantageous location for the initial seat of the Congress, New York City.[36]

His perception of the state's plight pinned Iredell to the ratification effort, as he again applied his talent as a political essayist to the cause of the new government, noting the dangers inherent in his state's status as independent not only of other nations but also of other states. The path chosen would, he said in a 1788 essay, "lead . . . to misery and ruin, if we continue to pursue it." One convention, though, could repair the mischief of another. "This fatal disunion," he concluded, should "last a very short time longer."[37]

This essay was not Iredell's only contribution to the literature of the post-Hillsborough ratification effort. He and Davie had hired a reporter to record the debates, and they published them at their own expense. The publication was widely circulated and aided in Federalist election victories of 1789.[38]

For personal and professional reasons, Iredell declined to become a candidate for the forthcoming General Assembly or a delegate to a second federal convention to consider the amendments proposed by North Carolina and other states. The voters imposed an additional constraint. When he ultimately sought election to a second ratification convention, he was defeated.[39]

Declinations and defeat notwithstanding, Iredell remained an energetic presence in the ratification effort. He joined fellow Federalists in circulating petitions requesting a second state convention. Improving prospects spurred their persistence. Shortly after the Hillsborough convention, William Hooper informed Iredell of Federalist successes in western county elections, and Maclaine notified him of a meeting in Wilmington with only one dissent to a call for a new convention.[40] Finally, the assembly decided to hold a second convention in Fayetteville in November 1789.

Shortly before the convention, Iredell was still providing allies with pro-ratification propaganda. With the new national government now operative, correspondents enlightened him regarding pending legislation and solicited his views. One sent him a copy of the proposed Judiciary Act of 1789 "principally drawn up by a Mr. Ellsworth of Connecticut," with whom Iredell would later serve on the United States Supreme Court. South Carolina senator Pierce Butler forwarded pending bills and requested Iredell's opinion.[41]

The Fayetteville convention quickly ratified the Constitution. Several factors influenced the reversal, not least among them educational efforts of leaders such as Iredell and Davie.[42] In the immediate afterglow of the Federalist triumph, Iredell was recognized as among its principal architects.[43] Later scholars would consider him "outstanding in debate,"[44] "the acknowledged leader for ratification,"[45] and the "ablest defender of the Constitution."[46]

Iredell undoubtedly derived satisfaction from this ultimate success. Shortly before the town of Edenton celebrated ratification, he was at ease about public affairs. "My heart," he stated, "is ... as light as a feather." He simultaneously admitted, however, that despair and apprehension had gripped him so thoroughly and long that he now found it difficult to relax.[47]

There would be little time for relaxation. George Washington was ambitious for the federal judiciary of the infant republic. Its initial arrangement, he said, was "essential to the happiness of [the] country, and to the stability of its political system." Consequently, he sought "the first characters of the Union" for his initial judicial appointments.[48]

Washington had named to the Supreme Court men with distinguished biographies, but his search was not over. Robert H. Harrison, prominent Maryland judge and the president's comrade in arms in the Revolution, declined his appointment due to health problems and a preference to be chancellor of Maryland. The president soon selected another "first character," James Iredell of North Carolina. Thirty-eight years old when appointed, Iredell remains one of the youngest persons to occupy the high bench.[49]

Iredell's limited experience as a state judge, while pertinent, hardly qualified him for this august station. His "Answers to Mason's Objections" had attracted national attention and was almost certainly a factor. The most significant reason, however, was the grasp of constitutional questions Iredell displayed in promoting ratification. The debates he had recorded at Hillsborough were widely read; Washington perused them and was impressed with Iredell's ability. Finally, the president wished to reward North Carolina for joining the union, and the prize appropriately went to the man who had done the most to accomplish it. North Carolina was underrepresented in the Federalist administration, and Iredell's appointment helped cement the state to the union; Washington candidly so acknowledged. He had appointed Iredell for his abilities, legal knowledge, and respectable character, but it had mattered that he was "of a state of some importance in the Union that ha[d] given *No* character to a federal office."[50]

Iredell's confirmation[51] commenced a near-decade of intimate relationships with, and stalwart support for, George Washington, John Adams, and their administrations. He helped solidify the new government whose establishment he had ably and vigorously assisted. Judicial service did not end his career as an essayist. When an excise tax produced domestic opposition, Iredell defended it.[52] When the administration suppressed an insurrection against it, Iredell's friends viewed it as his personal triumph.[53] His ratification-era utterances provided the philosophical roots for his support of administration policies and the measures used to enforce them. A union was necessary to the safety and prosperity of the states, and the union could not be preserved without reposing confidence in those entrusted with its government.[54]

Iredell's intimacy with the presidents was characteristic of jurists in the late eighteenth century. Federal judges, including Supreme Court justices, were seen as representatives of the Federalist administrations. It was through contact with judges sitting on circuit courts that the American people became acquainted with the federal judiciary, and it was through the judges' charges that the principles of the new Constitution and government became known to the public. While overt partisan charges from the bench violate modern concepts of judicial propriety, they were patriotic in motivation and consonant with the perceived needs of the time.[55]

Iredell was a consummate activist in this regard. As a jurist he was, as in the ratification period, a bellman for the union. Popular sentiment was not prerequisite to his praise for the government's measures. He rushed to defend even the Alien and Sedition Acts, despite mounting resentment to them in his home state and elsewhere.[56] His charges featured prods toward patriotic appreciation for the government.[57] "Notwithstanding all the efforts made to vilify and undermine the government," he once instructed a jury, "it has uniformly [risen] in the esteem and confidence of the people."[58]

Commitment to the union did not preclude multiple allegiances, however. The union, he instructed, contained two sovereignties, and the federal Constitution did not interfere with the internal regulations of a state in matters solely of state concern. "Each of these governments," he urged, "deserves our equal confidence and respect."[59]

This dual sovereignty theme was a font of Iredell's most significant Supreme Court opinion, his dissent in *Chisholm v. Georgia* (1793).[60] The issue was whether the Supreme Court had jurisdiction to determine a suit by a citizen of one state against another state. The question was important because of concerns as to whether the states had relinquished all their sovereignty.[61] The states also feared that if the citizen prevailed, there could be actions in the Supreme Court by Loyalist refugees for debts forfeited by acts of attainder and similar legislation. The potential liability of the states was considerable.[62]

Iredell's solitary dissent that would have disallowed such suits was consistent with his "Answers to Mason's Objections to the Constitution,"[63] his ratification convention arguments,[64] and his prior charges to grand juries.[65] While according with other Federalist thinkers—notably Alexander Hamilton, James Madison, and John Marshall,[66] it also reflected contemporary public opinion. As Marshall wrote later, "The alarm [over the majority opinion] was general."[67] This ensured passage of the Eleventh Amendment, which constitutionalized the result Iredell would have reached and protected the states from such suits.[68]

Scholars and jurists have debated who was "right" in *Chisholm*, as well as the rationale underlying Iredell's position.[69] In 1999 the Supreme Court said Iredell was right.[70] The questions are largely academic. The practical reality is that the Eleventh Amendment incorporated the outcome Iredell alone would have imposed and his concept of divided sovereignty[71] into the Constitution, where they remain over two centuries later.

As a justice Iredell participated in several other significant cases. In *Penhallow v. Doane's Administrators* (1795), the Supreme Court resolved an issue of state versus national sovereignty adversely to the contentions of the states, upholding the jurisdiction of the federal courts to decide prize cases. Iredell's opinion reflected a strongly nationalistic interpretation, as he reverted to his form as a Revolutionary period essayist. He stated that when acts of Parliament were thought unconstitutional or unjust and "hope of redress . . . appeared desperate," Americans formed "a common council to consult for the common welfare" regarding the British measures.

Congress, Iredell concluded, was the appropriate body to exercise the external national sovereignty. "I think *all prize causes* whatsoever ought to belong to the national sovereignty," he wrote. "They are to be determined by the laws of nations. A prize court is, in effect, a court of all the nations in the world, because all persons, in every part of the world, are concluded by its sentences in cases clearly coming within its jurisdiction."[72]

Penhallow marked a "notable beginning . . . in the assertion by judicial construction of national sovereignty in the federal government."[73] His dissent in *Chisholm* notwithstanding, it is not surprising that Iredell, who had championed independence and union, joined in spawning this "notable beginning."

In *Hylton v. United States* (1796), Iredell joined in holding that a tax on the use of carriages was not a direct tax required by the Constitution to be apportioned.[74] The case was the first in which the Supreme Court passed upon the constitutionality of an act of Congress and is significant in the history of the federal government's capacity to raise revenue.[75] Further, explicit declaration of an act's constitutionality implicitly proclaimed the Court's power to pronounce acts unconstitutional. "The signpost was up."[76]

Ware v. Hylton (1796) has similar import as the first case in which the Court declared a state law unconstitutional, having been superseded by the federal Treaty of 1783, which ended the Revolutionary War. Iredell, having sat on the case on circuit, recused himself. He nevertheless discussed the treaty power, again reverting to his style as a Revolutionary period essayist, saying of the treaty, "It insured so far as peace could insure them, the freest forms of government, and the greatest share of individual liberty, of which perhaps the world has seen any example."[77]

Finally, the case of *Calder v. Bull* (1798) is best known for the Chase-Iredell debate, in dicta, on whether natural law is a valid reference point for judicial review. Samuel Chase, drawing on the Preamble to the Constitution and "certain vital principles in our free Republican governments," posited that it was. It was "against all reason and justice," he said, to treat legislative powers otherwise. Iredell thought the framers had defined limits of legislative power with precision. A passion for certitude prompted this view. "The ideas of natural justice are regulated by no fixed standard," Iredell observed, and courts and legislatures thus could have divergent opinions on whether a measure was "inconsistent with the abstract principles of natural justice."[78]

The debate has reverberated through over two centuries of American constitutional law, a "running battle that never has simmered down completely." Iredell's view is generally considered to have prevailed for nearly a century but Chase's to have ultimately triumphed under such rubrics as "substantive due process."[79]

Thus, as the Supreme Court "set a pattern of constitutional adjudication that was to endure,"[80] James Iredell was a vigorous participant in its deliberations and decisions. One scholar concludes that among the early justices, Iredell and William Paterson "seem the most impressive." Iredell "receives favorable marks," he writes, "for his attention to history in *Chisholm* and for his opposition to limitless judicial nullification in *Calder*."[81] Another concludes that Iredell and James Wilson "possessed the finest legal minds on the high court during this period."[82] This is clearly a worthy legacy. It is equally clearly one of North Carolina's most significant contributions to the national founding.

Supreme Court service meant that Iredell would lead "the life of a post-boy," traveling as much as 1,900 miles in covering a federal circuit.[83] Under the Judiciary Act of 1789, federal circuit courts heard appeals from the district courts but mainly functioned as the primary trial courts for certain categories of cases. Two (later, one) of the six Supreme Court justices, together with the resident district court judge, composed the circuit court. Each justice thus traveled through one of the three circuits twice annually.[84]

On circuit Iredell joined colleagues in their role as "republican schoolmasters," carrying law to citizens and fashioning support for the new national government.[85] He spoke anew of constitutions as fundamental law and reiterated his belief in the power of judicial review. A constitution was "the fundamental law of the state" and "not alterable by its ordinary legislature [as] all other species of law are." "A constitution is one thing," he concluded, while "particular and repealable laws, subsisting under [it] are another."[86]

In a 1798 case in which he made his final appearance as a circuit justice in his home state, Iredell wrote an opinion replete with significant philosophical reflections, especially regarding judicial review. If unwarranted by the Constitution, an act was without authority and void, for the superior power must be obeyed. The Constitution, he said, "is a supreme law, paramount to all acts of assembly, and unrepealable by any." While legislation inconsistent with a prior act repeals the former, "when the constitution says one thing and an act of assembly another," the former law controls; it is "a supreme law unrepealable and uncontrollable by the authority which enacted the latter."[87]

A further Iredell pronouncement here reflects his motivating life force. An abiding belief that private interests must yield to the greater public good influenced his entire existence. He enunciated this creed with eloquence. Private and public interests would at times collide, he said, and the former should yield to the latter. The benefits derived "from a well-constituted society" are more than ample compensation "for any accidental sacrifice which the public interest may occasionally require of a subordinate private advantage to a superior public good."[88]

Iredell lived his adult life by this creed. As a consequence, he left an epistolary legacy considered "invaluable for an understanding of social and political affairs in the later eighteenth century."[89] His letters while on the Supreme Court "illuminate[d] the contemporary scene."[90] "Without Iredell, the chronicler," editors of *The Documentary History of the Supreme Court of the United States* acknowledge, "these volumes would not be possible."[91]

Further, despite the untimeliness of his death at age forty-eight, his Revolutionary period essays, his defense of judicial review and the Constitution, and his commitment to the residual sovereignty of the states were firmly chiseled into the fabric of the American experiment. He had come to America in his youth to seek his own fortune and had stayed to contribute significantly to the formation of ours.[92]

NOTES

1. *The Papers of James Iredell*, ed. Don Higginbotham, 3 vols. (Raleigh: Division of Archives and History, North Carolina Department of Cultural Resources, 1976), 1:xxxvii; Henry E. McCulloh to Francis Iredell, 3 March 1768, in ibid., 12.

2. Thomas Iredell to James Iredell, circa 1770, and David L. Swain to Griffith J. McRee, 1855, in Griffith J. McRee, ed., *Life and Correspondence of James Iredell*, 2 vols. (New York: Appleton, 1857–58), 1:74; Josiah Martin to Lord George Germain, 15 September 1777, in Walter Clark, ed., *The State Records of North Carolina*, 20 vols.,(Goldsboro, N.C.: Nash Brothers, 1895–1911), 11:765–66; Raoul Berger, *Selected Writings on the Constitution* (Cumberland, Va.: James River Press, 1987), 184.

3. See the following in *Papers of Iredell*: editorial essay, 1:lv–lvi ; William Hooper to Iredell, 26 April 1774, 231; Joseph Hewes to Iredell, 23 May 1775, 305; Samuel Johnston to Iredell, 5 April 1776, 348; Joseph Hewes to Samuel Johnston, 8 July 1775 and 11 February 1776, quoted at lxxv.

4. "Causes of the American Revolution," in ibid., 410–11.

5. Editorial essay, in ibid., lix–lxi; "Essay on the Court Law Controversy," in ibid., 163–65.

6. "Essay on the Court Law Controversy," in ibid., 165.

7. "To the Inhabitants of Great Britain," in ibid., 251–57.

8. Editorial essay, in ibid., lxxi; "Principles of an American Whig," in ibid., 328–38; Henry S. Commager, ed., *Documents of American History* (New York: Appleton-Century-Crofts, 1973), 1:100–102.

9. "Causes of the American Revolution," in *Papers of Iredell*, 1:370–411; "To the Inhabitants of Great Britain," in ibid., 264. On the latter essay's wide circulation, see editorial note, in McRee, *Life and Correspondence of James Iredell*, 1:283.

10. Jonathon Elliot, ed., *The Debates in the Several State Conventions on the Adoption of the Federal Constitution*, 5 vols. (Philadelphia: J. B. Lippincott Co., 1907), 4:100–101.

11. See "List of the Number of Persons in the Family of James Iredell in the Town of Edenton," dated 8 February 1786, in file marked "James Iredell, Sr.—miscellaneous," North Carolina State Archives, Raleigh (NCSA) (reference to fourteen slaves). The Iredell Papers are replete with references to assistance from his slaves, and the wills of Iredell and his wife suggest that both died owning slaves. As to manumission, see Hugh T. Lefler and Patricia Stanford, *North Carolina*, 2nd ed. (New York: Harcourt Brace Jovanovich, 1972), 251; and Maeva Marcus, ed., *The Documentary History of the Supreme Court of the United States*, 6 vols. (New York: Columbia University Press, 1985–98), 2:446n1.

12. *State Gazette of North Carolina* (Edenton), 13 August 1789, 4.

13. Iredell to Thomas Jones, 15 July 1776, in *Papers of Iredell*, 1:415.

14. Act of 9 May 1777, chap. 1, secs. 14, 21, 1777 N.C. Sess. Laws, reprinted in Clark, *State Records*, 24:3–5; and the following in *Papers of Iredell*: editorial essay, 1:xxx; John Johnston to Iredell, 4 July 1776, 412–13; Thomas Jones to Iredell, 23 July 1776, 415–16; "To His Majesty George the Third, King of Great Britain, &c," 427–43. On Iredell's exemption certificate and hiring a substitute, see *Papers of Iredell*, 462.

15. "To His Majesty George the Third," in *Papers of Iredell*, 1:427–43.

16. Oath, in ibid., 454–55; Edenton grand jury to Iredell, 1 May 1778, in ibid., 2:15; charge, in ibid., 2:16–23.

17. Samuel A. Ashe, *History of North Carolina* (Greensboro, N.C.: Charles L. Van Noppen, 1908), 1:591–92; "To the Commissioners of the King of Great Britain for Restoring Peace, &c," in *Papers of Iredell*, 2:45–48; editorial note, in *Papers of Iredell*, 48.

18. Iredell to Hannah Iredell, April 1783, in *Papers of Iredell*, 2:393; resolutions, in ibid., 430–32; instructions, in ibid., 446–51; editorial essay, in ibid., 1:xxxviii–xxxix.

19. Arthur Iredell to Iredell, 18 August 1783, in ibid., 2:438; Arthur Iredell to Iredell, 17 November 1783, in ibid., 458; Iredell to Thomas Iredell, ca. November 1783, in ibid., 469–72; Iredell to Thomas Iredell, 28 May 1784, in McRee, *Life and Correspondence of James Iredell*, 2:101–3; Iredell to Thomas Iredell, 23 February 1786, *Papers of Iredell*, 3: 200–203.

20. Charge to the Federal Grand Jury for the District of Virginia, Richmond, 23 May 1796, in McRee, *Life and Correspondence of James Iredell*, 2:484.

21. See the following in McRee, *Life and Correspondence of James Iredell*, vol. 2: William R. Davie to Iredell, 30 May and 19 June 1787, 161; Richard Dobbs Spaight to Iredell, 3 July 1787, 162; Hugh Williamson to Iredell, 8 July 1787, 163; William R. Davie to Iredell, 17 July 1787, 165; Iredell to William R. Davie, 19 July 1787, 165; Hugh Williamson to Iredell, 22 July 1787, 167; William R. Davie to Iredell, 6 August 1787, 167; Richard Dobbs Spaight to Iredell, 12 August 1787, 168; Iredell to Richard Dobbs Spaight, 26 August 1787, 172. See also Clinton L. Rossiter, *1787: The Grand Convention* (New York: W. W. Norton, 1987), 127, 150; Blackwell P. Robinson, *William R. Davie* (Chapel Hill: University of North Carolina Press, 1957), 180, 188–89; and Louise Irby Trenholme, *The Ratification of the Federal Constitution in North Carolina* (New York: Columbia University Press, 1932), 95, 97.

22. Editorial note, in McRee, *Life and Correspondence of James Iredell*, 2:170–71; Stephen Cabarrus to Iredell, 18 August 1787, in ibid., 171; Iredell to Cabarrus, 21 August 1787, in ibid., 172; Trenholme, *Ratification*, 100–102, 120.

23. Editorial note, in McRee, *Life and Correspondence of James Iredell*, 2:180–81; Grand Jury Address, in ibid., 181–83.

24. Robert A. Rutland, *James Madison: The Founding Father* (New York: Macmillan, 1987), 23–27.

25. "Answers to Mason's Objections," in McRee, *Life and Correspondence of James Iredell*, 2:214–15. For the entirety of "Answers," see ibid., 186–215.

26. Editorial notes, in ibid., 186, 219; John McLean to Iredell, 10 February 1788, Iredell Papers, Manuscripts Department, Perkins Library, Duke University, Durham, N.C. (hereafter IP); *State Gazette of North Carolina*, 27 March 1788, 3 (advertising "Answers"). Forty-nine of the eighty-five *Federalist* essays postdate Iredell's "Answers"; compare McRee, *Life and Correspondence of James Iredell*, 1: 186–215, with Jacob E. Cooke, ed., *The Federalist* (Middleton, Conn.: Wesleyan University Press, 1961).

27. "To the Freemen of the Town of Edenton," in McRee, *Life and Correspondence of James Iredell*, 2:220; Thomas Iredell to Iredell, 22 May 1788, in ibid., 224–25. Person quoted at Willis Whichard, *Justice James Iredell* (Durham: Carolina Academic Press, 2000), 54.

28. William R. Davie to Iredell, 1 May 1788, in ibid., 223–24; Archibald Maclaine to Iredell, 4 June 1788, in ibid., 225–26; Hugh Williamson to Iredell, 7 July 1788, in ibid., 227–28; William R. Davie to Iredell, 9 July 1788, in ibid., 230.

29. Elliot, *Debates*, 4:1–4.

30. Ibid., 4–7.

31. Ibid., 143, 228; Trenholme, *Ratification*, 147.

32. Editorial essay, in McRee, *Life and Correspondence of James Iredell*, 2:235; Samuel Johnston to Iredell, 20 November 1788, NCSA (published in part in McRee, *Life and Correspondence of James Iredell*, 2:246–47); David L. Corbitt, *The Formation of North Carolina Counties, 1663–1943* (Raleigh: North Carolina Division of Archives and History, 1950), 127–29.

33. See Hugh Williamson to Iredell, 5 January 1789, in McRee, *Life and Correspondence of James Iredell*, 2:248; Pierce Butler to Iredell, 11 August 1789, in ibid., 263–64; Hugh Williamson to Iredell, 12 August 1789, in ibid., 265; and John Steele to Iredell, 26 September 1789, in ibid., 267.

34. Iredell to John Steele, 17 February 1789, in ibid., 254.

35. Iredell to Hannah Iredell, 3 August 1788, IP.

36. William S. Powell, *North Carolina through Four Centuries* (Chapel Hill: University of North Carolina Press, 1989), 229; Trenholme, *Ratification*, 216–17, 226, 230–32.

37. Quoted in Hugh T. Lefler, ed., *A Plea for Federal Union: North Carolina, 1788* (Charlottesville: McGregor Library, University of Virginia, 1947), 21–22, 35–38. While this essay has not been definitively identified as Iredell's, Lefler was so convinced, as I am.

38. William S. Powell, *North Carolina: A History* (Chapel Hill: University of North Carolina Press, 1977), 91; Marcus, *Documentary History*, 1 (pt. 2): 649nl; John C. Cavanagh, *Decision at Fayetteville: The North Carolina Ratification Convention and General Assembly of 1789* (Raleigh: North Carolina Division of Archives and History, 1989), 11.

39. Editorial note, in McRee, *Life and Correspondence of James Iredell*, 2:236; Samuel Johnston to Iredell, 14 November 1788, NCSA; Iredell to Hugh Williamson, 22 January 1789, NCSA; Archibald Maclaine to Iredell, 15 September 1789, IP; Cavanagh, *Decision at Fayetteville*, 11; Clark, *State Records*, 21:94–95, 22:39; *State Gazette of North Carolina*, 2 April 1789, 3.

40. William Hooper to Iredell, 2 September 1788, in McRee, *Life and Correspondence of James Iredell*, 2:238; Archibald Maclaine to Iredell, 27 October 1788, in ibid., 243–44; Trenholme, *Ratification*, 199.

41. Tristram Lowther to Iredell, 1 July 1789, in McRee, *Life and Correspondence of James Iredell*, 2:260; Pierce Butler to Iredell, 11 August 1789, in ibid., 265; John Williams to Iredell, 11 September 1789, in ibid., 265.

42. Cavanagh, *Decision at Fayetteville*, 27; William Dawson to Iredell, 22 November 1789, IP; William R. Davie to Iredell, 22 November 1789, IP; Samuel Johnston to Iredell, 23 November 1789, IP.

43. William Dawson to Iredell, 22 November 1789, in McRee, *Life and Correspondence of James Iredell*, 2:272; Samuel Johnston to Iredell, 23 November 1789, in ibid., 272; Charles Johnson to Iredell, 23 November 1789, in ibid., 273; Albert R. Newsome, "North Carolina's Ratification of the Federal Constitution," *North Carolina Historical Review* 17, no. 4 (1940): 287, 297.

44. Trenholme, *Ratification*, 147.

45. Henry G. Connor, "James Iredell: Lawyer, Statesman, Judge, 1751–1799," *University of Pennsylvania Law Review* 60 (1912): 225, 236.

46. Trenholme, *Ratification*, 120.

47. Iredell to Hannah Iredell, 26 November 1789, NCSA.

48. George Washington to James Madison, circa 10 August 1789, in *The Writings of George Washington*, ed. Jared Sparks (Boston: Russell, Shattuck, and Williams, 1836), 10:26; George Washington to Edmund Randolph, 27 September 1789, in ibid., 34.

49. Richard B. Bernstein and Kym S. Rice, *Are We to Be a Nation? The Making of the Constitution* (Cambridge, Mass.: Harvard University Press, 1987), 260; Douglas S. Freeman, *George Washington: A Biography* (New York: Charles Scribner's Sons, 1954), 6:253, 253n95; Charles Grove Haines, *The Role of the Supreme Court in American Government and Politics, Vol. 1, 1789–1935* (Berkeley: University of California Press, 1944), 121.

50. Sidney H. Asch, *The Supreme Court and Its Great Justices* (New York: Arco, 1971), 18; *Biographical History of North Carolina: From Colonial Times to the Present*, ed. Samuel A. Ashe, 8 vols. (Greensboro, N.C.: Charles L. Van Noppen, 1905–17), 2:201; William Spohn Baker, *Washington after the Revolution* (Philadelphia: J. B. Lippincott, 1898), 171; Ernest Sutherland Bates, *The Story of the Supreme Court* (Indianapolis: Bobbs-Merrill, 1936), 46; Hampton L. Carson, *The Supreme Court of the United States: Its History* (Philadelphia: John Y. Huber, 1891), 154–55; Leon Friedman and Fred L. Israel, eds., *The Justices of the United States Supreme Court, 1789–1969: Their Lives and Major Opinions* (New York: Chelsea House in association with R. R. Bowker, 1969), 1:127–28; Donald Jackson and Dorothy Twohig, eds., *The Diaries of George Washington* (Charlottesville: University Press of Virginia, 1979), 6:28–29; Lefler, *Plea for Federal Union*, 12; Robert Shnayerson, *The Illustrated History of the Supreme Court of the United States* (New York: Harry N. Abrams, 1986), 65.

51. See Samuel Johnston to Iredell, 11 February 1790, NCSA; and Samuel Johnston to Iredell, 6 March 1790, IP.

52. "TO THE CITIZENS OF THE UNITED STATES" from "A CITIZEN OF PENNSYLVANIA," in McRee, *Life and Correspondence of James Iredell*, 2:307–20.

53. William R. Davie to Iredell, 15 December 1794, in ibid., 431.

54. "TO THE CITIZENS," in ibid., 320.

55. William R. Davie to Iredell, 15 December 1794, in ibid., 431, noting "conciliatory effect with respect to the government" of Justice Wilson's conduct while holding court; editorial essay, in ibid., 435.

56. Charge to United States Grand Jury for the District of Pennsylvania, 11 April 1799, in ibid., 551–70. As to resentment, see Herbert S. Turner, *The Dreamer: Archibald DeBow Murphey* (Verona, Va.: McClure Press, 1971), 53.

57. E.g., Charges to Grand Jury at Richmond, Virginia, 23 May 1796, IP; and 22 May 1797, in McRee, *Life and Correspondence of James Iredell*, 2:508–9.

58. Charge to United States Grand Jury for Pennsylvania, 11 April 1799, in McRee, *Life and Correspondence of James Iredell*, 2:569.

59. Charges to United States Grand Juries, Trenton, 2 April 1793, Philadelphia, 11 April 1793, and Annapolis, 7 May 1793, all at NCSA. The Annapolis charge is in McRee, *Life and Correspondence of James Iredell*, 2:386–87.

60. 2 U.S. (2 Dall.) 419 (1793).

61. Charles Warren, *The Supreme Court in United States History, Vol. 1: 1789–1821* (Boston: Little, Brown, 1922), 92–93.

62. Julius Goebel Jr., *History of the Supreme Court of the United States: Antecedents and Beginnings to 1801* (New York: Macmillan, 1971), 741–42; Kemp P. Yarborough, "Chisholm v. Georgia: A Study of the Minority Opinion" (Ph.D. diss., Columbia University, 1963; Ann Arbor, Mich.: University Microfilms, 1991), 33.

63. McRee, *Life and Correspondence of James Iredell*, 2:193; Yarborough, "Chisholm v. Georgia," 192–95.

64. Elliot, *Debates*, 4:35; Yarborough, "Chisholm v. Georgia," 192, 232–33.

65. McRee, *Life and Correspondence of James Iredell*, 2:348, 387; Yarborough, "Chisholm v. Georgia," 234–34, 235nl.

66. J. Cooke, ed., *The Federalist*, No. 9, at 55; No. 32, at 200; No. 81, at 548–49 (Alexander Hamilton); Elliot, *Debates*, 3:533 (James Madison), 555–56 (John Marshall). See also Samuel F. Miller, *Lectures on the Constitution of the United States* (New York: Banks and Bros., 1891), 380–82; and Yarborough, "Chisholm v. Georgia," 233–34, 240–41, 318.

67. Cohens v. Virginia, 19 U.S. (6 Wheat.) 264, 406 (1821).

68. Shnayerson, *Illustrated History of the Supreme Court*, 70; Francis N. Thorpe, *A Constitutional History of the American People, 1776–1850* (New York: Harper and Bros., 1898), 1:177. See also Jefferson B. Fordham, "Iredell's Dissent in *Chisholm v. Georgia*: Its Political Significance," *North Carolina Historical Review* 18, no. 2 (1931): 155, 162–63; William D. Guthrie, "The Eleventh Article of Amendment to the Constitution of the United States," *Columbia Law Review* 8 (1908): 183, 185–86; and Yarborough, "Chisholm v. Georgia," 180–87, 192–93.

69. See, e.g., John V. Orth, *The Judicial Power of the United States: The Eleventh Amendment in American History* (New York: Oxford University Press, 1987), 13–14, 22, 42, 69–70, 74–75, 137–38, 149, 159; and John V. Orth, "The Truth about Justice Iredell's Dissent in *Chisholm v. Georgia* (1793)," *North Carolina Law Review* 73, no. 1 (1994): 255–70. Orth's thesis is that Iredell's dissent rested on the absence of a statutory remedy, not on a lack of constitutional power.

70. Alden v. Maine, 527 U.S. 706 (1999).

71. Friedman and Israel, *Justices*, 131, 133.

72. 3 U.S. (3 Dall.) 54, 90, 91 (1795).

73. Haines, *Role of the Supreme Court*, 141.

74. 3 U.S. (3 Dall.) 171, 181–83 (1796).

75. Goebel, *History of the Supreme Court*, 778; Leonard W. Levy, *Original Intent and the Framers' Constitution* (New York: Macmillan, 1988), 59; Warren, *Supreme Court*, 146–47.

76. Friedman and Israel, *Justices*, 192.

77. 3 U.S. (3 Dall.) 199, 256–80 (1796); David P. Currie, *The Constitution in the Supreme Court: The First Hundred Years, 1789–1888* (Chicago: University of Chicago Press, 1985), 4, 39, 41.

78. 3 U.S. (3 Dall.) 386, 387–89 (Chase), 399 (Iredell) (1798).

79. Currie, *Constitution in the Supreme Court*, 47–48; Jethro K. Lieberman, *The Enduring Constitution: A Bicentennial Perspective* (St. Paul, Minn.: West Publishing Co., 1987), 263.

80. Currie, *Constitution in the Supreme Court*, 58.

81. Ibid., 57–58.

82. Don Higginbotham, "Iredell, James," in *Dictionary of North Carolina Biography*, ed. William S. Powell (Chapel Hill: University of North Carolina Press, 1988), 3:254.

83. Arthur Iredell to Iredell, 1 February 1791, in McRee, *Life and Correspondence of James Iredell*, 2:306.

84. See Wythe Holt, "'The Federal Courts Have Enemies in All Who Fear Their Influence on State Objects': The Failure to Abolish Supreme Court Circuit-Riding in the Judiciary Acts of 1792 and 1793," *Buffalo Law Review* 36 (1987): 301, 305–6.

85. See ibid., 307–8; Wythe Holt, "'To Establish Justice': Politics, the Judiciary Act of 1789, and the Invention of the Federal Courts," *Duke Law Journal*, no. 6 (1989): 1421, 1488–89, 1489n235; and Maeva Marcus and Emily F. Van Tassell, "Judges and Legislators in the New Federal System, 1789–1800," in *Judges and Legislators: Toward Institutional Comity*, ed. Robert A. Katzmann (Washington, D.C.: Brookings Institution, 1988), 31–32.

86. United States v. Mundell, 27 F. Cas. 23, 29–32 (C. C. D. Va. 1795) (No. 15, 834).

87. Minge v. Gilmour, 17 F. Cas. 440, 442 (C. C. D. N.C. 1798) (No. 9, 631).

88. Ibid. at 445.

89. William K. Boyd, *History of North Carolina: The Federal Period, 1783–1860* (1919; repr., Spartanburg, S.C.: Reprint Co., 1973), 2:385.

90. Archibald Henderson, author and ed., *North Carolina: The Old North State and the New*, 5 vols. (Chicago: Lewis Publishing Co., 1941), 1:418.

91. Marcus, *Documentary History*, 2:4.

92. With permission, which is gratefully acknowledged, I have drawn on my prior essay on Iredell contained in Scott Douglas Gerber, ed., *Seriatim: The Supreme Court before John Marshall* (New York: New York University Press, 1998), and on my full-length biographical treatment of him, *Justice James Iredell*.

IV

The Anti-Federalists

9

Samuel Spencer, Anti-Federalist

Jason Stroud

Historian Gordon Wood has observed that what was "extraordinary about 1787–88," the period that encompassed the struggles over the newly written Constitution, was the "political strength of Anti-Federalism."[1] Indeed, by late July 1788, when North Carolina's delegates assembled at Hillsborough to consider ratification of the Constitution, opponents of the new government had waged a spirited, if ultimately unsuccessful, campaign against the new national government. In several states, including Virginia, which ratified the document only a month before the Hillsborough convention, the opposition had nearly prevailed, failing by only a few votes. Despite its strength and popularity, though, it is easy in retrospect to view Anti-Federalism in general, and the eleventh-hour efforts of the opponents of the Constitution in North Carolina in particular, as a hopeless, sullen rearguard action, an attempt to derail or delay the inevitable consolidation of the federal union. Yet the Anti-Federalists at Hillsborough enjoyed more than a two-to-one majority, evidence that theirs was a significant movement, particularly in the Piedmont and the western counties.

At the center of this movement was Samuel Spencer, a jurist and Anson County planter who emerged as the most vocal critic of the Constitution and proponent of additional amendments at the Hillsborough convention. Spencer spoke frequently and eloquently throughout the convention, opposing immediate ratification and articulating a critique of the Constitution rooted in a profound skepticism about the nature of centralized political power. Yet despite his contributions at Hillsborough, Spencer's role in organizing and publicizing popular opposition to the Constitution in the state is not clear. No evidence suggests that Spencer was, like Willie Jones, the state's other leading Anti-Federalist, active in the often-rancorous public debates that preceded the convention in July 1788. This is perhaps because Spencer's Anson County constituents were already set against the new government—each of the delegates they sent to debate the Constitution was an Anti-Federalist. They would have required little persuasion to oppose the Constitution. Unlike Jones of Halifax and Thomas Person of Granville, who led the fight against the Constitution out of doors in their respective counties, Spencer's participation in the movement was largely limited to his speeches on the floor of the convention. Yet taken together, these speeches themselves were a significant contribution—a thoughtful (if in some instances intellectually inconsistent) critique of the Constitution. At the core of this critique was a program of amendments aimed at protecting the powers of the state governments, considered to be inherently friendlier to the liberties of the people. Spencer's speeches crystallize many of the concerns of Anti-Federalists everywhere who viewed the program of national consolidation envisioned by the framers of the Constitution with profound skepticism.

Spencer's opposition would likely have come as little surprise to North Carolina's Federalist leaders, but it is doubtful that they would have regarded him as a serious obstacle to ratification before the convention. It seems that many of Spencer's contemporaries—particularly the men who emerged as the Constitution's leading supporters at Hillsborough—held his talents as well as his character in very low esteem. James Iredell, an arch-Federalist who served with Spencer as a superior court judge for a time during the Revolution, once described Spencer to his wife as "the most obstinate fool in Nature," a remark typical of several others in his correspondence.[2] Iredell's opinions were shared by the pugnacious Wilmington Federalist Archibald Maclaine, who regarded Spencer by 1787 as an "apostate to his principles," if also a "man of firmness."[3]

Modern historians have struggled to draw meaningful conclusions regarding the judge. Few of Spencer's papers—official or otherwise—survive, a fact that seems to have tilted the scales in favor of his political adversaries in the eyes of scholars. For instance, Iredell's judgment of Spencer's character was repeated with gusto by nineteenth-century North Carolina historian Griffith J. McRee, who claimed, based entirely on Iredell's correspondence, that Spencer was "unacceptable to the bar" and that his behavior evinced "selfishness and avarice" rather than the genteel disinterestedness one expected of eighteenth-century political leaders.[4] One recent legal historian has remarked that, at least during his time as a superior court justice, Spencer was "notoriously indifferent to public opinion, whether about his professional or his private life."[5] Indeed, among the most interesting aspects of Spencer's life in modern accounts has been his death, which occurred under tragicomic circumstances—he was mortally wounded, according to tradition, during an attack by an agitated turkey.[6]

Yet the man privately derided by Maclaine as "that fool Spencer" was indisputably central to almost all of the notable events of the second half of the eighteenth century in North Carolina, including the Regulation, the Revolution, and—the subject of this essay—the fierce debates over ratification of the Constitution in 1788 and 1789.[7] In the debates at the 1788 ratification convention at Hillsborough, in particular, Spencer spoke for an Anti-Federalist majority that ultimately declined to ratify the new government in a gambit aimed at bringing amendments to the top of the new nation's agenda. Rather than simply delaying the inevitable progress of ratification, Spencer proposed major alterations in the Constitution consistent with a political philosophy that held that power was least destructive of individual rights when vested in state and local governments. His overriding interest, he claimed, was in "settling it [the Constitution] so as to exclude animosity and a contest between the general and individual governments."[8] In this sentiment, he represented a clear majority of North Carolinians, especially those in the Piedmont and backcountry, who viewed the Constitution with suspicion and skepticism.

Prior to the Revolution, Spencer made few claims to represent the interests of the majority of North Carolinians, particularly those in the backcountry. Born in Connecticut and educated at the College of New Jersey (later Princeton University), Spencer arrived in the Sandhills of North Carolina sometime in the early 1760s. By 1765, he had secured the post of clerk of court for Anson County.[9] In this capacity, he provoked the ire of the Regulators in that county, who alleged in a petition to Royal Governor William Tryon that Spencer, in collusion with other corrupt officials, charged "double and some times treble his due" in carrying out his duties.[10] Like Willie Jones, Spencer was among the militia commanded by Tryon at the Battle of Alamance. There he might have looked across the battlefield to see Thomas Person, who would become one of the state's other leading opponents of the Constitution, lined up with the Regulators. Despite his initial unpopularity, Spencer seems to have become a prosperous and influential man in Anson County. He owned large tracts of land throughout the southern Piedmont and was, by Anson County's admittedly humble standards, a wealthy man.[11] As a measure of the region's relatively modest economic development, Spencer's eighteen slaves listed in the 1790 census placed him among the county's largest slave owners. Many of the planters who dominated eastern North Carolina politics owned more than 100 enslaved people.[12]

In the wake of the Regulation, Spencer emerged as a leader in local protests against British policies, serving on the county Committee of Correspondence and chairing a local Revolutionary committee that enforced participation in the boycott of British goods instituted by the Continental Association of 1774 through coercion and, some alleged, threats of violence.[13] After the outbreak of the Revolution, Spencer served in the provincial congress at Halifax from 1776 to 1777. In 1777, he became a North Carolina Superior Court justice, a position that he held for the rest of his life.[14] In this capacity, Spencer served with fellow jurist James Iredell, with whom he traversed much of the state during the Revolution and who, as noted previously, did not relish his company. Along with Samuel Ashe and John Williams, Spencer was on the court in 1787 when it delivered what would become a landmark decision in *Bayard v. Singleton*. By overturning (albeit reluctantly) a state law that restricted the right of Loyalists to sue for confiscated property after the Revolution, Spencer and the other justices asserted the principle of judicial review. *Bayard v. Singleton* would be cited as precedent in subsequent American jurisprudence, most significantly in the John Marshall–led Supreme Court's decision in *Marbury v. Madison* (1803).[15]

Spencer, then, emerged from the Revolution as Anson County's most powerful political figure and an accomplished, if not universally respected, jurist. He was thus among the political leaders of a region that was, from the start, predisposed against support for any program of national consolidation. As historian Jackson Turner Main demonstrated in his seminal work on the Anti-Federalists, the opponents of the new Constitution in North Carolina overwhelmingly represented "those sections of the state which were not so immediately and directly concerned with mercantile or business affairs and who preferred inflation to a 'sound,' or deflationary financial system."[16] These men also had powerful and emotional reasons for opposing ratification, having nurtured a long-standing distrust of political power emanating from beyond their immediate control. To Piedmont and backcountry farmers, the robust new government proposed by the Constitution evoked memories not only of the imperial government shaken off by the Revolution but of the corruption of eastern North Carolina elites that had provoked the Regulator movement.[17] As noted previously, Spencer's record was hardly spotless in the latter uprising. Still, in the wake of the Revolution, he had achieved prominence in a county populated primarily by yeoman farmers and small planters who were powerfully inclined to oppose ratification.

In short, by the time the delegates convened at Hillsborough, Spencer was a well-placed—if often controversial—figure in North Carolina's notoriously fractious politics. Chosen along with Daniel Gould, Lewis Lanier, Thomas

Wade, and Frame Wood—all opponents of ratification—to represent Anson County at the convention, he emerged as the most vocal and arguably the most eloquent spokesman among the Constitution's critics.[18] He spoke more often—and longer—than any other Anti-Federalist delegate and, along with Willie Jones, was acknowledged by the Federalists at the convention as one of the leaders of the Anti-Federalist faction. The debates at Hillsborough provide us with our only meaningful glimpse into the mind of Spencer, who unfortunately left little correspondence and very few papers to posterity. We are forced to glean his views on the Constitution from his speeches as recorded in *The Proceedings and Debates of the Convention of North Carolina*, a highly problematic source inasmuch as it was commissioned—and subsequently altered—by Federalists William R. Davie and James Iredell, Spencer's chief rivals at the convention. Yet, as historian Pauline Maier recently observed, the *Proceedings and Debates* did not omit Anti-Federalist speeches, "even when they argued well," as Spencer often did.[19] This was not always the case—in Pennsylvania, for example, the published proceedings blatantly privilege a Federalist perspective on the debates.[20] Another issue stems from the political dynamics on the floor of the convention. Comfortable in their clear majority, most of the opponents of ratification at Hillsborough decided essentially to remain quiet as the Federalists gave one speech after another. If this strategy was rooted in a pragmatic assessment of the political terrain in 1788, it also, as one historian has observed, placed the Anti-Federalists "on the defensive in the debates" despite their overwhelming numerical majority.[21] Though the Federalists were often out of order in answering objections to the Constitution not raised on the floor of the convention, they used their time to mount a cogent and thorough apologia for the Constitution. The effect is that the modern student (or, perhaps more important, a North Carolina reader in 1789) is more likely to be struck by the eloquence and erudition of Davie and especially Iredell, which dominate the pages of the *Proceedings*, than by Spencer's appeals in opposition.

Still, whatever the biases in reporting the debates, Spencer emerges from the *Proceedings* as a thoughtful critic of the Constitution, one whose contributions to the debates deserve to be taken seriously by modern historians. He was, he professed, no knee-jerk opponent of national political reform. In his first major speech to the Hillsborough convention, he described the work done at Philadelphia as a "great performance" with "a great deal of merit in it." Unlike many critics of the Constitution, he did not argue that the convention had exceeded its mandate in developing an entirely new national government: the question was, he thought, academic if the states ratified the document.[22] He defended the prohibition of a religious test, laid out in Article VI of the

Constitution, against the criticisms of several prominent Anti-Federalists (and probably many of its critics out of doors) and argued that the inclusion of a bill of rights would rectify many of the wrongs in the document. Employing an analogy common among skeptics of ratification, he likened joining the new government to entering a legal "copartnership." It was a "principle of prudence," he argued, "not to assent to any obligation till its errors were removed."[23]

Repeatedly, Spencer stressed that the Constitution's most damning "errors" stemmed from provisions that, either by design or neglect, portended a dangerous reorientation of political power away from the states and toward a distant federal government. He delivered his first significant speech at Hillsborough on 25 July, when he rose to voice his opposition to Article I, Section 4, of the proposed Constitution (the convention proceeded in order through each article of the document) on the grounds that the power of Congress to alter the "times, places, and manner" of electing representatives (established by state legislatures) might facilitate a "consolidation of the government of the United States, when the state legislatures may entirely decay away."[24]

As Iredell and Davie pointed out, Spencer's remarks seemed to rest on an overly expansive reading of the word "time," which led him to the conclusion that, among other things, Congress was empowered to lengthen the terms of its members. But Spencer was not the only delegate who read the clause that way—Governor Samuel Johnston, a strong supporter of ratification, voiced similar concerns. In any case, the "time and place" clause was only one aspect of what Spencer saw as a clear pattern of federal consolidation. As the erudite Davie declaimed at length on the fates of confederations that failed to consolidate their power in a central government, citing such classical examples as the Achaean League and the Amphictyonic Council, the essential differences between Spencer and the supporters of the Constitution became clear. Despite the obvious need for revision and, indeed, replacement of the Articles of Confederation, Spencer responded, the people's liberties were still best protected by state governments, the very governments that the new Constitution was intended to restrain. Spencer did not, however, view protections for state governments as irreconcilable with a more robust federal union: "From all the notions which we have concerning our happiness and well-being, the state governments are the basis of our happiness, security, and prosperity. A large extent of country ought to be divided into such a number of states as that the people may conveniently carry on their own government. This will render the government perfectly agreeable to the genius and wishes of the people. If the United States were to consist of ten times as many states, they might all have a degree of harmony. Nothing would be wanting but some cement for their connection."[25]

Of course, Spencer and his fellow delegates were gathered to discuss precisely how much "cement" was required, and on this point, as with so many of the issues before the delegates, the devil was in the details.

The clause was, Spencer worried, dangerously vague in its wording, and many delegates—and, it appears, their constituents—shared his concerns. William R. Davie acknowledged that the clause was a "favorite theme of declamation out of doors" but claimed that the state's Anti-Federalists had "alarmed and agitated the public mind" by exaggerating and misrepresenting its "mischiefs."[26] Yet for men like Spencer, the clause was dangerous because it might be understood to countenance the usurpation of a time-honored prerogative of local elites like themselves—control of elections. The clause, he said, "strikes at the foundation of the governments on which depends the happiness of the states and the general government."[27]

To Spencer, the same principle applied to the new government's power to tax, generally viewed by Anti-Federalists as a power most safely vested in state legislatures. In the debate over the power to tax enumerated in Article I, Section 8, Spencer argued that "the most certain criterion of happiness that any people can have, is to be taxed by their own immediate representatives ... who intermix with them, and know their circumstances ... not by those who cannot know their situation." This was, many delegates agreed, a serious issue. As they well knew, the state suffered from a chronic currency shortage—a problem that had plagued North Carolina since the colonial period. There was simply no money in the state, Spencer maintained, and without the hard currency to satisfy whatever demands Congress imposed, North Carolina's propertied citizens (particularly, he might have added, yeoman farmers and small planters in places like Anson County) would see their "lands, negroes, stock and furniture" confiscated and sold at auction. Spencer's proposed solution to this problem was to allow the state legislatures to collect "articles proper for exportation" to satisfy the tax quotas established by Congress by payment in kind.[28]

Supporters of the Constitution argued, as did the proponents of a direct tax at the Philadelphia convention, that import duties would likely be sufficient to meet the needs of the federal government. Still, Spencer remained unconvinced.[29] The salient theoretical point, he said, was that state legislatures were best situated to ascertain local circumstances and could adjust modes of taxation to include methods that placed the least possible strain on the people while still raising the revenue that, he understood, the national government needed to function: "I wish to have the most easy way for the people to pay their taxes. The state legislature will know every method and expedient by which the people can pay, and they will recur to the most convenient. This will be agreeable to the people, and will not create insurrections and dissensions in the country."[30] While declaring them "odious to a free people," Spencer even reluctantly agreed that he would allow the federal government the power to levy excise taxes, which would prove disastrously unpopular with backcountry farmers in the early republic.[31]

Spencer's unthinking conflation of "negroes" with "lands, ... stock and furniture" in his remarks on taxation is jarring to the modern reader, particularly in light of the vehement defense of liberties and even "human rights" throughout his speeches to the convention. But there is no evidence that this spokesman for freedom and liberties imagined that these blessings would belong to anyone other than whites (or, for that matter, to anyone other than white men). In this, Spencer was no different from the majority of his contemporaries—though several delegates, in keeping with what one historian has termed the "emancipationist impulse" among Revolutionary gentlemen, expressed disgust at the institution, and particularly the slave trade.[32] Many, perhaps, agreed in principle with Iredell, who expressed his conviction that "the entire abolition of slavery," though "not attainable," was "an event that must be pleasing to every generous mind."[33]

Yet Iredell himself was a slave owner, and the issue of slavery seldom emerged in the debates except when Anti-Federalist delegates expressed their anxieties that the new Constitution might invest the federal government with the power of emancipation. Spencer, as mentioned previously, owned several enslaved people, and as a superior court judge, he frequently ruled on cases involving property in human beings. In one case in Rowan County, for example, he ordered the sale of "one Negro man ... fifty years of age ... very infirm," along with "goats, sheep, and furniture," to support the family of a Loyalist executed for treason during the Revolution.[34] Ultimately, it ought to be remembered that Spencer and his colleagues at Hillsborough rose to prominence in a slave society. Many, like Spencer, were active in policing and maintaining its legal boundaries, and most of the leaders in the convention, whatever their opinions of the new Constitution, profited from the labor they extracted from black bodies. Virginian George Mason (a large slaveholder himself) famously observed in the debates at the Philadelphia convention that "every master of slaves is born a petty tyrant."[35] If Spencer and the other delegates to the Hillsborough convention harbored such grave doubts about the institution, they did not generally choose to air them on the floor. Indeed, as historian Edmund Morgan famously argued for colonial Virginia, their dependence on slavery may have made some North Carolinians more, not less, sensitive to perceived threats to their own liberties.[36]

One of the gravest of these dangers, Spencer and the Anti-Federalists believed, lay in Article II of the Constitution. The national government under the Articles of Confederation had lacked an independent executive, and the powers granted to the president in the new Constitution evoked republican fears of abuse of power by designing and ambitious men. In a typically memorable speech to the Virginia ratifying convention just over a month before the North Carolina delegates convened at Hillsborough, Patrick Henry claimed that, among many other "deformities," the new government created by the Constitution "squints toward monarchy."[37] Spencer also worried that the president, armed with expansive executive powers, might become a despot. Yet unlike Henry (and several members of the North Carolina convention who railed against the powers granted to the president in the first section of Article II), he was primarily concerned with the relationship between the president and the Senate as laid out in the "advice and consent" clause of Article II, Section 2. On the one hand, Spencer feared that the power of the Senate to confirm appointments might make the executive unduly beholden to the wishes of factions within that body. On the other, he, like many other Anti-Federalists, doubted that the Senate would vote to remove the chief executive from office for unlawful actions that they had advised him to carry out. Thus a vital check on the power of the executive would be essentially toothless: "I cannot conceive, therefore, that the President can ever be tried by the Senate with any effect, or to any purpose, for any misdemeanor in his office, unless it should extend to high treason, or unless they should wish to fix the odium of any measure on him, in order to exculpate themselves; the latter of which I cannot suppose will ever happen."[38]

Here, as elsewhere, Spencer accompanied his critique of what he perceived as a potentially fatal flaw in the Constitution with a proposed remedy. Again, his solution reserved more power to the states, this time by proposing a "standing council," composed of one member from each state, which would perform the "advice and consent" role prescribed for the Senate by the Constitution. This, Spencer suggested, would create an executive that was truly independent of the Senate, preventing that body from sliding into "despotic aristocracy," which, he feared, was possible even though its "members be not hereditary."[39] As Davie quickly pointed out, this argument was founded on a rigid interpretation of the doctrine of separation of powers, one that he assured the convention that "the great Montesquieu" had not intended and that the experiences of several state governments had proved unworkable.[40] Concurring with Iredell's accusation that Spencer's avowed fears of aristocracy in the Senate were "uncandidly calculated to alarm and catch prejudices," Samuel Johnston would later remark on the irony of the convention's most vocal advocate of states' rights criticizing the powers of the Senate: "The Senate represents the states," Johnston said, "and can alone prevent this dreaded consolidation; yet the powers of the Senate are objected to."[41]

Historians have long recognized that North Carolina's Anti-Federalists, including Spencer, were concerned above all with leveraging amendments to the Constitution rather than rejecting the document outright.[42] After all, the momentum of ratification, especially once Virginia's convention approved the Constitution shortly before the delegates met at Hillsborough, left seeking amendments the only realistic political strategy for those with grave misgivings about the new government. Of primary concern, of course, was the addition of a bill of rights, which they understood as a sine qua non of representative government. Yet supporters of the Constitution discerned ulterior motives in demands for a bill of rights. Gordon Wood has written that many Federalists opposed the "frenzied advocacy of a bill of rights" because they saw in it a desire to "dilute the power of the federal government in favor of the states."[43] Indeed, this was precisely what Spencer had in mind, and his comments on the lack of a bill of rights in the document demonstrate the extent to which he viewed the states as bulwarks for individual liberties. Speaking against what he saw as the sweeping jurisdiction granted to the federal judiciary, he expressed his fear that, without a bill of rights, the state governments would be swallowed up by a continually grasping federal government, with disastrous consequences for the liberties of the people. "I can see no power," he declared, "that can keep up the little remains of the power of the states. Our rights are not guarded. There is no declaration of rights, to secure to every member of society those unalienable rights which ought not to be given up to any government."[44] At various points in the debates, Spencer referenced the rights of the people and the powers of the state almost interchangeably, revealing his conviction—common to many Anti-Federalists—that local institutions, under the control of local elites like himself, were essential to the preservation of liberties: "Such a bill of rights would be a check upon men in power. Instead of such a bill of rights, this Constitution has a clause which may warrant encroachments on the power of the respective state legislatures. I know it is said that what is not given up to the United States will be retained by the individual states. I know it ought to be so, and should be so understood; but, sir, it is not *declared* to be so. There ought to be a bill of rights, in order that those in power may not step over the boundary between the powers of government and the rights of the people, which they may do when there is nothing to prevent them."[45] In this formulation, "unalienable rights ... the *residuum* of human rights" were best protected by state governments, which, as he had argued throughout the convention, were most responsive to the people.[46] In the context of his comments on Article III, this meant that trial by "juries of the vicinage" must be maintained; further, the omission of this explicit protection could mean only that the framers of the Constitution intended that trial by jury "should be suppressed in the superior and inferior courts."[47]

Historian Saul Cornell has correctly warned that by training our focus on men like Spencer and other leading opponents of ratification, we risk losing sight of the diversity of Anti-Federalist thought, particularly the radical plebeian opposition that characterized "grass-roots" Anti-Federalism.[48] Yet it appears that the desire for a bill of rights was nearly universal among Anti-Federalists. According to Maclaine, the complaint that there was no bill of rights had "often been said out of doors" in North Carolina, and the issue had been crucial at other ratifying conventions, including those in Massachusetts, New York, and Virginia. These conventions had in fact proposed, in various forms, amendments for consideration after ratification, a fact not lost on the North Carolina Anti-Federalists.[49] The desire to safeguard individual liberties seems to have been, at least in Spencer's case, sincere. Reiterating that he was an "advocate for securing every unalienable right," Spencer spoke at length in support of the third clause of Article VI, which banned religious tests as a requirement for public office. This clause, he declared, forced religion to stand on its own inherent validity.[50] On this point, Spencer broke ranks with Anti-Federalist delegates Henry Abbot and David Caldwell, as well as, it seems, with many opponents of the Constitution among the general population of North Carolina. Iredell claimed to have discovered a hysterical pamphlet in the state that alleged that the "pope of Rome might be elected President," and Henry Abbot, who disagreed with the proscription of a religious test, claimed that many of his constituents feared the power to make treaties might enable the federal government to make a treaty "engaging with foreign powers to adopt the Roman Catholic religion in the United States."[51] Dismissing these concerns as unfounded, Spencer argued that without connection to "temporal authority . . . no kind of [religious] oppression can take place." Indeed, the convention's most vocal Anti-Federalist wished "every other" part of the Constitution was "as good and proper."[52]

If not as a knee-jerk opponent of the federal union, how, then, is Spencer to be characterized? Historian Cecelia Kenyon famously described the Anti-Federalists in general as "men of little faith," men so steeped in a fundamental distrust of human nature and classical republican fears of corruption and tyranny that they were incapable of imagining (or were unwilling to imagine) that the proposed Constitution could possibly work in the long term.[53] To Kenyon's Anti-Federalists, the mechanisms of checks and balances set up by the framers—the "rope-dancing, chain-rattling, ridiculous ideal checks and contrivances," as Patrick Henry memorably described them in the Virginia convention—would be insufficient to maintain republican government, which would surely be pulled apart by the centrifugal forces of faction, an inexorable process that would inevitably lead to despotism and tyranny.[54] Spencer largely shared these convictions, but while he harbored a belief that "men in power were apt to abuse it," he nonetheless placed a great deal of faith in "the people," who he said would keep honest men in office—and indeed the new government in existence—"if they shall behave themselves in such a manner as will merit it."[55] It was crucial, though, to erect firm, unambiguous constitutional barriers that the federal government could not usurp without arousing the populace. "If a boundary were set up," Spencer averred, "when the boundary is passed, the people would take notice of it immediately."[56]

Even given this point, it would be tempting, with the benefit of hindsight, to dismiss Spencer as a provincial politician, a rustic populist lacking the foresight and vision of more enlightened statesmen like Iredell and Davie. However, neither Spencer nor many of his vocal allies in the convention—with the possible and noteworthy exception of Willie Jones—seem to have envisioned a future without North Carolina in the national fold. As Spencer observed early in the debates, "No man wishes for a federal government more than I do. I think it necessary for our happiness."[57]

So Spencer's speeches and the efforts of the opponents of ratification in general were aimed at securing crucial amendments to the new Constitution. To this end, along with a Declaration of Rights that included twenty articles, twenty-six amendments were proposed at the end of the convention. Of these proposed additions to the Constitution, five were explicitly aimed at preserving state powers. At the top of the list was a statement echoed in what would become the Tenth Amendment, a stipulation that each state would "respectively retain every power, jurisdiction, and right, which is not by this Constitution delegated to the Congress of the United States." Other proposed amendments included guarantees for state control of the militia, limits on the powers of the federal judiciary, and restrictions on the power of Congress to set the time and place of elections. The penultimate amendment would have protected the right of states to redeem state-issued securities as they saw fit.[58]

The decision at Hillsborough "neither to ratify nor reject" the Constitution caused great consternation among Federalists in the state and beyond. "The Majority of this Convention, under the guidance of Willie Jones, were obstinate to an astonishing degree," Iredell wrote his wife in exasperation. "We are . . . for the present out of the Union, and God knows when we shall get in to it again."[59] Still, they were well aware that the strategy adopted by North Carolina's Anti-Federalists was essentially a gambit designed to force the new government to consider amendments to the Constitution.[60] Davie compared this tactic, which he characterized as a "dictatorial proposal," to a "beggarly bankrupt addressing an opulent company of merchants, and arrogantly telling them, 'I wish to be in copartnership with you, but the terms must be such *as I please.*'"[61] This was partially in response to a provocative speech by Jones in which the Halifax County delegate had dismissed the concerns of the Federalists by declaring, "It is objected we shall be out of the Union. So I wish to be."[62] Spencer was more measured in his remarks. He "acknowledged that exclusion from the Union would be a most unhappy circumstance" but was forced to vote against ratification since doing so seemed to him to be the "mode of proceeding" that was most likely to "hasten the amendments."[63] In any case, he had observed earlier, despite the disadvantages, a "short exclusion" from the new nation was "infinitely less dangerous than an unconditional adoption."[64]

The denouement to the ratification drama—and, in many ways, to Spencer's public life—came at the second constitutional convention at Fayetteville in November 1789. By then, the federal government had been established with George Washington at its head, and, crucially, James Madison had proposed many of the amendments demanded by Spencer and other Anti-Federalists throughout the new nation. Still, Spencer attended the convention, as did several other vocal opponents of ratification at Hillsborough, a group that included Timothy Bloodworth, Thomas Person, and William Lenoir. Willie Jones, perhaps sensing the ratification game was up, declined to stand for election as a delegate, and his absence was notable. Even then, according to Samuel Johnston shortly before the convention began, there was a "virulent and violent Opposition kept up to the new Constitution" in Fayetteville.[65]

The "Anties," despite their minority, attempted to get Spencer elected president but were outmaneuvered by the Federalists, who again secured the position for Johnston.[66] At the convention, Spencer voted with the decided minority against ratification but was selected (along with his rival Davie) to serve on a committee tasked with drawing up proposed amendments to the document. The work of this committee clearly reflects Spencer's influence, particularly the first amendment, which stipulated that "Congress shall not alter, modify, or interfere in the times, places and manner of holding elections for Senators and Representatives."[67] The presumed ability of Congress to meddle with the time and place of elections, it will be recalled, was among

Spencer's gravest concerns with the document at Hillsborough. Shortly after the convention, Spencer, frustrated with a long-running fight over compensation for his services as a superior court judge, apparently "expressed a wish to offer his Services to the United States," desiring to accept an "Appointment in their Courts."[68] If he did angle for a federal appointment, he was disappointed, and he spent the rest of his life on the superior court he had served since the Revolution.

In conclusion, Spencer's contributions to the debate over ratification place him squarely in the mainstream of Anti-Federalist thought, allowing for the narrowness of political options available to the Constitution's opponents at Hillsborough after eleven states had already ratified. If, as Pauline Maier has recently written, the speeches of James Iredell are "among the best glosses on the Constitution . . . anywhere in the ratification debates," Spencer's comments on the document represent a measured but thoroughgoing critique that encapsulates many of the most basic concerns of a significant portion of the Constitution's opponents. These men feared the consequences of ceding powers to a distant federal government, though they were not, for the most part, dismissive of the need for a stronger constitution. Most acknowledged that ratification was probably imminent in any case.[69] More specifically, Spencer represented a significant majority of North Carolinians who feared the influence of distant elites, who regarded political power as safest when it was vested in those closest to them, and who saw the necessity of a bill of rights and a number of structural changes to formally circumscribe the powers of the new government.

These reservations, shared by so many North Carolinians, underscore the contentious and divided nature of American politics at the founding moment. Historian Richard Hofstadter, summarizing what became known as the "consensus" interpretation of American history during the 1950s, once claimed that the United States, unique among nations, was fated "not to have ideologies, but to be one."[70] Yet at Hillsborough the terms of the debate revolved around the very nature, or at least the parameters, of what this ideology ought to be. Indeed, Spencer's speeches, while revealing a distinct faith in the people, evince little of an "exceptional" vision for the new nation and its people. Without stringent protections against encroachments by would-be tyrants, he made clear, the American republican experiment was doomed to failure. At the heart of his critique of the new government, and his advocacy for a bill of rights and other changes, was not so much a belief in American exceptionalism as old assumptions about human nature and the corrosive, almost metastatic nature of power. For Spencer, the "vague and uncertain" wording of the Constitution left open the possibility that men, inherently power-hungry, might "ultimately destroy the liberty of the whole United States" by arrogating power to a federal government that was little more than a vehicle for their ambitions.[71] Spencer may have believed that the United States "might yet hold a place of first importance in the unfolding course of human history," as historian Jack P. Greene has characterized the budding post-Revolutionary faith in American exceptionalism, but his speeches at Hillsborough are shot through with uncertainty and anxiety. For Spencer, the future of the new nation was far from divinely ordained or guaranteed by the putatively unique material circumstances found in the new United States.[72] Ironic, then, that the "decentralized institutional structure" of American government, in no small part a legacy of the Anti-Federalist critique, may well be, as political scientist Charles Lockhart has argued, among the most exceptional aspects of the American political system.[73]

One student of the Hillsborough convention has commented that Anti-Federalists "won the political battle, but . . . lost the philosophical war." Not only did the forces of national consolidation eventually prevail in North Carolina, but the Bill of Rights adopted in 1791 included only one amendment—the Tenth—that explicitly protected the rights of states.[74] But this was hardly Spencer's intent—as noted above, he gave his support to a program of amendments that included five explicit protections for the rights of the states, and virtually all of his speeches at Hillsborough advanced this principle. In the final analysis, his particular contributions to the Hillsborough convention had less to do with winning a battle—political, philosophical, or otherwise—than with, in his words, "ascertaining and securing the great rights of the states and the people."[75] With national consolidation very nearly a fait accompli, Spencer, like Anti-Federalists in several other states, sought to preserve the core elements of his political vision through amendments to a Constitution that most acknowledged would become the supreme law of the land. The battle, as it were, was lost before the Hillsborough convention even met. Spencer's efforts were aimed at securing a favorable and lasting peace.

NOTES

1. Gordon S. Wood, *The Creation of the American Republic, 1776–1787* (New York: W. W. Norton and Co., 1993), 498.

2. James Iredell to Hannah Iredell, 25 November 1779, in *The Papers of James Iredell*, ed. Don Higginbotham, 3 vols. (Raleigh: Division of Archives and History, Department of Cultural Resources, 1976), 2:129.

3. Archibald Maclaine to James Iredell, 6 March 1786, in *The Papers of James Iredell*, ed. Donna Kelly and Lang Baradell, 3 vols. (Raleigh: Office of Archives and History, North Carolina Department of Cultural Resources, 2003), 3:204.

4. Griffith J. McRee, ed., *The Life and Correspondence of James Iredell*, 2 vols. (New York: Appleton, 1857–58), 1:368–69. McRee, a Wilmington-area planter and lawyer who took up history as an avocation, was married to Penelope Johnston Iredell, the granddaughter of James Iredell. Clyde Wilson, "Griffith John McRee," in *Dictionary of North Carolina Biography*, ed. William S. Powell (Chapel Hill: University of North Carolina Press, 1994), 4:195.

5. Philip Hamburger, *Law and Judicial Duty* (Cambridge, Mass.: Harvard University Press, 2008), 454n.

6. Isaac Copeland and Jerry C. Cashion, "Samuel Spencer," in *Dictionary of North Carolina Biography*, 5:412–13.

7. Maclaine to Iredell, 15 September 1789, in *Papers of James Iredell, 1784–1789*, 3:523.

8. Jonathan Elliot, ed., *The Debates in the Several State Conventions on the Adoption of the Federal Constitution*, 5 vols., 2nd ed. (Philadelphia: J. B. Lippincott Co., 1836), 4:55.

9. Copeland and Cashion, "Samuel Spencer," 5:412–13.

10. "Petition from Inhabitants of Anson County Concerning Taxes and Fees for Public Officials," in William L. Saunders, ed., *Colonial Records of North Carolina*, 10 vols. (Raleigh: Josephus Daniels, 1890), 7:808.

11. "1790 Census: Heads of Households," in Walter Clark, ed., *State Records of North Carolina* (Raleigh: P. M. Hale, 1905), 26:243 (hereafter *SRNC*).

12. *SRNC*, 10:243. In 1790, Anson County included part of the lands that would later become Union County, in addition to its current size. See David Leroy Corbitt, *The Formation of the North Carolina Counties, 1663–1943* (Raleigh: Division of Archives and History, 2000), 10, 289. North Carolina governor Samuel Johnston, president of the conventions at Hillsborough and Fayetteville, owned ninety-six people and was the third largest slave owner in Chowan County. *SRNC*, 26:402.

13. See the depositions of Samuel Williams and James Cotton "concerning treatment of Loyalists in Anson County," 12–13 August 1775, in Saunders, *Colonial Records*, 10:125–29.

14. Copeland and Cashion, "Samuel Spencer," 5:413.

15. Hamburger, *Law and Judicial Duty*, 449–75. As Hamburger shows, Spencer and the other justices were nearly removed from office in the wake of the decision, which was very unpopular among many prominent politicians. Many, especially Archibald Maclaine, already privately detested Spencer, regarding him as uncouth and incompetent on the bench. Iredell, on the other hand, approved of the decision, if not Spencer's other behavior.

16. Jackson Turner Main, *The Antifederalists: Critics of the Constitution, 1781–1788* (Chapel Hill: University of North Carolina Press, 2004), 246–47.

17. Pauline Maier, *Ratification: The People Debate the Constitution, 1787–1788* (New York: Simon and Schuster, 2010), 406.

18. Stephen E. Massengill, *North Carolina Votes on the Constitution: A Roster of Delegates to the State Ratification Conventions of 1788 and 1789* (Raleigh: Division of Archives and History, 1988), 67.

19. Maier, *Ratification*, 408–9, 545–46n. In short, as Maier writes, the original stenographer lost interest in the project and gave his notes to a "little boy" to copy. Davie was predictably dissatisfied with the copy of the proceedings, and he and Iredell published a "corrected" version.

20. Ibid., 101.

21. Michael Lienesch, "North Carolina: Preserving Rights," in *Ratifying the Constitution*, ed. Michael Allen Gillespie and Michael Lienesch (Lawrence: University Press of Kansas, 1989), 349.

22. Elliot, *Debates*, 4:51.
23. Ibid., 227.
24. Ibid., 51.
25. Ibid.
26. Ibid., 66.
27. Ibid., 52.
28. Ibid., 75–77, 80.
29. Maier, *Ratification*, 413; Elliot, *Debates*, 4:76; Jack Rakove, *Original Meanings: Politics and Ideas in the Making of the Constitution* (New York: Alfred A. Knopf, 1997), 179–80.
30. Elliot, *Debates*, 4:80–81.
31. Ibid., 76.
32. Ira Berlin, *Many Thousands Gone: The First Two Centuries of Slavery in North America* (Cambridge, Mass.: Harvard University Press, 1998), 279.
33. Elliot, *Debates*, 4:100.
34. State v. Samuel Bryan, March 1782, Salisbury District Superior Court Minute Docket, 1782–86, 10, 13, 15, North Carolina State Department of Archives and History.
35. Quoted in Richard Beeman, *Plain, Honest Men: The Making of the American Constitution* (New York: Random House, 2009), 322.
36. See Edmund S. Morgan, *American Slavery, American Freedom: The Ordeal of Colonial Virginia* (New York: W. W. Norton, 1975).
37. Patrick Henry, speech to Virginia Ratifying Convention, 5 June 1788, in *The American Constitution For and Against: The Federalist and Anti-Federalist Papers*, ed. J. R. Pole (New York: Hill and Wang, 1987), 123.
38. Elliot, *Debates*, 4:117–18.
39. Ibid., 117–18, 131.
40. Ibid., 121.
41. Ibid., 121, 142.
42. For an early example of this interpretation, see prefatory notes to *SRNC*, 20:vi–vii.
43. Wood, *Creation of the American Republic*, 537.
44. Elliot, *Debates*, 4:137.
45. Ibid.
46. Ibid., 138. The italics are Elliot's.
47. Ibid., 154.
48. Saul Cornell, "Aristocracy Assailed: The Ideology of Backcountry Anti-Federalism," *Journal of American History* 76, no. 4 (1990): 1148.
49. Elliot, *Debates*, 4:141; Maier, *Ratification*, 206, 317.
50. Elliot, *Debates*, 4:200.
51. Ibid., 195, 191–92.
52. Ibid., 200.
53. Cecelia Kenyon, "Men of Little Faith: The Anti-Federalists on the Nature of Representative Government," *William and Mary Quarterly*, 3rd ser., 12, no. 1 (1955): 3–43.
54. Henry, speech of 5 June 1788, in *American Constitution*, 123.
55. Elliot, *Debates*, 4:68.
56. Ibid., 169.
57. Ibid., 55.
58. *SRNC*, 22:16–25.
59. Iredell to Hannah Iredell, 3 August 1788, *Papers of James Iredell*, 3:413.

60. Maier, *Ratification*, 423.
61. Elliot, *Debates*, 4:237.
62. Ibid., 225.
63. Ibid., 240.
64. Ibid., 228.
65. Trenholme, *Ratification*, 234; Samuel Johnston to James Iredell, 13 November 1789, in *Papers of James Iredell*, 3:536.
66. William R. Davie to Iredell, 16 November 1789, in *Papers of James Iredell*, 3:537.
67. *SRNC*, 22:52–53. By the time the Fayetteville convention met in November, James Madison had already proposed a series of amendments to the Constitution in Congress. The amendments proposed at Fayetteville were in addition to these amendments, which, according to an early motion made by James Galloway of Rockingham County, failed to address some of the "most exceptional" passages in the document. Ibid., 46.
68. Samuel Johnston to Iredell, 13 November 1789, in *Papers of James Iredell*, 3:536–37.
69. Maier, *Ratification*, 416.
70. Quoted in Seymour Martin Lipset, *American Exceptionalism: A Double-Edged Sword* (New York: W. W. Norton, 1997), 18.
71. Elliot, *Debates*, 4:55.
72. Jack P. Greene, *The Intellectual Construction of America: Exceptionalism and Identity from 1492 and 1800* (Chapel Hill: University of North Carolina Press, 1993), 135.
73. Charles Lockhart, *The Roots of American Exceptionalism: Institutions, Culture, and Policies* (New York: Palgrave-Macmillan, 2003), 30.
74. Lienesch, "North Carolina," 350, 364.
75. Elliot, *Debates*, 4:163.

10

Willie Jones

Kyle Scott

This chapter will situate the political thought of Willie Jones within the broader setting of the ratification debates and incorporate Anti-Federalists and Federalists from inside and outside North Carolina to clarify and contextualize Jones's beliefs. Several unique aspects of Jones's thought will be noted, but it is important to put his thinking in a proper perspective in order to chart a clear course through the nation's and North Carolina's political history.

This chapter has three sections. The first will provide a brief biography of Willie Jones. The next section will provide background with regard to North Carolina's role within the ratification debate and Jones's role within North Carolina during ratification. The third section will provide an analysis of Anti-Federalist thought more generally to situate Jones within the intellectual history of American political thought.

Armistead Gordon wrote, "Willie Jones, a Virginian by birth, was one of the most important and distinguished figures of the states in the Revolutionary period, and in some respects one of the most remarkable men of his time."[1] Gordon is not the only historian to have recognized Jones's prominence in Revolutionary era politics. "Willie (pronounced Wiley) Jones was the principal radical leader of North Carolina, a counterpart to Samuel Adams and Patrick Henry," Samuel Eliot Morison wrote. "A wealthy gentleman of aristocratic tastes but democratic principles."[2] Although I contest the claim that Jones was a radical, it is beyond dispute that Jones was a leading figure in North Carolina politics who played an important role during the Revolutionary period and the transition to statehood. Willie Jones was a constant fixture in North Carolina government before and after the war. His career included service in the first three provincial congresses and the Fifth Provincial Congress, where he worked on the committee to draft the state constitution.[3]

His father, Robert Jones Jr., served as the state's attorney general and sent Willie and his brother Allen to England to be educated at Eton, as he had been. After his return to North Carolina, Willie built his home, known as "The Grove," in Halifax. There, he married Mary Montfort and had thirteen children, eight of whom died before adulthood. "The Grove" grew into one of the largest plantations in the state, with nearly 9,900 acres and 120 slaves.

Jones began his career in public service as a delegate from Halifax County to the lower house of the assembly from 1766 to 1768 and again in 1771. Jones was then elected to the First Provincial Congress in 1774 and to the 1775 and 1776 congresses as well. Jones next served in the lower house of the General Assembly from 1777 to 1780 and in the North Carolina Senate in 1782, 1784, and 1788. For two years between 1780 and 1782 he was elected to the Continental Congress, during which time he also fought, holding the rank of lieutenant colonel, at the Battle of Guilford Courthouse in 1781.

Jones was elected as a delegate to the Constitutional Convention in Philadelphia but declined to attend, as did Richard Caswell. As a supporter of states' rights and North Carolina's sovereignty and a critic of centralized power, Jones did not want to attend a convention that he suspected would move the nation toward a more centralized system of government. Instead, after the Constitution was sent back to the states for ratification, Jones led the campaign to assure its defeat in North Carolina. He was elected as a delegate to the Hillsborough convention, where he helped delay ratification. Over his objections, the Constitution was ratified by North Carolina in 1789 in a second convention. Afterward, Jones never again held elected office but stayed active in North Carolina public life. Most notably, he led the effort to make Raleigh the capital of the state and served as a trustee for the University of North Carolina. He helped steer the university in a direction that reflected the Jeffersonian ideal of an enlightened public in a democratic republic.

The Fifth Provincial Congress, where state leaders drafted and ratified a state constitution in late 1776 after independence was declared, quickly divided itself into two factions. Willie Jones led one side, and luminaries like James Iredell led the other. Jones and the other radicals, as they were known, desired a more democratic polity, whereas Iredell and the conservatives were more interested in protecting traditional landed interests.[4] This division would persist all the way to the ratification debates over the U.S. Constitution. Thus, the debates surrounding the ratification of the Constitution were little more than a continuation of a debate that had taken place immediately following the Declaration of Independence, and perhaps even earlier. "From the earliest times, by geography and demography, in economics and social structure, North Carolina had been predisposed towards a politics of resistance to distant power and protection of local liberties," political scientist Michael Lienesch writes. "The colonial history of the state had been characterized by almost continuous conflict between imperial representatives and an activist lower house of the legislature. With the Mecklenburg Resolves of 1775, North Carolinians had become some of the earliest subscribers to the cause of colonial rebellion; and in the state's Constitution of 1776, they had sought to create a government, in the words of one set of delegate instructions, 'as near a simple democracy as possible.'"[5]

North Carolina's resolve to keep a decentralized and democratic system of government was reinforced by the experience of fighting for freedom and reflected the state's commitment to states' rights and individual liberty. "North Carolinians entered the period of debates swirling around ratification of the federal Constitution during a decade that had witnessed bloody fighting, the establishment of state government, and a judicial challenge to legislative authority," observes historian William S. Price. "These circumstances—coupled with the state's rural character, its lack of a major seaport, its diversity of religious denominations, the presence of large slave and Indian populations, and a tradition of self-sufficiency and independence—fostered strong Anti-Federalist sentiments in North Carolina."[6] Calling ratification opponents "Anti-Federalists" is a misnomer, however. The Anti-Federalists reflected the principles of federalism more accurately than did Federalists, a point that will be elaborated upon later in this chapter.

North Carolina first convened on the matter of ratification in 1788 in Hillsborough, but the state had geared up for the debate with the annual election for members of the General Assembly in August 1787, while the federal convention in Philadelphia was still in progress. The legislature would have to take action on what the federal convention created, so the election served as a proxy vote for whatever the federal convention would eventually give to the North Carolina General Assembly. Pamphlets and newspaper articles were widely circulated with both Federalist and Anti-Federalist views represented. The state, and the elections, divided into these two camps even before the Hillsborough convention. After the elections the Anti-Federalists maintained control in both branches of the General Assembly, ahead of the Hillsborough convention.

Following the elections, which were perceived to be a referendum on the Constitution, the state assembly authorized the election of delegates to the Hillsborough convention, which would decide the issue of ratification.

At the Hillsborough convention, Willie Jones demanded that a vote be taken immediately. Jones argued that a protracted debate was unlikely to change anyone's mind and would only waste the people's time and money.[7] Although perhaps not the most public figure with regard to rallying opposition forces, Jones was the chief architect in building and solidifying opposition to the Constitution. "Willie Jones," historian Louise Irby Trenholme writes, "was in the convention, not to convince others in debate, but to marshal the forces of the opposition." William Richardson Davie, also of Halifax and supporter of the Constitution and signer of the document, identified Willie Jones as the leading Anti-Federalist and termed the opposition's position as the "W. Jones System."[8]

Jones knew he had the votes to defeat the Constitution and wanted to move swiftly. Federalists such as Iredell did not agree to the tactic and spent considerable time debating ratification. On 30 July 1788, the final day of the first North Carolina ratifying convention, Jones and Iredell had a lengthy exchange in which Iredell wanted more time for deliberation. Jones made the competing claim that all arguments that could be made had been made and that no one's mind at that point would be changed. Jones implied that Iredell was using a stalling tactic to prevent the inevitable rejection of the Constitution that Iredell ardently supported.[9]

Iredell and other Federalists were worried that North Carolina would be marginalized if it did not ratify immediately. Jones, though, was not concerned about being left out of the union created by the Constitution. Jones made his point clear in a speech at the Hillsborough convention on 30 July 1788, when he replied to Iredell, "The gentleman further said that we could send no representatives, but must send ambassadors to Congress as a foreign power. I assert the contrary; and that, whenever a convention of the states is called, North Carolina will be called upon like the rest."[10] The statement reflects a more deeply held disposition as well. Jones did not think of the thirteen colonies as disunited, even if they did not all embrace the same Constitution. Rather, a shared heritage and experience united them. To Jones, the colonies were more like siblings who disagree but, when confronted with a severe problem, forget their differences and fight on behalf of one another. This was how independence was won, and this was how he thought it would remain. Jones could not conceive of being thought a foreign nation to the new union, even if North Carolina remained outside the legal boundaries of its Constitution. While it may seem an odd outlook to modern observers, and perhaps it does reflect Jones's lack of understanding of the legal implications of the Constitution, we must understand that the Constitution was new, and a large, united republic was a new and radical concept as well. Jones was familiar with the concept of a confederation or a national system. The federal system devised by the Constitution was a new formulation, which is why James Madison referred to it as "partly federal, partly national," for there was not yet a term that could define it precisely. Today we understand Madison's federal system as confederal and the overall formulation as federal.

Jones also knew that North Carolina had leverage. He recognized that North Carolina was a powerful state with value to add to the union and other member states. He also knew that other powerful states, most notably Virginia, would back North Carolina's admission at any time. Thus he failed to see the urgency of ratification. "Virginia, our next neighbor, will not oppose our admission," Jones predicted. "We have common cause with her. . . . South Carolina and Georgia are deeply interested in our being admitted. The Creek nation would overturn these two states without our aid. They cannot exist without North Carolina."[11] Geographically speaking, South Carolina and Georgia would need North Carolina's cooperation. Union troops would not be able to reach those two southernmost states without North Carolina's cooperation, and North Carolina could send assistance faster than the national government could if assistance was needed.

The style of government endorsed by Jones and other Anti-Federalists was more democratic, more concerned with individual rights, and more committed to a decentralized system of government than what they read into the proposed Constitution. And while he relied on the zealotry of his allies like Colonel Geddy, Jones was more statesmanlike, almost tempering the extreme Anti-Federalists to make their position more palatable to centrists.[12] But his respectable demeanor did not insulate him from insults by critics who opposed his politics. As a skeptical historian put it, "The leader of the radicals and the virtual dictator of the state was Willie Jones, a wealthy planter who lived like a prince but who talked and voted like a Jacobin."[13]

For all the reasons expressed by Anti-Federalists in other states, North Carolina Anti-Federalists, led by Jones, worked effectively to defeat ratification on the first try. According to scholar Alan D. Watson, "When the first ratifying convention met at Hillsborough on July 21, 1788, Anti-Federalists, led by Jones, Thomas Person, and Samuel Spencer, commanded a substantial majority, allowing them to pacify their opposition by proposing Governor Samuel Johnston, an avowed Federalist, as president of the meeting. Then Jones astonished Federalists by proposing a quick vote, claiming that the delegates were prepared for a decision and that delay would merely waste the public's money."[14]

The Anti-Federalist position eventually won at Hillsborough despite Federalists taking most of the floor time. Anti-Federalists had the advantage going into the convention. Most people in the state were uncomfortable adopting a constitution that lacked a bill of rights and promoted centralized political authority. "The margin of the vote against the Constitution (184–84) in August 1788 at Hillsborough was probably an accurate proportional reflection of sentiment against the new federal system in North Carolina as a whole," notes Price.[15] The resolution passed out of this convention neither ratified nor rejected the Constitution but proposed a bill of rights with twenty parts as well as twenty-six additional amendments.

North Carolina's initial refusal to ratify the Constitution was to be expected given its history with the Articles of Confederation and its commitment to states' rights and individual rights. North Carolina initially rejected some of the Articles within the Articles of Confederation, and the Continental Congress was even friendlier to states' rights than the Philadelphia constitution.[16] Furthermore, because North Carolina had adopted its own Declaration of Rights and the principle of codified natural rights was in operation within North Carolina as early as 1689 through the English Bill of Rights, those who fought for independence were uncomfortable adopting a document that did not explicitly guarantee certain rights, rights they had fought so hard to secure during the Revolution.[17]

In the words of Michael Lienesch, "That North Carolina did not fall in line should not have come as a surprise."[18] North Carolinians like Jones pushed the nation toward independence from England because they saw the debilitating and tyrannical effects of a centralized governing body abstracted philosophically and geographically from those that it governed. Therefore, the Articles of Confederation, the governing document during the early years of American independence and during the war, codified a decentralized system of government in which states and localities maintained control of the governing process.

The Constitution, on the other hand, was a more centralizing document, and the consequences of centralization were part of what American revolutionaries were fighting against. North Carolina led the way in American independence as it took the first official state action for independence among the thirteen colonies. On 12 April 1776, North Carolina's Fourth Provincial Congress had instructed North Carolina's delegates to the Continental Congress "to concur with the delegates of the other colonies in declaring Independency."[19] That such a freedom-loving state would be skeptical of, or initially resist, a centralizing governing structure should not be surprising to anyone.

As a vocal opponent of British rule, Willie Jones was a leader of the independence movement in North Carolina, and he later aligned politically with Anti-Federalists. What he saw as reprehensible in British rule he saw reflected in the new Constitution. Jones wanted local control through decentralized governing structures with guaranteed protections for individual rights. Moreover, he was concerned that the new Constitution would empower the mercantile class and alienate the landed gentry—the class to which he belonged. Jones saw no advantage to ratifying a constitution that could replicate what was wrong with British rule or one that violated the amendment procedures provided by the Articles of Confederation. The Articles of Confederation contained procedures for amendment that were ignored by the drafting and ratification procedures for the new Constitution in Philadelphia. The concern was that a new document borne out of disobedience to the law could itself be an instrument of tyranny.

Jones was not just a skillful tactician. He was motivated by a philosophical disposition that moved him to embrace a smaller agrarian system that reflected his populist sentiments. The new Constitution was too far removed from the principles he found important for sustaining self-government. Writing about Jones, Claude Bowers contends:

> In North Carolina [Thomas] Jefferson found a leader cut from his own pattern, an aristocratic democrat, a radical rich man, a consummate politician who made the history that lesser men wrote without mentioning his name—Willie Jones, of Halifax. His broad acres, his wealth, his high social standing were the objects of his pride, and he lived in luxury and wore fine linen while the trusted leader of the masses, mingling familiarly with the uncouth backwoodsmen, inviting, however, only the select to partake of the hospitality of his home. There was more than a touch of the Virginia aristocrat of the time in his habits—he raced, gambled, and hunted like a gentleman. Like Jefferson, he was a master of the art of insinuation, a political and social reformer. He loved liberty, hated intolerance, and prevented ratification of the Constitution in the first State Convention.... There he exerted a subtle influence that was not conspicuous on the floor. If he was neither orator nor debater, he was a strategist, disciplinarian, and diplomat who fought with velvet gloves with iron within.[20]

Jones had thrived under the system during and prior to the Revolution and did not want to see it upended by the mercantilist North, to be sure. But he was a lover of liberty and agrarian life for more than solely his material interests.

Jones was a mature force among the opposition. "If some of the Anti-Federalist arguments verged on the paranoid style," writes historian William Price, "leaders like Willie Jones, Samuel Spencer, and Timothy Bloodworth were skillful enough to bend them to their ends."[21] Jones helped direct and shape some of the more undisciplined arguments circulating among the Anti-Federalists.

Modern historians consider Jones to have been the leader of the Anti-Federalist movement in North Carolina, as did his contemporaries.[22] His affiliation with the Anti-Federalists was motivated by his strong democratic tendencies and opposition to the urban, aristocratic elite that he viewed as being more in line with British sensibilities. And Willie Jones was not simply a leader of democratic thought during his lifetime; his legacy lived on in North Carolina through such men as Nathaniel Macon.[23]

Jones's writings are sparse. So to better understand his political thought, we must approximate his political philosophy by comparing what writings and speeches of his that we do have to the political writings and thought of those we know more completely. This is the task of the next section, where I will situate Jones within Anti-Federalist thought more generally.

Like other Anti-Federalists, Jones made no qualms about his desire to stay out of the union if it meant having to ratify the Constitution in its original form: "It is objected that we shall be out of the Union. I wish to be." He rationalized his position, in part, on the basis that there was no need to hurry. There was more than enough time to deliberate and decide if ratification would be prudent. He remained unswayed by those saying it was a now-or-never proposition: "We are left at liberty to come in at any time. . . . I have no doubt we shall have it when we come in, as much as if we adopted now. . . . Gentleman need not be in such haste. If left eighteen months or two years without offices, it is no great cause of alarm."[24] This sentiment displays Jones's cautious pragmatism that buoyed up against, as he saw it, the headlong pursuit of ratification without consideration of the consequences. Jones was more like an elder statesman in the midst of Federalists who could be like young men more taken by promises than realistic expectations.

Jones's intention to stay out of the union was clear. He would be willing, however, to reconsider if time proved it necessary and if amendments were added. Indeed, Jones proposed a set of amendments: "We have a right, in plain terms, to refuse it if we think proper. I have, in my proposition, adopted, word for word, the Virginia amendments, with one or two additional ones. We run no risk of being excluded from the Union when we think proper to come in."[25] Jones, like most Anti-Federalists, was not a radical but cautious and conservative in his approach to change. To see this, however, one must look to other Anti-Federalists to gain a more complete picture.

Jones, whose political thought reflected Jefferson's, invoked Jefferson's name in defense of his position during his speech at the Hillsborough convention on 31 July 1788. He reasoned, "There is no doubt we shall obtain our amendments, and come into the Union when we please.... [Jefferson] in that letter [to Madison] ... said he wished nine states would adopt it, not because it deserved ratification, but to preserve the Union. But he wished that the other four states would reject it, that there might be a certainty of obtaining amendments. Congress may go on, and take no notice of our amendments; but I am confident they will do nothing of importance till a convention be called."[26] Again, Jones pressed the point that the urgency manufactured by the Federalists was artificial. In Jones's view the prudent course of action was to take more time to see how the Constitution would work in practice and whether a new governing document was necessary at all. Jones was trying to impress upon his fellow North Carolinians the need for prudence and patience. He was fighting against the reactionary tendencies of the Federalists.

While informative, it is not enough to know that Jones was an Anti-Federalist and what role he played in getting a bill of rights added to the U.S. Constitution. Readers must understand what it meant to be an Anti-Federalist and what those who were categorized as Anti-Federalists thought. To do this properly one must look within and beyond North Carolina to develop an understanding of the ratification debate more generally. Furthermore, understanding Willie Jones as an Anti-Federalist will help contextualize and illustrate his political philosophy and bring into focus the full scope of the ratification debate. It is only when this is done that we can demonstrate the importance of Willie Jones and thus justify an examination of his political life.

The immediate question one might ask is why a constitution was being written in the first place. When America declared its independence it wrote a constitution, the Articles of Confederation. In the 1780s there was a push, citing the need for a stronger, more united nation, to write a new constitution. Under the Articles of Confederation the central government had almost no power, and the states could not be forced to do anything they did not want to do. Without a centralized, coordinating power, the new nation seemed to be falling apart—at least according to the critics of the Articles of Confederation. The states could not organize their efforts for a national purpose. The risk was that the nation could not deal with all the problems it was facing. Not only was there domestic discord, but there were threats from abroad as well. Luminaries like Benjamin Rush and George Washington promoted the idea that the fledgling nation was on the brink of collapse.

Yet, these worries may have been overstated. There was a general sense of opportunity in the 1780s, a decade that saw the greatest population growth of any in American history. All the worries about paying back debts and collecting taxes could have been overstated, too. It is difficult to collect data from the period and know whether things were that bad. One state seemed to think they were not. Rhode Island refused to send any delegates to the Philadelphia convention; it was satisfied with the existing system. One New York Anti-Federalist, under the name "The Federal Farmer," wrote on 8 October 1787 to deny that the Articles of Confederation were failing and objected to the Constitution; even if a stronger government was needed, the Farmer argued, it was not, as Willie Jones also argued, an urgent issue.[27]

But, in this instance, perception became reality. The dominant view was that the Articles of Confederation were failing and something needed to be done. The perception perpetuated a sense of urgency and an impending crisis that was manufactured by those seeking a new constitution.

What happened in Philadelphia during the summer of 1787 was not what anyone would have admitted that they expected. With a narrow grant of power to revise the Articles of Confederation, the Philadelphia convention scrapped the Articles and wrote a new constitution. The challenge would be to convince the rest of the nation this was a good thing despite its dubious legal beginnings.

Under the Articles of Confederation, Section 13, all states had to unanimously agree to any amendment to the Articles. But the seventh article of the proposed Constitution required that only nine out of thirteen states had to agree to its adoption for it to take effect. Thus, the new Constitution violated existing law as established by Section 13 of the Articles of Confederation in the name of expediency. Anti-Federalists worried about what other laws might be put aside in the name of expediency.

Under the Articles of Confederation, the assembled Congress had to agree to an amendment and then submit it to the states for universal approval. According to Article VII of the Constitution, the Congress of the states under the Articles would have no official role. Rather, "the Ratification of the Conventions of the nine States, shall be sufficient for the Establishment of this Constitution between the States so ratifying the Same." Anti-Federalists like Willie Jones could not endorse a constitution that they believed so blatantly violated the Articles of Confederation. The worry was that if such a constitution were formed on the basis of extralegal means, then the precedent would be set for a government established through these means to govern through extralegal means as well. Anti-Federalist concerns were well founded; modern legal scholars have argued that violating the strict letter of the Constitution is keeping in the spirit of the Constitution as exemplified by the ratification process.[28]

Anti-Federalists could be found in every state to varying degrees. In North Carolina, Anti-Federalist sentiment was among the strongest and most effective thanks to leaders like Jones. North Carolina was one of the last states to ratify, and in part because North Carolina held out as long as it did, James Madison was forced to usher a bill of rights through the First Congress. North Carolina required a bill of rights as a condition of ratification. Near the end of the Hillsborough convention, Jones held up a list of rights he wished to see incorporated before ratification. "Jones himself presumed it would take about eighteen months to have the amendments ratified," observes Lienesch. "But he had 'rather be eighteen years out of the union,' he announced, 'than adopt it in its present defective form. . . . He referred [also] to one final right, the 'right to reject.'"[29] Jones was a cautious pragmatist. Although it may now seem radical for someone to oppose the Constitution, Jones was opposed to adopting a new order and preferred to maintain the governing document that brought the nation through the American War of Independence. If anything his position was conservative, even though he sometimes relied on rhetorical flourishes bordering on the revolutionary. Jones wanted to make sure that individual and states' rights would be preserved through a bill of rights in the new Constitution.

North Carolina's opposition to a new Constitution without a bill of rights played a pivotal, if not decisive, role in getting a bill of rights adopted. And Willie Jones's efforts can be credited for North Carolina's steadfastness in holding to its principles even when nine of the thirteen states had ratified, thus making the Constitution the law of the land and placing North Carolina outside the protection of the union.

What exactly did it mean to be an Anti-Federalist? Were Anti-Federalists simply contrarians, or was there a deeper philosophical grounding for their opposition? In general terms, writes Lienesch, "Anti-Federalists saw the proposed federal system as a threat to their freedom."[30] Anti-Federalists worried that a larger, more centralized system of government would deprive them of what they had fought to secure in the war against Britain. Most Anti-Federalists were under the impression that weakened state governments and a stronger central government would weaken individuals and deprive them of adequate representation, thus leading to a growth in government and diminished individual and community rights. For Anti-Federalists, states' rights and individual rights were inextricably linked.

Herbert Storing cites two fundamental principles held by Anti-Federalists: only a small republic can enjoy a voluntary attachment of the people to the government and a voluntary obedience to the laws, and only a small republic can provide a government by the people.[31] For the Anti-Federalists, the rules that dictated the policy process would determine whether the resulting policy decision was in the public good. The process was as important as the outcome in achieving the public good. And for the Anti-Federalists, the public good was determined by each local community determining what was in its own best interest, for the local community was more familiar with the needs and values of its citizens than was a centralized government overseeing a large number of communities. The logic of this formulation is that a small community shares similar values that lead it to a higher degree of agreement concerning the public good.[32]

But more important than sharing common views about the common good, Anti-Federalists understood the importance of scale and its relationship to consent. Only a small republic, they argued, could govern through consent, as a larger republic would either require passivity among the people or force interested parties to accept measures they disliked. Small republics enjoyed the active, voluntary engagement of their citizens.

On 24 July 1788, during the North Carolina ratifying convention, Joseph Taylor, with Jones's backing, expressed his concern over what he saw as the consolidating tendency of the Constitution and the problem of consolidating communities that did not share the same interests.[33] James Winthrop of Massachusetts wrote, "The idea of an uncompounded republic, on an average of one thousand miles in length, and eight hundred in breadth, and containing six million white inhabitants all reduced to the same standard of morals, of habits, and of laws, is in itself an absurdity, and contrary to the whole experience of mankind."[34] Winthrop went on to say that local interests are the most closely connected to self-interest; therefore, the citizen's bond is stronger at the local level because the same interests are shared. Decisions should be made through deliberation within the community. They should be made at the level closest to the people.

Echoing these sentiments, one of the most notable Anti-Federalists, Brutus, argued the states should retain control over their affairs because their smaller size made them more manageable and more accountable to the people. Brutus even argued that the local communities should be consulted before the state governments.[35] The general conclusion reached by Anti-Federalists was that the separation of powers was insufficient and that the state powers allotted by the Constitution would not stop the national government from growing beyond its intended sphere. Furthermore, the men and the institutions were not separated enough from the law. Whoever was in power had complete control over the law and could interpret and change it as they saw fit. And given that the institutions (especially the courts, because their members were unelected with life tenure) were properly insulated from the public, consent from the governed would not be needed under the new Constitution.

Where the Federalists opted for an extended republic, the Anti-Federalists argued for a confederation of small republics. For the Anti-Federalists, the best way to achieve public virtue was to preserve and promote individual virtue. Thus, the Anti-Federalists were able to promote the public good without sacrificing the good within the individual. The Anti-Federalists can be understood as being more concerned with cultivating character than with crafting laws: "More than their Federalist opponents, the Anti-Federalists inclined toward the ancient view that, just as the soul's excellent qualities have a natural title to rule over the base impulses, public spirit is entitled to govern private interests."[36] The mechanism for achieving this balance was the preservation of a small republic. This is why Anti-Federalists, including Willie Jones, linked states' rights to individual rights. If states retained their governing authority, argued Jones, individuals would retain their rights as well. If governing was abstracted to a large centralized body charged with the task of governing a multitude of competing interests, individual rights would be subjugated in the name of the public good. In small republics there would be less of a distinction between public good and individual liberty.

A small republic would be better equipped to preserve the individual and public good without sacrificing the liberty of either, providing a stable and long-lasting government and alleviating the tendency toward corruption that necessarily comes with the operation of a large republic, particularly one in which the ratio of representatives to citizens is reduced.[37] Some Anti-Federalists, including Jones, saw similarities between the size of the new American government and the British Empire and drew upon their experience under British rule to impress upon the American people the perceived dangers inherent in a large republic.[38] More influenced by their recent war over independence with the king of England than by examples from the classical world, the Anti-Federalists wanted sovereignty to reside within the states. They believed the greatest threat to liberty came from above. This threat was embodied in the Constitution, which the Anti-Federalists saw as establishing a system that would undermine the authority of the states and work to consolidate their varied interests.[39]

We know that the Federalists' answer to this problem would be new institutional restraints. They also argued that only the virtuous would have an interest in politics. For the Anti-Federalists, institutional constraints were not enough.

Anti-Federalists argued that the only way to make sure people were adequately represented was by tying both the people and the government to one another, and the best way to ensure the bond without coercion was through small size and close proximity. From the Anti-Federalists' point of view, the Constitution overlooked the differences that existed among local communities and the differences between the local communities and the national government by artificially manufacturing a large republic out of thirteen separate states.[40]

While the expressed concerns of the Anti-Federalists over the size of the nation and the lack of representation provides some insight into why smallness and closeness promote virtue, it does not complete the picture. The Anti-Federalist called Centinel I helps bring the point into focus when he writes, "A republican, or free government, can only exist where the body of the people are virtuous, and where property is pretty equally divided, in such a government the people are the sovereign and their sense or opinion is the criterion of every public measure."[41] To some degree the Anti-Federalists equated smallness with sameness. Thus, the perceived public good varied little between people, and that meant the public and the private were similar.

The ties between the representatives and the people diminish as do the ties among the people as the districts grow in size. The overriding point is that representative government must rest on a foundation of deliberation and fellowship. That is, one cannot be compelled to look out for someone else without being forced to subjugate his or her individual interests to those of the greater good, thus sacrificing individual liberty. Bonds of fellowship and deliberation, however, allow for citizens to align their individual interests with those of others in the community without sacrificing individual liberty or the public good. "They [Anti-Federalists] were far more likely than their antagonists to refer to government and society as 'natural.' Civic virtue was a central concern of their political argument, and they were zealous to defend true opinion and small states as the foundations of civic education," writes historian Carey McWilliams.[42] To this point, and others relating to the issue of scale, Anti-Federalists were on solid footing with historical and normative support stretching back to the Greek city-states. In *Politics*, Aristotle wrote, "Experience shows that a very populous city can rarely, if ever, be well governed.... To the size of states there is a limit, as there is to things, plants, animals, implements; for none of these retain their natural power when they are too large or too small, but they either wholly lose their nature, or are spoiled."[43] In small states—particularly in small republics—there is a sense of connection and fellowship that is absent in large states. Large states promote competition and domination through acting on one's self-interest; small states promote deliberation.

It is unlikely Jones relied upon Aristotle in deciding to oppose ratification. It is significant, however, to notice that Jones and the Anti-Federalists more generally were part of a consistent strand of political philosophy reaching back to ancient Greece—that is, scale is important. The argument was that to cultivate the proper disposition and engagement among citizens, to facilitate the proper relationship between officials and citizens, and to best approximate the public good and civic virtue, nations could not be too large or too centralized. Jones was seeking to preserve a more traditional view of government and community, whereas the Constitution was trying to make over anew how republics were constructed and conceived. Jones was anything but radical in this respect.

Early in May 1789 James Madison announced to Congress that he would submit a bill of rights for approval on 8 June in an attempt to persuade North Carolina to join the union. By a vote of 194–77, the Fayetteville convention did just that on 16 November 1789. The General Assembly approved the Bill of Rights on 21 December 1789. This action made North Carolina the next-to-last state to ratify the Constitution. Recognizing the inevitability of ratification, Willie Jones did not attend the Fayetteville convention. After all, he had fought for a bill of rights and had won.[44] Jones was not a radical, for he understood the importance of compromise and the benefit of accepting what victories he could without holding too steadfast to his opposition.

The addition of the Bill of Rights is evidence that there is value in dissent, and in fact, there is value in the struggle produced by the presence of dissent. If it were not for Anti-Federalists, there would not have been a discourse about the value of republican government, separation of powers, or American political ideals. Moreover, without dissent and the ensuing struggle, our Constitution may very well lack a bill of rights, and we would thus be living in a much different country. Modern observers may look askance at Anti-Federalists, for so many of us revere and hold dear the very document they opposed. But what all observers should remember is that without active and engaged dissent, there would have been no moderating force to keep the centralizing tendencies of the new document balanced against the more traditional views of the Anti-Federalists.

Jones was a gentleman statesman who fought hard for what he believed. He was not a charlatan. When he felt he could move the state in his preferred direction, he did. When he saw the tide moving against him, he stepped out of the way. Being able to accept defeat graciously is an underappreciated cornerstone of stable democracies. Jones lived the example admirably.

Once Jones left politics, he remained active in civic life within North Carolina. He was still a wealthy landowner with the leisure time and connections to pursue civic projects. He helped oversee the University of North Carolina as a trustee and worked to establish the state's capital in Raleigh in 1791, where he died on 8 June 1801.

Because Jones did not serve in high federal office or live too long beyond the ratification of the Constitution, it is easy to overlook his influence. Yet he was no less an influence on North Carolina's ratification debates than was Alexander Hamilton on New York's. Jones was every bit the gentleman statesman as Thomas Jefferson while embodying similar political leanings and sensibilities. Without North Carolina's willingness to hold out until a bill of rights was proposed in the first Congress, we might not have the Bill of Rights that we have today. And without Jones's force of character and political wherewithal, North Carolina may have ratified without demanding a bill of rights. If for no other reason, we must remember Jones for his influence on the structure of our nation's governing document.

NOTES

1. Armistead C. Gordon, *Old Halifax: A Series of Newspapers Clippings* (N.p.: American Historical Society, 1931), 6.

2. Samuel Eliot Morison, *John Paul Jones: A Sailor's Biography* (Boston: Little, Brown, 1959), 198.

3. He did not serve in the Fourth Provincial Congress. He had been appointed to Superintendent of Indian Affairs for the Southern Colonies.

4. Richard B. Bernstein, "Ratification of the Constitution," in *The Reader's Companion to American History*, ed. Eric Foner and John Arthur Garraty (Boston: Houghton Mifflin, 1991), 913; Pierce Robinson Blackwell, "Willie Jones of Halifax: Part II," *North Carolina Historical Review* 18, no. 2 (1941): 33–170, 134. For a general review, see also Hugh T. Lefler and William S. Powell, *Colonial North Carolina: A History* (New York: Charles Scribner's Sons, 1973).

5. Michael Lienesch, "North Carolina: Preserving Rights," in *Ratifying the Constitution*, ed. Michael Allen Gillespie and Michael Lienesch (Lawrence: University Press of Kansas, 1989), 343–44.

6. William S. Price, "North Carolina," in *The Bill of Rights and the States: The Colonial and Revolutionary Origins of American Liberties*, ed. Patrick T. Conley and John P. Kaminski (Madison, Wis.: Madison House, 1999), 436.

7. Useful accounts include Steven E. Massengill, *North Carolina Voters on the Constitution: A Roster of Delegates to the State Ratification Conventions of 1788 and 1789* (Raleigh: North Carolina Division of Archives and History, 1988); Louise Irby Trenholme, *The Ratification of the Federal Constitution in North Carolina* (New York: Columbia University Press, 1932); and Pauline Maier, *Ratification: The People Debate the Constitution, 1787–1788* (New York: Simon and Schuster, 2010).

8. Davie quoted at Trenholme, *Ratification*, 134. See also ibid., 148 and 201.

9. See generally Maier, *Ratification*; Massengill, *North Carolina Voters*; and Trenholme, *Ratification* for documentation of North Carolina's ratifying conventions and Maier, in particular, for a terrific treatment of the ratification period within each state.

10. Quoted in Trenholme, *Ratification*, 18.
11. Quoted in Massengill, *North Carolina Voters*, 129.
12. Steven R. Boyd, *The Politics of Opposition: Antifederalists and the Acceptance of the Constitution* (Millwood, N.Y.: KTO Press, 1979), 110.
13. William E. Dodd, "The Place of Nathaniel Macon in Southern History," *American Historical Review* 7, no. 4 (1902): 663–75, 665.
14. Alan D. Watson, "States' Rights and Agrarianism Ascendant," in *The Constitution and the States*, ed. Patrick T. Conley and John P. Kaminski (Madison, Wis.: Madison House, 1988), 260.
15. Price, "North Carolina," 436.
16. Lienesch, "North Carolina," 347.
17. Ibid., 350.
18. Ibid., 343.
19. Watson, "States' Rights," 251.
20. Claude G. Bowers, *Jefferson and Hamilton: The Struggle for Democracy in America* (Boston: Houghton Mifflin, 1925), 77.
21. Price, "North Carolina," 436–37.
22. Hugh T. Lefler and Albert Ray Newsome, *North Carolina: The History of a Southern State*, 3rd ed. (Chapel Hill: University of North Carolina Press, 1973), 283. See also Bernstein, "Ratification of the Constitution," 913.
23. Dodd, "Place of Nathaniel Macon," 665–64.
24. Quoted in Blackwell, "Willie Jones," 134.
25. *Elliot's Debates*, 4: 226; Trenholme, *Ratification*, 129–30. See also Massengill, *North Carolina Voters*, 6.
26. Quoted in Trenholme, *Ratification*, 130.
27. Ralph Ketcham, ed., *The Anti-Federalist Papers and the Constitutional Convention Debates* (New York: Signet Classics, 2003), 258.
28. See generally Bruce Ackerman, *We the People: Transformations* (Cambridge, Mass.: Belknap Press, 2000).
29. Lienesch, "North Carolina," 362.
30. Ibid., 355.
31. Herbert J. Storing, *What the Anti-Federalists Were For: The Political Thought of the Opponents of the Constitution* (Chicago: University of Chicago Press, 1981), 16.
32. See generally Herbert J. Storing, ed., *The Anti-Federalist: Writings by the Opponents of the Constitution* (Chicago: University of Chicago Press, 1981).
33. Jonathan Elliot, ed., *The Debates in the Several State Conventions on the Adoption of the Federal Constitution*, 5 vols. (Philadelphia: J. B. Lippincott Co., 1836), 4:24.
34. Paul Leicester Ford, *Essays on the Constitution of the United States, Published during Its Discussion by the People, 1787–1788* (New York: B. Franklin, 1970), 63.
35. Brutus, 27 December 1787, in Ketcham, *Anti-Federalist Papers*, 287.
36. Wilson Carey McWilliams, "The Anti-Federalists, Representation, and Party," *Northwestern Law Review* 84, no. 1 (1990): 19.
37. Speech of Melancton Smith, 21 June 1788, in David J. Siemers, *The Antifederalists: Men of Great Faith and Forbearance* (Lanham, Md.: Rowman and Littlefield, 2003), 144.
38. Speech of William Grayson, June 1788, in ibid., 217–18.
39. Brutus, 18 October 1787, in Bernard Bailyn, ed., *The Debate on the Constitution* (New York: Library of America, 1993), 1:165–67.

40. Brutus, 18 October 1787, in Storing, *Anti-Federalist*, 110.
41. Centinel I, 5 October 1787, in Siemers, *Antifederalists*, 80.
42. Wilson Carey McWilliams, "Democracy and the Citizen: Community, Dignity, and the Crisis of Contemporary Politics in America," in *How Democratic Is the Constitution?*, ed. Robert A. Goldwin and William A. Shambra (Washington, D.C.: American Enterprise Institution for Public Policy Research, 1980), 92.
43. Aristotle, *Politics*, trans. C. D. Reeve (Indianapolis: Hackett, 1998), 1325a4.
44. Price, "North Carolina," 438.

V

The Legatees of the Revolution

William R. Davie

North Carolina's Patriot Partisan

Scott King-Owen

As American patriots pressed the British closer to defeat at Yorktown in 1781, General Nathanael Greene selected Colonel William R. Davie as commissary general in charge of foraging for the Continental army. Unfortunately, North Carolina had been "reduced to a degree of poverty and distress by impolicy so as to be unable to supply her own inhabitants," Greene lamented.[1] Since Davie's power to seize goods from harassed citizens by "odious impressments" required the imprimatur of state authority, Greene requested North Carolina's Board of War to make the appointment.[2] "He [Davie] is not willing to engage," the general wrote, "unless his powers are ample; for he is not willing to hazard his reputation without a fair prospect of succeeding. His ambition, popularity, good sense, and activity, give great reason to hope he will execute the business to our satisfaction."[3] Although the Board of War made the appointment, it limited Davie's authority to one district until the state's General Assembly could give Davie more ample powers.[4] Davie's "arduous and disagreeable" yearlong service as commissary general proved quite formative in his subsequent career as a public figure, shaping his views on statesmanship.[5]

Davie applied the lessons his Revolutionary experience taught him in his quest for a balanced, hierarchical, and harmonious order in North Carolina and national politics from 1781 to 1805. He worked to build "decision and firmness" into state and national institutions, focusing his efforts on judicial reform, support for the Constitution, internal improvements, and the state's first university. The benefit of early education in the home of his uncle William

Richardson, a Presbyterian preacher, and further training at the College of New Jersey (now Princeton) gave Davie a decided advantage over his unlettered peers.[6] A colleague at the Constitutional Convention in 1787 described Davie as a "Lawyer of some eminence," a man with a "good classical education," and a gentleman "with considerable literary talents."[7] By the time of his final years in North Carolina, Davie came to lament the "gothic ignorance" of state leaders and the intensifying partisanship of the Federalist and Democratic-Republican Parties.[8] He blamed his failure to win a seat in Congress in 1803 on parochial partisanship that prevented citizens from submitting to his liberal, independent judgment. In 1805, Davie, a frustrated and melancholy anachronism, retired from politics to a plantation named Tivoli in upstate South Carolina, condemned as the "King of the Federalists to the Southward."[9]

In retirement at Tivoli, Davie wrote sketches of his Revolutionary exploits as well as a manual on the use of cavalry, nostalgically recalling his autonomy as the twenty-four-year-old leader of a light horse company.[10] After Davie replaced the worn-out Colonel Thomas Polk as commissary general, however, he fumed at the bureaucratic nightmare that characterized North Carolina's Revolutionary government. Unlike his quasi-independent light horse command, his new position thrust him into a tangled web of dependence on jealous local officials, petty state leaders, and incompetent politicians. Davie's first task—acquiring the approval of the Board of War for his appointment—underscored the state's lack of leadership. The board itself had originated from the governor's complaint that his executive council failed to function. Davie lampooned the board's members, later writing in his memoirs that "nothing could be more ridiculous" than the three men who composed it.[11] The General Assembly confirmed Davie's appointment, but its leadership was no more effective despite Davie praising the "ardent patriotism" of its members. Lawmakers had doubled their legislative output since the Revolution began, enacting a mass of statutes requiring repeated revision since the legislature reacted slowly to the vicissitudes of war. Davie concluded a section of his war sketches with the telling observation that "the advantages derived from an existing well organized government will never be forgotten."[12]

Other annoyances of Davie's wartime experience that became important to him in his postwar career concerned the inadequate transportation facilities of the state and the deranged condition of the state's finances. Davie's letters criticized the legislature for lack of foresight in making internal improvements for the efficient distribution of war matériel he collected.[13] Even more distressing to Davie was the state's method of impressing goods for the troops from an impoverished public, which he called "legal robbery, qualified by promissory note."[14] "There is no centralized power over everything," Davie lamented to Governor Thomas Burke in 1781.[15] Life-giving commerce shriveled under the ruinous policy of a previous executive, Governor Abner Nash, and Davie was forced to make purchases on his own personal credit, for which he petitioned the General Assembly in vain for reimbursement. Had Davie been compensated, it would have likely taken the form of fiat paper money, emitted on five occasions during the war and twice after the war. Fiat currency embittered Davie for the future, leading him to comment that "paper emissions without real funds of redemption are mere state tricks now detected by everybody."[16]

Davie's tenure as commissary general ended in 1782, after legislators complained that Davie's assistants abused their impressment powers. Davie then settled down in Halifax with Sarah Jones, daughter of a general under whom he had served early in the war.[17] As Davie told a friend in 1783, a man must have a "fixed plan" so that he could live "genteely" under a "frugal economy." Halifax had rapidly grown into a center of planter culture, influenced deeply by, but resentful of, Virginia's grandees. There, Davie became a lawyer-planter, building an estate that allowed him to live "genteely" by the labor of slaves while he tackled legal questions for his neighbors. Davie soon entered politics as a lower house representative from the neighboring county of Northampton.[18] He sponsored legislation to reform the tax code—a "difficult and unpopular" course of action that resulted in a boon for large landowners through taxation by acreage, not by value.[19] Davie still expressed dislike for paper money, which, he told a colleague, caused the profits of the merchant to vanish "like Magic." He relented, nonetheless, to the need for a circulating currency and offered an unsuccessful plan to emit £100,000 in funds as long as redemption was tied to taxes on sales of confiscated lands.[20] Davie's keen interest in legal reform can also be traced through assembly journals. Davie approved or sponsored legislation to increase the salaries of the superior court judges, called for a revisal of the state's laws, and insisted that the state repeal all state laws contrary to the Treaty of Paris.[21]

Davie's experience in the legislature through the 1780s confirmed his conclusion that the views of "young republicks" are "all local and limited."[22] Continued fights over legal reform, emission of paper money, confiscation of land from Tories, and taxation convinced Davie that his state careened toward a breakdown of law and order. As a lawyer, Davie favored an autonomous role for law, in which constitutional guidelines remained insulated from popular passions; he criticized the state's superior court judges for openly courting community approval in a series of cases involving Loyalists. Bitterness climaxed in the legislative session of 1786. Davie and his lawyer comrades dominated a committee investigating the state's three superior court judges for banishing three Tories who had returned to the state after the war.[23] One judge accused the lawyers of "scouring and hunting after fees."[24] The committee of lawyers, predictably, condemned the three judges and demanded that, in future, they adjudicate cases based on the "true spirit and meaning of the Constitution."[25] When the legislature rejected the lawyers' report, Davie fumed and entered a protest against the vote. Davie's role in the fight, however, earned him the praise of a colleague, Archibald Maclaine, who wrote a pamphlet dedicated to Davie that detailed every single reprehensible act of the legislature and the judges for the previous three years.[26]

A chorus of voices across the union lamented the state of public affairs by the late 1780s. To the men who became Federalists, the nation's woes seemed to multiply as they corresponded and commiserated over each travesty of law and justice. "At the eve of Bankruptcy and total dissolution of Government," North Carolinians joined with residents of other states to consider revisions to their national frame of government.[27] On 6 January 1787, the General Assembly selected Davie, along with four others, to represent the state at the Constitutional Convention to take place in Philadelphia in the summer. His Revolutionary experience had taught him that states needed "decision and firmness," with powers divided between governing bodies, while his experiences during the 1780s taught him the need to create a common interest—"the basis on which all the transactions of mankind are built"—that could help bind the states together. Soon to be thirty-one, Davie departed for Philadelphia.[28]

College of New Jersey alumni secured nine of the seats at the convention. We cannot know how many of Davie's contributions to the Constitution relied exclusively on an intellectual milieu shaped by the lectures of the university's Reverend John Witherspoon, whose homilies combined history, moral philosophy, political science, and religion. Davie's wartime experiences may have rekindled his appreciation for Witherspoon's four essential characteristics of a good government: wisdom, fidelity to the public interest, secrecy and dispatch, and unity and concord. Combining Scottish and Continental Enlightenment thought, Witherspoon told his students that every "good form of government must be complex, so that the one principle may check the other," and that a government must be "so balanced" that every party "draws to his own interest or inclination."[29] Davie's political ideas, filtered through his experiences, certainly owe something to Witherspoon's potpourri of Scottish moral philosophy, republicanism, and liberal thought.[30] Davie certainly agreed with the list of the "vices" of the Articles of Confederation proposed by another Witherspoon student, James Madison: the failure of the states to pay requisitions, states' encroachment on federal authority, violations of the law of nations and treaties, and states' trespasses on the rights of other states through paper money and debtor laws.[31] Paper money represented a personal annoyance for Davie, since it supplied the stingy budget of North Carolina's delegates, who complained to Governor Richard Caswell that North Carolina's paper currency was subject to "Considerable Decrements when reduced to Current Coin."[32]

North Carolina's delegates grasped the enormity of the task that lay before them, believing that their work constituted an unparalleled experiment, a chance to make an exceptional contribution to political philosophy.[33] Although Hugh Williamson led the delegation in completing its extraordinary task, Davie earned a spot on the Grand Committee that shaped the eventual Connecticut Compromise.[34] Davie's concerns about the structure of a national government, one that would be, in his words, "partly federal, partly national," he shared in brief remarks in late June. In a debate over the method of electing senators, Davie expressed grave doubts about a Senate composed of members chosen by the state legislatures; he argued that such a system would simply re-create the problems that existed under the Articles.[35] Davie's criticisms highlighted his insistence on "balance and security," as he told his friend and North Carolina lawyer James Iredell.[36] After much debate, delegates eventually crafted a balanced government that would "in some respects operate on the States, in others on the people," and narrowly approved the now well-known Connecticut Compromise by mid-July.[37] North Carolina's delegates, including Davie, provided the crucial swing votes for the compromise.[38] With the critical decision over the legislative structure of the national government secure, delegates could move on to other issues.

Handling the question of slavery's relationship to the new national government proved to be one of the more contentious difficulties raised at the convention, and it gave Davie his most noteworthy opportunity to speak. On 12 July, in a bitter back-and-forth argument over the issue of direct taxation as it related to representation, Davie decided it was "high time to speak out" as Gouverneur Morris, an implacable opponent of counting slaves for representation, finished speaking. In "stridency bordering on paranoia," in Richard Beeman's words, Davie told the delegates that the business of the convention would be "at an end" if the new government did not count slaves in determining representation. "N. Carola. would never confederate on any terms," Davie thundered, if the eastern states refused to support what became known as the Three-Fifths Compromise.[39]

Davie's "paranoia" reflected his status as a slaveholder, North Carolina leaders' growing unease about slavery in the late 1780s, and the threat of direct taxation. In 1784, when North Carolina voted to cede its western territories to Congress, it explicitly enjoined the national government from enacting regulations tending toward emancipation in the ceded lands.[40] Quaker petitions for general emancipation, combined with itinerant preachers declaiming against slavery, had led to a proposed general emancipation bill in 1787 that failed in the North Carolina Senate by a margin of two votes. At the time of his participation in the Philadelphia convention, Davie owned at least twenty-five slaves. In the context of Gouverneur Morris's comments concerning direct federal taxation, Davie's distrust arose from the very real chance that federal taxing power could indeed affect his livelihood as a planter.[41] Indeed, in their summary letter to North Carolina's governor in September 1787, North Carolina's delegates praised the Three-Fifths Compromise three times, mentioning that the state would now have "more security" for the return of its runaway slaves.[42] Davie himself saw no conflict in linking his own political "security" in the federal government to the lack of liberty and inherent social death in slavery, later defending the Three-Fifths Compromise as necessary for securing the South's due weight in representation.[43]

Davie did not sign his name to the Philadelphia delegates' final product. Instead, he returned to North Carolina in early August. Lest anyone accuse him of dereliction of duty, Davie explained that as general principles had been sufficiently settled, he felt at liberty to return to his law practice for the start of the autumn superior court term.[44] Undoubtedly, Davie eagerly wanted to find out how the momentous decision in the famous *Bayard v. Singleton* decision, rendered in May 1787, might affect his other cases.[45] The *Bayard* case originated in North Carolina's confiscation acts that had allowed the seizure and sale of the property of a New Bern Loyalist, Samuel Cornell, who fled to New York during the Revolution. Davie, along with lawyer Samuel Johnston, represented Elizabeth Bayard, heir of Cornell, against Spyers Singleton, the purchaser of the Cornells' New Bern property. After the General Assembly in 1785 had banned lawsuits for recovery of confiscated property, Davie and Johnston argued in superior court in May 1786 that such a ban violated the state's constitution. At the May 1787 court term, the judges agreed, declaring the law of 1785 unconstitutional for its denial of the right of trial by jury to Elizabeth Bayard. This case's assertion of judicial review affected other suits on the docket, suits that may have been the "business" that Davie said called him so "pressingly" from Philadelphia.[46]

In October 1787, the Constitution crafted by Davie and his colleagues appeared in North Carolina newspapers, and the General Assembly ordered the printing of 1,500 public copies by November.[47] Although Davie played a minor role in the work at Philadelphia, he became one of the foremost champions of the Constitution in North Carolina's ratification debates, set in the Piedmont town of Hillsborough in the summer of 1788. Davie and his coterie of nationalists, including Samuel Johnston, James Iredell Sr., Hugh Williamson, and Archibald Maclaine, won elections for seats in the convention and flooded the public sphere with pro-Constitution essays. Iredell and Maclaine both released pamphlets in early 1788 to influence the outcome of the elections and to counter now-lost pamphlets published by the state's soon-to-be denominated Anti-Federalists.[48] Voters, however, were suspicious and irascible. A riot in Dobbs County led to the destruction of election records, one Federalist had his eyes "blacked" in a street fight in Hillsborough, and affrays broke out in two other counties.[49] Anti-Federalist delegates arrived in Hillsborough in July with instructions from their constituents to vote immediately against the Constitution and thus save taxpayer money by avoiding a long convention. Arguing that their purpose was to debate the frame of government designed in Philadelphia, nationalists called for spirited inquiry and deliberation but often ended up posing and answering their own questions because Anti-Federalists generally refused to debate.[50]

Davie, the "great cannon from Halifax," as one critic labeled him, spared North Carolina not a whit in his comments: "The conduct of this state has been among the principal causes which produced this revolution in our federal government." The state chiefly sinned in issuing paper money, a "great political evil" and "iniquitous" in Davie's eyes.[51] Although wealth alone has not proven a significant predictor of support for ratification, support for paper money did. Of the thirty-six legislators who voted to emit paper money in 1785, thirty-one of them rejected ratification, while legislators who voted against paper money were more likely (nine out of twelve) to approve of the new Constitution.[52] Indeed, when North Carolina failed to ratify, Davie and others attributed the decision to the state's love for paper money.[53] His disgust at fiat currency may explain why Davie contributed specimens of North Carolina's paper money to the University of North Carolina Museum in 1802, as a reminder to future generations of the state's fiscal folly.[54] Davie's salvos against fiat currency hit a nerve among his opponents, who rushed to defend the state while criticizing the power of the new federal government to interfere with the state's internal policies. Davie replied that the Constitution would affect future monetary policies only and that the new federal judiciary would not interfere with the sanctity of existing contracts. The federal government would be powerful, but limited.[55]

Davie's praise for the Constitution rested on that document's careful balancing of powers. He defended the phrase "We the People" from criticism by arguing that the new government gave the people "an immediate interest and agency in the government," even as the whole structure still rested on the great "massy pillars" of the states. Unlike his opponents, Davie did not fear the development of a national "aristocracy" or federal meddling in the "internal policy" of the states. The Senate, with its "perfectly balanced" powers, could conduct its business, especially treaty making, with "secrecy, design, and dispatch," while the federal judiciary, with its "partial" powers," could resolve interstate disputes.[56] In discharging his "fire-balls" in defense of the Constitution at the convention, Davie was perhaps second only to James Iredell in the number of times he rose to defend the new frame of government. Yet their words failed to persuade. Davie's desperate last gambit, two days before the end of the convention, was to argue that if North Carolina failed to ratify at that moment, it would remain out of the union forever. Scoffing at Davie's threat, opponents of ratification called Davie's bluff and won the day by a margin of 100 votes.[57]

Momentarily defeated, the pro-Constitution forces developed a two-prong plan of attack. They marshaled the state's citizens in a petition campaign that ultimately garnered 3,359 signatures, collected to impress upon the General Assembly the need to call another ratification convention.[58] Davie and James Iredell, meanwhile, took up the task of publishing the debates of the Hillsborough ratification convention.[59] While the petition campaign did secure a second trial for ratification at Fayetteville in 1789, the published debates themselves contributed little to the burgeoning embrace of "federal" politics in the state. James Madison's introduction of a bill of rights, the stature of George Washington as the first president, and the return of relative prosperity (contrary to Anti-Federalist predictions) assuaged the public mind. Even after Anti-Federalists staged a walkout in the Fayetteville convention of 1789, delegates voted to join the union by a margin of 118 votes. As the representative for the town of Halifax, Davie now happily sat among the majority.[60]

With membership in the union secure, Davie turned his attention to the state's development. Davie, in contrast to the gruff parsimony of fellow planter Nathaniel Macon, envisioned enlightened state power, under the leadership of an educated elite, as a tool to promote material progress. Active and energetic government, one that harnessed the state's productive capacity for the good of the whole, rather than a negative government that took little and did less, defined Davie's vision. Davie focused his energy in three areas: internal improvements, legal reform, and education. Recalling the lack of transportation during the Revolution, Davie supported internal improvements through publicly sanctioned private corporations. He helped to lead the Roanoke Navigation Company, a chartered corporation tasked with clearing the Roanoke River so that Davie and his fellow planters could reduce North Carolina's economic subservience to Virginia.[61] Unfortunately for the champions of internal improvements, progress was slow.

Davie remained equally passionate about—and slightly more successful in—the cause of judicial reform during the 1790s. As a lawyer, Davie lamented the clogged dockets of the courts, the mixing of law and equity jurisdiction, and the lack of a final tribunal of appeal to resolve difficult questions for the entire state.[62] Despite asserting that change was "indispensably necessary," Davie witnessed only piecemeal reforms in the state's court system by 1800. The federal circuit courts, on the other hand, gave Davie a platform for success. In his most important victory, *Hamiltons v. Eaton* (1796), Davie argued that North Carolina had erred in confiscating the debts of two bona fide British citizens. The Treaty of Paris, not recognized by North Carolina until 1787, nonetheless trumped state statutes and required that Archibald and John Hamilton not meet with any bar to lawful recovery of their debts in the state's courts. Davie's victory inspired other creditors to ask his opinion on how they might sue North Carolina citizens for pre–Revolutionary War debts.[63] So highly regarded was Davie's legal acumen that President Washington offered him a spot on the Supreme Court. Fortunately, Davie remained in the state to work on his most important legacy: the development of a state university.

Backed by a state constitutional mandate, legislators had attempted to establish the university (as it was called) in 1784.[64] Where Davie's predecessors met with defeat, Davie triumphed in 1789 with a bill that called upon the legislature to "consult the Happiness of the arising generation" by equipping the members of that generation for "an honourable discharge of the social duties of life."[65] No other of Davie's contemporaries gave so much to the school that sprang up in rural Chapel Hill: Davie served on the board of trustees; proposed a curriculum; tirelessly corresponded with board members about buildings, faculty, and student discipline; and defended the university in the public prints. What critics saw as a "Temple of Folly, planned by the Demi-God Davie," represented, in Davie's eyes, a sanctuary for cultivating North Carolina's future republican leaders.[66] By combating aristocracy, superstition, and ignorance, the university promoted the "general diffusion" of knowledge in the state, furthering North Carolinians' progress to enlightenment.[67]

Davie's proposed curriculum did not conceal the enlightened vision he intended for the University. The school's leaders, particularly the Reverend Samuel E. McCorkle and later Joseph Caldwell, imagined a Presbyterian-centered curriculum that would counteract the progress of Deism and "Jacobine Morality" in the South.[68] Davie, instead, embraced a modern curriculum encompassing Enlightenment texts by Montesquieu, Vattell, Burlamaqui, and Hume, as well as practical courses in geography, physics, chemistry, agriculture, modern languages, and belles lettres. Practical subjects like these could mold self-governing citizens with a liberal and cosmopolitan view of the republic's future. Davie's curriculum mentioned religion only insofar as to require entering students to have a reading knowledge of Greek so they could read the Gospels; Caldwell's later curriculum specified the Gospels to be studied with examinations required for each, with the intent of creating a morally disciplined citizenry. Davie shepherded his curriculum design through board meetings and donated many volumes of the kinds of books he wished students to read, leading to acrimony with Dr. McCorkle and one of Davie's Federalist colleagues, John Steele.[69] Until 1804, when Joseph Caldwell became president, Davie's plan for producing enlightened statesmen partially guided academic study at the university.[70]

Unfortunately for Davie, his vision of an active, energetic government led by an educated elite faltered with the rise of the first American political parties, the Federalists and the Republicans. Davie played no small role—though it was at times unwitting and halting—in the building of the system that was also his political undoing. The men of Davie's generation did not welcome political parties. Nonetheless, the growing divide within President Washington's administration over Hamiltonian economic policies and foreign entanglements soon forced Davie and others to choose sides. Privately, Davie supported Hamilton's assumption plans but wanted the federal government to ease North Carolinians' pains by accepting the state's paper currency for federal tax payments. He feared that the heavy hand of the federal government imperiled the great experiment launched by the Constitution, breaking those affective bonds needed to give the people an "interest and agency" in the national government.[71]

The crisis over the Jay Treaty, designed to increase commerce with Britain, so aroused Davie's ire that he began to identify more with the Federalists. In the public hullaballoo over what many southerners saw as John Jay's betrayal of southern interests, Davie recognized that the Republicans were collecting "combustibles" in a "political Vesuvius" that he deemed the "most delicate and important [crisis] since the organization of our government."[72] The public's treatment of Jay, Davie noted, was a "satire upon humanity" that produced a "shameless... degree of ingratitude."[73] Even at the University, Davie and others in 1795 had to oust a "furious Republican" whose teachings threatened to undermine Davie's vision for the school.[74] In the election of 1796 that followed the Jay Treaty crisis, Davie noted with some dismay that "uncommon pains have indeed been taken by the Jacobin party" to ensure Thomas Jefferson's election.[75] By the time that President Washington retired, Davie was labeling those Republican members of the "Jacobin party" an "unprincipled faction" motivated by "factious views."[76]

Davie, like many in his Federalist coterie, believed that he stood for the right political principles, which justified his criticism of the Republicans as a faction while exonerating his own party from the charge of being a self-interested clique.[77] Reeling from the fallout over the Jay Treaty, Davie found himself drawn further into the polarization of politics in the next foreign policy crisis to shake the young republic: the XYZ Affair. Relations with France soured precipitously in 1797, as the French increased attacks on American ships. "The humiliating system of suffering and concession," Davie argued in a public speech, "has already disgraced our councils, and debased our national character; and that high rank which we lately held in the estimation of nations, is not to be recovered but by an active display of the spirit and energy of the people."[78] While Davie rejoiced that the French crisis had seriously disrupted the "Jacobin" faction in southern politics, he worried about the possibility of a coming conflict and the need for a man of "business and energy" to be at the helm of the state.[79] One of the most popular men in the state, so popular that legislator Samuel Johnston waited for Davie to appear in the House of Commons before introducing a resolution praising President Adams, Davie was soon selected as governor at the height of the crisis.[80] His correspondence with Secretary of State Timothy Pickering marked him as a committed Federalist, concerned with the most politically appropriate appointments to the new provisional army to be headed by George Washington and with circulating pamphlets to further undermine the "Jacobin" Republicans.[81] In the atmosphere of crisis, Davie galloped headlong into political partisanship.

At the height of his popularity, Davie made a surprising decision: he accepted a position as one of the American envoys to negotiate with the French, indicating that he undoubtedly preferred peace to war, even if it diminished the war hysteria that bolstered Federalist fortunes. Telling James Iredell that the "appointment of an Envoy is highly honorable to me," Davie made his way north in the fall of 1799, having resigned as governor on 10 September. Sailing with Oliver Ellsworth in November, the envoys met William Vans Murray in

Paris and spent the next year successfully negotiating claims for the $12 million in damages done by the French since 1796. Returning to the United States in October 1800, Davie spent some time in Washington, D.C., before arriving home 23 December. In his absence, however, a crisis in political affairs had dramatically altered the nation.[82]

The presidential election of November 1800 had provoked tremendous political passions. "Parties in this district," lawyer Charles W. Harris noted in 1800, "become more and more defined."[83] A Federalist newspaper editor engaged in fisticuffs with a Republican state official in Raleigh while newspaper editorials and pamphlets assaulted readers with apocalyptic predictions of the nation's future under the monarchical John Adams or the Jacobin Thomas Jefferson.[84] In the 1800 congressional elections, which were held in the summer, Federalists managed to win six out of ten seats, taking approximately 59 percent of votes cast. Average voter turnout reached just over 58 percent for congressional seats but dropped to just under 40 percent for the presidential contest that fall. North Carolinians gave Jefferson the election by a margin of 414 votes. Still, Adams managed to earn four electoral votes in North Carolina.[85] At the state level, however, affairs proved more ominous for Davie and his Federalist friends. The "anti-federals" had a "decided Superiority," and, consequently, they selected David Stone, one of Davie's law students, U.S. senator over Davie; they made Joseph Gales, Republican editor of the *Raleigh Register*, the state's printer; and they selected a native of France, Stephen Cabarrus, as Speaker of the House of Commons over his Federalist opponent. Federalist William Polk later lamented of this General Assembly that never had there been "so much ignorance collected in a legislative capacity since the days when laws were enacted prohibiting the frying of pancakes on Sundays."[86]

As the national contest over the presidential election extended into the next year because of the tie in the electoral college between Thomas Jefferson and Aaron Burr, Davie expressed deep doubts about the future of the republic. Siding more with the moderate Federalists, Davie at times blamed the Federalists and at others the "antifederal party." Critical of the "violence" of the Republicans and the "party rage" of the Federalists, Davie lamented that the "public mind" convulsed in the partisan tug-of-war. Conceiving of the public as a single body working together for the good of the whole under the influence of the nation's natural aristocrats, Davie pictured the American people as an organism, whose nerves were stimulated to the "highest pitch of irritation" by political factionalism. The eventual result, in Davie's estimation, would be the "destruction of the Constitution," once the "world's best hope" but now an "old woman's story." Searching for a solution, Davie turned to his Revolutionary past. Federalists needed to "act an open, manly and decided part" through disinterested leadership and dispassionate propaganda. As he did when he was a wartime partisan, Davie simply needed to mount his steed and show good men the way forward.[87]

As early as January 1800, Davie had already recognized the need for Federalists to coordinate and share information. From his brief stay in Washington, D.C., after the French negotiations, Davie learned about "some plans" of the Federalists to turn the "most influential men" into an epistolary phalanx. By correspondence, these "firm federalists" could circulate "useful information."[88] A year after the election of Jefferson, Davie was invited by Alexander Hamilton to a meeting to further these plans by focusing on "incorrect men with incorrect views." The death of Davie's wife, Sarah, in April 1802 probably precluded his attendance, but North Carolina's Federalists had already hatched a plan to tackle the problem of "incorrect views" among the people.[89] Lawyer Duncan Cameron discussed a plan in 1802 to raise money for the distribution of a Federalist newspaper, William Boylan's *Minerva*, to each county for "suppressing falsehood and disseminating truth." Cameron, quoting an unnamed source, argued that the "political opinion of a great portion of our citizens seems to me to grow out of hatred and party principles" imbibed from Republican newspapers. Indeed, Cameron noted, Republican newspaper editors had already been in the habit of distributing free newspapers.[90] No extant sources indicate the extent of Davie's approval or participation, but he probably expressed sympathy for the project. After all, the plan amounted to a campaign of political enlightenment that, if done correctly, could undo "incorrect views" through dispassionate and reasoned discourse.

Davie decided to act a "manly part" in pursuit of a congressional seat in the election of 1803. He requested information from Cameron in April 1803 of Federalist "prospects" in the western part of state, particularly after public confidence in the "Mammoth of Wisdom" (Jefferson) had faltered.[91] His printed electoral handbill espoused the classic principles of disinterested elite statesmanship: he wished for no voter support except from men who would allow him to "pursue the good of my Country according to the best of my judgment, without respect either to party men or party views."[92] He later told his friend John Steele that he had not sought the office but that gentlemen had called upon him to run and that he agreed on the condition that he never be called upon to surrender his "personal independence" or "principles."[93] These hallmarks of aristocratic, disinterested, and independent leadership had, however, become outdated by 1803. Davie lost the election by more than 800 votes, losing every county save one to his Republican opponent, Willis Alston.

Indeed, only one Federalist candidate, Samuel Purviance, won election in 1803. With electoral turnout averaging 70 percent, Republicans took 71 percent of the 42,444 votes cast in the races.[94] The Federalist phalanx crumbled.

Davie analyzed his loss in three separate letters to Federalist friends. To Duncan Cameron, Davie claimed that the Republicans had a better strategy. They convinced a second Republican candidate to drop out of the race and spread "frightful stories of kings and aristocrats" among the "ignorant and credulous."[95] Criticism of Davie as an aristocrat appeared in print as early as 1798 but flourished wildly in 1803.[96] An apocryphal electoral anecdote gave a scatological cast to Davie's elitism; Willis Alston circulated the story that Davie had returned from France with a fancy china bowl that he kept under his bed as a chamber pot.[97] Davie told John Steele that the election depended on keeping the people "cool and rational" by suppressing party spirit but that the "Demos" had denounced him as the "King of the Federalists to the Southward" and the personal enemy of Jefferson.[98] Davie rationalized his defeat in a letter to John Haywood, claiming that his loss was the "greatest favor" the Republicans could bestow.[99] Intraparty criticism of Davie's electoral handbill highlighted disunity in the Federalist ranks, indicating that internal problems of party organization as well the failure of their plan of public enlightenment doomed Davie's election.[100]

By 1805, Davie had settled upon retirement. "My Plan of life is to be completely changed," he told John Haywood, "and those measures which are to lead me to a *Repose* I have long sighed for, and which is becoming every day more necessary for me to commence this fall."[101] Davie departed for his plantation, Tivoli, in upstate South Carolina. Never again did he take up public office in North Carolina. As for politics, he told Duncan Cameron in 1808 that the Federalists were dead as a political party.[102] The Revolutionary War soldier, legislator, member of the Philadelphia convention, lawyer, governor, and diplomat devoted his remaining days to agricultural improvements and voluminous correspondence with his friends. Inclined to melancholy, Davie preferred the life of a planter to that of a politician.

The republic Davie helped to fashion had outgrown his political principles by 1805. The active, energetic, and, above all, independent state that Davie envisioned under the leadership of enlightened statesmen had given way, in his view, to indolence, illiberal partisanship, and a want of firm political principles. From his time as a youthful partisan in 1780 to his diplomatic post in 1800, Davie had constantly advocated a set of political principles emphasizing aristocratic leadership, the exercise of independent judgment, and harmony and balance among the different interests in society, values out of touch with the political realities of the Jeffersonian republic. Davie died 5 November 1820, mourned as the "Soldier, Jurist, Statesman and Patriot" who paternalistically preferred "the People's good to the People's favour."[103]

NOTES

1. General Nathanael Greene to William R. Davie (hereafter WRD), 26 November 1781, William R. Davie Papers, Southern Historical Collection (hereafter SHC), the Wilson Library, University of North Carolina at Chapel Hill.

2. WRD to the General Assembly, 7 July 1781, Davie Papers.

3. Nathanael Greene to the Board of War, 18 December 1780, in *The Papers of General Nathanael Greene*, ed. Richard K. Showman et al., 13 vols. (Chapel Hill: University of North Carolina Press, 1976–2005), 6:598–99.

4. *The Laws of North Carolina* (New Bern: Arnett and Hodge, 1786–1836): 1781, chapter 8, and 1782, chapter 2.

5. Blackwell P. Robinson, ed., *The Revolutionary War Sketches of William R. Davie* (Raleigh: North Carolina Division of Archives and History, 1976), 42.

6. Blackwell R. Robinson, "Davie, William Richardson," in *Dictionary of North Carolina Biography*, ed. William S. Powell (Chapel Hill: University of North Carolina Press, 1979–96), 2:28–29; Daniel W. Patterson, *The True Image: Gravestone Art and the Culture of Scotch Irish Settlers in the Pennsylvania and Carolina Backcountry* (Chapel Hill: University of North Carolina Press, 2012), 256, 324–25.

7. Max Farrand, ed., *The Records of the Federal Convention of 1787*, 3 vols. (New Haven: Yale University Press, 1911), 3:95–96.

8. WRD to John R. Eaton, 27 December 1801, in J. G. de Roulhac Hamilton and Kemp P. Battle, eds., "William Richardson Davie: A Memoir," *James Sprunt Historical Monograph*, no. 7 (Chapel Hill: University of North Carolina at Chapel Hill, 1907), 49.

9. Scott King-Owen, "To 'Write Down the Republican Administration': William Boylan and the Federalist Party in North Carolina, 1800–1805," *North Carolina Historical Review* 89, no. 2 (2012): 171–74; WRD to John Steele, 20 August 1803, John Steele Papers, SHC.

10. William Richardson Davie, *Instructions to Be Observed for the Formations and Movements of the Cavalry* (Raleigh: Abraham Hodge, 1799).

11. Alexander Martin to Nathanael Greene, 3 and 5 January 1781, and WRD to Nathanael Greene, 6 January 1781, in *Papers of Nathanael Greene*, 7:45, 54, 56; WRD to Nathanael Greene, 6 January 1781, Davie Papers; Robinson, *War Sketches*, 39; Fordyce M. Hubbard, *Life of William Richardson Davie, Governor of North Carolina* (Boston: Charles C. Little and James Brown, 1848), 53.

12. George Wesley Troxler, "The Homefront in Revolutionary North Carolina" (Ph.D. diss., University of North Carolina, 1970), 8; Robinson, *War Sketches*, 39, 43; Hubbard, *Life*, 55–59; Scott King-Owen, "The People's Law: Popular Sovereignty and State Formation in North Carolina, 1776–1805" (Ph.D. diss., Ohio State University, 2011), 450.

13. WRD to Nathanael Greene, 23 April 1781, and WRD to the General Assembly, 7 July 1781, Davie Papers.

14. Hubbard, *Life*, 69.

15. WRD to Thomas Burke, 30 August 1781, Davie Papers.

16. WRD to Nathanael Greene, 22 October 1781, Davie Papers; Hubbard, *Life*, 65, 72; King-Owen, "People's Law," 9; WRD to Alexander Martin, 3 November 1781, quoted in Hubbard, *Life*, 73.

17. Hubbard, *Life*, 5; Alexander Martin to William Bryan, 16 August 1782, in Walter Clark, ed., *The State Records of North Carolina*, 20 vols. (Raleigh: State of North Carolina, 1896–1905), 16:703; WRD to Charles Crockett, 20 July 1783, Davie Papers.

18. Blackwell P. Robinson, *William R. Davie* (Chapel Hill: University of North Carolina Press, 1957), 138, 141, 145–46.

19. King-Owen, "People's Law," 84–85; WRD to Nathanael Greene, 27 June 1784, Davie Papers.

20. WRD to John Gray Blount, 1 September 1782, in Alice B. Keith, William H. Masterson, and David T. Morgan, eds., *The John Gray Blount Papers*, 4 vols. (Raleigh: State Department of Archives and History, 1965–82), 1:29–30; Robinson, *William R. Davie*, 162.

21. Clark, *State Records*, 19:565, 675, 751; William Hooper to James Iredell, 15 March 1783, in *The Papers of James Iredell*, ed. Don Higginbotham, Donna Kelly, and Lang Baradell, 3 vols. (Raleigh: Office of Archives and History, 1976–2003), 3:37–38.

22. WRD to Nathanael Greene, 2 December 1783, Davie Papers.

23. King-Owen, "People's Law," 118–21; Archibald Maclaine to George Hooper, 9 February 1786, in Clark, *State Records*, 18:534.

24. Letter of Judge Ashe in Clark, *State Records*, 18:137–42.

25. Report of the Committee in ibid., 18:215–17, 361.

26. Two other protests likely reflect Davie's sentiments: Protest against the Unqualified Approbation of the Judges, in ibid., 18:477; and Protest against the Thanks to the Judges, in ibid., 18:478–82. Archibald Maclaine, *The Independent Citizen, or, the Majesty of the People Asserted against the Usurpations of the Legislature of North-Carolina in Several Acts of Assembly, Passed in the Years 1783, 1785, 1786, and 1787* (Newbern, N.C.: Francois X. Martin, 1787).

27. Address of Benjamin Hawkins to the General Assembly, 1787, in Clark, *State Records*, 20:241–43.

28. WRD to Nathanael Greene, 22 October 1781, Davie Papers; WRD to John Haywood, 14 January 1791, Ernest Haywood Collection, SHC; Robinson, *William R. Davie*, 37–89, 178–79; Jonathan Elliot, ed., *The Debates in the Several State Conventions on the Adoption of the Federal Constitution*, 5 vols. (Washington: Jonathan Elliot, 1836–45), 4:120–21.

29. John Witherspoon, *Lectures on Moral Philosophy*, ed. Varnum Lansing Collins (Princeton, N.J.: Princeton University Press, 1912), 91, 94.

30. Scholars of early American political history have concluded in the debate over America's liberal versus republican origins that both traditions were influential. Davie, in seeking the public good and disinterestedness, reflected key themes in republican thought but ultimately was the product of several traditions. See Richard Beeman, *The Varieties of Political Experience in Eighteenth-Century America* (Philadelphia: University of Pennsylvania Press, 2004); Lee Ward, *The Politics of Liberty in England and Revolutionary America* (Cambridge: Cambridge University Press, 2004); and Robert M. Calhoon, *Dominion and Liberty: Ideology in the Anglo-American World, 1660–1801* (Arlington Heights, Ill.: Harlan-Davidson, 1994).

31. Woody Holton, *Unruly Americans and the Origins of the Constitution* (New York: Hill and Wang, 2007), 108–23, 179–98; Jack Rakove, *Original Meanings: Politics and Ideas in the Making of the Constitution* (New York: Vintage Books, 1997), 35–56.

32. Delegates of North Carolina to Governor Caswell, 14 June 1787, in Farrand, *Records*, 3:46.

33. Ibid.

34. William Blount to Richard Caswell, 19 July 1787, in Paul H. Smith et al., eds., *Letters of Delegates to Congress, 1774–1789*, 25 vols. (Washington, D.C.: Library of Congress, 1976–2000), 24:363.

35. Farrand, *Records*, 1:487, 498; James H. Hutson, ed., *Supplement to Max Farrand's "The Records of the Federal Convention of 1787"* (New Haven: Yale University Press, 1987), 131–32.

36. WRD to James Iredell, 19 June 1787, in Farrand, *Records*, 3:279.

37. Farrand, *Records*, 1:487

38. Richard Beeman, *Plain, Honest Men: The Making of the American Constitution* (New York: Random House, 2009), 200, 219, 220–21.

39. Ibid., 211; Farrand, *Records*, 1:593.

40. King-Owen, "People's Law," 167, 239–40, 92.

41. Robinson, *William R. Davie*, 374.

42. North Carolina Delegates to Richard Caswell, 18 September 1787, in Smith et al., *Letters of Delegates*, 24:431–32.

43. Elliott, *Debates*, 4:31.

44. WRD to James Iredell, 17 July 1787, and William Blount to Richard Caswell, 20 and 23 August 1787, in Farrand, *Records*, 3:60, 71, 74–75.

45. Davie wrote to one of the parties in the case in early June to give her details and to tell her that he hoped to see her in New York. See WRD to Mary Edwards, 14 June 1787, Davie Papers.

46. King-Owen, "People's Law," 123–24; Philip Hamburger, *Law and Judicial Duty* (Cambridge, Mass.: Harvard University Press, 2008), 449–61.

47. *State Gazette of North Carolina* (New Bern), 4 October 1787; Sheldon F. Koesy, "Continuity and Change in North Carolina, 1775–1789" (Ph.D. diss., Duke University, 1963), 259.

48. Archibald Maclaine to James Iredell, 26 December 1787, in *Papers of James Iredell*, 3:336; *State Gazette of North Carolina*, 27 March 1788; King-Owen, "People's Law," 146–47.

49. King-Owen, "People's Law," 145, 147.

50. Elliot, *Debates*, 4:4, 30.

51. Ibid., 4:182, 159.

52. King-Owen, "People's Law," 150; William Clayton Pool, "Economic Interpretation of the Ratification of the Federal Constitution in North Carolina," *North Carolina Historical Review* 27, nos. 2–4 (1950): 119–41, 289–313, 437–61; Robert A. McGuire, *To Form a More Perfect Union: A New Economic Interpretation of the United States Constitution* (New York: Oxford University Press, 2002), 187–91.

53. WRD to James Madison, 10 June 1789, Davie Papers; John Swann to James Iredell, 21 September 1788, in Smith et al., *Letters of Delegates*, 25:381–82.

54. *North Carolina Minerva* (Raleigh), 7 December 1802.

55. Elliot, *Debates*, 4:182, 191, 160; Max Edling, *A Revolution in Favor of Government: Origins of the U.S. Constitution and the Making of the American State* (New York: Oxford University Press, 2003), 163–73.

56. Elliot, *Debates*, 4:16, 17, 21, 43, 58, 67, 120, 121, 157.

57. Ibid., 94, 238.

58. King-Owen, "People's Law," 157; James Iredell, "To the People of North Carolina," 18 August 1788, in *Papers of James Iredell*, 3:418–27.

59. King-Owen, "People's Law," 160–61; WRD to James Iredell, 4 June and 4 August 1789, in *Papers of James Iredell*, 3:498, 510.

60. Alan D. Watson, "States' Rights and Agrarianism Ascendant," in *The Constitution and the States*, ed. Patrick T. Conley and John P. Kaminski (Madison, Wis.: Madison House, 1988), 264; Penelope Sue Smith, "Creation of an American State: Politics in North Carolina, 1765–1789" (Ph.D. diss., Rice University, 1980), 601.

61. Robinson, *William R. Davie*, 294; King-Owen, "People's Law," 226; *Laws of North Carolina*, 1796, chap. 13.

62. Robinson, *William R. Davie*, 160; Clark, *State Records*, 21:220; *Journal of the House of Commons*, 1794 session (Halifax: Abraham Hodge, 1795), 42; *Journal of the House of Commons*, 1796 session (Halifax: Abraham Hodge, 1797), 40; Samuel Johnston to James Iredell, 15 April 1791, in Griffith J. McRee, ed., *Life and Correspondence of James Iredell*, 2 vols. (New York: Appleton, 1857–58), 2:331; WRD to John Haywood, 18 January 1791, Ernest Haywood Collection.

63. *Journal of the House of Commons*, 1791 session (Halifax: Abraham Hodge, 1792), 11; Hamiltons v. Eaton, 2 Martin 1 (N.C. 1796); New York Public Library, *Papers Relating to Samuel Cornell, North Carolina Loyalist* (New York: New York Public Library, 1913), 7–9, 16.

64. Darryl Lynn Peterkin, "'Lux, Libertas, and Learning': The First State University and the Transformation of North Carolina, 1789–1816" (Ph.D. diss., Princeton, 1995), 10; WRD to Spruce Macay, 3 September 1793, Macay and McNeely Family Papers, SHC.

65. R. D. W. Connor, *A Documentary History of the University of North Carolina, 1776–1799*, 2 vols. (Chapel Hill: University of North Carolina Press, 1963), 1:23.

66. Robinson, *William R. Davie*, 257.

67. WRD to Alexander Martin, 1 November 1790, in Clark, *State Records*, 22:801; *North Carolina Journal* (Halifax), 19 and 26 December 1792, 20 March 1793, 5 June 1793, 10 July 1793.

68. Joseph Caldwell to John H. Hobart, 8 November 1796, and Thomas Y. How to Joseph Caldwell, 27 December 1796, in Connor, *Documentary History*, 2:71; Samuel E. McCorkle to John Haywood, 20 December 1799, Ernest Haywood Collection.

69. Connor, *Documentary History*, 1:452–54; Robinson, *William R. Davie*, 244–50; Board of Trustees Minutes, 12 July 1804, in Board of Trustees of the University of North Carolina Records, University Archives, Chapel Hill.

70. John Steele to John Haywood, 19 September 1799, Ernest Haywood Collection; Robinson, *William R. Davie*, 249–51.

71. WRD to John Haywood, 14 January 1791, Ernest Haywood Collection; WRD to Alexander Martin, 1 November 1790, in Clark, *State Records*, 22:800; WRD to Alexander Hamilton, 17 November 1791, Alexander Hamilton Papers, microfilm reel 6, vol. 13, Library of Congress, Washington, D.C.

72. WRD to James Iredell, 4 September 1795, William R. Davie Papers, North Carolina Division of Archives and History (NCDAH); WRD to John Haywood, 7 March 1796, Ernest Haywood Collection.

73. WRD to James Iredell, 4 September 1795, Davie Papers (NCDAH).

74. Robinson, *William R. Davie*, 251.

75. WRD to James Iredell, 11 November 1796, in McRee, *James Iredell*, 2:480.

76. WRD to James Iredell, 1 February 1797, in ibid., 490.

77. Ronald P. Formisano, "Deferential-Participant Politics: The Early Republic's Political Culture, 1789–1840," *American Political Science Review* 68, no. 2 (1974): 473–85; John F. Hoadley, *Origins of American Political Parties, 1789–1803* (Lexington: University Press of Kentucky, 1986), 8–11, 141; Richard Hofstadter, *The Idea of a Party System: The Rise of Legitimate Opposition in the United States, 1780–1840* (Berkeley: University of California Press, 1969), 8, 18.

78. *North Carolina Journal* (Halifax), 2 July 1798.

79. WRD to James Iredell, 25 June 1797, in McRee, *James Iredell*, 2:514; WRD to James Iredell, 22 July 1798, Papers of James Iredell Sr., David M. Rubenstein Rare Book and Manuscript Library, Duke University, Durham, N.C.

80. Samuel Johnston to James Iredell, 28 November 1798, in McRee, *James Iredell*, 2:537–38.

81. William R. Davie's Recommendations for Appointments to the Provisional Army, 29 November 1798, and WRD to Timothy Pickering, August 1798, Davie Papers (NCDAH).

82. WRD to James Iredell, 10 September 1799, Papers of James Iredell Sr.; Robinson, *William R. Davie*, 319, 322, 324, 332, 336, 351, 356.

83. Charles W. Harris to Robert Harris, 12 May 1800, in J. G. de Roulhac Hamilton and H. M. Wagstaff, eds., "The Harris Letters," *James Sprunt Historical Publications* 14:1 (Durham: Seeman Printery, 1916), 71.

84. *Minerva and Raleigh Advertiser* (Raleigh), 24 June 1800; *North Carolina Mercury* (Salisbury), 24 September 1800; King-Owen, "People's Law," 338–40.

85. Lampi Collection of American Electoral Returns, 1787–1825, American Antiquarian Society, 2007, accessed 9 July 2009, http://elections.lib.tufts.edu/aas_portal/index.xq.

86. William Polk to John Steele, 28 November 1800, in H. M. Wagstaff, ed., *The Papers of John Steele*, 2 vols. (Raleigh: Edwards and Broughton, 1924), 1:190–91; William Blackledge to John Gray Blount, 25 November 1800, in Masterson, *John Gray Blount Papers*, 3:453; William Polk to John Steele, 20 November 1800, John Steele Papers.

87. WRD to John Steele, 2 and 22 February 1801, 7 January 1802, and 13 March 1802, in Hamilton, "William Richardson Davie," 43–44, 45, 50, 53; WRD to Duncan Cameron, 9 March 1801, Cameron Family Papers, SHC; WRD to Thomas Jefferson, 20 March 1802, Thomas Jefferson Papers, Library of Congress, Washington, D.C.

88. Charles W. Harris to Duncan Cameron, 9 January 1800, Cameron Family Papers.

89. Alexander Hamilton to Charles C. Pinckney, 15 March 1802, in *The Papers of Alexander Hamilton*, ed. Harold C. Syrett, 27 vols. (New York: Columbia University Press, 1961–86), 25:563; Robinson, *William R. Davie*, 370.

90. Duncan Cameron to John Moore, 1802, John Moore Papers, David M. Rubenstein Rare Book and Manuscript Library.

91. WRD to Duncan Cameron, 3 April 1803, Cameron Family Papers.

92. Electoral handbill, Davie Papers (SHC).

93. WRD to John Steele, 25 September 1803, in Wagstaff, *John Steele*, 2:414.

94. Lampi Collection of American Electoral Returns.

95. WRD to Duncan Cameron, 2 and 28 August 1803, Cameron Family Papers.

96. Hubbard, *Life*, 111–12; *Republican Star* (Easton, Md.), 6 September 1803.

97. Robinson, *William R. Davie*, 371.

98. WRD to John Steele, 20 August 1803, John Steele Papers.
99. WRD to John Haywood, 2 September 1803, Ernest Haywood Collection.
100. John Steele to WRD, 15 September 1803, John Steele Papers.
101. WRD to John Haywood, 9 June 1805, in Hamilton, "William Richardson Davie," 56.
102. WRD to Duncan Cameron, 9 February 1808, Cameron Family Papers.
103. Robinson, *William R. Davie*, 379, 396–97.

12

John Chavis

Quiet Leader of an Early Revolution

Benjamin R. Justesen

Just two decades after the ratification of the U.S. Constitution, soft-spoken educator John Chavis began sowing seeds for a quiet revolution in North Carolina's new capital city, Raleigh. Little was known for certain about his background, yet his unmistakable aura of leadership inspired trust in children of both the wealthy and the less affluent. In an age when private tutors held sway across the American South—where university-educated teachers were still rare—North Carolina's students were drawn to this man with classical training at the precursors of Princeton University and Washington and Lee University.

In 1807, Chavis was in his midforties: a respectable and respected black patriot claiming wartime experience as a Revolutionary soldier. Accredited by the Presbyterian synod since 1799 as a riding missionary, Chavis was a spellbinding orator, with the rhetorical skills of a seasoned politician; his skills as a secular schoolteacher would soon gain equal fame.

Less well known would be his elusive role as mentor and confidant to Willie Person Mangum, North Carolina's esteemed nineteenth-century statesman. A committed Federalist, Chavis offered a powerful example of the resilience of the founding fathers' message, offering thoughtful advice to new generations of North Carolina's leaders in the turbulent age of Jacksonian democracy, tinted by conservative Presbyterian principles. For Chavis, the risks of instability posed by popular rule tended to weaken safeguards installed by conservative prudence in the 1780s; his distaste for Jackson's preemptive, combative 1820s activism signaled a strong preference for the more prudent demeanor of George Washington and other founders. His quiet role as a founder of the new civil society of post-Revolutionary North Carolina would offer thoughtful reflections on the consequences of democratic excesses in a growing nation by channeling the famous voice of mentor John Witherspoon.

Was Chavis an early example of the American dream—a late eighteenth-century model for Horatio Alger's "rags to riches" fables after the Civil War?[1] Or was his life story a cautionary tale of the promises—and very real risks—afforded talented overachievers by the world's newest breeding ground for democracy? For his life was more Greek tragedy than modern success story, a reminder of glowing possibilities and darker pitfalls of success in this still-maturing nation. John Chavis, as fellow Raleigh residents learned, was both a gifted instructor and enigmatic symbol of the political obstacles awaiting America's free citizens of color.

John Chavis's small Raleigh school offered a classical curriculum similar to that of the larger Raleigh Academy. Opened either in late 1807 or early 1808, Chavis's school would prepare students of more prosperous families for higher education, perhaps at the new state university in Chapel Hill, at reasonable rates. Incorporating the increasingly popular instructional methods of Lindley Murray, Chavis's school at first had just one teacher and probably one room[2]—and one rare distinction: students of both races and genders.

Over the next three decades, Chavis attracted the sons of leading citizens of his adopted state: lawyers, businessmen, planters, politicians. Yet only a handful of parents may have heard his name before his carefully phrased advertisement for a new quarter appeared in the *Raleigh Register* in August 1808.[3] By then, John Chavis faced a practical dilemma: prospective parents did not all share his forward-thinking views on race. Few formal schools existed in Raleigh, and none before Chavis's had ever served both races.

In an age when free black men could still vote in North Carolina—mostly in its small urban areas—few of them dared advance beyond traditional trades: barbering, tailoring, carpentry and other crafts, and construction. Having transcended the race barrier in organized religion—a carefully selected black minister in a nearly exclusively white denomination—Chavis now sought to break ground as an educator. To dampen potential dissatisfaction among white clients, Chavis would continue teaching both races but under stricter rules of racial segregation: same building, same teacher, separate times (whites by day, African Americans by night). In mid-September, his school planned to reopen under its new schedule, with tuition at $2.50 per quarter (roughly $43.00 in 2015).[4] The text of his advertisement was clear, polite, and carefully phrased:

EDUCATION

John Chaves[5] takes this method of informing his Employers, and the Citizens of Raleigh in general, that the present Quarter of his School will end the 15th of September, and the next will commence on the 19th. He will, at the same time, open an EVENING SCHOOL for the purpose of instructing Children of Colour, as he intends, for the accommodation of some of his Employers, to exclude all Children of Colour from his Day School.

The Evening School will commence at an hour by Sun. When the white children leave the house, those of colour will take their places, and continue until ten o'clock.

... Those who think proper to put their Children under his care, may rely upon the strictest attention being paid, not only to their Education but to their Morals which he deems an important part of Education.[6]

Was this an act of desperation or another act of personal daring—or both—in a career of so many unusual achievements? Chavis's race had so far not bothered white parents. But to keep his school open, Chavis was now forced to confront the racial prejudice he had always sought to rise above, even using a white merchant as an intermediary to collect fees across the racial divide.[7]

Tradition locates Chavis's first school near a public city park later renamed for him, along with his state historic highway marker.[8] Chavis reportedly owned significant acreage in Raleigh, including a house at East Cabarrus Street and Person Street ("Lot 46"), described decades later as "where the teacher lived." A black postwar Presbyterian church, built a block away, prepared freed slaves for higher education, perhaps even at Shaw University, a predominantly black Baptist college offering extensive academic training.[9]

The Raleigh known to John Chavis in 1808 was far different from the bustling metropolis of the twenty-first century. Already the state's fifth-largest town, largely white Raleigh did not number even 1,000 residents until 1820. Roughly one-third of its residents were slaves, but a handful of free blacks also lived there. An 1807 city census published in the *Raleigh Minerva* listed 33 free persons of color in a city population of 726—a small increase in free blacks since the 1800 federal census. Nearly 300 free blacks lived outside the city in sprawling Wake County.[10]

Raleigh's school-age population in 1800 was also small, barely 100 white children sixteen years or younger. Perhaps half a dozen free black children also lived there in 1800, likely more in 1807. How well Chavis's new strategy might work for either racial group remained to be seen. But if any black teacher could attract significant numbers of whites, Chavis possessed the best chance of long-range success. With high hopes, he concluded optimistically, "He hopes to have a better School House by the commencement of the next quarter."[11]

Chavis himself was among a tiny group of free blacks in North Carolina, just 7,000—about 5 percent of all African Americans—recorded in the 1800 census, mostly in twenty-five coastal and Piedmont counties. Literacy rates for these free blacks are unknown, although historian John Hope Franklin believes the apprenticeship system—governed by a 1762 law requiring masters to teach their free wards to read and write—made the level far higher than it might have been.[12] How many other free blacks were schoolteachers is also unknown; the only other known prewar black schoolmaster, John Stewart Stanly, taught free black children in New Bern until about 1850.[13]

Free blacks did enjoy many benefits of citizenship—including, until 1835, the right to vote—but their status became increasingly precarious in the early nineteenth century. Free blacks were forbidden to enter North Carolina after 1826, and in 1830 emancipated slaves were ordered to leave the state within ninety days "and never return." Those remaining endured a reduced status that was "little better than slavery" by 1835, according to one well-regarded account.[14]

Yet for a quarter century, Chavis persistently weathered all obstacles in and around Raleigh. By 1832, when new political circumstances severely restricted his continued teaching, John Chavis would have helped educate some of the state's most noteworthy young white men, including a future governor, sons of the state's chief justice, and perhaps three future U.S. congressmen and two future U.S. senators—thus assuring himself a secure place in the secondary ranks of state historical figures.

But where had he come from? How had he been educated? His early life remains a mystery, with no facts verified before 1792, when he entered the College of New Jersey: no birthplace or birth year, names of parents or siblings, early education, or military background. Even the correct spelling of his name—often Chaves, sometimes Chavos—still eludes researchers.

Two theories of origin compete for authenticity; both attribute John Chavis to free parents—perhaps of mixed race, with Indian ancestry—but born either in southern Virginia or a northern-tier county in North Carolina, probably in the early 1760s.[15] The family name Chavis, with its many variants, certainly resembles the Spanish surname Chavez, suggesting early links with Spanish explorers and Native Americans who roamed through territories that became the United States and later links with both slaves and free blacks.

Historian Barbara Parramore sets his birth in Mecklenburg County, Virginia; biographer Helen Chavis Othow suggests Granville County, North Carolina. Professor Othow's research makes John Chavis the son of Lottie Chavis—for whose 1818 marriage John served as bondsman—and great-grandson of landowner Gibrea Chavis, of Cherokee Indian blood, through Gibrea's son and grandson, both named William Chavis.[16]

Born free but in poor circumstances, John Chavis was likely apprenticed to a prosperous master at an early age. The first credible public mention of a John Chavis occurs in 1773, in papers from the estate of Halifax County attorney James Milner, owner of a large private library. According to Parramore, attorney Milner moved to Halifax from Sussex County, Virginia, in 1766. At his death in 1773, he bequeathed Latin and Greek books to his former minister, Reverend William Willie of Sussex County. Did Willie also assume custody of Milner's indentured servant John Chavis, perhaps ten years old? If so, that relationship ended with the Anglican clergyman's death in 1776.[17]

Southern Virginia is an equally plausible origin. Genealogist Paul Heinegg names ancestors Thomas Evans (as grandfather) and Jacob Chavis (probable father), citing contemporary documents, including a will and a chancery case.[18] In either scenario, the American Revolution could only have complicated Chavis's situation, as a minor unable to travel alone to rejoin his family or support himself by working. His only practical option, perhaps, was military service.

Chavis never publicly described his life as a soldier, making only one known reference to military service in an 1832 letter to Senator Willie Person Mangum: "If I am Black I am free born American & a revolutionary soldier."[19] At least one Virginia man named John Chavis enlisted in the Fifth Virginia Regiment in 1778, serving for five years. Parramore cites a March 1783 warrant by Captain Mayo Carrington, who "certified that [John] Chavis had 'faithfully fulfilled [his duties] and is thereby entitled to all immunities granted to three year soldiers,'" including a reenlistment bounty. But was this a different, older John Chavis, born in 1755, leaving a widow and five children in 1787?[20] If the younger John Chavis was also a soldier, official records of time and place of service offer no evidence of application for a military pension.

By 1789, this younger John Chavis boasted just one possession, a horse, on the Mecklenburg County, Virginia, tax rolls. Chavis reportedly hired himself out that year as a tutor to orphaned children of Virginia planter Robert Greenwood[21]—no mean feat for the nation's first black tutor of white children. Informally educated but a voracious reader, seemingly acquainted with Greek and Latin, Chavis would have been an excellent choice as a tutor and a promising candidate for formal education.

But how did John Chavis advance from itinerant tutor to respected educator and friend of influential North Carolinians? Othow believes that Chavis returned to Granville County, where Presbyterian clergyman Henry Pattillo's home served as a Latin classical school for boys, modeled after his earlier school in Orange County. Pattillo's poor health had kept him from enrolling at the College of New Jersey, but he had studied privately in the 1750s under Reverend Samuel Davies, its future president.[22] Perhaps Pattillo and others endorsed Chavis as a scholarship student at the era's most famous Presbyterian college.

Parramore suggests instead that Chavis's pre-1792 education was limited to instruction by Milner, perhaps by Willie. The two theories converge with Chavis's introduction to the life-changing experience of academia—at the College of New Jersey, now Princeton University. Historian Edgar W. Knight, whose fastidious "Notes on John Chavis" formed the first comprehensive portrait in 1930, was first to document the "strong tradition" of his early affiliation with Princeton. The school's early records could not document Chavis's actual enrollment, but its secretary confirmed to Knight that Chavis was on its alumni list as a "non-graduate."[23]

What brought Chavis to the notice of college president John Witherspoon? The signer of the Declaration of Independence had headed the school for two decades before Chavis appeared, at a time when Princeton had recently undertaken its transformation from training site for Presbyterian clergymen into a spawning ground, under new, tighter academic standards, for a new generation of national leaders. The Edinburgh-educated Dr. Witherspoon had immigrated to Princeton in 1768 as the college's sixth president, soon becoming an active member of the colonial body politic. After signing the Declaration in 1776, he went on to serve in New Jersey's provincial and state legislatures and the Continental and Confederation Congresses and as a member of the New Jersey delegation that helped draft the U.S. Constitution in 1787.[24]

Chavis was one of a select group of private pupils of minority heritage, African Americans and Native Americans who benefited from Witherspoon's iconoclastic quest for racial diversity. As early as 1774, he brought free black students into his Princeton home for private tutoring. Witherspoon's biographer Varnum Collins declares that Chavis "was sent to Princeton as an experiment" and was "the most remarkable of his pupils in this group."[25]

Witherspoon may have publicly argued with colleague Thomas Jefferson over calling King George III a "tyrant" in the Declaration but tended to agree privately with Jefferson on the nettlesome issue of slavery. Both men were slaveholders, although Jefferson owned far more; Witherspoon's estate listed just two slaves—farmhands at his 500-acre country estate, Tusculum—in 1794. Witherspoon never subscribed to the immediate goals of abolitionism but instead expressed reservations about the consequences of hasty action to "make them free to their own ruin." Yet before his death, his position had softened enough to favor gradual emancipation in 1790, as chair of a statewide committee on abolition.[26]

Even in his declining years, Dr. Witherspoon still impressed his students, both by force of personality and intellect; John Chavis echoed his views four decades later. "Perhaps more than any other single founder, Witherspoon embodied all of the major intellectual and social elements behind the American founding," wrote Jeffry Morrison in 2005. "Witherspoon was literally peerless among his founding brothers when it came to combining religion, education, and politics, and seldom in American history have so many key vocations been formed in one man."[27]

Othow cites Presbyterian Church records claiming Chavis was "sent by gentlemen in Oxford [county seat] to Princeton University," perhaps even as part of a friendly wager over his chances of academic success. Parramore cites Charles Lee Smith's account, with no Granville connection, of a "1792 recommendation of the Reverend John Blair Smith [to college trustees] that 'Mr. John Todd Henry of Virginia and John Chavis, a free black man of that state . . . be received' on the Leslie Fund" (a bequest by James Leslie of New York City to provide for education of "poor and pious youth").[28]

A detailed chapter in Smith's 1888 monograph describes Chavis as "one of the most remarkable characters in the educational history of North Carolina. . . . His life finds no parallel in the South, nor, so far as the writer is aware, in any part of our country," and offers the longest known physical description of Chavis: "of dark brown complexion, without any admixture of white blood in his veins. . . . A robust, corpulent man, with large, round clean-shaven face, expressive of benevolence and its kindred virtues. His stature was about 5 feet 7 inches in height. He was always neat in dress and usually wore a suit of black home-spun, with spotless linen and a nicely-tied white cravat. In his latter years his woolly hair was as white as driven snow, adding to the dignity of his appearance."[29]

After 1792, Chavis presumably lodged with Witherspoon and his second wife. In failing health, Witherspoon was already blind, no doubt dependent on students as readers and secretaries; he died in November 1794.[30] By 1795, Chavis would soon appear at another school with strong Presbyterian ties in Lexington, Virginia: Liberty Hall Academy, now Washington and Lee University.

Historian Theodore Delaney believes that Chavis entered an environment remarkably similar to that of Princeton: "Life in western Virginia could not have been very different from life in New Jersey," he said in 2001. In his well-regarded biographical entry on Chavis in *American National Biography*, Delaney also asserted that "more than likely, Chavis's religious fervor and potential for scholarship attracted the attention of Presbyterian leaders in Virginia, who believed a black clergyman might do a better job of evangelizing slaves and free blacks . . . than white ministers."[31]

Chavis's arrival coincided with the final year of William Graham's twenty-year career as academy rector, allowing Chavis to witness Graham's spirited defense of the institution of slavery and his views that blacks were generally unfit for liberty—although Delaney believes Graham may "have found free-born blacks like Chavis much more acceptable." A 1773 graduate of Witherspoon's College of New Jersey, Graham may even have admitted Chavis to Liberty Hall in 1795 as a final tribute to his own late mentor. Within a year, Graham resigned, and Chavis studied under two new rectors: first, trustee Dr. Samuel Legrand Campbell, then Reverend George Addison Baxter, once a fellow student of Chavis's. Before Chavis left, Liberty Hall Academy changed its name to Washington Academy, honoring George Washington's generosity.[32]

Most of the college's early records were later destroyed, but other documents indicate that Chavis completed his studies there with some distinction by 1800, perhaps even graduating. Parramore cites "a certificate made out in Rockbridge County, Va., on 6 Apr. 1802 [which] attests that John Chavis was known to the court and considered a free man and 'also that he has been a student at Washington Academy where he went through a regular course of Academical studies.'" A similar 1802 certificate "acknowledged that Chavis was a free black, forty years of age (indicating that his birth was in 1762 or 1763)."[33]

Delaney believes that Chavis's emerging religious fervor was shaped and profoundly strengthened by experiences in New Jersey and Lexington, declaring that "Chavis was a deeply religious man, who had been evangelized by the Presbyterian Church. Presbyterian ministers worked hard to evangelize black southerners during the early national period, particularly in Virginia. And they must have had a powerful effect on Chavis."[34]

In some ways, this impetus was a mixed blessing. For while "like many Americans of the Revolutionary Era, most Presbyterian ministers viewed slavery as inconsistent with the principles of the American republic . . . [and] favored the principle of universal liberty and prayed for a final abolition," even those progressive Presbyterians were rarely ardent, committed abolitionists. "Instead the Church warned that the transition from slavery to freedom required education," Delaney continued. "Without education, they argued, freed slaves would most certainly represent a danger to the community."[35]

In 1801, the Presbyterian General Assembly hired Chavis as "a missionary among people of his color, until the meeting of the next General Assembly," with "some prudential instructions . . . issued to him by the Assembly."[36] For five years, he would be officially reported as a licentiate—in essence, a licensed apprentice, not an ordained minister—of the same presbytery and recommended periodically for missionary service "for the times and on the routes specified in the report." His travels took him across Virginia and into North Carolina. The Synod of Virginia reported in 1805 that "Mr. Chavis, a missionary to the blacks, itinerated in several counties in the south part of the state; but owing to some peculiar circumstances, stated in his journal, his mission to them was not attended with any considerable success." That same year, he was authorized to "employ himself chiefly among the blacks and people of color," including those in Maryland; in 1807 it was ordered that he be employed for three months among the blacks in North Carolina and Virginia, with his choice of routes.[37]

But in 1955, scholar Margaret Burr Deschamps discovered an unusual wrinkle, concluding that Chavis's success in preaching to white congregations—drawing significant crowds, as revealed in his presbytery journal—far outweighed his early appeal to slaves and disappointed presbytery leaders. "So well did the white population attend his services that Presbyterian leaders soon came to regard Chavis's popularity as a problem," wrote Deschamps. Small wonder, then, that sometime after 1805, the Hanover Presbytery permitted Chavis's transfer to the Orange Presbytery in North Carolina, which received him as a licentiate. He now began "performing missionary service among the Negroes and preaching from time to time to white congregations" in Granville, Wake, and Orange Counties.[38]

By 1807 or 1808, he settled in Raleigh, where he preached intermittently. But his primary livelihood long remained the school he opened there. Over the years, Chavis's continuing work as a teacher in Raleigh drew favorable public remarks, including an April 1830 review by Joseph Gales, fellow Presbyterian and influential *Raleigh Register* editor: "On Friday last . . . we attended an examination of the free children of colour, attached to the school conducted by John Chavis, also colored, but a regularly educated Presbyterian minister. . . . The exercises throughout, evinced a degree of attention and assiduous care on the part of the instructor, highly creditable, and of attainment on the part of the scholars almost incredible."[39]

In his separate classical training to white students, Chavis used what he called "the theory of the English language," and Lindley Murray's spelling book "which no other Teacher in this part of [the] Country Teaches but myself & I think it preferable to the English Grammar." According to Gales, Chavis also regularly reminded his students that "they occupied inferior and subordinate station in society and were possessed but of limited privileges; but that even they might become useful in their particular sphere by making a proper improvement of the advantages offered them."[40]

No official records give their names, but many chroniclers list a remarkably influential group of white students. According to historian Stephen Weeks, "among those who are known to have attended his school were Priestly H. Mangum, brother of Senator [Willie Person] Mangum and himself a lawyer of distinction; Charles Manly, governor of North Carolina; Abram Rencher, U.S. minister to Portugal and governor of New Mexico; and Mr. James H. Horner, founder of the Horner School." Smith adds Willie P. Mangum and others to Weeks's list, including "Archibald E. and John L. Henderson, sons of Chief Justice [Leonard] Henderson; Rev. Williams Harris; Dr. James L. Wortham; and the Edwardses, the Enlows and the Hargroves . . . politicians, lawyers, preachers, physicians, and teachers."[41]

Several students duly recalled educational debts to their early teacher. One student's son—James Horner, himself a respected school principal—told Smith in 1883 that his father "not only went to school to him [Chavis] but boarded in his family." Chavis was considered a good scholar and a good teacher and "hence was patronized by the best people of the country. . . . The school was the best at that time to be found in the State." According to Granville lawyer George Wortham, Chavis "was said by his old pupils to have been a good Latin and a fair Greek scholar. He was a man of intelligence on general subjects and conversed well. He had a small but select library of theological works, in which were to be found the works of Flavel, Buxton,

Boston, and others," including "two volumes of Dwight's Theology" owned by Wortham.[42]

Wortham also described the venerable teacher's command of the language: "His English was remarkably pure, contained no 'negroisms'; his manner was impressive, his explanations clear and concise, and his views, as I then thought and still think, entirely orthodox."[43] Such refined language could only have impressed possible patrons such as Orange County planter William Person Mangum, whose sons Willie and Priestley became Chavis favorites.

The teacher's correspondence with Willie Person Mangum—illustrious congressman, longtime Whig member of the U.S. Senate, and presidential candidate in 1836—began by 1825 and continued until 1837.[44] A number of Chavis's letters to Mangum are contained in Mangum's papers at the Library of Congress[45] and offer fascinating insights into their unusual personal relationship, one documented by Weeks:

> His relations with Judge Mangum were very intimate. I might say they were affectionate, even fatherly. He was an occasional visitor at the house of the Judge and was treated with all deference and courtesy, so much so that it caused astonishment and questioning on the part of the younger children, which was met in turn by, "Hush, child, he is your father's friend."
>
> The letters of Chavis to Judge Mangum which have come down to us indicate no social inequality. They are written in the frank friendship which has bridged all social distinctions, and when read between the lines give us glimpses of the power of intellect and character to overcome the mere conventionalities of society.[46]

Letters preserved by Mangum paint a cryptic portrait of their relationship, more like that of doting but frank uncle and headstrong nephew, alternating personal advice and pleas for financial assistance with unashamed, occasionally tart criticisms of Mangum's actions. In 1831, for instance, Chavis chastised Mangum for political vacillation: "I have told you to put on your coat [of] Federalism again. You know that you have been for some time past, hoping & shifting about, showing your coat, to be sometimes Federalism, sometimes Democracy, sometimes Republicanism. Now you know this won't do, because you know that no political stratagem whatever can shake the foundation of Federalism. Then why will you be afraid & cast & shift about? If you will now repent of your sins & promise to do better I shall hope that those of the Washington school, will forgive you."[47]

In 1832, Chavis refers to Mangum fondly as "my son," a term elsewhere reserved for former students, such as Abraham Rencher and Mangum's brother

Priestley.[48] Chavis's familiar tone has persuaded most scholars that their special relationship resembles one born of classroom instruction. Who else but a revered teacher could talk to Willie Mangum that way?

Willie Mangum's family members have long confirmed an affectionate relationship between the two men, but none has ever publicly agreed that Mangum studied under Chavis; at least one descendant vigorously denied it.[49] Yet the facts make an early connection plausible: Willie Mangum did attend the Raleigh Academy and taught there in 1812, before entering the University of North Carolina, according to Charles Coon.[50] Given their long-standing acquaintance, it is conceivable that academy principal Reverend William McPheeters asked Chavis to tutor Mangum for future university studies; it is generally accepted that Chavis taught his brother Priestley before or at the academy. In 1825 and 1826, Chavis invited Congressman Mangum to visit his Wake County school and even urged him to attend an 1827 school examination, confident that Mangum would enjoy the visits.[51]

According to writer Joseph L. Seawell, Mangum may have owed Chavis his life, if a legend recounted by an admirer of Chavis's "good sense, tact, and diplomacy, wielded without the knowledge of his former pupil," were true: Chavis may actually have helped prevent Mangum's participation in an imprudent duel.[52] Whatever their precise relationship, Chavis considered Mangum his friend—and pointedly reminded Mangum that he had never wished for his protégé to become a politician. Far better that he remain a prosperous lawyer in North Carolina (and hire Chavis to educate his own children): "You know, that I have ever opposed every stage of your political life, preferring your continuance at the bar until you had acquired a competent fortune," he wrote Mangum in 1827.[53]

Well aware of Mangum's deteriorating relationship with President Andrew Jackson in 1832, Chavis—still an old-line Federalist sympathizer, like Witherspoon—warned him to be resolute. "I disapprove of three of your votes. Van Buren, the Bank & the fast day, but my greatest grief is that you should be in favour of the election of General Jackson for the Presidency," Chavis wrote. "Let G. J. be elected & our Government is gone, and even in its present situation, it would require a Hamilton; a Jay and an old Adams, bottomed upon G. Washington to repair its ruins. This Clay knows, & nothing but conscious integrity & a united love of Country, could possibly induce him to undertake the management of such a rotten & decayed Government. I hope he [Clay] will be elected, & even if he should, I shall pity his situation."[54]

During 1832, Chavis also sought unsuccessfully to persuade Mangum to enroll his daughter Sallie in Chavis's rural school.[55] Mangum demurred;

whether his reluctance to oblige his old friend was politically motivated is unclear. But indeed, much had changed since the two men had first met. In the near future lay tight restrictions on teaching, along with an outright ban on preaching, by African Americans in North Carolina, both born of fear after Nat Turner's bloody Virginia slave rebellion.

That Chavis had mixed feelings about slavery is apparent from comments in correspondence with Mangum, as Congress considered petitions to abolish slavery within the District of Columbia. Chavis, born free, had preached to slaves for three decades; he must have sympathized with the plight of fellow blacks who had never known freedom but remained firmly practical, declaring to Mangum as late as 1836, "That slavery is a national evil no one doubts, but what is to be done? It exists & what can be done with it? All that can be done, is to make the best of a bad bargain. For I am clearly of the opinion that immediate emancipation would be to entail the greatest earthly curse upon my bretheren according to the flesh that could be conferred upon them especially in a Country like ours. I suppose if they knew I said this they would be ready to take my life, but as I wish them well I feel no disposition to see them any more miserable than they are."[56]

Here Chavis continued to channel explicit views of mentors Witherspoon and Graham, among others—a pragmatic, if counterintuitive, position for a free African American to espouse. Doubtless aware of abolition's troublesome implications, Chavis stood to gain little and lose much more by taking a more defiant stand. Faced with financial ruin after losing his livelihood in 1832, Chavis could have moved north, perhaps even to New Jersey. But advancing age and poor health made any move unthinkable; long ago, he had cast his lot with the South, and it was there he must remain.

Instead, he appealed to Orange Presbytery colleagues for assistance. Their response: "Mr. John Chavis, a free man of color, and a licentiate under the care of the presbytery, stat[ed] his difficulties and embarrassments in consequence of an act passed at the last session of the Legislature of this State, forbidding free people of color to preach: Whereupon, *Resolved*, That presbytery, in view of all the circumstances of the case, recommend to their licentiate to acquiesce in the decision of the Legislature referred to until God in His providence shall open to him the path of duty in regard to the exercise of his ministry."[57]

Presbytery leaders like McPheeters, pastor of Raleigh's First Presbyterian Church, were privately sympathetic and by 1834 were collecting funds to alleviate his poverty.[58] The presbytery resolved that year to "provide a competent support for Mr. Chavis, during the year ensuing, by private contributions, or otherwise," under a project committee including McPheeters, Reverend M. Osborne, and lay leader John Primrose.[59]

McPheeters had known Chavis for forty years when he recounted two letters from "our Old Friend Chavis" in an 1834 missive to Samuel Smith Downey of Raleigh. Chavis "makes known to me his difficulties, distresses, and wants—Says he is a miserable man—old and infirm —his wife a dying— or at least on her deathbed—in want of the necessities of life—and without money to procure them." McPheeters dutifully delivered monies collected for Chavis the previous fall ("about $20"), plus funds from Downey. But he was dismayed at Chavis's claim that Downey had recently sent even more money to McPheeters ("I have not as yet received it"); Chavis was simply mistaken or confused. McPheeters estimated the need for a minimum pension of five dollars per month, or sixty dollars per year; "I see no other chance for him but the Poor House."[60]

In 1836, Reverend Robert Burwell was "appointed the agent of this Presbytery to supply the wants of John Chavis, a superannuated licentiate." In 1837, an annual pension of fifty dollars began, to continue until death, financed through assessments on various churches. But even this could not shore up Chavis's dire straits. Unable to attract white students, his tuition income from as many as sixteen students in 1828—cited in a letter to Mangum—had dwindled to thirty dollars in 1833.[61]

Grateful for support from the presbytery but citing heavy debts, Chavis had appealed to Mangum in October 1832 to hire him to educate daughter Sallie near the Mangum home, if his neighbors near Rogers' Store failed to hire him as a teacher first. The school Chavis proposed "must not exceed a quarter of a mile from your door & let it be less if possible," and tuition should be paid twice a year. Mangum preferred a cheaper option, to educate Sallie near the family's home at Red Mountain (Rougemont), and told his wife he could not afford to board Sallie near Oxford.[62]

The teacher's grim situation gradually worsened. His wife, Sarah Frances, or Fannie, whom he had married around 1815, was now an invalid; his own health was declining. Yet he still dreamed of teaching children of both races— either in Reavis Crossroads, near the intersection of Orange, Wake, and Granville Counties, or in homes of prospective clients—and of writing. Barred from preaching, perhaps despondent over losing his voting rights in 1835, Chavis grew more determined to publish his final thoughts.[63]

In his last year, despite long opposition from Orange Presbytery colleagues, he published an illuminating sermon, "Letter upon the Doctrine of the Extent of the Atonement of Christ," offering a summary view of his religious beliefs and hinting at his somewhat unorthodox views on slavery.[64] The complicated story of that letter's long-delayed publication epitomizes the sad fate of an aging Chavis: denied the right to continue working, discouraged from issuing a profitable private treatise, and forced by circumstance to appeal to friends and strangers for what amounted to charity.

Chavis had first requested Orange Presbytery permission in April 1832 to publish the sermon, but its leaders declined, claiming the subject had been thoroughly discussed by others and Chavis's offering would have no "real interest to the reading public."[65] In fact, the letter was controversial, Othow argues, for its implied criticisms of slaveholders denying the fitness for Christianity of their human property.

Essentially, Chavis argued that Jesus Christ himself had directed his followers to "go Ye into the world and preach the gospel to every creature, and he that believeth and is baptized shall be saved, and he that believed not, shall be damned." Christ had made no distinction between those who could hear the gospel and those who could not hear it and act on it. "Can it possibly be believed that the Saviour would send his ministers to preach to any part of the human family for whom he did not die . . . ? The character of the Saviour, the plan of Redemption, reason and common sense forbid such a belief."[66]

Like Witherspoon, Chavis was no ardent abolitionist, with no explicit brief for immediate freedom for slaves. Yet by insisting that every human being had the right to hear the gospel and act on it, he was challenging traditional beliefs—as espoused by the Old Side (Old School) of Presbyterianism—that certain humans, the elect, were predestined to receive God's grace, and others were condemned to be deprived of it. Many on the Old Side—in the throes of a new battle with New Light proponents over doctrine versus experimentation—were perfectly willing to count themselves among the elect and their slaves among those forever lost in what Chavis and others might easily have interpreted as a cynical rationalization of prejudice. Chavis believed instead that every man, whether free or enslaved, held his fate in his own hands, that by his actions each man might either be saved or damned, "willingly . . . and not from motives of compulsion."[67]

Whatever the true reason for official Presbyterian opposition, Chavis's letter languished for four years. In 1837, secular publisher J. Gales and Son of Raleigh printed it as a pamphlet. But by then, any appeal to the general reading public had probably disappeared, with Presbyterianism descending into schismatic conflict. Few southern Presbyterians would have displayed it against the express wishes of their leaders. Few copies survive; whatever sales it generated, the modest publication had little time left to help its author.[68]

In early 1837, Chavis wrote Mangum a long, rambling letter—the last on record—about a number of subjects, including his imminent move to Granville County from Rogers' Store: "I expect to leave the neighborhood the last of March, and I wish to be prepared to meet malicious reports. Col. Rogers can tell you all about the business."[69] This followed a cryptic reference to lingering hopes of teaching free black students in Raleigh, a move now forbidden by state law, and previous comments opposing abolition in letters to Mangum. He pleaded for a response, obviously hoping for Mangum's intercession with state authorities to allow an exception.

Troubled by Mangum's resignation from the Senate in late 1836, he wondered if "our government is too corrupt for you ever to attempt to go into Congress again, with a hope of producing a reformation? I would be glad that you would give Col Rogers your definition of States rights." In closing, he mentioned a possible visit: "Give my respects to Mrs. Mangum & tell her if [I] do go to Granville to live she may expect to see me at her house some time in July if I can get any cloaths fit to wear for I am naked at this time, & how I am to be cloathed I dont know."[70]

But that promised visit never materialized. The disjointed letter, perhaps reflecting his own deteriorating physical condition, was the last to his longtime friend. Chavis never resumed teaching at his new Granville County home, nor did he live to see Mangum's reelection to the U.S. Senate in 1840 or his two-year stint as de facto vice president when Vice President John Tyler become president upon the death of William Henry Harrison. In June 1838, Chavis died at home at age seventy-five, almost certainly of natural causes. (A persistent rumor that he died a violent death, after being beaten by a local mob, has never been substantiated, despite its mention in a best-selling account of a twentieth-century murder in nearby Oxford.) A contemporary obituary in a Richmond, Virginia, publication reports only his "very infirm" condition.[71]

His widow received a reduced pension of forty dollars a year until 1842. It is not certain whether the couple had children, although Othow lists three; historian Tekla Johnson says one son survived Chavis. Nor has his burial site ever been located. Family members declare he lies in an old family cemetery on remnants of Mangum's plantation near Rougemont, in Durham County. Othow speculates that an unmarked stone near the graves of Mangum and his parents belongs to Chavis, but her theory remains unproved.[72]

A brief, respectful remembrance of his life graced the Oxford, North Carolina, newspaper *The Torchlight* in 1880. Responding to "inquiries about the remarkable man" in the *Raleigh Sentinel*, the article recalled Chavis's death "at his residence between Oxford and Williamsboro, leaving descendants who are yet in the county. The writer remembers to have seen him when a short time before his death several of his old white pupils, prominent gentlemen, called to see him.... His manners were dignified yet respectful and entirely unassuming and his conversation sprightly and interesting."[73]

In Smith's 1888 retrospective, Chavis was simply a rarity in southern history: "His contemporaries admired him for his noble bearing as a gentleman, revered him for his fervent piety as a Christian, and respected him for his eminent ability as a teacher and preacher."[74] Chavis was remarkably free of either arrogance or pretension, in the opinion of Paul C. Cameron, who recalled him vividly as "received by my father and treated with kindness and consideration, and respected as a man of education, good sense, and most estimable character.... He seemed familiar with the proprieties of social life, yet modest and unassuming, and sober in his language and opinions. He was polite—yes, courtly; but it was from his heart and not affectation."[75]

And yet, for all his intellect and astuteness, he was surprisingly naive. "I remember him as a man without guile," Cameron wrote. "His conversation indicated that he lived free from all evil or suspicion, seeking the good opinion of the public by the simplicity of his life and the integrity of his conduct."[76]

How can one best summarize the life of such a man, who transcended the racial divide as a teacher, a preacher, and a writer and was able to conduct spirited and intelligent political arguments with men far above his own station? Was he simply a diehard Federalist, trapped within outdated beliefs of a long-gone era, offering pointless advice? Were his political views, however sincere, hopelessly unrealistic? Or was he actually more farsighted than his students, now redefining themselves as Whigs, temporarily successful but facing eventual irrelevance in a rapidly changing political environment?

Within southern history—indeed, within the broader context of American history—John Chavis represents a uniquely talented example of the heroic innocent, trapped by rules he had no hand in writing, unable to argue effectively in his own defense, ultimately doomed to suffer without appeal, saved only by the charity of those who remembered his superior performance.

His historical legacy bespeaks both success and failure in the republic's earliest decades; rewards for merit and punishment for accomplishments; the delicate balance between personal advancement and pitiful rejection by a nation obsessed with both its concept of personal freedom and perplexing political and social rules governing race; and the unforeseen limits of an unfulfilled democratic gospel once preached by the founding fathers he championed.

NOTES

1. Horatio Alger's novels, beginning with *Ragged Dick* in 1868, popularized a "rags to riches" theme in the lives of young heroes.

2. American-born grammarian Lindley Murray, popular textbook author, published *English Grammar* (1795) and *An English Spelling Book* in 1804. See http://en.wikipedia.org/wiki/Lindley_Murray.

3. Charles L. Coon, "Wake County Schools: John Chaves' School, 1808," *North Carolina Schools and Academies, 1790–1840: A Documentary History* (Raleigh, N.C.: Edwards and Broughton, 1915), 515.

4. See Download Conversion Factors, https://liberalarts.oregonstate.edu/spp/polisci/faculty-staff/robert-sahr/inflation-conversion-factors-years-1774-estimated-2024-dollars-recent-years/download-conversion-factors.

5. As noted below, the family name was subject to variant spellings.

6. Coon, "John Chaves' School." As noted, "The terms of teaching the white children will be as usual, two and a half dollars per quarter, those of colour, one dollar and three quarters . . . to be paid in advance to Mr. Benjamin S. King." Ibid., 515.

7. King operated his profitable dry goods store until a major fire in 1833. "Raleigh Fire Department History, 1792–1849," http://legeros.com/ralwake/raleigh/history/timelines/1792–1849.shtml.

8. John Chavis Memorial Park and Community Center, on Martin Luther King Jr. Boulevard, was dedicated in 1937; in 1938, a historical marker rose two blocks away. See North Carolina Highway Historical Marker Program, http://www.ncmarkers.com/Markers.aspx?MarkerId=H-13.

9. Helen Chavis Othow, *John Chavis: African American Patriot, Preacher, Teacher, and Mentor, 1763–1838* (Jefferson, N.C.: McFarland, 2001), 86. Othow cites a 1988 statement by Raleigh resident Mrs. Asa Turner. Davie Street Presbyterian Church, built in 1875, stands nearby. The Tupper Institute, founded in 1865, was renamed Shaw University in 1875 and housed both medical and law schools.

10. North Carolina City populations at North Carolina Business History, http://www.historync.org/NCCityPopulations1800s.htm; Census Online, North Carolina–1800 Census Records, U.S. census, Wake County, N.C., 1800; John Hope Franklin, *The Free Negro in North Carolina, 1790–1860* (Chapel Hill: University of North Carolina Press, 1943), 7. Raleigh had 699 residents, Wake County 13,383; 18 "other free persons" (nonwhite) lived in Raleigh. The *Minerva* census of 23 March 1807 listed 270 city slaves and 33 free blacks, a population growing faster than that of whites. See US GenWeb Archives, http://files.usgwarchives.net/nc/wake/census/1807cen.txt.

11. Coon, "John Chaves' School."

12. Franklin, *Free Negro in North Carolina*, 165.

13. Catherine W. Bishir, *Crafting Lives: African American Artisans in New Bern, North Carolina, 1770–1900* (Chapel Hill: University of North Carolina Press, 2013), 11.

14. Jeffrey J. Crow, Paul D. Escott, and Flora J. Haley, *A History of African Americans in North Carolina* (Raleigh: Division of Archives and History, 1992), 49.

15. James C. Ballagh, "John Chavis," in *Dictionary of American Biography*, ed. Allen Johnson (New York: Charles Scribner's Sons, 1929–30), 4:44–45. A once-popular theory that John Chavis emigrated from the West Indies was discredited after 1900.

16. Barbara M. Parramore, "Chavis, John," in *Dictionary of North Carolina Biography*, ed. William S. Powell (Chapel Hill: University of North Carolina Press, 1979), 358–59; Othow, *John Chavis*, 86.

17. "James Milner," in "Historic Halifax: The People," North Carolina Historic Sites, http://www.nchistoricsites.org/halifax/people.htm; Parramore, "Chavis, John," 1:358; "Notes from Albemarle Parish Register, Sussex County, Va.," *William and Mary College Quarterly* 14, no. 1 (1905): 1–6. Parramore says Willie "may have played a role" in Chavis's training and education after Milner's death.

18. Paul Heinegg, *Free African Americans of North Carolina, Virginia, and South Carolina from the Colonial Period to about 1820*, vol. 1, 5th ed. (Baltimore: Clearfield Company by Genealogical Publishing, 2005), 313–15. "John Chavis . . . , born say 1764, was called John Chavis, Junior, in 1786 . . . taxable on one tithe and a horse in Mecklenburg County, Virginia . . . a grandson of Thomas Evans who named him in his 22 May 1787 Mecklenburg County, Virginia will . . . [an] heir of Jacob Chavis . . . named in a Mecklenburg County chancery case in 1819." Ibid., 313.

19. John Chavis (JC) to Willie P. Mangum (WPM), 10 March 1832, in *The Papers of Willie Person Mangum*, ed. Henry T. Shanks, 2 vols. (Raleigh: State Department of Archives and History, 1950), 1:506–8. Chavis asked Mangum to contact North Carolina congressmen Abraham Rencher and Daniel Laurens Barringer: "Tell them I . . . ought not to be thrown intirely out of the scale of notice." Ibid., 507.

20. Parramore, "Chavis, John," 358. See also Free African Americans of Virginia, North Carolina, South Carolina and Delaware, http://www.freeafricanamericans.com/Chavis_family.htm.

21. Parramore, "Chavis, John," 358.

22. Durward T. Stokes, "Henry Pattillo," in *Dictionary of North Carolina Biography*, 5:38–39. Pattillo died before Chavis arrived. Davies headed the College of New Jersey from 1760 to 1761.

23. Edgar W. Knight, "Notes on John Chavis," *North Carolina Historical Review* 7, no. 3 (1930): 326–45.

24. Jeffry H. Morrison, *John Witherspoon and the Founding of the American Republic* (Notre Dame: University of Notre Dame Press, 2005), 2–3.

25. Ibid., 76; Varnum L. Collins, *President Witherspoon* (1925; repr., New York: Arno Press, 1969), 217.

26. Morrison, *John Witherspoon*, 76; Collins, *President Witherspoon*, 167–68.

27. Morrison, *John Witherspoon*, 127.

28. Othow, *John Chavis*, 40–41, 41n26; Parramore, "Chavis, John," 358.

29. Charles Lee Smith, *The History of Education in North Carolina: Bureau of Education Circular of Information No. 2, 1888*, Contributions to American Educational History No. 3, ed. Herbert B. Adams (Washington, D.C.: Government Printing Office, 1888), 138–41. Professor Charles Phillips compiled "materials for a sketch of Mr. Chavis, and the data for this account are drawn principally from correspondence . . . from well-known citizens who were personally acquainted with the negro divine (and) remembered by them as an old man." Ibid., 138.

30. Theodore C. Delaney, "Founder's Day Lecture: John Chavis: Washington and Lee's First African American Student," delivered at Washington and Lee University, Lexington, Va., 19 January 2001.

31. Ibid.; Theodore C. Delaney, "John Chavis," in *American National Biography*, ed. John A. Garraty and Mark C. Carnes (New York: Oxford University Press, 1999), 4:761–62.

32. Delaney, "Founder's Day Lecture"; collection overview, Graham Family Papers, 1773–1885, David M. Rubenstein Rare Book and Manuscript Library, Duke University, Durham, N.C., http://library.duke.edu/rubenstein/findingaids/grahamfamily/#c01_1. Campbell was interim rector until 1799; Reverend Baxter served until 1829.

33. Parramore, "Chavis, John," 358–59.

34. Delaney, "Founder's Day Lecture."

35. Ibid.

36. Stephen B. Weeks, "John Chavis: Antebellum Negro Preacher and Teacher," *Southern Workman* (February 1914), 101. Weeks cites *Acts and Proceedings of the General Assembly of the Presbyterian Church in the United States* (1801).

37. Weeks, "John Chavis," 104.

38. Margaret Burr Deschamps, "John Chavis as a Preacher to Whites," *North Carolina Historical Review* 32, no. 2 (1955): 167–68; Weeks, "John Chavis," 105.

39. *Raleigh Register*, 22 April 1830.

40. JC to WPM, 3 September 1831, *Mangum*, 1:413; Edgar Knight, "John Chavis: A Negro Teacher of Southern Whites," *(Baltimore) Sunday Sun*, 8 December 1929.

41. Weeks, "John Chavis," 103; Smith, *History of Education*, 140.

42. Ibid. Prof. J. H. Horner wrote Stephen Weeks on 14 May 1883. The elder Horner was probably the last of Chavis's white students to live with him.

43. Quoted in ibid., 140.

44. Mangum served in the House from 1823 to 1826 and the U.S. Senate from 1830 to 1836, when he received presidential electoral votes from South Carolina. Reelected to the Senate in 1840, he became president pro tempore in May 1842, second in line to President John Tyler from 31 May 1842 until March 1845. "Biography of Willie Person Mangum" at U.S. Senate, https://www.senate.gov/artandhistory/art/artifact/Painting_32_00022.htm.

45. Chavis's letters to Mangum, between 1825 and 1837, appear in the first two volumes of the *Papers of Willie Person Mangum* along with two earlier letters: Chavis to North Carolina state treasurer John Haywood (1822) and Haywood to Mangum (1824).

46. Weeks, "John Chavis," 104–5.

47. JC to WPM, 3 September 1831, *Mangum*, 1:412.

48. JC to WPM, 10 March 1832, ibid., 1:506.

49. Great-grandson Preston Mangum Weeks denied the claim outright in the *Greensboro (N.C.) Daily News* ("Senator Mangum's Education," letter to the editor, 20 March 1920): "However well John Chavis was educated and regardless of North Carolinians whom he may have tutored, he did not have the honor of teaching Willie P. Mangum ... [and] was not one of his teachers."

50. Coon, "Introduction," *North Carolina Schools and Academies*, xiv; "Seven teachers employed at the academy, 1812" (reprinted from *The Star* [Raleigh], 24 April 1812), 432. Mangum taught in the Male Department. Willie Mangum and younger brother Priestley graduated from the university in 1815.

51. JC to WPM, 25 October 1825, 24 May 1826, and 18 December 1827, *Mangum*, 1:202, 287, and 317; Albert Edwards, "William McPheeters," in *Dictionary of North Carolina Biography*, 4:200. McPheeters, the academy principal in 1810, founded Raleigh's First Presbyterian Church by 1816.

52. Joseph L. Seawell, "Black Teacher of Southern Whites: A Negro Parson Who Educated a Senator, a Judge, and a Governor of North Carolina," *New York Times Magazine*, 18 May 1924. Seawell, longtime clerk of the North Carolina Supreme Court, quoted Paul Cameron's account of an averted 1819 duel between Mangum and another legislator; Chavis and Cameron's father, Duncan—Mangum's legal tutor—apparently prevented it.

53. JC to WPM, 18 December 1827, *Mangum*, 1:317–18.

54. JC to WPM, 21 July 1832, ibid., 564.

55. JC to WPM, 10 March, 21 July, and 5 August 1832, ibid., 506–7, 563–64, 574–76.

56. JC to WPM, 4 April 1836, *Mangum*, 2:418–19.

57. Quoted in Weeks, "John Chavis," 105.

58. Minutes of the 128th Session, Orange Presbytery, 30 April 1834; Minutes of the 129th Session, Orange Presbytery, 17 September 1834, Historical Foundation of the Presbyterian and Reformed Churches, Montreat, N.C.

59. Minutes of 129th Session, Orange Presbytery.

60. Deschamps, "John Chavis as a Preacher to Whites," 171–72. McPheeters's letter to Downey, dated 3 September 1834, appears in the Downey Papers at Duke University Library, Durham, N.C.

61. JC to WPM, 6 February 1834, *Mangum*, 2:103.

62. Minutes of the 135th Session, Orange Presbytery, 25 August 1837; JC to WPM, 1 October 1832, *Mangum*, 2:576–77; WPM to Charity A. Mangum, 18 February 1832, *Mangum*, 1:486–87.

63. Marriage Records, Granville County, N.C. According to county records, John Chavis and Sarah Anderson received a marriage bond on 3 June 1815; "Frances" was presumably her middle name. In 1835, a statewide constitutional convention barred voting by free persons of color, amid unease over Nat Turner's rebellion. But the narrow 66–61 vote also reflected grave doubts about the wisdom of disenfranchising blacks. See North Carolina History Project, http://www.northcarolinahistory.org/encyclopedia/32/entry/.

64. John Chavis, *Chavis's Letter upon the Doctrine of the Extent of the Atonement of Christ* (Raleigh: John Chavis, James H. Horner, J. Gales and Son, 1837).

65. Othow, *John Chavis*, 119–26.

66. Quoted in ibid., 124.

67. Ibid., 140.

68. Elizabeth T. Adams, "Divided Nation, Divided Church: The Presbyterian Schism, 1837–1838," *The Historian* 54, no. 4 (1992): 683–96. A pamphlet copy appeared in the University of North Carolina at Chapel Hill's Wilson Library in the late twentieth century, according to Robert P. Forbes ("The Enigma of John Chavis," Yale Conference on Line Singing, 6 May 2005).

69. JC to WPM, 1 February 1837, *Mangum*, 2:270. "Col. Rogers" was probably Colonel Allen Rogers, political ally of Mangum's, postmaster at Rogers' Store in Wake County from 1831 to 1838, and perhaps Chavis's landlord. Chavis tartly calls Rogers "a trifling numskull of a fellow."

70. Ibid.

71. Reelected to the Senate, as a Whig, by the General Assembly in November 1840, Mangum retired in 1853. Chavis's obituary appeared in *Watchman of the South*, Richmond, Virginia, 19 July 1838. Timothy B. Tyson recounts the legend in *Blood Done Sign My Name: A*

True Story (New York: Crown, 2004), 132–33: "The Chavis children grew up hearing that white opponents bashed in his skull because he [John Chavis] refused to stop educating black children."

72. Parramore, "Chavis, John," 358–59; Othow, *John Chavis*, 105–6, 108; Tekla A. Johnson, "John Chavis (1763–1838)," at BlackPast.org, http://www.blackpast.org/aah/chavis-john-1763-1838. Othow lists "John Chavis, Sallie Chavis, and Lizzie . . . Alston" as Chavis's children; Johnson names the surviving son as "Anderson Chavis."

73. "The Colored man who was the friend of Judge Gaston and the schoolmaster of Senators Mangum and Haywood," *The Torchlight* (Oxford, N.C.), 28 September 1880. William Joseph Gaston served on the North Carolina Supreme Court after 1833; William H. Haywood Jr., briefly U.S. senator in the 1840s, attended the Raleigh Academy.

74. Smith, *History of Education*, 140.

75. Quoted in ibid.

76. Quoted in ibid.

13

Two North Carolinians, Same Goal, Different Approaches

An Examination of the Political Lives and Philosophies of Nathaniel Macon and Archibald D. Murphey

Troy L. Kickler

If a town or institution in the southeastern United States is named Macon or has Macon in its name, it is more than likely named after Nathaniel Macon. Examples include Macon, Georgia; Macon County, North Carolina; and Randolph-Macon College. Although few, other than history enthusiasts, have heard of the former United States Speaker of the House, Macon's name was once synonymous with North Carolina, and he acquired a national reputation and wielded national influence and power. In contrast, Archibald D. Murphey's popularity was confined, more or less, in the Old North State. Not as many places are named for Murphey, an esteemed attorney, jurist, statesman, and promoter of North Carolina. Two examples, though, are Murphy, North Carolina, and Murphey Hall on the campus of the University of North Carolina at Chapel Hill (different spellings will be explained in a subsequent paragraph). While Macon has been considered resistant to change, Murphey has been seen as a visionary, at least an intellectual generation ahead of his time. Although Macon and Murphey inherited the Federalist and Anti-Federalist debates and differed regarding government's role at their respective levels of public service, both men worked to better the lives of North Carolinians as they deemed beneficial.

In many ways, it can be argued that current political philosophies in North Carolina originated and flowed intellectually downstream from the headwaters of Archibald D. Murphey and Nathaniel Macon. Even if North Carolinians are unaware, Macon's and Murphey's general political ideas continue to be invoked in modern political discourse. Although Nathaniel Macon was twenty years older than Murphey, both men were leading figures in the early republic—an era in which the first generation of Americans were remembering the founding and interpreting and exploring the proper authority and boundaries of not only the United States government but also state government. Both had ideas concerning what government should do (or not do). Both expressed concerns regarding what was best for North Carolina and its citizens.

Modern-day historians have offered mainly critical interpretations of Nathaniel Macon. In the last pages of a recent North Carolina history text, *The Tar Heel State*, scholar Milton Ready portrays Maconite thought and a similar Jeffersonianism as the main ideologies that have hamstrung American and North Carolinian progress: "Lastly the figure of Nathaniel Macon . . . looms over an enduring yet limited vision of what state government can and should do," writes Ready. "Frugal to the point of cheapness," Ready continues, "Macon believed that the state should not only govern sparingly but also tax and spend grudgingly, and then only in public and not private spheres." Historian William Powell offers a more straightforward and less bombastic interpretation regarding Macon's political views. To him, the Warren Countian "typified conservative North Carolinians." During all his thirty years in Congress as an exemplar of Old Republicanism, Macon, writes Powell, championed "economy in government, strict construction of the Constitution in favor of the states, and the interests of the masses."[1]

North Carolina histories usually offer approving interpretations of Murphey's political legacy. Powell, the dean of North Carolina history, has written that the teacher, attorney, planter, legislator, and judge inaugurated an era of progress that included constitutional reform and internal and educational improvements. Murphey, however, passed away too early and was unable to experience what he had envisioned. Ready praises Murphey for appealing to the state legislature and trying, as he puts it, to "awaken North Carolina from its Jeffersonian slumber." Historian Harry Watson has described Murphey as "the most forceful and persuasive advocate of change" in what was unfairly labeled by others as the "Rip Van Winkle" state.[2]

In contrast, Macon is often considered to be a statesman lacking vision. Harry Watson presents Macon as one who had failed to understand the value of federal internal improvements and who also misunderstood internal improvements on the state level. To Macon, state internal improvement projects were, as Watson writes, "gaming shops and get-rich-quick schemes" that had potential to "undermine the morals of the country." Macon and his political allies believed that economic change might unleash societal forces that would eventually question existing institutions and possibly undermine republicanism. In other words, the status quo, the argument goes, favored the existing ruling class, who worked to keep things the same. In the words of Macon biographer William E. Dodd, Macon led a "continued protest" against what became known as Henry Clay's American System.[3]

Macon, however, could be an agent of change, albeit less than radical. His service at the 1835 North Carolina constitutional convention provides an example. The aging politician, two years from his death, was respected across the state, so much so that convention delegates unanimously elected him to preside over the assembly as president. At one point in the convention, delegates discussed the religious qualifications for office, and Macon said that he did not care about a politician's religious belief. Macon simply wanted honest men to hold public office. After a passionate speech by William Gaston, a well-respected Catholic from New Bern, delegates replaced "Protestant" in Article 32 of the state constitution with "Christian." (The 1868 state constitution later banned only atheists from holding public office.)[4]

No matter what historians write concerning Macon or Murphey, both were respected among their colleagues and peers, for each man had much to say and influenced the times in which he lived. "There is no name in the history of this country which is destined to a higher or a more perpetual fame than that of Nathaniel Macon of North Carolina," declared the *United States Magazine, and Democratic Review* on 1 October 1838, approximately three months after the Tar Heel passed away at his plantation, Buck Spring. The account went on to praise Macon for leading a "life of principle" and for exhibiting "principles of democracy." The *Raleigh Register*, whose editors were often critical of Macon's political stances, succinctly evaluated Macon's legacy: "He has filled a large space in the history of the State, and doubtless some one content to the task will do justice to his memory in a biographical sketch." This was a necessary historical and literary project, as the *Enquirer*, a Democratic paper, suggests, for Macon was of national significance, and he was principled and resolute. When historian William E. Dodd accepted the long overdue challenge and published a much-needed in-depth manuscript in 1901, he opened by reminding readers that Macon was an important leader who influenced state and national affairs; he ended the biography with these words: "He actually believed in democracy." Macon was indeed nothing less than an icon in his time.[5]

Judge Jesse Turner, a former Murphey law apprentice, once remembered his mentor as a Renaissance man with achievements, not simply a dilettante with varied interests. He was, Turner writes, "a man of genius." As a well-respected attorney, he had a large caseload while earning a reputation as a "learned scholar," a "wise and sagacious legislator," and a statesman among "distinguished Carolinians of his day." In Turner's opinion, Murphey was an ideal candidate for the state supreme court, but the eastern interests and representatives controlled most of the public offices. As result, the Piedmont judge missed out on a prestigious opportunity. Murphey was also known as a historian. Many, including U.S. chief justice John Marshall and James G. M. Ramsey of Knoxville, Tennessee, a doctor and historian of early Tennessee history, respected Murphey for assuming the task of writing a history of North Carolina.[6]

Like Macon, it would be some time before a biographer penned an in-depth manuscript exploring Murphey's life and legacy. (This scholarly delay contributed to the misspelling of his name as "Murphy" among North Carolinians and to the reason the western North Carolina town in Cherokee County is erroneously spelled "Murphy.") Judge Turner lamented how Murphey's legacy was being forgotten in North Carolina memory, and he hoped that at least a monument would be erected in the visionary's honor. The *Daily State Chronicle* editor thought similarly and expressed dismay that Murphey's published speeches were not archived or republished for public consumption. Although William Graham wrote a Murphey biography in 1860, it would be shortly after the turn of the century before Murphey's papers were compiled and published and a little over a century later when an extensive biographical work appeared.[7]

Before proceeding into an examination of the differences and similarities between Macon's and Murphey's political philosophies, a brief biographical sketch of each man is needed.

Nathaniel Macon was born in what became Warren County, North Carolina. Little is known of his early life until he enrolled at the College of New Jersey (now Princeton). While there, the American Revolution began, and Macon left school and volunteered to fight. He signed up again in 1780 at the age of twenty-three and more than likely fought the British at Camden, South Carolina. A little while later, while encamped on the Yadkin River in North Carolina, he learned that his neighbors near Warrenton had elected him to the North Carolina Senate. He reluctantly obliged in this position until 1786, the year he also turned down an invitation to the Continental Congress. During his service at the state level, Macon was identified with Willie Jones—"the Jefferson of North Carolina"—the man whom many consider to be the leading force behind North Carolina's refusal to neither ratify nor reject the

U.S. Constitution at Hillsborough in 1788. A neighboring Halifax Countian, Jones influenced Macon's political ideas until the Warren Countian's death. Many constitutional interpretations of the early 1800s, according to historian William Price, were anathema to Macon, one who "cut his political teeth on Anti-Federalism."[8]

With twenty-four years in the House of Representatives and thirteen years in the U.S. Senate, Macon served his state and country from 1791 to 1828. In the House, he functioned as Speaker from 1801 to 1807. He also chaired the Foreign Relations Committee (1809–10). In the Senate, he was chairman of the Foreign Relations Committee from 1818 to 1826 and president pro tempore from 1826 to 1828. He was, according to one historian, the "dominant personality of the predominant Democratic-Republican Party."[9]

Macon's political and public service had three eras: Jefferson Republican (1791–1807), tertium quid (1807–15), and elder statesman in the U.S. Senate and at the state level (1815–28, 1835). In all three, he opposed taxes, internal improvements at national expense, all expenditures he deemed unnecessary to fulfill the necessary services of the national government, and a national bank. He further opposed executive patronage and compromises with the antislavery movement. Macon's fear of personal debt influenced his votes regarding public expenditures. He was considered by many to be the embodiment of Old Republican principles.[10]

In possibly 1777, Archibald DeBow Murphey was born in what is now Caswell County. Like Macon, little is known of his early life until he attended university—in this case, the University of North Carolina. A precocious student and scholar, he graduated in 1799, and he worked shortly afterward, among other duties, as a tutor and then as a professor. He started studying law in 1801 and relocated to Hillsborough.[11]

Murphey was an industrious individual in various fields. In addition to building a successful and busy law practice in Hillsborough, he had acquired approximately 2,000 acres, a gristmill, a sawmill, and a distillery. He also ran a transportation business with wagons hauling freight and products to Petersburg, Virginia. And like Macon, he owned slaves. In 1812, Murphey decided to run for public office. He served in the North Carolina Senate from 1812 to 1818, and in the latter year, the General Assembly elected him to the superior court. After two years, financial circumstances necessitated that he return to practicing law. Meanwhile, the versatile Murphey decided a history of the state should be written, and the legislature authorized a lottery to help fund the research and writing. But here again, financial circumstances prevented Murphey from completing the task. (Readers will not be surprised to learn that an ailing Murphey eventually ended up in debtors' prison in 1829 and that earlier, as a legislator, the attorney had advocated that imprisonment for debt be no more.)[12]

In education and internal improvements, Murphey made his biggest mark—although not immediately. He wanted the towns of North Carolina to be united by a system of canals and roads, and he believed such a system would foster the growth of major commercial areas that would attract outside commerce. The state would benefit from this system. A few years later, the idea of railroads emerged to unite the state, and influenced by Murphey's broad transportation vision, politicians later started implementing a connected transportation system in the Old North State during the 1840s. In 1817, Murphey proposed a publicly funded education system that provided social and economic uplift for the state's poor children. He argued that such a system would also benefit the state's economy. Murphey is often considered in histories as a prophet who died prematurely and never was able to see the realization of his vision.[13]

Macon and Murphey communicated with each other only a few times. In particular, Macon fielded an information request from Murphey when the younger man was writing a history of North Carolina—a topic Macon no doubt approved of. But Macon's personal, archival practices prevented him from thoroughly fielding Murphey's research requests: "Some years past," Macon relayed to Murphey, "a few confidential letters were I thought improperly published; This fact, induced me to burn, the correspondence of my life, together with notes on living characters, with whom I had been associated in public business." On Murphey's behalf, Macon, however, solicited historical information from Thomas Jefferson and John Randolph of Roanoke. The former's health prevented him from assisting, and the latter did not possess any pertinent and needed material for the proposed history. Macon also took the opportunity to tell the budding historian that one of North Carolina's delegates at the Constitutional Convention, Hugh Williamson, received most of the important papers from Warren County so that he could write his history of North Carolina, a work some of Murphey's colleagues deemed full of inaccuracies.[14]

Murphey and Macon appreciated the concept of constitutions and cherished the founding of the United States of America. Although Macon presided over the 1835 North Carolina constitutional convention, his public positions required him to devote more attention to interpreting the U.S. Constitution. In contrast, Murphey's public positions and interests dealt primarily with North Carolina; in fact, many in the early 1800s considered state politics to be as prestigious as national public service, if not more. In a national sense, Macon, generally speaking, defended the U.S. Constitution as ratified and properly amended. He wanted to execute the Constitution as it was written and in no other fashion; however, he also knew that strict construction allows for amendments to change the Constitution. Macon feared "grand notions and magnificent opinions" and thought they chipped away at a strict constructionist interpretation. Murphey did have "grand notions," yet he valued the Constitution as well. In regard to the state level, he also believed the North Carolina Constitution needed to be amended, and he led a call for reform.[15]

Informed by Anti-Federalism, Nathaniel Macon put forth a consistent and strict constructionist interpretation of the U.S. Constitution, for he feared broad interpretations encroached on individual liberty. To him, Americans needed to be on constant watch to secure freedom. The ratification debates undoubtedly influenced Macon's constitutional interpretations, his suspicion of government intervention, and his defense of individual liberty. He later became a palpable link to certain aspects of the American Revolution and to Anti-Federalism. In 1788, North Carolina refused to ratify the Constitution and remained out of the union for a year, and it was Willie Jones, more than any one individual—possibly other than Samuel Spencer—who persuaded North Carolina not to ratify initially the Constitution and later mentored Nathaniel Macon.[16]

Macon kept alive his intellectual mentor's political philosophy and constant suspicion of government action; such misgivings ensured liberty's existence. As he said in an 1816 Senate speech, "Ours is a government of suspicion; every election proves it; the power to impeach proves it; the history of Caesar, of Cromwell, and Bonaparte, proves that it ought to be so to remain free."[17]

Macon believed strict constructionism to be the best way to keep the nation together. In one of his longest congressional speeches, he elaborated this general argument when debating the admission of Maine and Missouri into the union. After providing a cursory history of the founding and recounting the origins of the Constitution to his fellow senators, Macon queried, "Destroy it, and what may be the condition of the country[?] No man, not the most sagacious, can even imagine. It will surely be much worse than it was before it was adopted, and that must be well remembered." In Macon's opinion, any major change might divide the nation, and divide its citizens in a regional way. Correct or not, Macon sincerely believed that his strict constructionist practices benefited the union and individual Americans. He contended that preserving the Constitution would "promote the happiness of the people" while ensuring that the "union of the States, and the Constitution, may be as lasting as the Alleghany."[18]

Visionaries, in particular, alarmed Macon; their goals were accomplished only by stretching the Constitution to expand the size and scope of the national government. Exhorting a young Bartlett Yancey, a U.S. congressman from North Carolina and later a prominent senator in the state legislature, to remain true to original intent, Macon warned him to "be not led astray by grand notions or magnificent opinions." A literal interpretation, according to Macon, checked what he described as dreams that would lead not to utopia but to an apocalyptic doom. Any deviation from the Constitution, Macon argued, led the nation one step closer to despotism. Using biblical examples, Macon penned once again to Bartlett Yancey, "The rising generations forget the principles of their forefathers, hence the destruction of free government in every age. Of what benefit was the law to the children of Israel when they departed from it, or what benefit are written constitutions if they be departed from[?]" Macon believed only honest people abided by constitutions.[19]

Like many North Carolina Anti-Federalists at Hillsborough, Macon considered unconstitutional taxation (and high taxation) as the biggest threat to the American republic. From the beginning of his public career on the national stage, Macon earned a reputation as a fiscal conservative; as a freshman congressman in 1791, he questioned unnecessary government spending and asked the Treasury Department to provide a statement of how unaccounted funds had been spent. His request should not be a problem, for an honest man, Macon believed, should not fear an investigation. From his first year in the House to his last in the Senate, Macon battled increased taxation, for it accompanied government growth; the latter needed the former. The relationship produced a debt cycle that was a "great evil" influencing the "moral as much as it does the political world." With this in mind, Macon adamantly opposed increased taxation during the Sixteenth Congress: "Our strength is in proportion to the smallness of our taxes; encumber and overload us with debt, and we are ruined." He further added, "It has so happened, that all the free government of old times has passed by; and all of them probably from the same causes, to wit—Debt & extravagance; can a remedy be found for this great evil, which affects the moral as much as it does the political world."[20]

As chairman of the committee on calling a convention for the purpose of amending the constitution of North Carolina, Archibald Murphey praised the founding of the United States of America and how the budding nation might actually foster a society in which people governed themselves while public safety and "Private Rights" were ensured. Even though the United States and the respective states, more or less, achieved that goal (or were on their way to doing so), Murphey commented that fallible humans endeavored to create a government in a short time. The existence of deficiencies or areas of improvement should not have surprised anyone. In turn, Murphey wondered whether the state constitution needed to be updated or amended to ensure republican principles. He, of course, concluded that it needed revision.[21]

His main concern was the inequality of representation in the legislature. Since 1776, eastern North Carolina had an advantage, but as the state's population grew the inequality increased. The Piedmont and western regions, he claimed, were underrepresented in the state house. (Readers should remember that Judge Turner believed that Murphey was a great candidate for the state supreme court; however, eastern interests prevailed in public office selections.) According to the committee's tabulations, "one-third of the white population" elected a majority in the General Assembly. The underrepresentation and political inequality threatened what the committee described as "the first Principles of a Republican System of Government."[22]

Murphey then pointed out other defects in the North Carolina Constitution, but he was willing to postpone action if the convention focused on the inequality of representation. What Macon wanted, to be specific, was a resolution in the next General Assembly that allowed voters to decide whether they wanted a constitutional convention. He also wanted sheriffs, or other local public officials, to tally the votes and report the results to appropriate government officials. The subsequent legislature would then learn "the vote of the Freemen of the State."[23]

Although historians have considered Murphey a dreamer and a visionary, he was in some ways a calculating politician. Writing to Thomas Ruffin, a fellow attorney in Hillsborough, Murphey predicted the unsuccessful outcome of his committee's overall report. He possessed assurance, however, that his proposal would prompt public discussion on whether the state constitution needed to be amended. Nineteen years later, delegates proved him correct as they convened to revise the state constitution, with Macon presiding over the proceedings. Murphey had presented some other ideas during the 1816 legislative session, but he was most optimistic concerning the eventual adoption of his ideas regarding education.[24]

Murphey and Macon disagreed, in more than a few ways, regarding government's role in society and individuals' lives, but they had commonalities that many modern-day historians overlook. Murphey was more favorable regarding government involvement and programs, while Macon distrusted giving even a small amount of power to the government. They also had different visions for how the economy in their beloved North Carolina should operate. But while they approached matters from different perspectives, Murphey and Macon championed the improvement of individuals and North Carolina. Macon was an agrarian planter, while Murphey was a budding jack-of-all-trades with many entrepreneurial pursuits, including farming.

When Archibald Murphey starting experiencing serious financial difficulties, he debated whether to sell his slaves. In 1820, he had approximately sixty remaining slaves, and not all sixty helped him make a profit—more than likely, some were elderly, some were very young, and some were afflicted with ailments. Although Murphey was in dire financial straits, he did not realize, according to him, how some slaves were "attached" to him. Selling them troubled and pained him. He wrote to Colonel William Polk and acknowledged Polk's offer to purchase the slaves. Murphey, more than likely, would give him first choice.[25]

A year later, Murphey regretted his entrepreneurial mistakes and wished only to keep a "few servants for my wife, and begin anew." (He was a better lawyer and jurist than a businessman and entrepreneur.) In 1821, urgent financial circumstances necessitated that he sell his slaves, and he claimed to have an opportunity to acquire ten to fifteen thousand dollars in bonds. Such an amount would have alleviated much of his immediate debt problem. Yet in 1821, Murphey anticipated a plentiful corn harvest and preferred not to sell his slaves until after it was gathered.[26]

Nathaniel Macon reportedly maintained a fairly paternalistic and benevolent relationship with slaves, even at times working alongside them in the fields. Among his congressional peers, he invited his antislavery colleagues and political opponents to travel the South and observe the master-slave relationship and then form an opinion. Macon in some respects argued that the southern slave society was more benevolent than a free market one. "The owner can make more free in conversation with his slave," Macon opined, "than the rich man, where there is no slave, with the white hireling who drives his carriage." The North Carolinian also believed wholeheartedly that slave owners were as moral and religious as those who hired laborers, if not more so.[27]

Macon strongly believed slavery's fate should be decided by the states and that Congress had no authority over whether the Missouri Territory, for instance, should be slave or free. The people of Missouri should have the same opportunity as other and previous territories, for if it was denied, there would, he predicted, be discontent in the nation because states had been treated differently. If Congress intervened, the Constitution, Macon argued, was threatened, and he feared a domino effect in other political matters and a growing dissatisfaction that might threaten the existence of the union. He reminded fellow senators that "there is no power in the General Government to touch it [slavery] in any way." And as American colonists, Macon pointed out, maintained their English rights across the Atlantic, so did Missourians maintain their constitutional rights as they moved westward.[28]

During the early 1800s, the African colonization movement started gaining some popularity. In 1816, the American Colonization Society was founded with the idea to settle former slaves in Africa and expedite the end of slavery. Other antislavery white Americans speculated whether former slaves should participate in the American economy and society. (Not all motives were altruistic and humanitarian.) Many free blacks opposed the colonization movement; America was home, and they feared a widespread deportation. Still, the American Colonization Society established Liberia in 1822, and the colony became independent in 1847.[29]

Although both men owned slaves, Macon and Murphey had possibly divergent views regarding colonization. In his personal correspondence, Macon is silent concerning the matter. In one letter, though, he questions whether an equal number of whites and blacks can live in a free country: "Whether the whites [and] the blacks can live peaceably [and] happily in the same country, where the numbers are nearly equal, is a problem yet to be solved." And in one congressional speech, Macon discusses the movement to help him reveal that free blacks were treated like second-class citizens in the United States. According to Macon, there seemed to be "no place for the free blacks in the United States." Wherever they lived, especially in large cities, Macon claimed, free blacks were "degraded." If a welcoming place existed in a country wanting more inhabitants for a growing economy, no desire to form colonization societies would exist.[30]

Archibald Murphey supported colonization for emancipated slaves under the supervision of the United States government. It was suggested that the colony be located out west, near the Pacific Ocean. The United States would establish a government, including a constitution and laws, and provide transportation for existing free blacks to travel out west. More than a few North Carolina legislators believed this idea was the humane course of action.[31]

Murphey believed the founding era was a singular time: the literature of the era reveals the special nature of the revolutionaries and distinguishes that time period from all others in English and United States history. Ordinary men, Murphey claimed, produced unparalleled writings and speeches. Even the personal correspondence of George Washington inspired and motivated. Murphey compared founders' ordinary letters to the works of Tacitus and Cicero. Any educated American, if not all people, Murphey argued, should be familiar with George Washington and the founders and what American soldiers experienced during the conflict. Murphey also praised the writings of North Carolina founders, including William Hooper, Joseph Hewes, Samuel Johnston, and Richard Caswell. They contributed to what Murphey considered the high mark of North Carolina literature. When the North Carolina founders left the public arena, great literature "disappeared with them." In 1827, Murphey relayed these thoughts to the Dialectic Society at the University of North Carolina. The *Cape Fear Recorder*, however, criticized the interpretation of North Carolina founders and pointed out that Caswell's literary ability was not impressive.[32]

Macon and Murphey worked for what they deemed best for North Carolina. Murphey believed in the progression of freedom in human history and that the diffusion of wealth allowed people the opportunity to acquire an education and appreciate the arts. He adopted a somewhat more Whiggish interpretation of history—that the economy and the justice system, to name two examples, continually improve through time. His history of North Carolina presented a story of progress via personal freedom. This understanding undoubtedly influenced his political ideas regarding educational reform, constitutional reform for democracy's sake, and publicly funded internal improvements.

Nathaniel Macon protected individual liberty by defending First Amendment rights. The plain and direct language of that amendment satisfied the North Carolinian, who remained baffled that his colleagues misunderstood the express wording of the Constitution. He opposed attempts to muzzle public opinion most impressively during the 1798 Sedition Bill debates.

The Sedition Bill was intended to eliminate opposition to war preparations and the undermining of any war effort, but Thomas Jefferson and Macon's other political allies believed the legislation aimed directly at Republican presses. When he delivered his supportive speech and read excerpts from the Republican *Aurora*, John Allen, a Connecticut Federalist, may have proved them right. Allen accused the paper and Democratic-Republican leadership of printing "shameless falsehoods" that were "hostile to free government and genuine liberty, and of course to the welfare of the country." He and other Federalists believed the paper's provocative language was insurrectionary and was liberty misused.[33]

As he often did, Macon seemed most concerned with preserving the overall Constitution while emphasizing the importance of the freedom of the press and speech and expressing a concern for the erosion of constitutional liberties. Americans could be fined or imprisoned not only for obstructing the execution of a law but also for "writing, printing, publishing, or speaking anything libelous, scandalous, or tending to defame the government or its officers." Macon remained perplexed that no Federalist addressed the bill on constitutional grounds, and he warned Congress that by limiting the "liberty of the press" the Sedition Bill set a precedent for Congress to establish such things as a national religion; "if [the Constitution] be violated in one respect, it may as well be violated in others."[34]

Macon believed that the Sedition Bill would not silence government's critics. Unlike Europeans, Macon asserted, Americans were a politically aware citizenry that questioned government action and cherished the liberty of the press in which they, "as free men, ought to be extremely jealous." Such a citizenry would "suspect something is not right when free discussion is feared by government. They know that truth is not afraid of investigation." If the Sedition Bill passed, Macon forecast that Americans would recapture the spirit of 1776, "establish corresponding societies throughout the Union," and communicate "in secret instead of publicly." The bill should not pass, said the "Plain Republican," as he was sometimes known, because Americans have as much right to discuss politics as the men whom they elect "to do their business."[35]

More than frustrated that the bill's advocates refused to offer constitutional arguments, the Tar Heel legislator anticipated that Federalists would cite common law and state laws as legal justification. Harrison Otis of Massachusetts did exactly that. Otis cited state actions to limit the press and encouraged the states to continue punishing, "when necessary, licentiousness of the press." Macon disagreed. The national government had not the constitutional right to restrict the press, the Tar Heel pointed out. If the bill passed, Macon predicted a future in which groundless charges of licentiousness abounded. Macon remarked that the Federalist paper *Cobbott's* was equally as culpable as the Republican *Aurora*. (He needed to read one to counteract the lies of the other.) Macon once again challenged the bill's supporters to offer a constitutional argument; whatever they offered to prove it constitutional, he could easily offer more evidence to prove its unconstitutionality. And he suggested that the best way to determine the bill's constitutionality was to consider the ratification debates.[36]

Macon was surprised that an account was needed, so he read the First Amendment and asked, "How can so plain language be misunderstood or interpreted into consistency with this bill before us[?]" He remained baffled how in such a short time Congress thought it had the constitutional authority to assert such power. Nowhere in the ratification debates, Macon testified, did a state relinquish to the national government its power to prosecute libel. To support his argument, he even quoted James Iredell, a leading Federalist from North Carolina and a U.S. Supreme Court justice (who had written essays encouraging ratification before many of *The Federalist* essays were penned).

Iredell had written that the national government cannot prosecute authors for treason, for the power was not enumerated. Macon declared the bill as dangerous, for Congress was stepping on "forbidden ground" and endangering the liberty of the press.[37]

Macon then went on and revealed the crux of his opposition to the Sedition Bill. Not only did the bill threaten individual liberties, it challenged the nature of the United States government. Regarding the regulation of the press, Macon remarked, "The States have complete power on the subject, and when Congress legislates, it ought to have confidence in the States, as the States also to have confidence in Congress, or our Government is gone. This Government depends upon the State Legislatures for existence." Federalists knew, however, that certain state legislatures might never censure the press, and therefore Federalists, Macon believed, submitted the Sedition Bill to muzzle critics, not to solve a genuine problem.[38]

This speech contains, as William Dodd writes, Macon's political creed concerning the nature of the states and the Constitution—that is, the nation is a product of the states and relies on them for its existence. The Warren Countian's arguments for First Amendment rights harked back to the ratification debates, and he and his political allies defended states' rights, in many ways, as the best defense to protect individual liberties. Yet despite Macon's valiant defense of First Amendment rights and the liberty of the press, the House passed the Sedition Bill (44 to 41 votes).[39]

When the Committee of Revival and Unfinished Business in 1801 recommended the Sedition Act's continuation, Macon once again defended the First Amendment liberty of the press. To Macon, the press was "amongst the best gifts bestowed on man," and Congress had not power over it—that is, any constitutional power. Macon's speech against continuation can be divided into three parts: a history of the ratification debates of 1788, a defense of the press being a major means for citizens to have freedom to discuss government action, and the unconstitutional nature of the Sedition Act. While Federalists intermittently interrupted Macon, Macon argued specifically that the states never gave the national government authority to regulate the press. He furthermore claimed that no government had ever been destroyed by lies and that Federalists benefited most from the continuation of the Sedition Act. Macon reminded congressmen that they had repeatedly said that principled actions cannot bring shame; therefore, there should be no need for the Sedition Act, Macon articulated, because in contested accounts, truth prevails.[40]

During the speech, Macon may have been most effective when he criticized Federalists and challenged them to offer constitutional justifications.

When panned for being contrary, Macon again defended the way he questioned the constitutionality of most laws; it was necessary because some in the House never doubted any bill's constitutionality. He further objected to the selective application of the law to Republicans, who criticized Federalists. Macon spoke for some time (possibly one of his longest speeches, for which he apologized at its end), but every word hinged on his belief that Congress "was prohibited from legislating on the subject of the press by the Constitution." By demanding constitutional arguments from his opponents, Macon ensured that the Sedition Act died a natural death in 1801.[41]

Macon put forth these arguments when political parties were forming in the United States. Like Macon, Archibald Murphey believed political parties threatened republican values and that the "true Source of all Our evils," as he put it, was placing incompetent men in public office. He feared politicians who emphasized party ambition before the good of the country or honor. In a letter to Thomas Ruffin, a pessimistic Murphey envisioned nothing but "ruin and confusion" for the nation if it continued proceeding down its current path. At the time, 1814, some New England states were contemplating leaving the union, and Murphey feared North Carolina would be in a predicament deciding whether to join. Earlier that year, he had reported his concerns to his constituents regarding the growing party spirit in the nation. In his mind, it threatened all that was decent and good. Murphey was never one, at least publicly, to criticize political opponents, for he believed it undermined political goals and soured political discourse. He remained baffled with those who constantly quarreled, especially if the expressed goals—the betterment of the state and its people—were espoused by both parties. "Party spirit" had to be monitored; it posed a threat, he believed, to the existence of the government: "Party spirit has ruined all the free governments which have heretofore existed: It will ruin ours, unless constant efforts be made to check its influence."[42]

An affection for North Carolina and a concern for North Carolinians motivated Murphey. In particular, he genuinely believed that education would improve North Carolinians' lives, so in 1816, Murphey presented a comprehensive report promoting public education. A republic rested on its citizens' virtue, so citizens needed a solid education. Only knowledge, Murphey believed, shed light on necessary civil duties. To secure virtue, Murphey suggested a graduated and integrated system of education, from the rudimentary knowledge of the three R's to the most scientific education. (During the time, at the University of North Carolina many debated whether students should learn primarily by classical instruction or by the latest vocational and scientific methods.)[43]

For the betterment of the nation, Murphey believed that the school system was to be an instrument of social and even religious instruction. The state of North Carolina, according to Murphey, had a duty to confer these "blessings . . . upon her children." Public education, then, was considered a means of social uplift for many underprivileged children whose parents, according to Murphey, were unaware of education's economic and social benefits. If North Carolina's genius could be set free from the bonds of poverty, suggested Murphey, the state's economy would benefit from more and more ideas from its growing and enterprising citizenry. He even proposed that public school alumni return to teach without pay at their alma mater. Murphey's comprehensive plan also included the "humane attentions of the government" and the education of those he labeled "deaf and dumb." Explicit suggestions for African Americans and other population groups are absent from Murphey's report.[44]

Although Murphey's plan was not implemented while he served in the state senate, it influenced later politicians, including Bartlett Yancey, who proposed a bill establishing the Literary Fund, a system of common schools funded by various stocks, taxes, and sales of public land. The fund, however, suffered from financial mismanagement and political resistance.[45]

Although Nathaniel Macon suggested no system of education and his personal correspondence includes few mentions of education, the Warren Countian served as a trustee for the University of North Carolina during 1826–27. Macon was involved actively in 1826 with seeking character and professional references for prospective professors at the university. In the process, he learned that one applicant as a language instructor was considered more a "smatterer of languages than a real scholar." On another occasion, Macon reported the intellectual ability of one applicant yet stated his abilities as a teacher were unknown. In all, Macon acted diligently on behalf of the academic interests of the University of North Carolina until other duties and health prevented him from doing so.[46]

Archibald Murphey also championed internal improvements. Readers must be reminded that education, the arts, and improvements were interwoven in Murphey's mind; each represented a component of a comprehensive approach to improve North Carolina and its status in the United States. In a time of peace, Murphey recommended that Americans and North Carolinians focus on improvement in all three areas. Such an approach would foster a love of country among Americans and thereby increase the chances of its survival. Such a comprehensive undertaking also required diligence, Murphey thought, and the blessings of a higher power.[47]

In 1826, the *Raleigh Register* described Murphey as the "father of Internal Improvements" in the Old North State. Murphey's internal improvement plans included mainly an organized system of roads and canals. Although private companies had been building plank roads and the Dismal Canal, Murphey argued that North Carolina failed to compete with its neighboring states. The Old North State's diverse geography necessitated a more organized and comprehensive approach to improve the transportation system. More specifically, Murphey desired better roads to facilitate traffic; a network of market towns in strategic locations; a network of canals and channel locks that made rivers (particularly Piedmont rivers) navigable; and swamplands converted into workable farms. Murphey's transportation vision, however, was postponed until after his passing, when legislators started connecting the state via roads and railroads.[48]

Murphey initially believed a mixture of public and private funds should pay for the endeavor, but he later suggested the state take out loans. In time, North Carolina hired an engineer from England, Hamilton Fulton, who started working to execute Murphey's internal improvement plan, and public opinion became more favorable regarding such improvements. The public, through various local agencies at a convention, even recommended that the state borrow up to $6 million from banks. The legislature thought differently. The Board of Internal Improvements recommended, with increasing amounts up to $6 million, during the 1820s, that the state borrow money to complete the various projects. In the end, the Board of Internal Improvements suffered from mismanagement of funds, declining bank stock, and unsuccessful debt collection for the sale of Cherokee land; furthermore, as William Powell points out, local interests and pet projects competed with and distracted from a statewide implementation of an internal improvement network.[49]

Nathaniel Macon believed, in particular, that internal improvement bills at the federal level threatened Old Republican principles and that all parties, at times, violated the Constitution and undermined original intent. In many ways, an aging and politically jaded Macon labeled his political philosophy as a third thing—something different from the two major political parties. Macon predicted an ominous future, especially with a majority in Congress who believed in implied powers. To him, politicians of this stripe would turn Congress into a band of "bargainers [and] traders." Macon believed in a common argument uttered by southern politicians, that federal improvements might take advantage of his home state and make it pay an unfair share for improvements that benefited another state. If a state had power to fund internal improvements and so did the national government, what was North Carolina's interest in helping fund national internal improvements?[50]

As he did with issues of the press and the national bank, Macon feared a cascade of what he considered unconstitutional acts if internal improvement legislation were passed at the federal level. If one deemed it constitutional for Congress to establish a national bank or internal improvements, Macon reasoned, then what prevented Congress from intervening in other matters? In particular, he wondered whether it would set precedent for Congress to interfere with slavery in the states. Commenting that states were debating the existence of slavery and that it was an act of piracy to participate in the international slave trade, Macon sincerely believed that the major political question was what the extent of the power of the federal government was. He referenced *The Federalist Papers* and remarked that no such power was listed in the authoritative constitutional commentary. In many ways, Macon believed that the bank law and internal improvement legislation had set forth a new interpretation of the Constitution that essentially established a new constitution, a new form of government. The pessimistic senator deemed the original Constitution as ratified to be dead.[51]

Nathaniel Macon and Archibald Murphey, North Carolinians who cherished their beloved Old North State, interpreted government's role in societal affairs differently. In a somewhat paradoxical fashion, Macon championed limited government on the national scene, while Murphey promoted government support and involvement at the state level. Macon's chief concern was to defend the U.S. Constitution as it was ratified, for he deemed that priority tantamount to preserving what was best regarding the United States and North Carolina. Murphey's concern was to encourage state government involvement to improve North Carolina's economy and society and thereby foster an appreciation for the state among North Carolinians so that it participated (and was appreciated) in the growing American economy. In the end, one Tar Heel believed the U.S. Constitution was dead while fearing what lay ahead for his nation and state; and another Tar Heel anticipated his state's participation in what seemed to be a budding American economy and society.[52]

NOTES

1. Milton Ready, *The Tar Heel State: A History of North Carolina* (Columbia: University of South Carolina Press, 2005), 389; William S. Powell, *North Carolina through Four Centuries* (Chapel Hill: University of North Carolina Press, 1989), 235.

2. Powell, *North Carolina*, 266; Ready, *Tar Heel State*, 163; Harry L. Watson, "'Old Rip' and a New Era," in *The North Carolina Experience: An Interpretive and Documentary History*, ed. Lindley S. Butler and Alan D. Watson (Chapel Hill: University of North Carolina Press, 1984), 219–20.

3. Watson, "'Old Rip' and a New Era," 223; William E. Dodd, *The Life of Nathaniel Macon* (repr., New York: Burt Franklin, 1970), 401.

4. Ready, *Tar Heel State*, 172–74, 389; Dodd, *Nathaniel Macon*, 387–89.

5. Dodd, *Nathaniel Macon*, 399, xiii, 401.

6. Judge Jesse Turner to Judge Archibald Murphey Aiken, no date listed, in *The Papers of Archibald D. Murphey*, ed. William Henry Hoyt, 2 vols. (Raleigh: E. M. Uzzell, 1914), 2:426–30; James G. Ramsey to Archibald Murphey, 9 April 1827, and Chief Justice John Marshall to Archibald Murphey, 6 October 1827, in ibid., 1:355–56, 365–66.

7. *Papers of Archibald Murphey*, 1:423–24; Henry Snipes Turner, *The Dreamer, Archibald De Bow Murphey, 1777–1832* (Verona, Va.: McClure, 1971).

8. Dodd, *Nathaniel Macon*, 2–44; Clyde Wilson, "Nathaniel Macon," in *Dictionary of North Carolina Biography*, ed. William S. Powell (Chapel Hill: University of North Carolina Press, 1979–96), 4:185–87; William S. Price Jr., *Nathaniel Macon of North Carolina: Three Views Regarding His Character and Creed* (Raleigh: North Carolina Office of Archives and History, 2008), 51.

9. Wilson, "Nathaniel Macon," 185–87.

10. Ibid.; Stephen J. Barry, "Nathaniel Macon: The Prophet of Pure Republicanism, 1758–1837" (Ph.D. diss., State University of New York at Buffalo, 1996), 292–95.

11. H. G. Jones, "Archibald DeBow Murphey," in *Dictionary of North Carolina Biography*, 4:345–46.

12. Ibid.

13. Ibid.; Ready, *Tar Heel State*, 163–67; Powell, *North Carolina*, 253–66.

14. Nathaniel Macon to Archibald Murphey, 25 October 1825, Nathaniel Macon Papers, North Carolina Department of Archives and History, Raleigh; Nathaniel Macon to Archibald Murphey, 26 February 1826, Nathaniel Macon Papers, Special Collections, William R. Perkins Library, Duke University; Ramsey to Murphey, 9 April 1827, *Papers of Archibald Murphey*, 1:355; Dodd, *Nathaniel Macon*, 401.

15. Wilson, "Nathaniel Macon," 185–87; Nathaniel Macon to Bartlett Yancey, 15 April 1818, in Edwin Mood Wilson, *The Congressional Career of Nathaniel Macon* (Chapel Hill: University of North Carolina, 1900), 46–47; Watson, "'Old Rip and a New Era," 219–21, 235; Ready, *Tar Heel State*, 168–70.

16. Price, *Nathaniel Macon*, 27–51.

17. Quoted in ibid., 36.

18. *Annals of Congress*, 16th Cong., 1st Sess., 220, 232 (1820).

19. Nathaniel Macon to Bartlett Yancey, 15 April 1818, 31 March 1826, in Wilson, *Congressional Career of Nathaniel Macon*, 46–47, 86.

20. Dodd, *Nathaniel Macon*, 65–66; Nathaniel Macon to Willie Person Mangum, 14 January 1827, in *The Papers of Willie Person Mangum*, ed. Henry Thomas Shanks, 2 vols. (Raleigh: State Department of Archives and History, 1950–56), 1:305–7.

21. *Report of the Committee on Calling a Convention for the Purpose of Amending the Constitution of North Carolina*, in *Papers of Archibald Murphey*, 1:57.

22. Ibid., 58.

23. Ibid., 60.

24. Archibald Murphey to Thomas Ruffin, 22 December 1816, in *Papers of Archibald Murphey*, 1:90–91.

25. Archibald Murphey to William Polk, 18 February 1820 in ibid., 1:158.

26. Archibald Murphey to Thomas Ruffin, 28 July 1821, in ibid., 1:218.

27. *Annals of Congress*, 16th Cong., 1st Sess., 226 (1820); William J. Cooper Jr., *Liberty and Slavery: Southern Politics to 1860* (repr., Columbia: University of South Carolina Press, 2000), 128, 137.

28. *Annals of Congress*, 16th Cong., 1st Sess., 222–25, 239 (1820).

29. Paul S. Boyer, ed., *The Oxford Companion to United States History* (New York: Oxford University Press, 2001), 146.

30. Nathaniel Macon to Bartlett Yancey, 8 December 1825, in Wilson, *Congressional Career of Nathaniel Macon*, 77; *Annals of Congress*, 16th Cong., 1st Sess., 227–28 (1820).

31. "Resolution of the General Assembly Proposing a Colony for Free Negroes," in *Papers of Archibald Murphey*, 2:61–62.

32. Archibald D. Murphey, "An Oration Delivered in Person Hall, Chapel Hill, on the 27th June, 1827, the Day Previous to the Commencement under the Appointment of the Dialectic Society," in ibid., 2:347–51.

33. Dodd, *Nathaniel Macon*, 122–23; James Marvin Helms Jr., "The Early Career of Nathaniel Macon: A Study in 'Pure Republicanism'" (Ph.D. diss., University of Virginia, 1962), 174–80.

34. Dodd, *Nathaniel Macon*, 123.

35. Ibid., 124.

36. Ibid., 124–25.

37. Ibid., 125–26.

38. Ibid., 126–27.

39. Ibid., 126; Helms, "Early Career of Nathaniel Macon," 174–80.

40. Dodd, *Nathaniel Macon*, 151–53.

41. Ibid., 153–54. For further discussion regarding Macon's role in the Alien and Sedition Acts debate and his rise to House leadership, please refer to Helms, "Early Career of Nathaniel Macon," 195–200; and Barry, "Nathaniel Macon," 51–68.

42. Archibald Murphey to Thomas Ruffin, 24 November 1814, in *Papers of Archibald Murphey*, 1:75–76; Archibald Murphey, "Circular Letter to the Freeholders of Orange County," 3 June 1814, in ibid., 2:14–18.

43. Archibald Murphey, *Report on Education Made to the General Assembly of North Carolina at Its Session of 1816*, in ibid., 2:51–53; Robert M. Calhoon, "An Agrarian and Evangelical Culture," in *North Carolina Experience*, 172–74.

44. Murphey, *Report on Education*, in *Papers of Archibald Murphey*, 2:53–56.

45. Powell, *North Carolina*, 258–59.

46. William Staughton to Nathaniel Macon, 22 March 1826, and Nathaniel Macon to William Polk, 3 May 1826, University Papers, Nathaniel Macon Correspondence, University of North Carolina at Chapel Hill.

47. Murphey, *Report on Education*, in *Papers of Archibald Murphey*, 2:64.

48. Archibald Murphey to Victor Moreau Murphey, 12 August 1826, in ibid., 1:337–39, 339n2; Powell, *North Carolina*, 261; *Memoir on the Internal Improvements Contemplated by the Legislature of North Carolina and on the Resources and Finances of That State*, in *Papers of Archibald Murphey*, 2:105–51.

49. *Mr. Murphey's Report to the Legislature of North Carolina on Inland Navigation, December 1816*, in *Papers of Archibald Murphey*, 2:44; *Memoir on the Internal Improvements*, in ibid., 2:182; Powell, *North Carolina*, 260–65.

50. Nathaniel Macon to Thomas Jefferson, 21 May 1824, in Elizabeth Gregory McPherson, ed., "Unpublished Letters from North Carolinians to Jefferson," *North*

Carolina Historical Review 12, no. 3 (1935): 354–80; Nathaniel Macon to Bartlett Yancey, 26 December 1824, in Wilson, *Congressional Career of Nathaniel Macon*, 71–73.

51. Nathaniel Macon to Bartlett Yancey, 8 December 1826, and Nathaniel Macon to Bartlett Yancey, 3 November 1827, in Wilson, *Congressional Career of Nathaniel Macon*, 93–95.

52. Murphey wrote in an 1821 letter to Joseph Graham, "I love North Carolina, and love her more, because so much injustice has been done to her. We want pride. We want independence. We want magnanimity. Knowing nothing of ourselves, we have nothing in our history to which we can turn with feelings of conscious pride. We know nothing of our State, and care nothing about it." *Papers of Archibald Murphey*, 1:211–12. Macon wrote to a young Bartlett Yancey in 1818, "Add not to the constitution nor there from; no coincidental power can stand alone, whatever can stand alone is substantive, not incidental; Be not lead astray by grand notions or magnificent opinions, remember you belong to a meek State and just people who want nothing but to enjoy the fruits of their labor honestly and to lay out their profits in their own way." Macon to Yancey, 15 April 1818, in Wilson, *Congressional Career of Nathaniel Macon*, 46–47.

Afterword

Jeff Broadwater & Troy L. Kickler

We believe the preceding essays illustrate the essential role our ordinary founders played in the American Revolution. There could have been no revolution in North Carolina without them. Continental figures alone, even someone of George Washington's stature, could not have mobilized a largely parochial population to fight a long war against imperial Britain or to support a new national government. These North Carolinians were ordinary only in the sense of being overshadowed by a small cadre of more famous founders.

A few other observations might be made in closing. First, while their influence lingers, our North Carolina founders, for the most part, enjoyed relatively brief political careers. North Carolina experienced a changing of the political guard in the 1790s. Partly, it was a result of ill fortune. William Hooper, Joseph Hewes, John Penn, and James Iredell all died in their forties. Richard Caswell, one of the older founders when the Revolution began, died in 1789. Changing circumstances and a more democratic political culture also played a role. When Tennessee became a separate territory, John Sevier went with it. The polymath Hugh Williamson left North Carolina for the more cosmopolitan environs of New York City in 1793. Although he did not abandon public life, Willie Jones never again sought political office after 1789. William R. Davie served briefly as governor in the late 1790s, but after losing a race for Congress in 1803, he left the state in 1805, disgusted at the voters' rejection of his brand of aristocratic leadership. Richard Dobbs Spaight, who occupied the governor's office from 1792 to 1795, was cut from the same cloth as Davie, but Spaight became identified with Jeffersonian Republicanism, only to find himself embroiled in a partisan feud that led to a fatal duel in 1802. Historical periods can sometimes be arbitrary, but with the establishment of a new federal government, North Carolina clearly entered a new political era.

Second, North Carolina's founders were a diverse group, encompassing men, women, whites, free blacks, and Native Americans. They held to differing political philosophies, even differing in the degree to which ideas influenced their actions. William Hooper was well versed in political theory. Joseph Hewes apparently was not. For John Sevier, liberty meant little more than the right of white men to own property and to vote. For the Catawba, the Revolution represented another phase in their struggle for survival, not an exercise in political philosophy. As a free black man, John Chavis sought primarily the right to pursue a career as a minister and teacher. Most of our founders, however, did share one trait. Few if any of them could be fairly described as extreme nationalists. No one supported ratification of the Constitution more enthusiastically than did James Iredell, but his best-known opinion as a Supreme Court justice was his defense of state sovereignty in his *Chisholm v. Georgia* dissent. Archibald Murphey, the most ambitious reformer of his era, urged state lawmakers to improve North Carolina's transportation and educational systems, but he showed scant interest in national politics.

Finally, opportunities for future research abound. Limitations of space led us to exclude any number of important figures: Thomas Burke, a wartime governor and highly influential member of the Continental Congress; Samuel Johnston, a conservative stalwart who was one of North Carolina's most durable politicians; and Cornelius Harnett Jr., whom the Massachusetts Whig Josiah Quincy called "the Samuel Adams of North Carolina," are only a few of the most obvious omissions.[1] A systematic study of political thought in Revolutionary era North Carolina might yield surprising fruit, as Kyle Scott's fresh look at Willie Jones suggests. As we have seen in Scott's chapter, he argues that a politician long regarded as North Carolina's preeminent radical was in fact a cautious pragmatist. Another potential topic: a modern, comprehensive study of North Carolina's role in the Constitutional Convention and the ratification debate.[2] Additionally, we need to know more about how North Carolina's state government actually operated. The essays in this volume demonstrate the critical role local officials played in dealing with Native Americans, but what about other state functions?

Nevertheless, the picture our contributors have drawn of eighteenth-century North Carolinians as an independent people with conflicting views of a post-Revolutionary political order and a deep-seated suspicion of distant rulers seems unlikely to change.

NOTES

1. Quincy quoted in Donald R. Lennon, "Harnett, Cornelius Jr.," in *Dictionary of North Carolina Biography*, ed. William S. Powell (Chapel Hill: University of North Carolina Press, 1988), 3:37.

2. The most recent treatment we have of North Carolina and the ratification debate is an excellent journal article: Thomas L. Howard III, "The State That Said No: The Fight for Ratification of the Federal Constitution in North Carolina," *North Carolina Historical Review* 94, no. 1 (2017): 1–58.

Contributors

JEFF BROADWATER recently retired as professor of history at Barton College. His publications include *George Mason, Forgotten Founder* (2006) and *James Madison: A Son of Virginia and a Founder of the Nation* (2012).

JENNIFER DAVIS-DOYLE is currently an adjunct history instructor at Campbell University.

LLOYD JOHNSON is professor of history and director of historical studies at Campbell University.

BENJAMIN R. JUSTESEN is currently a freelance editor and writer. He has taught at various institutions, including the University of North Carolina at Chapel Hill and Heritage Bible College. His publications include *George Henry White: An Even Chance in the Race of Life* (2001), *Broken Brotherhood: The Rise and Fall of the National Afro-American Council* (2008), and *Union Institute and University at 50: Leaders Realizing a Dream* (2015).

TROY L. KICKLER is a research historian at the North Carolina Office of Archives and History and author of *The King's Trouble Makers: Edenton's Role in Creating a Nation and State* (2013).

SCOTT KING-OWEN has worked for the Bexley City School District in Ohio since 2011. He teaches Advanced Placement courses in United States history, psychology, and Latin. In 2018, he was selected as Bexley Educator of the Year.

JAMES MACDONALD is professor of history at Northwestern State University in Natchitoches, Louisiana.

MAGGIE HARTLEY MITCHELL is currently associate director for programming and events at the National D-Day Memorial Foundation.

KARL RODABAUGH is emeritus professor of history at Winston-Salem State University. He currently is an adjunct professor at East Carolina University, where formerly he was a tenured history professor.

KYLE SCOTT teaches political science at the University of Houston and serves as vice chair on the board of trustees for the Lone Star College System. He has written four books exploring American political thought and the founding. His current research focuses on professional ethics, which he explores as an associate faculty member at the Baylor College of Medicine, Center for Health Policy and Medical Ethics.

JASON STROUD is supervisor of social studies for the Guilford County Public School System.

MICHAEL TOOMEY is chair of the Department of Humanities and Fine Arts at Lincoln Memorial University. He is a former editor of the *Journal of East Tennessee History*.

WILLIS P. WHICHARD is currently an attorney with Tillman, Hinkle, and Whichard in Chapel Hill, North Carolina. He was formerly an adjunct professor of law at the University of North Carolina at Chapel Hill and dean and professor of law at Norman Adrian Wiggins School of Law, Campbell University, from 1999 to 2006. Before then, he sat on the Court of Appeals of North Carolina and the North Carolina Supreme Court.

Index

Abbot, Henry, 209
Adams, John, 53, 56, 118, 119, 248; and *Thoughts on Government*, 54
Alien and Sedition Acts, 188
Allen, John, 290
American Colonization Society, 289
Annapolis Convention (1786), 14–15, 121, 170
Anti-Federalists, 16, 124–25, 138–39, 147, 182–85, 202, 219, 221–22, 227–30; as "men of little faith," 209–10. *See also* Jones, Willie; Spencer, Samuel
Aristotle, 18, 230
Articles of Confederation, 13–14, 170, 182, 225–27
Attakullakulla (Cherokee leader), 67–68, 74

Barker, Penelope. *See* Edenton Tea Party
Barker, Thomas, 29
Bayard v. Singleton (1787), 145, 214n15, 242
Bill of Rights (U.S.), 2, 148, 185, 208–9, 213, 231
Blount, William, 103–4, 137, 139, 169, 171–72, 175
Boston Tea Party. *See* Tea Act
Boykin, Samuel, 72–73
Brutus (Anti-Federalist writer), 228–29
Bryan, William, 167
Burke, Thomas, 12–13, 14, 302
Burr, Aaron, 248

Calder v. Bull (1798), 189
Caldwell, Joseph, 246
Cameron, Duncan, 249
Caswell, Richard, 8, 137, 159–75, 290, 301; early life and education, 159–60; elected to assembly, 160; elected speaker, 161; and French and Indian War, 161–62; as colonial treasurer, 162; praised by Josiah Martin, 162; advocates court reform, 162–63; elected to Continental Congress, 163; criticized by Josiah Martin, 163, 164; becomes minuteman commander, 164; and Battle of Moore's Creek Bridge, 164–65; elected governor, 165; attempts to avoid war against Cherokee, 165; as wartime governor, 165–67; and Battle of Camden, 167–68; elected to state senate, 168; returns to governor's office, 169; faces problems in the West, 169–70; supports stronger central government, 172; elected to Hillsborough convention, 174; death of, 175; proposes Fayetteville convention, 175
Catawba, 67–83; and South Carolina authorities, 67, 70–71, 80–81; decline of, 68–69; and defense of Charleston, 70–74; and Cherokee War of 1776, 75–78; in Carolina campaign of 1780–81, 79–81; impact of American Revolution

on, 81–82; assessing role in American Revolution, 82–83
Centinel I (Anti-Federalist writer), 230
Cession Act (1784), 14, 99–100
Charleston, South Carolina: fall of, 95
Chase, Samuel, 189–90
Chavis, John, 257–73, 302; and Willie Person Mangum, 257, 267–70; Federalist views of, 257–58, 268; opens Raleigh school, 258–60, 266–67; early life and education, 260–61, 262–64; military service of, 261; and John Witherspoon, 262–64; employed by Presbyterian General Assembly, 265; licensed by Orange Presbytery, 265; criticizes Andrew Jackson, 268; banned from preaching, 269; views on slavery and evangelism, 269, 270–71; death of, 272
Cherokee, 67–83, 163; and Transylvania Land Company, 67–68; divisions among, 67–68, 83, 91; land cessions by, 68; and Cherokee War of 1761, 68–69; Cherokee towns, 69; Cherokee War of 1776, 74–78. *See also* Native Americans
Chisholm v. Georgia (1793), 188
Coercive (Intolerable) Acts (1774), 8, 30, 31, 47–48, 116, 180
Common Sense (Paine), 52–53, 54
Conservatives: in North Carolina, 13–16, 138, 218–19; and North Carolina constitution of 1776, 10–12, 53–55
Constitutional Convention (1787), 15, 144–46, 171, 172–74, 240–41; and the Great (Connecticut) Compromise, 15, 241; and the Three-Fifths Compromise, 15–16, 242
Continental Congress, 8, 10, 48, 162–63
courthouse rings, 3–4, 11, 44, 56
Currency Act (1764), 5–6

Davie, William R., 79–80, 182, 183–84, 203, 204–5, 207, 211, 220, 237–51, 301; early life and education, 237–38; later years, 238, 250–51; frustration as commissary general, 238–39; elected to state legislature, 239; urges fair treatment of Loyalists, 240; influence of John Witherspoon on, 240–41; supports Connecticut Compromise, 241; supports Three-Fifths Compromise, 241–42; wins *Bayard* case, 242; elected to Hillsborough convention, 243; opposes paper money, 243–44; at Fayetteville convention, 244; advocates internal improvements, legal reform, and education, 245–46; identifies with Federalist Party, 246–47; elected governor, 247; helps negotiate settlement with France, 247–48; loses race for Congress, 249–50
Deane, Silas: on William Hooper and Joseph Hewes, 48–49; questions loyalty of Hugh Williamson, 118–19
Declaration of Independence, 10, 43, 52–53, 179–80, 263
Democratic-Republican Party, 149–50, 246
Dobbs, Arthur, 134–35, 161
Dumplin Creek Treaty (1785), 101. *See also* Cherokee; Watauga settlements
Dragging Canoe (Cherokee leader), 68, 74–75, 78
Drayton, William Henry, 67, 72

Edenton, town of, 4, 25–26
Edenton Tea Party, 8, 25–39; and Anne Horniblow, 27; and Elizabeth Beasley, 27; and Mary Blount, 27; and Elizabeth Ormond, 27–28; and Ruth Benbury, 27–28; and Sarah Littlejohn, 27–28; and Margaret Cathcart, 28; and Sarah (Winfried) Hoskins, 28, 30; and Penelope Dawson, 28, 30, 31; and Penelope Barker, 28–29, 30, 34; and Elizabeth King, 30, 33–34; Barker's letter to *Morning Chronicle and London Advertiser*, 32–33; and Abigail Cherlton, 33; Barker and leadership of, 33–34; Philip Dawe's sketch of, 34–36; Arthur Iredell's criticism of, 37–38
election of 1800, 149–50, 248–49
Enfield Riots, 160

Fanning, David, 12–13
federalism, 1–2, 18n1, 18–19n2, 213, 219, 221
Federalist Party, 149–50, 246–47

Federalists (supporters of Constitution), 15, 124, 138–39, 147–49, 182–84
Ferguson, Patrick, 93–94
foreign attachment controversy, 2, 7–8, 45–46, 162–63, 179
Franklin statehood movement, 100–102, 169–70
free blacks, in North Carolina, 9, 11, 139, 259–60, 277n63. *See also* Chavis, John
French and Indian War, 5, 161

Gales, Joseph, 266, 271
Gaston, William, 281
General New River (Catawba leader), 80, 81
Graham, William, 269
Greene, Nathanael, 81, 237

Halifax Resolves, 2, 53
Hamilton, Alexander, 16–17
Hamiltons v. Eaton (1796), 245
Harnett, Cornelius, 302
Harvey, John, 7, 9
Henderson, Richard. *See* Transylvania Land Company
Henry, Patrick, 207, 210
Hewes, Joseph, 10, 301; early life and business ventures, 46; in Continental Congress, 49–50; and Naval Board, 51; response to *Common Sense*, 52–53; and Halifax Resolves, 53; supports Declaration of Independence, 53; on republics, 53–54; loses congressional seat to John Penn, 56; allegations of financial misconduct against, 56, 63n52; death of, 57
Hooper, William, 10, 11, 301, 302; early life and education, 43–44; and Regulators, 44–45; in colonial assembly, 45–46; opposes British colonial policy, 46–48; in Continental Congress, 49, 50; and Declaration of Independence, 53; and North Carolina constitution of 1776, 54–56; decline and death of, 56–59
Hutcheson, Francis: political philosophy of, 136–37
Hylton v. United States (1796), 189

Iredell, James, 178–91, 203, 212, 220, 291–92, 301; early life and education, 178–79
—and ratification debate: writes "Answers to Mason's Objections," 182–85; supports ratification of Constitution at Hillsborough convention, 184–85; publishes record of Hillsborough convention, 185; continues to support ratification, 186
—as Revolutionary leader: criticizes parliamentary supremacy, 179; and foreign attachment controversy, 179; writes "Principles of an American Whig," 179–80; writes "Causes of the American Revolution," 180; and slavery, 180, 192n11; defends American Revolution, 180–81; supports Treaty of Paris of 1783, 181; disinherited by uncle, 182
—and Supreme Court: appointed to Supreme Court, 186–87; as activist judge, 187–88; dissent in *Chisholm v. Georgia* (1793), 188; supports federal jurisdiction in prize cases, 188–89; supports federal carriage tax, 189; opposes judicial reliance on natural law, 189–90; supports judicial review, 190

Jay Treaty (1795), 246–47
Jefferson, Thomas, 13, 263, 284; on William Hooper, Joseph Hughes, and John Penn, 43; on Richard Dobbs Spaight Sr., 140–42, 150
Johnson, Samuel, 46, 50, 182, 207–8, 214n12; as conservative leader, 11, 12, 56, 138, 204, 211, 221, 302
Jones, Willie, 18, 29, 184, 203, 210, 217–32, 282–83, 285, 302; declines appointment to federal Constitutional Convention, 218; early life and education, 218; leader of so-called radicals, 218–19; opposes ratification at Hillsborough convention, 220–22, 224–25, 227–28; political philosophy of, 222–24; as pragmatist, 224, 227, 231; cites Thomas Jefferson at Hillsborough convention, 225; supports

bill of rights, 227, 232; later years, 231–32. *See also* Anti-Federalists
Judiciary Act of 1789, 185, 186, 190

Kershaw, Joseph, 67, 72–73, 82
King's Mountain, Battle of, 95–98

Laurens, Henry, 72
Lincoln, Benjamin, 167
Loyalists, 9, 12–13, 139, 166, 188; confiscation of property, 93–94, 137; executions of, 96–97

Maclaine, Archibald, 146, 200, 209, 240
Macon, Nathaniel, 224, 279–96; contrasted with Archibald Murphey, 279, 287–88, 290, 296; criticism of, 280–81; sympathetic assessments of, 281; early life and education, 282; historiography on, 282; identified with Willie Jones, 282–83; service in Congress, 283; correspondence with Archibald Murphey, 284; advocates strict construction of Constitution, 285; as fiscal conservative, 286; and slavery, 288–89, 296; opposes Sedition Bill, 290–93; as University of North Carolina trustee, 294; opposes federal internal improvements, 295–96
Madison, James, 211, 221, 231, 241, 244
Mangum, Willie Person: relationship with John Chavis, 257, 267–70, 276n44
Marshall, John, 188
Martin, Alexander, 15, 169, 173
Martin, Josiah, 7–9, 45–48, 162–64
Mason, George, 182–83. *See also* Iredell, James
McCorkle, Samuel E., 246
Mecklenburg Resolves, 9
Mercer, John, 142
Mercer, John Francis, 141, 144
militia: criticism of, 167–68
Monroe, James, 142
Moore, Maurice: and *The Justice and Policy of Taxing the American Colonies* (1765), 6
Moore's Creek Bridge, Battle of, 9, 10. *See also* Caswell, Richard
Moultrie, William, 70–71, 72, 73, 82

Murphey, Archibald D., 279–96, 302; contrasted with Nathaniel Macon, 279, 287–88, 290, 296; sympathetic assessments of, 280, 282; early life and education, 283; varied professional interests of, 283–84; correspondence with Nathaniel Macon, 284; supports internal improvements and educational reform, 284, 293–95; calls for state constitutional reform, 286–87; and slavery, 288–89; praises founders, 289–90; criticizes political partisanship, 293

Native Americans, 9; and the American Revolution, 69–70; military potential of, 70–71. *See also* Catawba; Cherokee
New Bern, town of, 4, 135, 160
North Carolina: constitution of 1776, 2, 10–12, 165, 218–19; lack of development in, 3–4; diversity of, 3–5; postwar economic issues in, 13–14
North Carolina Provincial Congress: First Provincial Congress, 8, 29, 30, 47–48, 163; Second Provincial Congress, 9, 163; Third Provincial Congress, 9, 164; Fourth Provincial Congress, 10–11; Fifth Provincial Congress, 11–12
Northwest Ordinance of 1787, 103

Oconostota (Cherokee leader), 67–68, 83
Olive Branch Petition, 51
Otis, James, 44
Overmountain Men, 96

Paine, Thomas. See *Common Sense*
Penhallow v. Doane's Administrators (1795), 188–89
Penn, John, 10, 301; elected to Continental Congress, 50; early life and education, 51; and *Common Sense*, 52–53; supports Declaration of Independence, 53; and North Carolina constitution of 1776, 54–56; replaces Joseph Hewes in Congress, 56; criticism of, 57; death of, 57
Person, Thomas, 50, 54, 138, 183, 184, 200, 201, 221

Philadelphia Female Anti-Slavery Society, 34
Presbyterians: and slavery, 264–65
Princeton University (College of New Jersey), 262–64, 282. *See also* Witherspoon, John
Proceedings and Debates of the Convention of North Carolina, 203
Proclamation of 1763, 5, 9

radicals: and North Carolina constitution of 1776, 10–12, 54–56; in North Carolina, 13–14, 218–19
Raleigh, town of, 218, 259–60; John Chavis's school in, 258–60, 266–67
Raleigh Minerva, 249
Raleigh Register, 258–59, 266, 281, 295
Regulators, 5, 44–45, 146, 164
religion: in North Carolina, 4–5, 12
republics: optimum size of, 227–31
Rhode Island, 141, 147, 173, 226
Rutherford, Griffith, 75, 77, 78

Sedition Act (1798), 290. *See also* Macon, Nathaniel
Sevier, John, 17, 88–107, 169, 302; and War of 1812, 88, 105; interest of in western land, 89; and Watauga settlements, 89–92; builds Nolichucky fort, 92; wartime legislative service of, 93; and Watauga petition, 93, 99; and Loyalists, 93–95; assassination plot against, 94–95; and Battle of King's Mountain, 95–98; as "Scourge of the Cherokee," 98; historiography on, 99; and Franklin statehood movement, 100–102; and "Spanish Intrigue," 102; appointed brigadier general of territorial militia, 103; elected to territorial assembly, 104; as governor of Tennessee, 104–5; elected to Congress, 105; and slavery, 105–6; and concept of liberty, 107
slavery: proposals for emancipation, 139; and the Constitution, 205–6, 241–42
Spaight, Richard Dobbs Sr., 3, 4, 9–10, 132–51, 173, 182, 301; ranked as "ordinary founder," 132–33; political philosophy of, 133–34, 138, 150–51; recommends reconsideration of votes at Constitutional Convention, 134, 144: early life and education, 134–37; and slavery, 135–36, 141–43; aide to Richard Caswell, 137; elected to assembly, 137; elected speaker, 138–39; elected to Congress, 140; and Thomas Jefferson, 140–41, 153n23; feud with David Howell, 141–42, 155n64; leaves Congress, 144; service in Constitutional Convention, 144–45; criticizes judicial review, 145; supports ratification of Constitution, 146–48; rebuttal to William Lenoir at Hillsborough Convention, 147–48; becomes Democratic-Republican, 149; duel with John Stanley, 150
Spencer, Samuel, 199–213, 285; at Hillsborough convention, 199–200, 201–10; and *Bayard v. Singleton* (1787), 201; criticism of, 200–201; early life and education, 201; defends ban on religious tests, 203–4, 209; opposes federal regulation of elections, 204–5; criticizes federal power to tax, 205–6; and slavery, 206; criticizes relationship between president and Senate, 207–8; supports a bill of rights, 208, 212–13; at Fayetteville convention, 211–12
Stamp Act (1765), 6–7
Stanly, John Stewart, 260
Stuart, John, 67, 69, 71, 74–75, 78
Sugar Act (1764), 5
Sycamore Shoals Treaty (1775), 67–68, 78, 79, 90–91

Tea Act, 8, 30, 47–48; and boycotts of English tea, 31. *See also* Edenton Tea Party
Toby (slave of John Sevier), 106
Townshend Acts (1767), 7, 163
Townshend Duties. *See* Townshend Acts
Transylvania Land Company, 74, 90–91
Treaty of Hopewell (1785), 79, 83
Treaty of Long Island (1777), 78, 95
Treaty of Paris (1783), 13–14, 58
Tryon, William, 5, 6, 7

United States Constitution, 2–3, 190; ratification of in North Carolina, 16–17, 146–49, 174–75, 182–86, 202–13, 219–24, 231, 243–44
University of North Carolina: William R. Davie and, 245, 247; curriculum at, 246; Nathaniel Macon as trustee of, 294

Ware v. Hylton (1796), 189
Washington, George, 16, 88, 104, 119, 186, 244
Washington and Lee University (Liberty Hall Academy), 264
Watauga settlements, 89, 95; and Cherokee, 74, 90–91; creation of Watauga Association, 90; and outbreak of American Revolution, 91–92; Washington District organized, 92; annexation of by North Carolina, 93
Williamson, Andrew, 75–78
Williamson, Hugh, 14–15, 113–28, 182, 301; appraised by contemporaries, 113–14; early life and education, 114; as advocate for education, 114–15; enters public service, 115; settles in Edenton, 115; death of, 115–16, 128; serves in federal Congress, 127–28; opposes spread of slavery, 142; and Richard Dobbs Spaight, 145
—and American Revolution: and Boston Tea Party, 116; writes *Plea of the Colonies* (1775), 116–18; accused of disloyalty, 118; elected to state legislature, 119; as North Carolina surgeon general, 119; serves in Continental Congress, 119–21; supports Land Ordinance of 1784 and ban on slavery, 120; opposes Cession Act, 121
—and constitutional reform: appointed to Constitutional Convention, 121; misses Annapolis Convention, 121; accepts Connecticut Compromise, 122; supports stronger central government and proportional representation, 122; supports Three-Fifths Compromise, 123; advocates checks and balances, 123–24; campaigns for ratification of Constitution, 124–27; as North Carolina's unofficial representative to the new federal government, 126–27; as delegate to Fayetteville convention, 127
Wilmington Resolves, 47
Wilmington Tea Party, 38
Witherspoon, John, 240–41, 258, 262–64
Woodmason, Charles, 3, 4
Wortham, George, 266–67

XYZ Affair, 247

www.ingramcontent.com/pod-product-compliance
Lightning Source LLC
Chambersburg PA
CBHW030523230426
43665CB00010B/738